T0360917

ROUTLEDGE LIBRARY EDITIONS:
BUSINESS AND ECONOMICS IN ASIA

Volume 25

THE MICRO-ECONOMICS OF
PEASANT ECONOMY

THE MICRO-ECONOMICS OF PEASANT ECONOMY
China, 1920—1940

THOMAS B. WIENS

Routledge
Taylor & Francis Group

LONDON AND NEW YORK

First published in 1982 by Garland Publishing, Inc.

This edition first published in 2019
by Routledge
2 Park Square, Milton Park, Abingdon, Oxon OX14 4RN

and by Routledge
52 Vanderbilt Avenue, New York, NY 10017

Routledge is an imprint of the Taylor & Francis Group, an informa business

British Library Cataloguing in Publication Data
A catalogue record for this book is available from the British Library

ISBN: 978-1-138-48274-6 (Set)
ISBN: 978-0-429-42825-8 (Set) (ebk)
ISBN: 978-1-138-36885-9 (Volume 25) (hbk)
ISBN: 978-0-429-42899-9 (Volume 25) (ebk)

Publisher's Note
The publisher has gone to great lengths to ensure the quality of this reprint but
points out that some imperfections in the original copies may be apparent.

Disclaimer
The publisher has made every effort to trace copyright holders and would welcome
correspondence from those they have been unable to trace.

The Microeconomics
of Peasant Economy
China, 1920–1940

Thomas B. Wiens

Garland Publishing, Inc., New York & London
1982

Library of Congress Cataloging in Publication Data

Wiens, Thomas B.
The microeconomics of peasant economy.

(China during the interregnum, 1911–1949)
Bibliography: p.
1. Agriculture — Economic aspects — China — History.
2. Peasantry — China — History. I. Title. II. Series.
    HD2097.W5   338.1′0951   80-8837
    ISBN 0-8240-4692-7   AACR2

For a complete list of the titles in this series,
see the final pages of this volume.

All volumes in this series are printed on acid-free,
250-year-life paper.

Printed in the United States of America

The publication of this dissertation seven years after its completion arouses mixed feelings in its author. In retrospect, there are many elements deserving revision to reflect the usual maturation of understanding. There are portions which may be confusing, excessively academic, or simply incorrect. There are false starts, deadends, and candid emphasis on the consequences of faulty data, such as are usually edited out of more "finished" work.

The alternatives to unrevised publication are not appealing, however. A complete revision would be too costly of time and effort, in view of the size and scope of the manuscript. On the other hand, valuable ideas and information and many positive and negative lessons lie buried in the text and appendices. These merit a wider audience than the dissertation committee.

This dissertation represents a unique attempt to wed sophisticated microeconomic theory and econometric technique to cross-sectional data on the Chinese peasant economy in the pre-Communist period. The major goal was the revision and testing of theories and hypotheses applicable to comparable economies, rather than peculiar to the Chinese case. Indeed, most of the latter are dynamic in nature, whereas my approach was essentially static. It was and is my belief that the quality of Chinese statistical data in this period was too weak to provide definitive evidence on dynamic trends, whereas it does lend itself to cross-sectional analysis.

There are a number of points in the text where the reader would be well-advised to refer to published papers which fully-develop ideas first expressed below. For example, the impact of risk on the decisionmaking behavior of peasants, considered in Chapter II and Appendix II-B, was more completely and rigorously demonstrated in "Uncertainty and Factor Allocation in a Peasant Economy," Oxford Economic Papers 29:1 (March 1977). Chapter VII, inappropriately based on a mathematical derivation which is valid only for infinitessimal risks, was entirely redone on much stronger foundations (and with more conclusive results) and published as "Peasant Risk Aversion and Allocative Behavior: A Programming Experiment," in American Journal of Agricultural Economics, November 1976. Appendix VI-F, itself a mini-study applying some pre-1949 findings to an assessment of the development of agricultural productivity during the 1950s, was the seed from which grew "The Evolution of Policy and Capabilities in China's Agricultural Technology," in Joint Economic Committee, U. S. Congress, eds., Chinese Economy Post-Mao (Washington, D.C., 1978).

My gratitude must be expressed to those who helped to shape the dissertation--to Dwight Perkins for overall guidance, Lance Taylor for reading and commenting on it, and my former colleagues, G. Bierwag, M. Grove, and C. Khang, for steering me through the mathematics of the theory of risk aversion.

THE MICROECONOMICS OF PEASANT ECONOMY

CHINA, 1920-1940

A thesis presented

by

Thomas Burnett Wiens

to

The Department of Economics

in partial fulfillment of the requirements

for the degree of

Doctor of Philosophy

in the subject of

Economics

Harvard University

Cambridge, Massachusetts

May, 1973

CONTENTS

I   INTRODUCTION   1

II   A THEORY OF DISTRIBUTION IN THE
        AGRARIAN SECTOR   12

III   THE LAND MARKET IN PREWAR CHINA   76

IV   THE LOAN MARKET IN PREWAR CHINA   123

V   THE LABOR MARKET IN PREWAR CHINA   156

VI   THE AGRICULTURAL PRODUCTION FUNCTION
        AND FACTOR PRODUCTIVITY IN PREWAR
        CHINESE AGRICULTURE   198

VII   AN ACTIVITY ANALYSIS APPROACH TO
        PRODUCTIVITY MEASUREMENT:
        MI-CH'ANG VILLAGE SAMPLE   260

VIII   SUMMARY AND CONCLUSIONS   314

APPENDIXES

II-A   Proof of Relation between Number of
        Constraints and Number of Techniques   324

II-B   Factor Allocation in the Presence
        of Uncertainty   328

III-A   Choice-Theoretic Approaches to
        Rental Deposits   332

IV-A   Average Family Incomes and the
        Distribution of Income in the
        Chinese Peasant Economy   341

V-A   Estimation Procedure for Industrial
       Wage Structure Model   349

V-B   Relationship between Capital/Land
       Ratio and Size of Farm   352

VI-A   Notes on Data Derived from John
       L. Buck, Land Utilization in China,
       Statistical Volume   357

VI-B   Weighted Output Data and the Estimation
       of an Aggregate Production Function   363

VI-C   Specification of Land in Production
       Function Estimation   369

VI-D   Locality Intercepts   377

VI-E   The Simultaneous Equation Problem
       in the Estimation of the Chinese
       Agricultural Production Function   383

VI-F   Response to Fertilizer Applications
       and Technological Change in China   387

VI-G   Grain Prices in Prewar China:
       Data and Sources   450

NOTES   475

BIBLIOGRAPHY   500

TABLES

1.1 Distribution of farm households by crop
    region, nationally and in Buck sample,
    1930s   9

1.2 Distribution of farms by ownership status,
    various surveys, 1930s   9

3.1 Distribution of land ownership among farm
    families, China, early 1930s   78

3.2 Tenancy rates and hired labor, various
    provinces, 1936 and 1933   80

3.3 Comparison of distribution of land by
    ownership and farm size, various pro-
    vinces, 1934 and 1935   81

3.4 Distribution of rental systems among
    tenants, by province, 1934   85

3.5 Sharecropping and other indices, by
    crop region   92

3.6 Rate of return on investment in land,
    China, 21 localities, 1921-1924 and
    1934-1935   105

3.7 Gross and net rates of return on land,
    by tax class   108

3.8 Estimate of net rate of return to
    landlord, three rental systems, China,
    1930-1934   110

3.9 Average rent as a proportion of average
    value of the main crop, various pro-
    vinces, 1934   113

3.10 Rent relative to income and expense,
     tenant farms, various localities,
     1926-1935   114

3.11 Rent relative to farm income, twelve
     tenant farms, Kiangsu, Wu-hsi, 1940   115

3.12   Rent relative to farm income and
       direct expense, various localities,
       1921-24   117

4.1   Farm family borrowings, survey of
       15,112 farms, 1929-1933   125

4.2   Distribution of loans by purpose,
       Li Village, Tsingtao district,
       Shantung, 1940   126

4.3   Distribution of loans by source,
       850 counties, 22 provinces, 1933   128

4.4   Economic characteristics of debtor
       and creditor families, Li Village,
       Tsingtao, Shantung, 1939   137

4.5   Results of regressions of value of
       family debt (-) or credit on variables
       reflecting economic status   140

4.6   Distribution of village families and
       sampled families by land ownership
       status, Li Village, Tsingtao, 1939   143

4.7   Relationship between rate of interest
       and average size of loan, 240 loans,
       Hopei   145

5.1   Proportion of farm families with income
       from subsidiary work, by category of
       work, 15,316 farms, 144 counties,
       1929-33   158

5.2   Non-farm earnings by occupation, Li
       Village, Tsingtao, Shantung, 1938   166

5.3   Average monthly wage levels: regional
       and industrial rankings   173

5.4   Average daily wage levels: regional
       and industrial rankings   174

5.5   Predicted and actual daily wages,
       Shanghai, 1933   176

5.6   Male and female daily wage rates,
       Shanghai, 1933   176

5.7   Wages of farm labor by provinces, 1931-32   178

5.8   Farm daily wage levels (including non-cash
      compensation) and regional wage relatives
      (estimated)   179

5.9   Correlation coefficients, Chinese farm
      survey data, 16,000 farms, 1929-33   186

5.10 Relation of size of farm to percent of
      operators having side-occupations,
      2109 farms, 1922-25   191

5.11 Off-farm labor income as a percent of
      total net family income, 15,215 farms,
      1929-33   191

5.12 Percentage of hired labor cost to total
      labor cost by size of farm, 2866 farms,
      1921-25   191

6.1   Characteristics of eight crop regions   202

6.2   Mean value of input ratios by region   203

6.3   Parameter estimates: Cobb-Douglas
      equation, no locality dummies   225

6.4   Production function: Cobb-Douglas
      form, without interactions   226

6.5   Production function: Cobb-Douglas
      form, with interactions   227

6.6   Linear production function with
      exponential scale factor and uncon-
      strained locality dummies   228

6.7   Marginal response of output to inputs
      of ammonium sulphate equivalent from
      manure and nightsoil   232

6.8   Relationship between scale factors and
      parcel size elasticities   238

6.9   Real wage, marginal and average physical
      product of labor, by crop region, China,
      1929-1933   248

6.10   Estimated value of marginal productivity of
       land and estimated rental value, by
       crop region, China, 1929-1933   250

7.1   Product and factor prices and indices,
       Mi-ch'ang village, 1937-1939   269

7.2   Cobb-Douglas aggregate production
       functions, Mi-ch'ang village sample,
       1937 prices   272

7.3   Estimates of factor marginal value
       product at 1937 prices, based on Cobb-
       Douglas equation   273

7.4   Frontier techniques, Mi-ch'ang village
       sample   284

7.5   Weighting scheme for objective function   291

7.6   Shifts in land allocation among crops,
       1937-1939, Mi-ch'ang village sample   295

7.7   Observed, Cobb-Douglas predicted, and
       allocative-optimal output in 1937
       prices, Mi-ch'ang sample   298

7.8   Summary measures of sub-optimality of
       production   300

7.9   Comparison of actual and "optimal" land
       allocation among crops, Mi-ch'ang
       village sample   302

7.10   Frequency distributions and means of
       shadow prices of land and labor, at
       "allocative optimum"   307

FIGURES AND GRAPHS

2.1   Leibenstein "backwards-bending" effective
      demand curve for labor   20

2.2   Optimization of production over time,
      land-poor and land-rich farms   41

2.3   Investment schedule of peasant farm
      under uncertainty   70

3.1   Sharecropping related to risk   94

4.1   Regional distribution of interest rates,
      Kiangsu, 1932   147

5.1   Scatter diagram, relationship of profits
      /mou to average size of farm, North
      China, 1921-1923   185

5.2   Frequency distributions, labor/land
      ratios, 62 farms, Wu-hsi, Kiangsu,
      1939   193

6.1   Indices of prices received, farm wages
      and land value, North and South China,
      1920-1933   245

7.1   Derivation of "expected efficiency
      frontier"   279

7.2   Wholesale price indices, cotton and
      corn, Nanking, 1913-1939   294

CHAPTER I. INTRODUCTION

The objectives of this study are to elaborate a microeconomic model which adequately explains the interrelationships among economic forces determining the distribution of
income in a peasant economy in the early stages of transition
to industrialization, taking prewar China as a reasonably
typical example of such a society; to examine, using in part
econometric techniques, the degree to which statistical and
other data pertaining to the prewar Chinese economy are consistent with this model.

The intended contributions of this study lie in four distinct directions: First, the general equilibrium theory of
production and markets of comparative statics is extended to
the special case of a peasant economy. Second, descriptive
information on the institutional structure of the Chinese
peasant economy is assembled within an analytical framework
which provides a comprehensive economic explanation of structural interrelationships. Third, a considerable body of information is developed on the application of econometric methods
to the analysis of the processes of production in peasant
agriculture. Finally, useful and interesting empirical results are added to those derived from studies of other peasant
economies.

The point of departure for this study is the theories of

development of the "dual economy", by which is meant an
economy composed of a large peasant agricultural sector, with
its ancillary handicraft sector, both traditional in techniques and institutions, and a small but growing modern (industrial) sector. Income recipients in such an economy may include landlords, owner-cultivators, tenants, landless laborers
and part-time handicraftsmen, in addition to the industrial
capitalists and laborers of the modern sector on whom the
attention of economists has usually been lavished. A study
of the economic relationships determining the distribution of
income in a "dual economy" ought to provide a cogent account
of the economic roles of each of these groups and the interrelationships between them.

Wholesale application to this problem of those distributional theories designed for a modern, capitalist industrial
economy has often led to hypotheses which do not seem to accord
with data derived from direct observation. This has led a
number of economists to devise models which are in better
accordance with the realities of the "dual economy". However,
such models have generally focussed on intersectoral relationships, treating the determinants of the income distribution
within the predominant agricultural sector as either "institutional" or based on producer motivations differing radically
from those presumed to apply in developed economies.

In Chapter II, I will argue that while naive application

of neoclassical equilibrium distribution theory to peasant
economies is inappropriate, the understanding of the traditional sector implicit in the "dual economy" theories is contra-
factual and implausible. There is thus a need to arrive at a
model which avoids both extremes. Viewing the peasantry as
economically rational family producer-consumer units, subject
to social, institutional and economic constraints and market
imperfections, I attempt to develop an explanation of market
participation and equilibrium returns to each type of participant in the economic process which responds to this need.

Chapters III - V apply this theoretical model to an analysis
of the Chinese peasant economy as documented for the years
1929-1940. This choice of case study was based on the belief
that this economy was among those to which the "dual economy"
approach, if valid, should apply. That is, it is generally
considered to be among those economies of the "labor-surplus,
resource-poor variety in which the vast majority of the population is typically engaged in agriculture amidst widespread disguised unemployment and high rates of population growth."[1]
During this period, at least 70 percent of the population was
engaged in agricultural work; less than 15 percent was urban.[2]
Moreover, it was an agriculture characterized by "acute population pressure" and "technological backwardness and resultant
low labor productivity," hallmarks of the archtypical "labor-
surplus" economy.[3]

However, a choice-theoretic approach to the peasant economy,
that is an approach based on the decision-making behavior of
the peasant family as the primary economic unit, is not fully
applicable to every "labor-surplus" peasant economy. It is
necessary, after all, that there be genuine decisions to be
made, which in turn implies that there are alternatives among
which a family may choose with a certain degree of freedom.
Where social institutions or limited technologies seriously
constrict the range and significance of economic alternatives,
a choice-theoretic approach is irrelevant. Historically, it
is relevant where systems of exchange on a contractual basis
(i.e. markets) have become central features of economic activity, with greater than ritualistic significance.

A major purpose of these chapters is to establish that the
Chinese peasant economy of the prewar period was in essence an
early market economy -- early in that the system of exchange
was to a certain extent still limited by the geographically
fragmented nature of markets. I intend to provide evidence
that ample institutional arrangements existed for "readjustment
of factor proportions and activity mix; enough to permit meaningful decision-making on the part of economic units and to
give the concept of "optimization" with respect to participant
goals genuine content. I hope to demonstrate that market prices (and thus incomes) were set through the operation of
supply and demand in relatively competitive contexts and that

relative prices in different markets are consistent with theoretical expectations. I will also demonstrate that the nature and extent of participation in exchange were related to relative resource endowments in ways consistent with a "choice-theoretic" interpretation of peasant economic behavior.

Since theoretical analysis of equilibrium relationships in the factor markets of a peasant economy makes possible some fairly specific predictions concerning the quantitative relationships in those markets, it was possible to put the theory to a more rigorous test on the basis of survey data from the prewar period. The primary issue is whether or not there existed consistent relationships between the values of factor marginal productivities and their market prices, differing according to size of farm. The former are not directly observable, but could be derived from econometric estimates of agricultural production functions. Chapter VI describes the methods and results of such estimation, using data from a large-sample, cross-regional survey. However, there were sufficient theoretical and practical problems with this work to justify exploration of alternative methods and data. This "follow-up" forms the basis of Chapter VII.

The Nature of the Data

The analysis which follows can be no more reliable than the data on which it is based. Unfortunately statistical information available on the prewar peasant economy, while quite ex-

tensive, frequently leaves something to be desired in terms
of accuracy, representativeness and/or documentation of
collection methods. Open, preliminary discussion of this
issue should help the reader place the proper confidence
coefficients on what follows.

We can roughly classify the data employed in this work
into four types: (1) information on conditions in particular
localities collected through researchers and their assistants;
(2) compilations of nation-wide data collected on a county
basis by official organs, usually through a questionaire procedure relying on the responses of local officials; (3) medium-
to-large sample surveys employing interviewers and taking the
family or farm as the basic unit, with extensive methodological documentation; (4) small-sample surveys made by various
organs of the Japanese South Manchurian Railway (hereafter
Mantetsu) during the Occupation, generally well-documented as
to methodology and survey procedures.

Each of these data types has its respective strengths and
weaknesses: Type (1) data are at best probably quite accurate,
but frequently are not known to be based on careful or statistically valid sampling methods (information on sampling methods
is infrequently provided) and so may be quite unrepresentative.
Since these surveys are generally based on quite small samples
and since astonishing variations in economic and other conditions frequently occured in China within seemingly small
geographical areas, this sort of data does not lend itself

readily to generalizations concerning large geographical
units. It is useful for indicating the range of conditions
which occured and for generalizations concerning behavioral
relationships which are not so likely to have serious interlocality variance.

Type (2) data more probably can be questioned on the
grounds of accuracy rather than representativeness. Since
central organs had no real way of checking the accuracy of
responses or supervising the respondents, it is unlikely that
individual responses represented more than the informed guess
of local officials, who may or may not have taken their infor-
mation-gathering responsibility seriously. Where responses
could reflect on bureaucratic performance (for example, surveys
of practices which were nominally illegal), the direction of
biases is predictable. For instance, after describing a
variety of abuses or feudal customs occuring in Kiangsi
landlord-tenant relations, one author states: "Of the fifty-
four counties surveyed, no more than six reported such circumstances; either the others haven't experienced them, or have
but the informants were unwilling to report them."[4] On the
other hand, where local officials should have been well-in-
formed concerning conditions surveyed and where no reflection
on performance was involved, type (2) data may be taken
seriously, with the expectation that individual errors or
misimpressions would tend to average out.

The best known of the type (3) survey data are the work

of John Lossing Buck and his students and colleagues at Nan-kai University (especially those published in Chinese Farm Economy, 1930; Land Utilization in China, 1937). These materials were the product of surveys of large numbers of individual farms (2866 in CFE; 16,786 in LUC) by trained interviewers (Buck's students) over large geographical areas; detailed data and survey methodology have been published. As a result, information from these surveys has been commonly treated as both the most accurate and the most representative available by many students of the prewar peasant economy.[5] However, although the accuracy cannot easily be challenged, the representativeness can: Averages and aggregations based on the Buck data differ systematically from most examples of type (1) and (2) data, as a result of which Dwight Perkins has treated his yield data as unrepresentatively high and Alexander Eckstein his tenancy rate data as too low.[6] Myers found no discernable statistical relationship between crop yield data based on Buck and on a type (2) survey for the provinces of Hopei and Shantung, suggesting that one or both surveys did not accurately capture the true population characteristics because of sampling error.[7]

Certain biases in the sample taken for the Farm Survey (in LUC) can be pinpointed: First, the geographical distribution of the sample by crop region differs significantly (at the 99% level) from the corresponding distribution of the farm population (see Table 1.1). This involved an over-

Table 1.1 Distribution of Farm Households by Crop Region,
          Nationally and in Buck Sample, 1930s

Region	Percent of Farm Households	Percent of Sample
North China:		
Spring wheat	3.64	8.55
Winter wheat-millet	6.63	13.16
Winter wheat-kaoliang	28.41	23.03
South China:		
Yangtze rice-wheat	16.88	20.39
Rice-tea	18.89	14.47
Szechwan rice	10.77	4.61
Double-cropping rice	9.51	7.89
Southwestern rice	5.28	7.89

Source: Buck, LUC, Statistical Volume, pp. 418-410; farm house-
    hold data originally from Statistical Monthly, January-Febru-
    ary, 1932 and Kwangsi Yearbook, 1933.

Table 1.2 Distribution of Farms by Ownership Status, Various
          Surveys, 1930s

Region	Percent of farms which are: Owner-Cultivator	Part Tenant	Tenant
Wheat Region: Farm Survey	76.1	17.6	6.3
Wheat Region: Agricultural Survey	64.9	17.9	17.2
North China (10 provinces)	60.7	20.3	19.0
Rice Region: Farm Survey	38.3	37.1	24.6
Rice Region: Agricultural Survey	27.1	26.6	46.3
South China (11 provinces)	28.5	29.0	42.5

Sources: Farm Survey and Agricultural Survey from Buck, LUC,
    Statistical Volume, p. 57; N. and S. China survey results
    cited in Hsueh Mu-ch'iao, Chung-kuo nung-ts'un ching-chi
    ch'ang shih (1937), p. 27. The two major crop regions
    correspond roughly to the north-south division in Chinese
    usage. The Buck Agricultural Survey was based on interviews
    with three well-informed local residents in selected counties,
    and was intended to represent county-wide conditions; the
    Farm Survey, by contrast, was based on samples of local farms.

sampling of North China and a serious undersampling of many
Southern provinces. Second, the survey considerably under-
sampled tenant farms and oversampled owner-cultivators and (in
the South) part-owners (see Table 1.2). This is verifiable even
on the basis of Buck's accompaning Agricultural Survey, which
was explicitly intended to investigate county-wide conditions
in an approximate way. Third, it can also be shown that the
counties sampled by Buck tended to lie along major routes of
transportation (rail or water). It can therefore be presumed
that they were more commercialized and probably more prosperous
than the "average" county.

The existence of the above sampling biases in the Buck
survey data lead us to conclude that type (2) surveys are
frequently a more reliable source of averages and aggregates
intended to represent broadly generalized conditions. On the
other hand, like the type (1) survey data, the Buck data need
not be presumed biased or unrepresentative with respect to
behavioral relationships between population characteristics
sampled cross-sectionally. For this reason we do not hesitate
to take advantage of the quantity and detail of this data for
econometric estimation purposes in Chapter VI.

The type (4) (Mantetsu) surveys suffer from geographical
biases of a similar nature: Most of the villages studied in
detail lay within a few miles of major rail routes and market
towns or cities, implying unusual commercialization and opportunities for off-farm employment. Moreover, these surveys

were made under wartime conditions of rapid inflation and dis-
rupted urban and rural economy, with probable effects on
peasant economic behavior. Finally, surveys were made primarily
in the two provinces of Hopei and Shantung, a region of very
low tenancy (about 13 percent[8]) with relatively large farms
and considerable use of hired labor.[9] In view of these problems, the Mantetsu data must be used with considerable caution,
yet it is the only survey data available in published form
which permits analysis of the economic status and activities
of individual households in a consistent way, and as such is
too valuable to neglect. This data forms the basis for the
analysis contained in Chapter VII.

CHAPTER II. A THEORY OF DISTRIBUTION IN THE AGRARIAN SECTOR

In the past twenty years, a considerable body of literature has grown up with relevance to any attempt to explain the determinants of the distribution of income in "overpopulated" agrarian economies. Most of this literature has naturally centered around the issue of to what extent the marginal productivity theory of distribution, developed for modern, industrialized societies, holds also in such agrarian economies The discussants can be sharply divided into those who hold that the marginal productivity theory applies without amendment and those who allege that, because the marginal productivity of labor in such economies is observedly below subsistence and quite probably zero, this theory cannot adequately explain returns to labor which are greater than subsistence.[1]

A debate about the validity of the observation that the marginal productivity of labor is zero occupies the greatest proportion of the literature on the subject. The primary test criterion has been the extent of the "volume of workers who can be transferred out of agriculture without affecting agricultural output," ceteris paribus.[2] Much confusion has arisen, however, over differences of opinion as to which "ceteris" should be assumed "paribus": Navarrete permits the introduction of some capital into the production function, Nurkse the consolidation of scattered strips and plots of land, Dovring any institutional reforms (e.g. in cropping schemes,

farm size, land layout, etc.) which don't involve significant capital cost.[4] But there is no contradiction between
"disguised unemployment" in this sense and a positive marginal productivity of labor in the sense defined by Viner:

> I find it impossible to conceive of a farm of any kind
> on which, other factors of production being held constant
> in quantity, and even in form as well, it would not be
> possible, by known methods, to obtain some addition to
> the crop by using additional labor in more careful selec-
> tion and planting of the seed, more intensive weeding,
> cultivation, thinning and mulching, more painstaking har-
> vesting, gleaning and cleaning of the crop.[5]

A deliberate social choice of inefficient techniques and
an "unnecessary" spreading of labor is in fact the intuitive
meaning attached by most economists to "disguised unemployment".
But, since the marginal productivity of labor must be measured
in terms of constant techniques and common efficiency units
of labor (else it will not be a single-valued function of
inputs), the existence of "disguised unemployment" is compati-
ble with any value of the marginal productivity of labor.
The existence of work-spreading ("featherbedding"), if not
due to a desire to mix leisure and work (a rational and feasible strategy for laborers in a society with little or no institutional limitation on work-hours or days) or some other deviation from the Protestant ethic, might represent an effort

by a society in which population growth has outrun the rate
of capital accumulation to prevent a decline in the share of
aggregate returns to labor in total product, in total absolute
returns to labor[*] or in some mix of wages and leisure.

If the leap from intuitively plausible "disguised unemployment" to a zero marginal productivity of labor is conceptional-
ly inaccurate, empirically oriented case studies have only
further muddied the waters. Most of the studies purporting
to measure the extent of "disguised unemployment" or prove
the zero MP_L hypothesis have been criticized on the grounds
of weaknesses in methodology or data.[6] By contrast, attempts
to estimate production functions from cross-sectional data
from Indian farms have consistently found significantly positive elasticities with respect to labor.[7] Similar results may
be cited for farms in Taiwan in the 1950s[8] and, as we shall
see below, for the China Mainland in the 1930s. Thus the
empirical evidence for zero marginal productivity of labor
is far from convincing.

Considerable ingenuity has gone into the construction of
theoretical explanations of the existence of zero MP_L and
"disguised unemployment". As Kao, Anschel and Eicher suggest, these explanations must suggest answers to the following
questions:

_____

* plausible only if the elasticity of the marginal productivity
of labor with respect to labor is greater than unity.

First, if labor is unemployed or otherwise wasted, why
are techniques not introduced which use less land and
capital relative to labor? Second, with given technology (fixed capital-land-labor ratios), why is labor used
to the point where no returns are forthcoming? Employers
of hired labor lose money when they pay a wage to labor
whose product is zero or negligible. The self-employed
who produce nothing would do better to hire out their
surplus labor for a wage. Third, why are wages higher
than the marginal product? If large numbers of people
produce nothing or very little, wages normally would be
bid down to the marginal product of labor.[9]

The first of these questions is dealt with by Eckaus:
Given the total available stock of capital and labor in a
society , some part of the labor force may remain unemployed
if a limited stock of capital and limitations on the substitutability of labor for capital over parts of the production
surface result in zero MP_L occuring before all labor is
absorbed into productive uses; and/or structural rigidities
in either factor price or factor supply may in any case limit
the demand for labor to a less than full employment level.[10]
The first explanation might indeed apply to the industrial
sector, but, as Eckaus admits[11], seems less applicable to
agriculture (compare, for instance, Viner's statement quoted
above), which accounts for the greatest part of economic acti-

vity in economies to which the theory should be most applicable
Moreover, the types of structural rigidities mentioned by
Eckaus -- including unionization and reluctance to change
location or occupation -- do not accord with the picture
normally presented of, for instance, Asiatic economies, where
union power is relatively undeveloped, minimum wage legislation largely evaded, and major industries are asserted to
carry on in the midst of substantial under- or overemployment.
Finally, the two explanations offered by Eckaus would seem
contradictory: If employers are as rational as he assumes,
then structural rigidities in the labor market would indeed
result in unemployment, but at a level of MP_L equal to the
prevailing wage (even though, if all unemployed labor were
hired, an MP_L of zero might be reached).

A more comprehensive attempt to deal with these issues is
to be found in a seminal article by W. Arthur Lewis,[12] which
makes three key assertions: that members of peasant families
will not leave the farm to seek employment unless the wage
available is greater than the individual's share of net family product; that employers in the "traditional" or non-capi-
talistic sector, because of social pressure, employ workers
whose contribution to product is less than their compensation;
that landlords are willing to accept less than the marginal
productivity of their land, the rent level being adjusted to
permit tenants a bare subsistence. These assertions are mutually consistent, constitute an answer to all the questions

raised by Kao, Anschel and Eicher and in themselves represent a theory of distribution in the traditional economy.

Examining the propensity for stability of such an equilibrium, however, it becomes clear that only the inability of landlord or employer to resist social pressure to maintain an army of unproductive retainers prevents its breakdown. For although given a subsistence wage paid to employees, neither a freeholder nor a tenant could be induced to abandon his farm,[*] it always pays for an employer to reduce his work force or for a landlord to manage the land himself if he can freely determine the number of laborers he hires. Further, a landlord would find it in his interest to force or induce members of tenant families to leave the farm, since he could then charge higher rent.

To accept Lewis' view of the distributional equilibrium in the traditional agricultural sector, then, one must accept his belief that the motivations of the traditional "ruling class" are shaped by an ethical code not in their interests as individuals, but itself adapted to the existence of overpopulation. Overpopulation, however, may be too recent a phenomenon historically to have influenced the ethical code and the motivations of the elite. Fundamentally Lewis is arguing that relatively unrestrained income maximization

---

[*] If the wage becomes greater than the net return to tenants, it pays both tenant and freeholder to leave the farm, the latter to maximize earnings by renting out land and simultaneously working for others.

is a goal peculiar to the recently-arisen capital class.

The most disappointing aspect of the Lewis model is the difficulty of devising a definitive test of its hypotheses against, for instance, the alternative neoclassical model. In part this is because the equilibrium relationships in the traditional sector (e.g. between the wages of farm laborers and the net return to tenants) are similar to those in the neoclassical model. Moreover, the fungibility of the concept of a subsistence wage further robs the model of predictive and testable implications, for there is no reason to assume that the level socially defined as "subsistence" should not vary geographically and over time. Nor is invariance of the wage with respect to productivity required, since, as Marglin points out, if the _daily_ wage is institutionally set, any increase in agricultural productivity (such as further extension of irrigation or double-cropping) which requires or permits more days per year of work for agricultural laborers will result in a rise in the _yearly_ wage, so that annual wage series may show growth over time and may be correlated with productivity trends, as they of course would be under neoclassical hypotheses.[13] This would seem to imply non-zero MP_L, but then Lewis only requires that MP_L be less than subsistence. Because of this possibility (and despite other evidence alleged to be inconsistent with the Lewis model), an attempt by Jorgensen to refute this model on the basis of Japanese data by subjec-

ting it to a "rigorous" test proved unconvincing to supporters
of the "surplus labor" theory.[14]

However, another test of the two theories (by Bent Hansen)
utilized Egyptian time series for daily wage averages, and
found that variations in labor productivity statistically
explained variations in money wages better than did variations
in prices (the latter, however, being a dominant influence
in value productivity changes); that the share of wages in
the value of output was more constant over time than were
real wages; and that seasonal variations in agricultural
daily wages were highly correlated with seasonal labor demands.[15]
These findings are clearly more consistent with the marginal
productivity theory than with the subsistence wage theory.

Is it necessary, however, to assume totally different
motivations in traditional societies to arrive at an explanation of "underemployment"? Leibenstein suggests that it may
be rational for landlords to pay a wage greater than subsistence even if excess labor is available at a subsistence
wage level, if a higher real wage level raises the marginal
productivity of labor through a positive feedback on energy,
motivation and efficiency.[16] The effect is best understood
by reference to the diagram in Figure 1.1. Here a different
marginal productivity of labor curve is applicable for each
different wage level between subsistence (w_s) and some level
w_3 above which the "feedback" becomes unimportant. For a
given wage level the level of employment which maximizes

employer net income is shown by
the intersection of the wage
line with the corresponding
marginal productivity curve,
creating a "backwards bending"
effective demand curve for labor. However, the net revenue
of employers (the area between
corresponding marginal productivity curves and wage lines)
will in general be maximized at
only one combination of wage
level and number of employees,

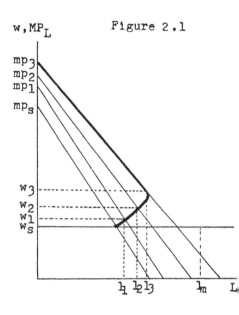

Figure 2.1

and this <u>may</u> be above the subsistence wage w_s, say at w_2.
Therefore, viewing the curves in Fig. 2.1 as the aggregate
supply and demand curves for all employers and laborers, it
pays employers (individually and as a group) to limit employment to l_2 at a wage w_2, despite the availability of a larger
number of laborers (l_m) at the lower subsistence wage (w_s).

The question then arises as to whether employers could
maintain the wage at a level higher than subsistence in the
face of competition between the employed and the unemployed
for the limited jobs available. Leibenstein supposes that
it might be possible for employers to find some compromise
wage level above subsistence but below the optimum at which
they could offer to employ the total labor force, yet still

be better off than at the subsistence wage. Even if such a
compromise existed (if unemployment were at all significant,
it would require an extraordinarily large feedback effect
to compensate for the loss due to employment of labor with
marginal productivity less than the wage)[17] it could only
be obtained by collusion among employers, since the natural
reaction to any bidding down of the wage level would be con-
traction of employment rather than expansion. Since no obvious examples of employer collusion to maintain higher wage
levels come to mind, I suspect that either the feedback effect
is not sufficiently significant or that employers don't
perceive it, behaving as if the marginal productivity curves
of their employees were unilinear. For example, 19th century
British employers vehemently opposed legislation to reduce
the length of the workday (which had the effect of raising
wages per unit time), yet found ex post that the resulting
productivity increase adequately compensated for the increased
cost (legislative restriction having the same effect as
collusion in maintaining the higher standard).[18]

When applied to the traditional agricultural sector, the
Leibenstein theory seems even less useful. For, if farm
laborers and tenants are paid a wage above subsistence and
yet all given employment, in what sense could the supply
curve of labor be considered to remain at the subsistence
level? If the owner-cultivator could simultaneously increase the "wage portion" of his income and the "rent por-

tion" by taking advantage of the feedback effect, he surely would not be willing to give up self-employment for a wage less than the "optimum" (w_2). In short, the Leibenstein model in this context breaks down into the neoclassical theory and we are left with the same questions.

One of the most stimulating articles on the distribution of income in peasant economies is that of Georgescu-Roegen.[19] The author accepts a priori the propositions that the factor proportions in peasant economies are such that the MP_L is below subsistence if labor is fully utilized (subsistence is biological subsistence in his definition, since it is the income level below which Malthusian forces begin to operate). Given the assumption that leisure is of no personal utility under such conditions, he establishes that maximum social product is obtainable at full utilization of all labor potential or, if the MP_L becomes zero previous to this point, at the level where marginal productivity of labor becomes zero. To determine the share of labor in total product, he posits the existence of a non-productive class monopolizing political power and extracting their income from the working peasantry. This class is assumed to collectively maximize its share of income, limited by a reluctance to drive the peasants below subsistence and a willingness to spread the work among all potential laborers (implying that all potential workers can receive at least a subsistence and that unemployment, as opposed to disguised unemployment, is

excluded). This maximum is of course attained at the same
labor input as maximum social product, and with each laborer
receiving a subsistence wage.

Georgescu-Roegen's solution is, then, essentially the same
as Lewis', and similar difficulties arise. If the subsistence income is in the form of a wage, and if the ruling
class does not consist of drones but of landlords or owner-
managers, then individual income maximization differs from
collective income maximization principles, and the result
would tend to break down for reasons cited earlier. The author
is apparently bothered by this possibility, since he emphasizes the feudal tithe as an institutional alternative to
the fixed wage which reconciles individual and class interests
(an income-maximizer who must pay a percentage of production
to his laborers reaches his optimum by employing labor up
to the point where their marginal productivity goes to zero).
While he is no doubt correct in suggesting that an overpopulated society in which land arrangements are not contractual,
opportunities for wage labor are absent, and all who farm the
land must pay a tithe to the ruling class would find a stable
equilibrium at a MP_L below the prevailing subsistence return
to labor, the relevance of this to contemporary peasant
economies which do not share these characteristics (and
often haven't for centuries) is questionable. Contrary to
Georgescu-Roegen's claim that "agricultural overpopulation
has usually been manifest in countries where feudalism was

late in being supplanted by capitalism,"[21] in China, at least,
the transition from a feudal agriculture to a system chara-
racterized by contractual relationships, including considerable use of hired wage labor, occured at about the same
time as in England, and accompanied increasing population
density.[22]

The author additionally asserts that an economy characterized by a MP_L less than subsistence "cannot possibly function
according to the principles of marginal productivity theory,"
i.e. paying each factor a return equal to its marginal productivity.[23] This is obviously untrue for an agrarian economy
composed primarily of owner-cultivators, and/or one in which
variation in factor proportions among production units exists
(permitting variations in factor marginal productivities).
Again, the assertion boils down to the truism that laborers
cannot survive if their only source of income is a wage which
is below subsistence, so that a low-productivity economy
based entirely on a landless rural proletariat indeed could
not function on marginal productivity principles.

The limitations of the existing literature on the determination of the distribution of income in "overpopulated" agrarian
economies can be succinctly summarized: First, the empirical
evidence that the marginal productivity of labor is either
zero or below subsistence and that the marginal productivity
theory can therefore not be applied is weak. Nevertheless,
the possibility of these propositions being true cannot be

readily dismissed, since it is apparent that the average
productivity is quite low in such economies and that capital
and land are exceedingly scarce relative to labor, by comparison with more advanced economies, so that the marginal productivity of labor is likely to be the smaller fraction of
average product. Yet a wage greater than or equal to subsistence is paid to hired labor and tenants manage to subsist,
suggesting that the wage may be greater than the MP_L and
the rent less than the marginal productivity of land.

However, attempts to devise theoretical explanations of
these facts, assumed to be inconsistent with the neoclassical
theory of distribution, are at best based on social sanctions
assumed to conflict with but effectively constrain the maximizing behavior of the individuals monopolizing power in
these societies. It is impossible to deny that religious and
social codes often imply such sanctions, yet these codes are
generally "remnants" of earlier social forms (such as
Georgescu-Roegen's feudalism) and there is some doubt as to
the extent to which they are observed when conflicts with
individual or family interests arise.

The strength of social sanctions may of course differ
from country to country (e.g. Hinduism today is probably
stronger than Confucianism was in China during the period
under study); sanctions may be applied discriminately (e.g.
among relations or clansmen) or observed more closely among
the very rich (for whom it serves as a form of conspicuous

consumption). Such exceptions notwithstanding, it is my
belief that decisions affecting significantly the livelihood
of peasants of all classes are and have in the past been
made largely on the basis of economic considerations and
without meaningful "class collusion". Considerable indirect
evidence in support of this belief will be offered below for
the Chinese case.

Since the possibility that the marginal productivity of
labor may be below subsistence and/or the wage level in
peasant economies of the "overpopulated" sort must be accepted, but the viability of essentially noneconomic theories
of distribution has been questioned, it is necessary to
develop a revised variant of neoclassical marginal productivity theory capable of accounting for deviations from the
equilibrium relationships commonly considered applicable
to developed capitalist economies.

The Neoclassical Theory Revisited: A Revisionist Approach

The fact that in "overpopulated" peasant economies, wages
paid to hired farm labor (and urban unskilled labor) seem
about as high as average productivity of labor (on small
farms) is an anomaly on which the marginalist distribution
theory appears to founder, since it seems to imply that
wages are greater than the value of the marginal productivity of labor. To account for this, "labor surplus" theorists
have opted for institutionally-determined wage and rent

levels, implying implausible employer/landlord motivations.

An alternative explanation which has found some favor is based on the observed negative correlation between labor intensity and farm size. It is argued that large farms, worked with a partly hired labor force, operate on roughly neoclassical principles, paying a wage equal to the value of marginal productivity. By contrast, small family farms are willing to exploit family labor to its limits in farm production, since no wage costs are born directly.

While this approach restores a measure of economic rationality to the large farm enterprise, thus avoiding our previous objections, it leaves the behavior of small farms to be explained. If opportunities for wage labor off the farm exist (as indeed they do), why does the small farm ignore marginalist criteria in allocating its labor force between on and off-farm labor? Since in reality the families operating small farms also _supply_ most wage labor, why are not wages bid down to the level of farm marginal productivity of labor?

The following section will attempt to provide explanations of the covariation of labor intensity with farm size which do not differentiate among farms in terms of _motivation_, but rather _situation_. I hope to show that it is more the arguments than the form of the peasant family's objective function which differs with farm size. Three lines of argument, each reinforcing the other, will be developed, as follows:

(1) The availability of a variety of crops and production
techniques, some of which are both labor and capital intensive
and others land intensive, leads to production isoquants
exhibiting stable marginal rates of substitution over a wide
range of factor proportions. If farms are constrained by
endowments of land and capital, and if the ratio of endowed
capital to endowed land declines with farm size, then despite
a free market in wage labor, small farms will optimally utilize
higher labor (and capital) intensities than larger farms.
It can be argued that such variation in endowed capital/land
ratios is a direct consequence of net additions to family
income/acre on small farms due to the hiring out of family
labor and net drains on income/acre on large farms due to
hiring in of wage labor, provided that the wage is above
average consumption per adult.

Even if a market in land also exists, it is possible that
equilibrium relative factor prices are approximately the same
as marginal rates of substitution along the portion of multi-
product isoquants having nearly constant rates of substitution,
in which case again a wide range of factor proportions may
be optimal, with little or no incentive for readjustment of
factor proportions by most farms beyond the range dictated
by "endowments".

(2) Increasing returns to scale, empirically observable
at farm sizes found in most "overpopulated" peasant economies,

should also tend to exhibit itself in greater labor and
capital intensity on small farms than on large, to the extent that indivisibility and imperfect rental markets prevent
marginal adjustments of factor proportions or farm scale.
This is true also of decreasing returns at large farm size
due to differences in quality of hired and family labor (and
possibly lower average land quality on large farms).

(3) A high degree of uncertainty together with risk
aversion which is a decreasing function of income levels
leads, for a variety of reasons, to greater labor and capital
intensity on small farms than large. Moreover, this to a
large extent accounts for the persistence of an institutional
form (sharecropping) which is not easily explained in a neoclassical framework. Firdly, this also accounts for the
persistence of a wide range of farm sizes, despite substantial
increasing returns which should, on neoclassical assumptions,
lead to uniformly larger scale of farming.

Factor Endowments, Farm Size and Market Opportunities

The seminal attempt to apply the neoclassical marginalist
theory of distribution to a peasant economy was that of A. V.
Chayanov (Tschajanow), a recently rediscovered Russian agricultural economist.[24] Starting from the assumption that a
peasant family attempts to allocate its resources (labor,
land and capital) in such a way as to maximize its utility
(viewed as a function of income and leisure per capita),

Chayanov arrived at a theory of peasant economic behavior which accounted rather well for the deviations from "ideal" capitalistic behavior observable in the extensive statistics he presented on Russian family farms.

An important proposition of the Chayanov theory is that peasant families allocate their resources so as to achieve equivalent marginal returns for various uses, behaving in that respect like capitalist firms. Thus, for instance, in deciding the proportions of labor to allocate to own-farm and off-farm uses, "the peasant farm takes for the realization of its labor from both agriculture and crafts and trades those opportunities which guarantee it in total the highest payment per marginal labor unit," i.e. the marginal productivity of labor on the farm will, in equilibrium, be equated with the wage rate available for off-farm labor.[25] Given fixed land assets and a low off-farm wage, the peasant family will "force its labor intensity far beyond the optimal limits" through "intensification of work methods or by using more labor-intensive crops and jobs."[26] "Optimal" here refers to the capitalist farm, which operates at lower labor intensity -- giving the impression that smaller farms are not optimizing their use of labor.

Chayanov's theoretical explanation of the observed difference in labor intensity is not necessarily correct, however, even if we grant his conditions -- which are apparently that the size of the farm be unadjustable in the short run

(i.e. no land market) and more than one production technique
be available (the condition of a low off-farm wage is irrelevant since, without the other conditions, it should induce
all scales of farm to employ equally labor-intensive techniques).

Assume that the different production techniques may be
represented as different, first-degree homogeneous production functions, producing a common product with two factors
of production, land and labor. Different farms have different
endowments of these factors and, additionally, may sell or
purchase labor services in the market at a fixed wage. If
all farms operate in such a way as to maximize total returns
to owned factors of production, then the conditions for optimizing the proportions of the endowment of each factor devoted
to own-farm use are identical for all farms, whether net
sellers or purchasers of labor services; namely, maximize
the net return to land (the total value of production minus
the value of labor used, evaluated at the market wage) subject to the land constraint and the condition that labor be
used only up to the point where its marginal productivity
equals the wage. These conditions, under the above assumptions, lead to the choice of one and only one production
function or technique and a unique factor ratio; nor is this
choice affected by the initial factor endowment of the farm,

given constant returns to scale for each technique.[*]

It is true, on the other hand, that in an n-factor world, with more than one necessary, non-marketable factor and unequal relative endowments among production units, that different mixes of production techniques will be employed, and different factor intensities will be observed depending on endowments. In fact the following theorem will hold in such a world:

Assume n techniques of producing a single good, each technique consisting of a linear homogeneous production function utilizing m factors of production. Assume that r of these m factors are available on the market at a uniform price for each, but that m - r factors constitute fixed endowments for each firm: Then it will be true that a revenue maximizing solution for each firm can be found which utilizes no more than (m - r) techniques (a proof is sketched in Appendix II-A).

This rule, which is analogous to a familiar theorem of linear programming, does suggest an explanation of widely varying degrees of labor intensity which is at least superficially plausible: Suppose there exist two linear homo-

---

* Optimization with respect to labor leads, for each production function, to a net revenue function which is linear homogeneous with respect to land alone; full optimization requires choice of the net revenue function with the highest slope (marginal value-added per unit land).

geneous production functions in the factors labor, land and
capital, one more "favorable" to labor than the other;[*] that
labor services are freely marketable at a fixed wage but
capital and land are available to farms in fixed endowments:
Then, if the labor-intensive production function is also more
"favorable" towards whichever of the other two factors is
least scarce on small farms, farm optimization would be observed to lead to use of labor-intensive production processes
on small farms to a greater extent than on large farms. In
fact, although it is not intuitively obvious, consideration
of specific examples leads to the conclusion that relatively
small variations in the ratios of fixed factor endowments,
combined with slight differences in production function elasticities with respect to the fixed parameters, could lead to
more significant variations in labor intensities between

---

* "Favorable" to labor may be interpreted as meaning that more
labor is required to equate the MP_L to a given real wage, for
any given amounts of capital and land, than is true for other
production functions (this need not hold for all wage levels
or factor proportions). In our case, it is only necessary that
the full optimization conditions for the production mix, which
additionally require equal marginal productivities of factors
in all uses, lead to a higher labor/land ratio for one technique than for the other.

producing units.[*]

The empirical evidence on factor proportions in peasant farming does not in itself contradict this explanation. Statistical data on peasant production from areas as different as Switzerland, Russia,[27]India[28] and China (see Chapter V and Appendix V-B) imply that it is universally true that small

---

* Consider two Cobb-Douglas production functions, $q_1 = \lambda L^{.5} K^{.3} A^{.2}$ and $q_2 = \lambda L^{.3} K^{.3} A^{.4}$, where L, K and A represent labor, capital and land respectively. Suppose additionally that the real wage level equals 5 units of output. Optimization conditions require that, if both production functions are used, the capital/land ratio must fall between 1.53 and 0.77. Farms with an endowment in the former, more capital-heavy proportion will produce using the first technique alone, and will employ labor sufficient to reach a labor/land ratio of 1.81; farms with endowment in the latter proportion will utilize only the second technique, and with a labor/land ratio of 0.56. Farms with endowments between the two extremes will employ a mix of techniques, with the labor/land ratio related to the capital/land ratio linearly, with a slope of 1.75. This range of variation in factor ratios is, coincidentally, strikingly similar to that between smallest and largest farms in a Swiss survey cited by Chayanov (p. 116). If $q_2 = \lambda L^{.3} K^{.4} A^{.3}$, a 13% variation in the K/A ratio leads to a 250% variation in optimal labor/land ratios.

peasant farms have a higher capital/land ratio than larger
ones, and that this holds also for most of the various elements
lumped together in the category of capital -- including material
inputs, irrigation, labor animal services, tools and implements,
and buildings. If this variation is a consequence of absolute
constraints (rather than the result of optimization with
respect to marketed capital and land inputs); if labor intensive production processes in peasant agriculture are also
by nature more "favorable" to capital (relative to land), as
previously defined; and if the range of relative factor endowments and forms of available production functions are such
that technique switching and mixing should optimally occur
over the range of farm sizes, we could then explain the equally
universal negative correlation between labor intensity and
farm size.

To consider the first of these conditionals, suppose that
peasants are forced to work within the constraints of their
endowments of capital[*] and land: Is there any reason to suppose that the ratio of these two endowments will generally
be negatively correlated with farm size? There is, if we
consider the statistical facts that (1) given their land constraints, small farms generally have a greater labor endowment

---

[*] With no rental market in land, and wages paid ex post, working capital is required only for maintenance and replacement of
farm implements and current inputs; hence is treated here as
both finance and service of physical inputs.

than can be profitably used on the farm, so that some part of the labor force works off the farm as laborers, craftsmen or tradesmen; (2) large farms conversely find it profitable to hire labor from outside; (3) farm families with larger holdings may maintain a larger proportion of unproductive (or less productive) family members and certainly a higher standard of per capita consumption (in consequence of greater wealth).[29]

We will employ an elementary mathematical comparison of the situations of a family with limited land assets and one with extensive land assets to establish that the former will, ceteris paribus, have a higher capital/land ratio than the latter. Two simplifying assumptions are necessary: First, since a capital market by assumption does not exist, the family must depend for this year's farm investment on a sacrifice of part of this year's asset holdings (this year's income plus net savings; the latter may be neglected if we assume that the family desires to maintain constant net worth, so that net additions to savings out of current income and subtractions for farm investment are identical). To avoid introducing the utility function (involving a rate of time preference) of the family, we assume that the family attempts to maintain a particular level of per capita consumption, c, and devotes the remainder of current income to working capital and capital maintenance, so that $K_t = Y_{t-1} - cL$ where K_t is capital services, Y_{t-1} is (last year's) real

family income (net), and L is the family labor force (no
dependents are assumed to exist).

Secondly, to avoid the infinite regress of current capital
expenditure depending, via income, on previous capital expenditure and on the labor/land ratio (which, after all, is supposed
to be optimized with respect to the capital expenditure),
we assume temporarily a single linear homogeneous production
function for both farms as well as initially identical labor/
land and capital/land ratios, so that yields are identical:

$$Q_t/A = f[L/A, K_t/A]$$

is the same for both large and small farm, even though A, the
size of landholding, differs.

Supposing that the small farm hires out and the large farm
hires in an equal amount of labor, L_h, at wage w, we can
express the net family income per unit land of small and
large farms as, respectively:

$$Y_{st}/A_s = f[(L_s-L_h)/A_s, K_{st}/A_s] + wL_h/A_s \qquad (1.1a)$$
$$Y_{1t}/A_1 = f[(L_1+L_h)/A_1, K_{1t}/A_1] - wL_h/A_1 \qquad (1.1b)$$

Since $K_{t+1} = Y_t - cL$, for small farms we may write
$Y_{st} = K_{st+1} + cL_s$ and for large, $Y_{1t} = K_{1,t+1} + cL_1$, so that

$$K_{s,t+1}/A_s = f[(L_s-L_h)/A_s, K_{st}/A_s] - cL_s/A_s + wL_h/A_s \quad \text{and}$$
$$K_{1,t+1}/A_1 = f[(L_1+L_h)/A_1, K_{1t}/A_1] - cL_1/A_1 - wL_h/A_1$$

We may use the assumption that the operational labor/land
ratios are identical, that is $(L_s-L_h)/A_s = (L_1+L_h)/A_1$, to
rewrite the last two terms in a form permitting comparison
of the two equations:

$$K_{s,t+1}/A_s = f[(L_s-L_h)/A_s, K_{st}/A_s] - c(L_l+L_h)/A_l$$
$$+ (w-c)L_h/A_s \qquad (1.2a)$$

$$K_{l,t+1}/A_l = f[(L_l+L_h)/A_l, K_{lt}/A_l] - c(L_l+L_h)/A_l$$
$$+ (c-w)L_h/A_l \qquad (1.2b)$$

If desired per capita consumption levels are identical on the small and large farm, clearly the first two terms of eqs. 1.2a and 1.2b are identical; the future capital/land ratios of small and large farm will diverge according to the magnitudes of the remaining term, which may be taken to measure the extent to which the hiring in or out of labor detracts from or contributes to the surplus for capital formation. Only if $w = c$, that is, the wage is equal to "subsistence" (here, average consumption per worker) will the capital/land ratios remain identical on small and large farm. If, as seems more probable, the wage is greater than the subsistence level for small farms, then the latter will tend to have a higher K/A ratio than large farms.

But suppose that, because of their higher wealth or larger number of dependents, land-rich families maintain a higher per worker consumption level than land-poor families: Then we may replace the term c in eq. 1.2b with $c' = c + \delta$, where c remains the consumption level of small farms. The equations remain identical with the exception of a term, $-\delta L_l/A_l$, added to eq. 1.2b, further reducing the capital/land ratio for large farms as compared to small.

All this, of course, depends on the assumptions of equal
initial yields and labor/land ratios for both farm sizes;
but it is reasonable to assume that farms adjust their labor
intensity (and thus yields) to optimize with respect to
differences in capital availability (and consumption standards). These adjustment operate on the first two terms
of eqs. 1.2a and 1.2b in such a way as to narrow the disparity in K/A ratios, but not to eliminate it, since a
bound is placed on the tendency towards equality by the
disparity in the ratio of family labor endowments to land
endowments and by differences in desired consumption levels
reflecting these relative endowments. It should also be
noted that increasing returns to scale could also reduce
the disparity.

To reiterate in more intuitive terms, in the absence of
a labor market, it is difficult to see why the greater labor-
intensity of small farms could be matched by greater capital-
intensity, since capital must be accumulated out of a surplus
above family consumption requirements. If, however, the
off-farm wage labor of family members on small farms adds
to the surplus available for capital formation, and on
large farms, the expense of hired labor and/or the higher
consumption levels per family-worker detracts from this surplus, then the resources available for capital formation may
well be higher on a per acre basis on small farms than on
large, and higher labor-intensity is likely to be accompanied

by higher capital-intensity on small farms.

If a land market exists, of course, it is possible that part of the higher per acre surplus will be diverted into land acquisition. However, if the existence of multiple production techniques permits considerable flexibility of factor proportions, as discussed above, this need not be the case. In demonstrating this below, we may also permit intertemporal optimization of consumption and investment with respect to peasant family "utility functions".

Suppose all farms have a choice of either or a mixture of two linear homogeneous production techniques, have fixed but different land endowments, initially equal yields (i.e. last period's L/A and K/A ratios were identical for all farms) and family-labor/land endowments which dictate that land-poor farms hire out some portion of available family labor supply (and land-rich farms hire in additional labor).

Referring to Fig. 2.2, consider first the land-rich farm: Net family income per acre at time t is represented by y_t'. This income may be consumed or invested, in varying proportions, to yield varying net incomes at time t+1 represented by the corresponding production possibilities frontier (ppf). From our earlier analysis, we know that this frontier will have a linear segment, where a mix of the two production techniques is profitably employed and along which the marginal productivities of capital, land and labor will be constant

(the slope of the ppf is the
marginal value productivity
of capital investment).

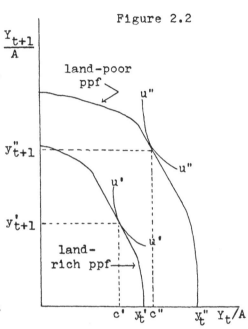

Figure 2.2

To consider the land poor
farm: Since last period's
K/A ratios, and thus farm
labor/land ratios (given a
uniform wage level) were
identical for all farms, so
was the portion of family
income/acre which can be
identified as a return to
capital and land. Total net
family income includes also
payments to family labor which, on or off the farm, can be
evaluated at the market wage (equated to the marginal value
product of labor), so that total income per acre of the
land-poor family (y_t'') is equal to that of the land-rich
family (y_t') plus the difference in family labor earnings
per acre of land holdings (i.e. $y_t'' - y_t' = wL_s/A_s - wL_1/A_1$).
Assuming no change between t and t+1 in family labor force
or the wage level, for any given level of investment per
acre, the same differential in per acre total net incomes
will be maintained over time, so that the ppf for land poor
families is identical to that of land rich families, except
that it is shifted outwards and upwards by the difference

in family labor earnings.

Corresponding to the respective ppf's of land-poor and
land-rich families, we may visualize indifference curves
representing family preferences with respect to different
combinations of present consumption and future income (both
per acre). Since land-poor families have a greater number
of consumers per acre, we can suppose a priori that, for any
particular combination in Fig. 2.2, the indifference curve
of land-poor families passing through such a point has a
higher slope and represents a lower degree of satisfaction
than the corresponding one for land-rich families. However,
if we can again assume that the per capital consumption level
for at least land-poor families which results from subjective
optimization of investment and consumption with respect to
time is less than the market wage, we can disregard the actual
shapes and locations of indifference curves since, in any
case, the difference between c" and c' must be less than
$y_t'' - y_t'$, since $c_s(L_s/A_s - L_1/A_1)$ is less than $w(L_s/A_s - L_1/A_1)$.
In that case, the investment/land ratio for land-poor families
must be higher than that for land-rich families, and if a
mix of techniques is employed, the former will employ the
more capital-favoring of these in greater proportion than
the latter (in Fig. 2.2, it may be observed that at the
subjective equilibrium, the land-poor family operates at a
point closer to the capital-favoring end of the linear segment -- i.e. closer to point a in Appendix II-A., Figure A.).

Note that if we relax the assumption of equal last-period yields and assume instead that the land-poor family has also previously been operating at higher capital-intensity and higher yield, the result is only to shift their ppf to the right (but not upwards). If, as we would intuitively expect, future income is not an "inferior good" compared to present consumption, the capital-intensity of land-poor families would then be expected to be higher than before.

We have so far assumed that no market exists which would permit the exchange of money capital for land and vice versa. Yet a theory which breaks down under the influence of a market is open to the same criticisms brought forward against the anti-neoclassical theories of a peasant economy in the previous section. Moreover, for most contemporary peasant economies, it is impossible to argue that such a market is non-existent, since even where social disapproval of, for instance, land sales can be established, one commonly finds quite sophisticated devices or institutions for evading the spirit of the taboo, if not the letter.[30] If, as is often the case, such transactions are not nearly as frequent as strictly neoclassical assumptions would lead on to expect, given wide disparities in factor endowments, then a meaningful theory certainly must account for this fact.

Let us consider then a closed peasant economy, with for any given period a fixed stock of homogeneous, consumable

capital,[*] of labor and of land; a set of production opportunities as previously described; and the opportunity to exchange
assets at the beginning of every period before the onset of
the productive process. To introduce slightly greater realism,
we may allow for land rentals (a fixed rent payable at the
end of the production period) as well as sales. I assume
no borrowing of capital, although its existence would not
affect our results in this case.

Under the usual neoclassical assumptions about producer-
consumer motivations, equilibrium factor prices -- market
clearing prices which, after initial transactions, leave no
incentive for further exchange of factors among producers --
will be determined by the ratios of total stocks of each
factor in the economy. There are two possibilities: If
aggregate factor proportions fall outside the range within
which it is optimal for producers to use a mix of production
functions, the result of trading will be to define a unique
set of factor proportions shared by all producers (who will
also use only one production process). If, on the other
hand, the aggregate factor proportions fall within that

---

* Defining capital as a homogeneous good with numeraire price
(instead of using heterogeneous capital services) is a matter
of convenience (as is its interchangeability with consumption
goods), not affecting our conclusions so long as production
functions allowing a high degree of substitutability can be
assumed.[31]

range, unique factor prices will be defined, but individual
producers may reach their optimal positions at any set of
factor proportions within that range.

In either case, the following distributional relationships
will hold at equilbrium: Producers will adjust their use of
capital services, land and labor, internally and externally,
so as to define a uniform "internal rate of return" (i.r.r.)
to money capital equal to the marginal value productivity of
capital in production and equal to the marginal rate of time
preference. Land price will adjust so that the value of land
times the i.r.r. is equal to the marginal value productivity
of land, which will also be equal to the rental price of land.
Finally, if labor is paid in advance of production, the m.v.p.
of labor will also equal the wage times one plus the i.r.r.
That is, no matter whether money capital is invested in working
capital (wage payments), physical capital services or land,
it will bring the same rate of return at the margin and will
reflect the marginal willingness to sacrifice current consumption for future income. We have arrived, then, at the
conventional distributional conclusions of neoclassical theory.

It is worthwhile, before continuing, to summarize the
development of the theory present above and examine the
picture it presents of equilibrium in a peasant economy in
a historical light. It is apparent that in an economy which
possess alternative linear homogeneous production techniques
that there will be one set of factor prices which allows

some degree of variation in factor proportions for individual producers at an economic optimum. If aggregate factor
proportions for such an economy are fixed and fall within a
range defined by the technical characteristics of the production functions, this particular set of factor prices will also
be the equilibrium factor prices for the economy. Once these
equilibrium factor prices have been established, individual
producers with factor proportions within this range will have
no incentive to utilize the market to change their factor
proportions, but given an unequal distribution of land endowments relative to family sizes, land-poor peasants will tend
to operate at a more capital-intensive end of this range than
land-rich peasants; and, again if the technical characteristics
of the production functions are appropriate, a similar distinction in labor intensity will be observed. Since capital
accumulation in peasant economies is at best a slow process
(and may in any case be kept pace with by labor force growth
and opening of new land), aggregate factor proportions and
consequently equilibrium prices are likely to remain virtually
constant over long periods.[*] Under this circumstance, all
factor markets except the labor market (where there is a high
rate of turnover) are likely to be quite inactive; indeed

---

[*] Barring natural catastrophes which, in many peasant economies,
cause occasional drastic losses of labor force, the consumption of "edible capital" (such as labor animals), and destruction or nonreproduction of physical capital.

individual transactions will only occur when families are
pushed out of the optimal range of factor proportions, by
calamity or windfall, "acts of God" or, probably less frequently, by gradual accumulation or loss of capital or labor
force. Most such gradual changes, however, may be adjusted
to through choice of technique mix and proportion of family
employed full-time on the farm.

The Significance of Returns to Scale

The theory developed above seems so far consistent with
such statistical patterns as I have cited for peasant
economies, particularily the significant variation in factor
proportions observable on peasant farms. But in fact a
serious discrepancy remains to be explained, the nature of
which is pointed up by a contradiction between my theory
and Chayanov's reasoning: Contrasting the differences in
labor and capital intensity on land-poor and land-rich farms,
he asserts that "similar forcing up of intensity is quite
unacceptable to the capitalist farm, since in this event
the land rent, in the economic sense [i.e. measured as a
residual, with returns to other factors measured at market
prices], per hectare falls almost one and a half times."[32]
But the linear homgeneity we have assumed guarantees that,
whether or not mixed techniques are employed and no matter
what the factor intensities (so long as they are optimal),
per unit returns to each factor are uniform among farms. As

there is considerable statistical evidence that excess
(residual) profits are often negative for small farms,
rising to substantial positive figures for large farms,[33]
it would appear that either the linear homogeneity assumption
is unrealistic or the behavioral assumptions of the theory
are inaccurate.

If the remaining assumptions of the theory are correct,
the statistical evidence is consistent with the existence
of increasing returns to scale at the lower range of farm
sizes, turning into decreasing returns at larger farm sizes.
This, of course, suggests the U-shaped marginal cost curves
of elementary economic theory. Is there a priori reason to
believe that such a cost configuration will prevail in
peasant agriculture? The answers of Western agricultural
economists are quite ambiguous.

The concensus seems to be that the nature of agricultural
technology is such that constant returns to scale is attainable over the range of farm sizes that a single family can
manage without substantial use of hired labor.[34]The main
source of increasing returns, it is argued, would be indivisibilities of inputs; but almost all the inputs used in traditional agriculture are highly divisible, and such indivisibilities as remain can generally be overcome by a well-
organized rental market, the existence of off-farm part-
time employment opportunities, or equivalent institutional
arrangements.

It must be kept in mind, however, that these arguments
are given in the context of a rebuttal of the belief in
economies of scale so prevalent in underdeveloped countries
and therefore tend to be overdrawn. Indeed, Mellor admits
that increasing returns are likely to prevail at farm sizes
below that which can fully employ a family-size labor force
and its complement of capital (especially work stock) and
that cooperative arrangements or custom hiring which would
increase effective divisibility have "proved difficult to
achieve."[35] Achievable or not, such alternatives surely involve greater cost per unit service and/or lesser efficiency
than can be attained by full owners of physical capital
operating at a scale sufficient for full utilization, which
fact translates into declining marginal costs with increasing
output. Moreover, even if family labor power can be made
divisible through off-farm employments, can the "managerial
input" (a slippery concept at best) be considered similarily
divisible?

On the other end of the scale, it is generally accepted that,
at a size of operation requiring considerable hired labor,
decreasing returns are likely to set in, due to the difficulties of management of larger labor forces and their lack
of skills or incentives. Hired agricultural labor is on the
average younger, less experienced, less skilled and probably
less motivated than other components of the labor force.

Qualitative differences in other inputs may also be correlated with farm size and lead to apparent deviations from the constant returns hypothesis. Among the most significant is the degree of fragmentation of farms: Not only do differences in plot size lead to differences in the efficiency of, for instance, work animal utilization, but excessive distances between plots involves considerable wastage of human and animal worktime.   This cost in turn should lead to differences in the intensity of cultivation of near and far fields and therefore to differences in average yield between farms with greater or lesser fragmentation.

There are reasons for expecting fragmentation cost to decline with farm size and therefore to contribute to increasing returns to scale. First, consider costs due to travel between plots: Take a simple model of land divisions -- for example, a chessboard patter -- and suppose travel between plots on a single farm is planned so as to minimize total distance travelled in working all plots, so that a sequential working pattern will be chosen, with travel occuring only between the most contiguous plots. Then it is obvious that, even with random placement of plots, expected average distance travelled between plots goes to zero as the number of plots owned per unit area goes to 100% of available plots, so that total distance travelled will not rise as fast as farm size. This conclusion of course breaks down if travel is always from a single reference point, such as the family compound.

Secondly, land inheritance patterns (which are most
influential in determining the pattern of landholdings of
small farms) are generally geared for equitable distribution
of landholdings among heirs, who will frequently receive
a piece of each type or quality of land even though the
resulting holdings are more dispersed than optimal for
efficient farming. Subsequent land acquisition and disposal,
generally leading to growth in farm size over the life cycle
of the heir, will be more oriented to income maximization,
and may well involve disposal of distant, less-intensely
worked plots and acquisition of adjacent plots, permitting
field consolidation and expansion (elimination of boundary
strips adds additional land at no cost). Larger, more
"mature" farms will thus display lower per acre costs of
production as the outcome of this process of farm evolution.

U-shaped marginal cost curves are therefore likely to
be observed in "real" peasant economies and are sufficient
to account for the observed relationship between profits
and farm size. Indeed, peasants are not unaware of these
facts: "At Su Hsien, Anhwei, the farmers realize the advantage of large farms in using men, animals and equipment
efficiently and there is a saying that for a farm of 100 to
125 mow three men, three animals, one plow, one harrow, and
one cart are used to maximum capacity, but that for a farm of
200 to 250 mow ... five men, five animals, two plows, two
harrows, and one cart are enough."[36] Farms of even the former

size (15 - 20 acres) were exceptionally large by Chinese
(and other Asian) standards.

How does the existence of increasing or decreasing returns
to scale affect the productive equilibrium in a peasant
economy? The answer depends on the source of deviation from
neoclassical assumptions. Returns to scale due to indivisibilities of inputs are the most unfortunate source inasmuch as
they mar the predictive precision of the theory. These are
best classed as "economic" (as opposed to technological)
returns, since they are quite consistent with production
functions characterized by constant returns to scale (when
inputs are defined in units of constant utilization efficiency). Their existence implies that, although the use
of an additional, indivisible unit of some factor may be
economically rational insofar as its marginal productivity
is greater than its market price, the addition of that unit
will lower marginal productivity to well below the price of
the factor. With constant returns production functions,
applying Euler's Theorem, with some factors having an opportunity cost greater than their (point) marginal productivity,
the farm will be taking an accounting loss (negative profits).
Unless there is a free and perfect market in every factor,
the existence of an accounting loss need not constitute an
incentive for a family farm to abandon operations, as it
would in the world of perfect competition and neoclassical
assumptions. But it does mean that the farm operates either

with a single or mixed production technique but in any case
with an internal rate of transformation of one factor for
another which may differ between production techniques and
will certainly differ marginally from the ratios of market
prices of factors, although not so much so that it pays to
trade a discrete and indivisible unit of one factor for
another.

Note, however, that the existence of multiple techniques
of production (including different crops) should permit the
use of productive factors to be so divided among techniques
as to achieve full effective divisibility internally, without
reference to the market. Only the inconvenience of growing
more than one crop simultaneously on the same plot (except
where the crops are complementary in the sense that inter-
planting is feasible) and the qualitative suitability of
particular types of land for particular crops limits this
internal substitutibility. However this does not guarantee
that the internal marginal rates of substitution so achieved
will be consistent with market factor price ratios. For
example, the services of a water buffalo may be divided
among crops in such a way as to bring the same marginal
returns for each crop, but these returns may only be sufficient to justify the ownership of a fraction of a water
buffalo given market prices of labor animals. Such a
situation may nevertheless be economically optimal if the
market makes no provisions for rental of animal services

and cooperative ownership arrangements are not feasible.

Of the remaining sources of deviation from constant returns, the influence of land fragmentation and, at large farm sizes, the effects of a fixed managerial constraint may be assumed to operate indiscriminately, regardless of the mix of production techniques used, to bias farms away from the use of otherwise optimally labor-intensive techniques to the degree to which distance of travel and less careful management lowers the marginal productivities of labor and (secondarily) other factors.

Finally, a qualitative difference between hired labor and own-labor will have the same effect as would a difference between the prices paid for and received by farm laborers: Hiring farms will be paying relatively more per unit of labor performed and, even if their production functions are the same, will use relatively less labor intensive techniques than farms which do not hire labor. Marginal productivity per laborer will remain the same on all types of farm, but marginal productivity per unit of labor of homogeneous quality will be higher on hiring farms than on family labor farms.

In sum, the relaxation of the unrealistic constant returns assumption in favor of varying returns to scale, besides accounting for the notable correlation between accounting profits and farm size, generally reinforces our earlier conclusion that small farms worked with family labor will, for economically rational reasons, employ more labor and capital intensive techniques than larger farms, operated with some hired labor and with more nearly full utilization of owned factors of production. Only a negative correlation between farm size and average distance between plots would work in the opposite direction, since then labor and capital -- the mobile factors of production -- would be relatively less productive on small than on large farms.

At the same time, we lose much of the uniformity and precision of the neoclassical results on the relationships between marginal productivities of factors and their market prices. Nevertheless, the deviations from these results are basically predictable and, given adequate data, we now have many new clues as to what sorts of patterns to expect if the theoretical discussion is valid.

Uncertainty in the Peasant Economy

The model developed thus far in this chapter is appropriate to a world of complete certainty -- that is, in which a known, one-to-one relationship exists between economic decisions and their consequences, which are universally known. Such a picture overlooks the primal role played by vagaries of nature and fortune in an otherwise relatively static economy and the degree of risk-aversion characteristic of a peasantry whose incomes are all too close to subsistence levels. The presence of an uncertain relationship between inputs and out-

puts and their prices affects resource allocation and thus
income shares through its impact on individual decision
making and through institutions such as sharecropping developed to deal with risk; moreover it lies behind the capital
constraint which preserves differentials in farm scale and
factor intensity in the peasant economy.

To simplify the following discussion, we shall confine
ourselves to a consideration of "pure" uncertainty or risk,
which we define as a situation where each action taken by a
decision-making unit is associated with a range of possible
outcomes of known or unknown probabilities. Thus, for instance, because of the variability of weather, the output of
a farm remains a random variable regardless of the input
allocations chosen by the peasant, although the latter will
generally affect the characteristics of the distribution of
outcomes. We exclude an alternative view dear to some economists,[37] under which there is a one-to-one relationship between decision variables and outcomes, but incomplete knowledge of this relationship exists, permitting an "entrepreneur"
presumed to have superior knowledge or "luck", to reap "pure
profits" as a reward for his endeavors. "Uncertainty" in
this sense is difficult to distinguish from variations in
managerial efficiency, particularily in economies where the
impact of technical and societal change is trivial in the
short run.[38]

The near-stationary condition of peasant economies and
the central position of weather variability as the origin
of most uncertainty in these economies further suggests
that we can safely assume an approximate awareness of the
probability distribution of uncertain consequences on the
part of the peasant, based on historical experience. That
is, the peasant will generally be aware of the past frequency
distribution of weather conditions, of their relationships
to crop yields and their further ramifications on economic
variables such as crop prices, wages, labor supply and demand
and so forth.

If we could further assume "risk-neutrality" as characteristic of peasant "utility functions"[*], uncertainty could
be conveniently incorporated into our earlier model by using
expected values of economic variables rather than their cer-
tainty-values, permitting maximization of the mathematical
expectations of net incomes as the primary motive of decision
makers, and leading to a productive equilibrium which is
independent of the stochastic "disturbances" caused by
weather.[39] This result does not follow, however, from the

---

* Implying that their utility functions of income are linear,
that they will accept a "fair gamble" (expected value of
outcomes equal to cost of gamble), and that the expected
utility of the distribution of outcomes can be decomposed into
the utility of the expected value of the outcomes.

assumption that peasants are risk-averters (i.e. that the
utility function of income is concave, or the marginal
utility of income decreases with increased income).[40] Rather
if risk-averting peasants are assumed to maximize the expected
utility of the stochastic consequences of their decisions, the
presence of uncertainty should induce them to (1) shift
resources in the direction of the least risky activities;
(2) decrease the absolute commitment of resources with fixed
(nonstochastic) unit costs to activities with uncertain outcomes.[41]

These assertions should be qualified slightly: They are
based on the assumption that the stochastic disturbance
affects the gross value of output in the production process
as a multiplicativie scale factor, and that the disturbance
is itself independent of the level of inputs, although its
impact on output is not. In fact certain types of inputs
have value as "insurance" of stable yields, and the presence
of uncertainty will induce greater use of such inputs, compensating wholly or in part for the reduced use which would otherwise be optimal for a risk-averter. The reader may refer to
Appendix II-B for a formal proof of these assertions.

Applying the above to the peasant farm economy, we immediat
ly arrive at some interesting hypotheses: First, of the three
aggregate factors of production, land, labor and capital,
only land has no obvious "insurance effect" (that is, additions of land will not in general reduce the impact of

uncertainty.[*] By contrast, more intensified applications of
labor and capital in the proper directions can afford
considerable protection against variations in natural conditions. Consequently, if risk-aversion induces a reduction
in input utilization, land inputs will be reduced more than
labor and capital inputs (which conceivably could be increased). Labor and capital-intensity will thus be greater
than would be expected if inputs were being employed to the
extent that their prices were equal or equi-proportional to
their expected marginal value productivity.

Secondly, uncertainty appears also in the factor markets
in the sense that the expected value of returns to factors will
generally be less than their nominal price (for labor, the
number of days or years of employment per unit time is a
random variable; for land and capital, even with fixed absolute
rents and interest rates, the rate of default on rent, principal and interest payments is a random variable). Thus,
while hirers of factors will take nominal prices or rental
rates as nonstochastic parameters in their net income func-

---

* unless landholdings are so dispersed as to take advantage of
the reduction in variance of average yields which results. A
fully effective dispersal of landholdings would be incompatible
with centralized management, but reduction of the impact of
geographically localized risks is often achieved at the expense
of lowered efficiency of cultivation.

tions, sellers of factor services will consider their returns
to be stochastic parameters with expected values lower than
nominal prices. Consequently poor peasants, with endowments
of labor and capital relative to land greater than those of
rich peasants, will rationally be induced to employ their
endowed factors in own-farm production to a greater extent
(i.e. to the point where they have a lower expected marginal
value productivity) than rich peasants would be inclined to
employ hired factors (with higher and certain opportunity
cost). The same rule applies to rich peasants, with their
relatively high land endowments. Therefore, with no assumed
differences in the degree of risk-aversion, the impact of
uncertainty, together with differences in initial endowments
of factor inputs, leads to parallel differences in own-farm
factor ratios, despite the existence of a common set of
factor markets.*

However, neglect of possibly systematic differences in the
degrees of risk-aversion among peasants is no longer justified,
since uncertainty combined with risk-aversion has the effect
of destroying that neoclassical separability which permitted
us to disregard the peasant's "utility function" and assume
only income maximization (although the utility function has

---

* We may surmise that the effects of uncertainty on the labor
and capital markets are significantly greater than on the
land market, since nominal rates of return on land are well
below those on money loans.

previously entered via the "rate of time preference", and would also have to be involved in a consideration of the labor-leisure choice).[42] For relative and absolute factor utilization will depend as much upon the degree of risk-aversion of the decision maker as on the extent of uncertainty. Since the capital constraint assumed implies increasing short-run marginal cost, the greater the uncertainty and the greater the degree of risk-aversion, the smaller the proportion of total output value attributable to marketable or purchased factors of production, and the larger the proportion consti-tuting residual, accounting profits. Conversely, risk-takers (i.e. those least risk-averse) will come closer to maximizing the absolute level of expected profits, although the per unit profit margin will be smaller.

The extent of risk-aversion is, commonsensically, related to one's income or asset position; in general, a definable relationship can be established between an individual's economic behavior under uncertainty and the shape of his "elementary utility function," U(C) (a "cardinal preference scale for consumption incomes under certainty").[43] "Risk-aversion" itself implies that, for $U'(C) > 0$, $U''(C) < 0$ over the relevant range of C. The "degree" of risk-aversion is commonly measured by either of two indices:

$$R_A(C) = - U''(C)/U'(C) \qquad \text{(absolute risk aversion) and}$$
$$R_R(C) = - CU''(C)/U'(C) \qquad \text{(relative risk aversion).[44]}$$

If observation or intuition permit us to deduce the behavior of individuals of different incomes faced with simple
risk-choices, we may employ these relationships to place
restrictions on the form of U(C) sufficient to predict
differences in behavior in more complex uncertainty situations.

Now it is generally accepted that humans (including
peasants, presumably!) display decreasing absolute risk
aversion with increasing income (for instance, if an individual will pay a certain amount, or "premium", to escape
a gamble with given values of outcomes and their probabilities,
an individual with higher income will generally pay less to
escape the same gamble).[45] This assumption is not sufficient, however, to make deductions about the behavior of
peasants of varying incomes in the presence of uncertainty
in the productive process, since the stochastic outcomes
faced tend to be _proportional_ to scale of operation and thus
almost proportional to income, rather than having constant
absolute variance. We therefore argue, more controversially,
that peasants display decreasing _relative_ risk aversion:
It seems intuitively plausible that, faced with a gamble
offering alternative outcomes involving a gain which is a
large proportion of income, or a loss which is a large proportion of income, a poor peasant would demand highly favorable odds (since the loss would leave him without the means
of subsistence), whereas a rich peasant would demand less

favorable odds (since the loss might still leave his income
above subsistence); thus the rich peasant would display less
relative risk aversion than his poor cousin. Against this
intuitive notion, the argument for increasing relative risk
aversion rests primarily on the convenient but unnecessary
restrictions on the mathematical form of the utility function
which it permits.[46] In addition, welfare systems which provide
security of subsistence in advanced societies (but not in
peasant societies) and belief among the poor in "hunches"
or "infallible systems" (relevant in gambling, but not in
productive activity under uncertainty) both may be asserted
to lower the degree of absolute and relative risk aversion
of lower income groups, but may be disregarded here.[47]

If decreasing relative risk aversion is associated with
increased income (or wealth) positions in peasant economies,
it follows that the richer peasants will come closer to ful-
filling the neoclassical optimization conditions (with
expected values replacing certain parameters), while the
previously described deviations from these conditions will
be most characteristic of poorer peasants. Consequently
richer peasants will have higher expected profits than
poorer peasants (who could easily take accounting losses,
both because of the latters' greater attention to the "insurance effects" of inputs and the effects of uncertainty on
expected returns, as opposed to nominal prices, in the factor markets) and factor shares and proportions will show the

closest relationship to market prices and the parameters
of the production function for rich peasants.

Uncertainty combined with risk-aversion not only affects
the allocation of resources and distribution of income within
the framework of an ordinary market economy; it also accounts
for the existence (or persistence) of an institution less
frequently found in developed agricultural economies,
namely sharecropping systems. Although sharecropping can be
thought of as a relic of an earlier, "feudal" period, its
persistence within peasant economies where the more "modern"
fixed (cash or commodity) rent system is prevalent begs for
an economic explanation. Since the main economic distinction
between a fixed and a proportional rent system is that under
the latter a portion of the risk in production is transferred
to the landlord and the variance of tenant income is consequently reduced, differences in the incidence of uncertainty
and extent of risk aversion would seem to be the core of such
an explanation.

It seems difficult to make much sense of sharecropping
using a strictly marginalist approach, so we begin with the
following basic propositions: Sharecropping reduces the
variance of net income for the tenant, by comparison with
a fixed rent system in which the same level of expected
rent payments prevails; consequently a risk-averting
peasant should be willing to accept a lower expected value
of income net of rent payments in return for the coinsurance

provided by the sharecropping system (the difference could
be considered the "premium" cost for the coinsurance). Conversely, the variance of the rent receipts per unit of land
is increased under the sharecropping system, hence a landlord would presumably require a greater expected value of
rent receipts before he would be willing to rent out a unit
of land under this system. The greater the degree of uncertainty (or the variance of output), and the greater the risk-
aversion of the tenant, the higher the "premium" which a
tenant would be willing to pay and which a landlord would
require to make a choice of the sharecropping system mutually
satisfactory to both parties.

However, the independent variable here is the _proportion_ of
the crop, not the expected value of the landlord's share.
Obviously the landlord's evaluation of this proportion, compared with a fixed absolute rent, depends on the yield, determined in part by the amounts of complementary inputs employed
by the tenant. Here lies the rub, since the tenant's optimization conditions under sharecropping require him to use
land up to the point where its marginal productivity becomes
zero, and to employ other inputs only up to the point where
their marginal productivity _times_ the tenant's share equals
their unit cost (with uncertainty and risk-aversion, even
further reduction of complementary input use can be expected).
Not only does this result seem counterintuitive (in a land-
scarce, overpopulated peasant economy), but if we examine

the landlord's willingness to rent out a marginal unit of
land under this system at a point near the tenant's equilibrium, it becomes clear that he will never do so if he
can receive a non-zero rent under the fixed rent system
(since the additional unit of land adds nothing to the tenant's
product at equilibrium). Thus Bardhan and Srinivasan argue
that, with neoclassical production functions and tenant
decision making in production, a sharecropping and a fixed
rent system cannot coexist in the same locality.[48]

To escape these results, it is necessary to assume that
under sharecropping either the landlord makes all production
decisions[49] or available production functions and/or contractual arrangements are such as to greatly restrict the decision-
making sphere of the tenant. The latter possibility seems
more realistic, and may be what Rao had in mind when he argued
that "under uncertainty situations where the scope for
entrepreneurial functions is limited" sharecropping arrangements
may prevail.[50] In any case, for a sharecropping system to
exist where a non-zero level of fixed rents is institutionally
permissible, it is necessary and sufficient that the share-
cropper be unable to optimize, in fact, be unable (or unwilling)
to lower the marginal productivity of land below a level of
expected returns to the landlord sufficiently above the
prevailing fixed rent to compensate him for the increased
uncertainty he is forced to bear.

Empirically, then, one would expect sharecropping to prevail

in localities where productive uncertainty is high only if
conditions such as the following exist: rent contracts
specifying type of crop, or land and environmental qualities
requiring particular crops and/or techniques; capital services provided at least in part by the landlord or "attached"
to the land (e.g. irrigation facilities), with their economic
returns included in the landlord's share of the crop (so
that the tenant has no incentive to reduce capital use);
lack of part-time off-farm employment opportunities (so that
all family labor assets will be applied on the farm); limited
knowledge of alternative techniques or crops (so that the
production function is or is perceived as being of fixed
proportions); share-pricing in other than the land market
(as where harvest labor, etc. receive a specific fraction of
the harvest, rather than a fixed wage).

Since such a system could only coincidentally approach a
Pareto-opimal allocation of resources, the widespread assumption that sharecropping is inefficient still holds, although
it will not then be as inefficient as simple optimization
models imply. Moreover, since many of the requisite conditions are associated with relatively backwards agricultural
societies, it is understandable that sharecropping should
prove increasingly disadvantageous to the landlord as modernization proceeds and the conditions preventing the tenant
from optimization break down. Paradoxically, the tenant
may find the sharecropping system increasingly favorable as

these restrictions break down in the course of modernization,
since the expected value of the landlord's share per unit
of land decreases more rapidly than yield as the tenant
adjusts his input proportions in the direction of greater
land intensity to approach his net-income maximizing position.

Uncertainty and the Capital Constraint

In the earlier discussion of the peasant economy in the
absence of uncertainty, it was assumed without explicit
justification that the peasant has no access to a loan market for productive purposes, so that he is confined by a
budget constraint to a scale of operation which may be less
than optimally efficient (i.e. where decreasing marginal
costs may prevail). In a certain world, with no particular
restrictions on the market, it is difficult to explain why
such a loan market wouldn't develop, especially in view of
the existence of markets for individual factor services. It
seems to be the case that peasants rarely look to the market
for funds which would permit them to increase their scale
of operation, presumably because the "marginal efficiency
of investment" is less than the high nominal rates of interest
prevailing. But if such is the case, one would expect that
large numbers of peasants would find it profitable to enter
the market as lenders, driving down the rate of interest
and raising the m.e.i. At equilibrium, the m.e.i. should
equal the rate of interest, individual peasants should be

indifferent between marginal lending and borrowing and there
should be a tendency (with U-shaped cost curves) towards
uniformity in scale of operation, as borrowers reach the
size of farm enterprise which minimizes average costs.

The existence of uncertainty provides a discontinuity
in the capital market sufficient to explain why this does
not occur. As we have seen, the expected rate of return to
the lender is considerably below the nominal rate of interest.
If the uncertainty attached to loans on the market is imilar
in magnitude to that attached to direct investment in own-
production, we would expect a peasant to distribute his
funds in such a way that the expected rate of return from
both types of investments would be equalized if the peasant
engages in any lending at all; otherwise the return to
investment in own production will be the higher of the two.
Yet it will rarely be as high as the nominal rate of interest.
Consequently, the peasant will rely only on his own funds
(or those from unusually low interest sources, such as family
or friends) for productive purposes, so that he effectively
operates within a budgetary constraint.

This situation is graphically depicted in Fig. 2.3 (for
a risk-neutral peasant). The expected marginal rates of
return available to a peasant from investment in expansion
of his own production are depicted as the m.e.i. schedule,
ab. His total investment opportunity schedule, agh, includes
loans with expected return, E(i). On the other hand, his

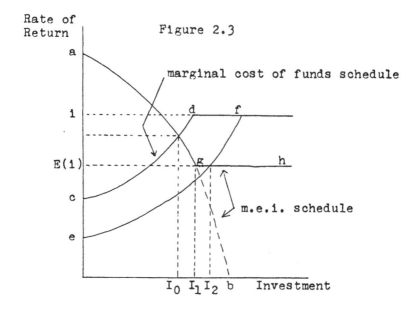

Figure 2.3

subjective, "internal" marginal cost of funds schedule (or
marginal rate of time preference) is cd or ef, but he can
also borrow at nominal rate i. Depending on which schedule
is appropriate, he may invest I_0 in expansion of his own
production, neither borrowing nor lending in the market, or
he may invest I_1 internally, loaning out $I_2 - I_1$ in the market. Only if as a result of some "emergency" his marginal
cost of funds schedule shifts drastically upward will he be
willing to borrow for productive purposes (e.g. if funeral
costs leave him insufficient funds to cover family consumption and seed).

It should be pointed out that the peasant's unwillingness
to borrow for productive purposes does not mean that he is
not "capital-starved" nor that the return to expansion of

productive scale is not high, compared with "reasonable" rates
of time preference. Obviously the gap between nominal and
expected rates of return on loans must be quite substantial
before this argument rings true. But, in this respect, it is
worth noting that, although returns to labor, land and
capital all have uncertain values, loans involve greater
risk in two respects: The "principal" of the loan is at
stake, as well as the interest (or return to "capital services");
it is difficult to insure that loans are used for "productive
purposes" (creating the means of repayment) instead of
consumptive ends. Thus with interest charges sufficient to
cover these greater risks, the markets for land, labor and
physical capital services may be quite active where peasants
are simultaneously unwilling to borrow to expand their
production.

Conclusions and Testable Implications

The introduction of uncertainty and its implications completes
a theory of equilibrium relationships in the peasant economy
which deviates from neoclassical assumptions about the
motivation and behavior of the atomistic decision unit only
in the direction of introducing greater realism in the assumptions made concerning the opportunity set faced by the
decision makes. The major departures from the neoclassical
model are a consequence of the emphasis on the peasant
family as the primary unit of decision making in production

and consumption. Other distinctions between economic relationships in modern, industrial societies and peasant economies are a consequence of quantitative differences in the distribution of productive resources, degree and impact of uncertainty, and factor productivity.

I have previously stated that one of the weaknesses of the "anti-neoclassical" theories of the "labor-surplus economy" is that they are not easily susceptible to test on the basis of statistical data. It may be useful to summarize the major testable propositions (or assumptions) which have emerged from the previous discussion:

(1) The productive opportunity set available to peasants is characterized by quite high elasticities of substitution among major factors of production over the range of factor proportions found on most farms. This permits optimization of factor proportions with respect to market prices by farms possessing a wide range of relative factor endowments largely by choice of mix of crops or techniques, although factor indivisibilities may make this impossible on small farms;

(2) Within the context of traditional agricultural technology, capital-intensive techniques tend also to be labor-intensive. Despite their small size (or rather because of it), small farms derive a higher surplus per acre for capital formation from income added by off-farm family labor than do wealthier, larger farms, which not only are forced to pay for wage labor but also consume a larger amount per

unit of family labor because of greater wealth and a larger
number of dependents. Although this result may be counteracted by the effects of increasing returns to scale, the
greater per acre availability of capital contributes to
the greater capital and labor intensity of small farm production.

(3) Decreasing marginal cost curves (increasing returns
to scale) characterize peasant agricultural production
largely because of indivisibilities of factor inputs and
greater consolidation of plots on larger farms. The rate
of decline of marginal costs will be reduced and eventually
reversed with increasing farm size as a consequence largely
of increasing dependence on hired labor. The increasing
returns will be manifest in a strong correlation of residual
profits with farm size (which is also due in part to the
effects of uncertainty on input utilization).

(4) The pervasiveness of uncertainty and risk-aversion
will lead to equilibrium relationships in which nominal
market prices are greater than the expected values of returns
from sales of factor services, and to factor use which keeps
the expected marginal value productivity of purchased factor
inputs above their nominal market prices. The latter is
counteracted by an "insurance effect" which induces greater
use of labor and capital services in order to stabilize
output and income levels, hence one can only predict that
the m.v.p. of land will be higher than the nominal rental

cost for farms which rent land. On the other hand, peasants
who are not net purchasers of factor services will tend to
use relatively more of such factors and may have an expected
m.v.p. less than market price if uncertainty in that factor
market is sufficiently high. This is likely to affect the
labor and capital markets more than the land market, and
leads to the prediction that small farms will use labor and
large farms money capital in own-farm production to an
extent greater than nominal wage and interest levels would
seems to dictate.

(5) Because of lower risk aversion, richer peasants (i.e.
larger farms) will generally come closer in equilibrium to
equating expected m.v.p. of factor services with their market
prices, and to maintaining the factor proportions implied by
risk-neutrality and profit maximization.

(6) The expected value of the landlord's share under the
sharecropping system will be greater than that of a fixed-
rent on the same land; inputs under sharecropping will show
less relationship with market prices and m.v.p.'s. Cross-
sectionally, restrictions on marketability and substitutability
of factors will be correlated with the prevalence of the
sharecropping system.

(7) The gap between nominal and expected rates of return
in the loan market will be larger than in other factor markets, while the market for loans for productive purposes
will be notably inactive. Rates of expected return to

investment in own-farm production will be significantly
less than nominal loan rates from commercial sources, less
also than the expected rate of return on loans, as a result
of risk-aversion on the part of potential lenders.

Many of these propositions will find ready acceptance,
as they agree with well-known facts concerning the peasant
economy. The explanations, however, may not be so readily
accepted, nor is it obvious that the quantitative significance of the effects predicted will be sufficient to
account for the magnitude of deviations from neoclassical
hypotheses presumed to be characteristic of the "labor-surplus"
economy. The following chapters will examine available data
on the Chinese peasant economy as it existed in the period
1920-1940 in an attempt to provide a convincing assessment
of the value of these revisions of neoclassical distribution
theory in interpreting the workings of traditional rural
economy.

CHAPTER III. THE LAND MARKET IN PREWAR CHINA.

The economic institutions of peasant economies are frequently treated as "givens" by economists. Analysis of their origins, geographical incidence, reasons for persistence and interrelationships is generally left to historians and anthropologists. Yet the institutional framework of an economy is the product of human choice and bears a relationship to the economic interests of participants, particularily where alternative frameworks coexist. Moreover, economic analysis developed for the institutional framework of an advanced capitalist economy cannot be readily applied to a traditional peasant economy without consideration of the impact of differences in institutions on that analysis.

This chapter will take as "given" only the distribution of land ownership in the prewar Chinese peasant economy. It will seek to account in economic terms for the origins, geographical incidence, reasons for persistence and interrelationships among various forms of land tenure prevailing in this economy. Such a narrow approach will of necessity ignore non-economic aspects of a highly complex reality.

Because the intent is to generalize, the range of discussion will be broad and sometimes lacking in depth. But while excellent studies of particular institutions or geographical regions exist, what has heretofore been lacking is a general framework within which institutional relationships and geographical differences are integrated.

The framework we are attempting to establish is one of comparative statics. While many of the more interesting economic issues concerning the Chinese peasant economy relate to trends over time, the data is lacking which would permit firm conclusions within a dynamic framework. Furthermore, unless one first understands how the pieces interlock at a given point in time, one is unlikely to be able to describe structural change over time with any accuracy.

Land Tenure in Prewar China

The extent of activity which existed in the land and other markets in factor services in the prewar Chinese peasant economy was fundamentally due to two causes: the existence of a highly unequal distribution of land owner-ship and a high and increasing density of rural population. The first of these facts is documented in Table 3.1: It is apparent that fifty percent of all farm families (including landless elements) owned only something over 10 percent of all land, whereas 5 percent owned thirty per-cent or more. There appears to be slightly less inequality in North China than in the South, but the difference between Anhwei and the northern provinces is surprisingly small, given the difference in the tenancy rate. The

southeastern provinces of Kwangtung and Kwangsi should be
treated as special cases, as much of their cultivated area
was opened up in recent centuries by tenants immigrating
for that purpose and also because the permanent tenancy

Table 3.1   Distribution of Land Ownership Among Farm
Families, China, Early 1930s.

Percent of land owned by:

	Lowest 50%	Highest 5%
Average, 17 provinces[1]	11	36
North China:		
Hopei (2)	14	29
Shansi (2)	15	27.5
Shensi (2)	10	30
South China:		
Anhwei (2)	12	31
Chekiang (2)	10	44
Chekiang, Ts'ung-te hsien [3]	13	34
Kwangtung (2)	5	61*
Kwangsi (4)	6	37.5

*Includes 12% institutional land
Sources:
(1)   1935 survey by National Government, Nei-cheng pu,
cited in Hsueh Mu-ch'iao, Chung-kuo nung-ts'un
ching-chi ch'ang-shih, p. 26. Figures may be unweighted averages.
(2)   1933 survey, Nei-cheng pu, cited in Feng Ho-fa,
Chung-kuo nung-ts'un ching-chi tzu-liao, Vol. II,
p. 501.
(3)   Survey of 399 households, 9 villages, 1933. Cited in
Ibid., Vol. II, pp. 461-462.
(4)   Survey of 242 hsien, 2,857 households, 1934, cited in
Ibid., Vol. II, p. 453.
Note: Sources (3) and (4) break land ownership down by
size categories; to estimate percent of total land, we
used the modal size for each group as weight. In all
cases, the figures given above were extrapolated from
hand drawn Lorenz curves to permit comparability.

(yung-tien) system of land tenure resulting from this practice gave tenants partial property rights not reflected in the ownership statistics (see below for discussion of this system).

The maldistribution of property rights in land, in conjunction with lack of adequate land resources, forced a majority of the agricultural population to seek means of subsistence through some combination of land rental, farm or non-farm wage labor or subsidiary enterprise (handicraft activities). The effects of tenancy and the use of hired labor in equalizing the distribution of the use of land may be seen in Table 3.2. On the whole, this effect was small in North China: If the wage-laboring group is removed from the "less than 10 mou" category of ownership and the percentages readjusted to the 10 percent smaller base, it remains apparent that the percentage of large landholdings is not reduced -- i.e. large landholders in the North generally chose to farm their land rather than rent it out. In the South, by contrast, a greater proportion of the large landholdings were broken up and rented out (however, Shensi and Kwangsi appear exceptions to these patterns). The general pattern of smallholdings remained, with about half the farms of less than 10 mou (1.65 acres) though with a tendency in the North towards farms of between 10 and 30 mou (1.65-5 acres) in size.

Table 3.2 Tenancy Rates and Hired Labor, Various Provinces,
1936 and 1933.

Area	% of farm families who were:			Hired Labor as % of Rural Population
	Tenant	Part Tenant	Owner Cultivator	
All China	30	24	46	10.3
North China:				
Kansu	18	18	64	12.5*
Shensi	18	20	62	19.8
Shansi	16	23	61	10.4
Hopei	10	18	72	11.6
Shantung	10	15	75	10.2
Honan	20	21	59	9.4
South China:				
Kiangsu	30	25	45	8.8
Anhwei	42	23	35	8.2
Chekiang	47	33	20	9.3
Fukien	42	44	31	5.8
Kwangtung	46	33	21	11.4
Kiangsi	40	33	27	10.9
Hopei	41	26	33	6.0
Hunan	50	28	22	11.1
Kwangsi	38	23	39	12.1
Szechwan	51	20	29	10.6
Yunnan	36	25	39	8.5
Kweichow	45	28	27	6.0

*average for Ch'inghai, Kansu and Ninghsia.
Sources:
  Tenancy data: National survey, 1936, cited in Yen
    Chung-p'ing et al., eds, Chung-kuo chin-tai ching-chi
    shih t'ung-chi tzu-liao hsuan-ts'e, p. 262.
  Hired labor data: 1933 survey, 354 localities. Includes
    both long and short-term labor, so that there may be
    some overlap in numbers with tenants and owner-
    cultivators. Cited in Ibid., p. 263. Refers to farm
    labor only.

The prominent differences in patterns of land ownership and operation between North and South China suggest an
approach to the unresolved issue of why tenancy rates were
consistently higher in the South. Dwight Perkins has argued

Table 3.3 Comparison of Distribution of Land by Ownership
          and Farm Size, Various Provinces, 1934 and 1935.

Province		Percent of families with:				
		<10 mou	10-29.9	30-49.9	50-99.9	>100 mou
Hopei:	Owned	51.4	28.4	12.7	5.8	1.7
	Farmed	40.0	41.4	10.8	6.1	1.7
Shansi:	Owned	37.1	30.3	17.7	11.1	3.8
	Farmed*	16.9	41.0	20.3	16.1	5.7
Shensi:	Owned	47.5	22.3	15.9	11.7	2.5
	Farmed	38.7	35.9	12.8	10.1	2.5
Anhwei:	Owned	55.0	26.4	12.0	5.0	1.6
	Farmed	47.0	38.2	9.6	4.5	0.7
Chekiang:	Owned	76.4	15.4	5.3	2.2	0.6
	Farmed	67.0	27.8	3.5	1.4	0.3
Kwangtung:	Owned	68.3	21.5	7.2	2.4	0.7
	Farmed*	87.4	12.3	0.3	**	-
Kwangsi:	Owned	79.7	16.6	2.2	0.9	0.6
	Farmed	51.1	37.7	7.2	3.0	0.9

* sample only includes two hsien.   (1 mou = .1647 acres)
** less than .05%
Sources:
  Ownership: See Table 3.1. Lowest group includes farm
     laborers.
  Farmed: Yen Chung-p'ing et al., eds., op. cit., p. 285.

that this fact can be largely accounted for in terms of the
better transport network and resulting higher degree of
commercialization in the South: With high transport costs,
the value of land to a subsistence producer was higher than
to a large landowner (either landlord or owner-cultivator)
who must market a major portion of the produce. Given this
gap, landlords in the North were presumably priced out of

the market (relative to the rates of return on alternative
uses of their capital).[1] However, this line of reasoning
founders on the evidence of Table 3.3 that both large landholdings and large-scale farming (necessarily non-subsistence
oriented) were noticeably more prevalent in the North than
in the South. Clearly the wealthy were not averse to
holding much wealth in land in the North: The question is
rather why did they choose to farm it as a unit rather than
subdivide it and rent it out, as in the South? The most
plausible explanation is agro-technical: With the relatively
land-intensive grain crops of the North, large landowners
could profitably farm their holdings with a minimal supplement of hired labor (compare the somewhat higher population
proportion of hired labor in North China, in Table 3.2).
In the South, paddy rice and economic crops such as tea, silk,
tobacco and, near urban areas, vegetables required the use
of both labor and capital-intensive production techniques.
Large-scale farming with hired labor would have involved a
substantial fixed wage cost, with losses due to crop yield
fluctuations absorbed by the managerial landlord; the
requirement of close supervision of a large labor force
involved impossible diseconomies; the use of unmotivated and
unskilled hired labor was simply not suitable to the
relatively sophisticated agro-technology employed in the
South. Subdivision and rental of the land shifted these
burdens to the tenants and provided a more motivated and

skilled labor force. Moreover, the comparatively heavy requirements for working capital were also shifted to the tenants, freeing landlord capital to take advantage of better opportunities for investment in the urban commercial economy of the South.

This explanation of the difference in tenancy rates between North and South China also provides an explanation for higher tenancy rates in parts of the North: around the cities, where alternative opportunities for capital were available and labor and capital-using garden crops were of greater importance; in commercial tobacco and cotton-growing counties, such as Feng-jun hsien (Hopei) and Wei-hsien (Shantung), for the same reasons.[2] In the more mountainous areas, large farms were geographically un-feasible, and extremely low-yield, high-risk farming (with correspondingly low rent and land prices) meant that extra-ordinarily (and unmanageably) large holdings were required to provide income equivalent to that of a smaller owner-cultivator or landlord on the plains.

Four major categories of rental system coexisted in the prewar peasant economy, although the fourth was rarely employed. These were the fixed (commodity) rent, cash rent, proportional rent and labor rent systems, of which the first was by far the most common system (see Table 3.4). Under the first two systems, capital and labor were generally

provided by the tenant, the landlord being responsible only
for the land and improvements thereto. Rental payments were
made in terms of set amounts of the major crop(s), of cash
or, in a transitional variant, at the cash value of a set
quantity of crops. The major difference between commodity
and cash rental systems was, of course, that under the
former the landlord bore the expense and risk of marketing
(and reaped any speculative or monopoly gains). Where the
landlord was a local resident and expected to consume large
quantities of the crops produced by his tenants, there was a
clear advantage to commodity rent, since it eliminated the
twofold middleman's margin (on sale by tenants and purchase
by landlords). Conversely, cash rent was often preferred by
institutional or collective landlords and absentee landlords in the cities or where high transport costs were
involved; also for crops other than foodgrains.[3] On the
other hand, commodity rent was more subject to landlord
abuses (such as use of unofficial measures of volume in
collecting rent, or the requirement of uncompensated grain
transport labor services of the tenant)[4] and could be bene-
ficial to those landlords, absentee or local, who could
obtain better prices for produce, due to greater transactions volume, personal influence or market "savvy".[5] As
for cash conversion of commodity rent (notably popular in
Kiangsu, Wu-hsi and K'unshan hsien),[6] there was scope for

abuse in the choice of conversion rate, sometimes set in
advance of the harvest.[7]

Table 3.4 Distribution of Rental Systems Among Tenants, By
Province, 1934.

Province	Cash Rent (%)	Commodity Rent (%)	Proportional Rent (%)
Chahar*	18.7	51.6	29.7
Suiyuan*	31.2	23.1	45.7
Ninghsia*	46.1	18.5	35.4
Chinghai*	10.6	53.8	35.6
Kansu	14.3	51.2	34.5
Shensi	15.1	59.0	25.9
Shansi	27.0	46.3	26.7
Hopei	52.3	21.6	26.1
Shantung	30.4	30.5	39.1
Honan	16.5	39.5	44.0
Kiangsu	27.6	52.9	19.5
Anhwei	14.1	52.5	33.4
Chekiang	27.2	65.7	7.1
Fukien	19.2	55.5	25.3
Kwangtung	23.9	58.4	17.7
Kiangsi	7.1	80.1	12.8
Hopei	20.2	58.0	21.8
Hunan	7.4	74.2	18.4
Kwangsi	6.3	65.2	28.5
Szechwan	26.4	57.8	15.8
Yunnan	14.0	61.1	24.9
Kweichow	9.6	39.9	50.5

Source: Yen Chung-p'ing et al., eds., op. cit., Table 24.,
p. 289.

The relative advantages of cash versus commodity rent
varied to some extent with price trends. Cash rental levels
were periodically adjusted: In western Chekiang, this was
done on a yearly basis, with some exceptions, and other
data make it clear that cash rents at least kept up with
the general price level over the long run.[8] But in periods

of rapid inflation there was a substantial tendency to switch back to commodity rent systems.[9]

Both cash and commodity fixed rent systems sometimes included provision for rent reduction in case of an extremely poor harvest, although this provision may have depended on somewhat higher rental payments or on payment of rental deposits.[10]   However, the "insurance" involved was probably minimal: Analysis of Mantetsu data for a village in Wu-hsi hsien, Kiangsu, reveals that, of 39 tenancies, of as long as 50 years in duration, 29 had never experienced major rent reduction; four had experienced reductions involving a long-run (or "expected") loss to the landlord of from 1 to 5 percent; five a loss of 6 to 10 percent; and one a loss of 17 percent. None of the 18 tenancies begun after 1930 had experienced any reductions (by 1940).[11] Nor was this a consequence of absenteeism, as two-thirds of the landlords lived in or reasonably near the village surveyed. Yet it is conceivable that outside coastal China landlords were forced to be more lenient on this issue.[12]

The proportional rent system (fen-tsu), while less common than the fixed rent system, was still in use among about one out of three tenants and moreover showed no clear tendency to decline over this period.[13] This system could be subdivided into two types, one in which the landlord supplied both capital and basic management while the tenant was responsible only for the labor input, and one in which the landlord was responsible for little more than the land. The former system, found most frequently in the northwestern provinces and Honan, is best treated as a substitute for use of hired labor by managerial landlords, in which some of the risks and rewards of cultivation were shifted onto the shoulders of the tenant and the landlord was not responsible for wage or board.[14] This system was frequently called the two-eight or three-seven system, representing the respective shares of tenant and landlord. For example, in northwest Honan's cotton-growing areas, labor's share was 30 percent for cotton but 20 percent for wheat;[15] these shares, which should represent "pure return to labor" under marginal productivity theory, will be of interest in the following chapter.

The second variety of proportional rent system was the more frequent sharecropping system, the theoretical interpretation of which has been discussed in the previous chapter. In this case the tenant was responsible for all or most of the capital and management; the tenant's share depended on region, crop and, most important, the proportion of capital he provided. For example, in Kwangtung, if the tenant provided all the capital, his share was 70 percent; if very little, closer to 40 percent. The proportions were applied to the major crop, unless subsidiary crops were an important part of total receipts.[16] Nationally, about 60

percent of tenants under this system received between 40

and 50 percent of the crop.[17]

As discussed in the previous chapter, this system was

distinguished from fixed rental systems primarily in that the

landlord assumed a share of the risk (i.e. provided "co-

insurance" to the tenant). We would therefore expect it to

be practiced on fields or in regions where risk of crop

fluctuation or major calamities was high. However, the

system theoretically creates an incentive for minimum

possible use of labor and capital by the tenant, so that we

should also expect close landlord supervision; restrictions

or lack of opportunities for alternative uses of tenant

labor and capital. There is considerable evidence to con-

firm these hypotheses: According to Feng Ho-fa, "Wherever

the sharecropping system is implemented, the tenants are

frequently guilty of the malpractices of clandestinely

reducing their labor, and allowing the land to become barren

and overgrown, thus influencing the yield, so that the land-

lord has to frequently inspect the farm personally to

prevent this. From the point of view of the landlord's

profit, it is not as convenient as collecting a definite

quota under the fixed rent system. Moreover no sooner do the

losses due to calamitous harvests become extremely expensive

than this system ceases to be very popular."[18] In Kiangsu it was reported that, under this system, the landlord had to inspect while the crops were growing, to "point out or correct the omissions of the tenant".[19] In West Chekiang sharecropping was confined to economic crops _for_ _which_ _the_ _landlord_ _supplied_ _the_ _capital_.[20] And in Kwangsi, the system was employed only on land where the harvest was relatively unpredictable and where the landlord lived in the same village; where absentee landlordism and stable yields were the rule, fixed rent was preferred.[21]

We have attempted a crude test of the hypothetical relationship between risk and the prevalence of the share-cropping system in prewar China on the basis of the Buck survey data. For empirical testing purposes, we suggest that the proportion of tenants on the sharecropping system should vary cross-regionally inversely with the expected yield/_mou_ of land (measured at market values) and directly with the standard deviation of the distribution of yields over time, a measure of variability and thus risk (that is, tenants are likely to prefer sharecropping if the risk is high _relative_ _to_ the yield). Deviations from this relation-ship should be explainable by factors bearing on the ability of landlords to supervise or restrict the tenant tendency to limit labor and capital use on the land: High absenteeism, urbanization, commercialization, and labor and capital-intensive farming technologies are all such factors, limiting the advantages to the landlord of this system.

We have used Buck's data on the frequency of flood,
drought, wind, insects, frost, hail and other calamities
affecting crops and the average percentages of crop lost at
each occurrence (see Statistical Volume, Table 9., pp. 13-
16) for each of 150 localities over the period from 1904 to
1929; treating the frequencies as probabilities of occurrence,
we computed the expected percentage of crop loss and the
standard deviation of this percentage, which we take as a
risk index. We have ignored the (small) probability of more
than two calamities occurring the same year, and treated
each type of calamity as a statistically independent event.
The consequence of a double-calamity is arbitrarily assumed
to be equal to the crop loss from the worst of the two
calamities plus one-half the loss from the milder calamity.
The computed values of $E(X)$, the expected percent of normal
yield realized over the long run, vary from .3 to 1.0 while
δ, the standard deviation and measure of risk, varies from
0 to .41 among localities, being highest where calamities
are severe and frequent, but not so frequent as to be the
norm.

For a definitive test, we need also data on the
"normal" yield of tenant farms (yields vary tremendously
among farms and localities) to permit computation of
expected yield and its standard deviation ($E(X) \cdot \bar{Y}$ and
$\delta \cdot E(X) \cdot \bar{Y}$ where $\bar{Y}$ is normal yield). This data, however, is

not available from Buck and perhaps because of this
omission, the analysis which follows is less than satisfactory: We attempted, for a collection of localities, to
measure the relationship between the percentage of tenant
farms on the sharecropping system and the computed E(X) and
δ; we also attempted to estimate $\delta \cdot E(X) \cdot \overline{Y}$, choosing as a
proxy for $\overline{Y}$ the value of production (measured in grain-
equivalents) per labor unit in each locality at the time of
the survey on farms roughly corresponding in size to the
mean size of tenant farms.[22] We found no systematic, significant relationships, although one point became very
apparent: Interlocality yield variations are so great that
they are likely to outweigh variation in δ in a risk index.
That is, small variations in the distribution of actual
yields around the "normal yield" are likely to be of less
relevance in choice of rental system than large variations
in the extent of surplus above subsistence represented by
the differences in "normal yield" among localities.

Averaging the data by crop region, however, brought out
some at least "suggestive" relationships between sharecropping and risk (a "suggestive" relationship, in our
usage, is one in accordance with expectations, but to which
no statements of statistical confidence can be applied).
The regional data is summarized in Table 3.5 below.

Table 3.5 Sharecropping and Other Indices, by Crop Region.

Crop Region:	1	2	3	4	5	6	7	8
Sharecropping (1)	.31	.13	.44	.13	.10	.05	.12	.30
Sharecropping (2)	.38	.30	.36	.25	.15	.15	.23	.38
E(X)	.82	.82	.73	.80	.66	.90	.89	.86
Sigma (σ)	.22	.22	.23	.26	.28	.15	.20	.21
$\bar{Y}$ (Yield/Man) (3)	.74	1.11	1.44	1.36	1.67	1.66	1.54	1.83
$(1-\sigma)\cdot E(X)\cdot\bar{Y}$ (4)	.48	.71	.81	.80	.79	1.26	1.10	1.25
Commercialization Proxy (5)	.43	.53	.50	.62	.57	.54	.64	.46

(1) Percent of tenants sampled who were on the share-
     cropping system; Buck, Statistical Volume, Table 24.,
     p. 61.
(2) Based on Table 3.4. Provincial figures averaged, with
     weights in approximate proportion to their importance
     in Buck's samples of crop regions.
(3) Production per man-equivalent in thousand kilograms of
     grain-equivalent; Buck, SV, Table 13., p. 301.
(4) The value of yield/man one s.d. below the expected
     yield.
(5) The percentage of marketed crop which is sold immedi-
     ately after the harvest. Buck, SV, Table 1., p. 343.
Crop Regions:
1 -- Spring wheat area: Kansu, Ninghsia, Suiyuan,
     Chinghai, and N. Shensi and Shansi.
2 -- Winter wheat-millet: Shansi, Shensi, NW Honan.
3 -- Winter wheat-kaoliang: Honan, Hopei and Shantung.
4 -- Yangtze Rice-wheat: Anhwei, Kiangsu, Hupei.
5 -- Rice-tea area: Chekiang, Hunan, Kiangsi and N. Fukien.
6 -- Szechuan Rice: Szechuan.
7 -- Double-cropping rice: Fukien, Kwangtung and Kwangsi.
8 -- Southwestern rice: Kweichow and Yunnan.
     Small portions of other provinces overlap between
     regions.

There are a variety of ways of examining the relationship between sharecropping and the risk variables, depending

first on which estimates of the extent of sharecropping we accept (we are inclined to assume that Buck's sample underestimated sharecropping for much the same reasons that it underestimated tenancy, and therefore here use the alternative national survey results) and what sort of functional relationship between these and $E(X)$, σ, Y and other variables is assumed to exist.* To conserve the few degrees of freedom available, we have used $(1 - \sigma) \cdot E(X) \cdot Y$ as the risk measure. If actual yields are normally distributed around their expected value, actual yields will be above this value about 85% of the time. Clearly the closer this benchmark is to "subsistence" -- that is, the lower its value -- the more likely a tenant is to prefer the risk-sharing feature of sharecropping, ceteris paribus.

The values of this measure are plotted against the percent of tenants on the sharecropping system in Figure 3.1. It is apparent that a negative relationship exists, although, with so few degrees of freedom, it is statistically negligible. It is of interest to examine the deviations from this relationship. The regions which lie above the

---

* In all cases (including the use of Buck's sharecropping data), the signs of statistical relationships are correct -- i.e. σ is positively correlated and $E(X)$ negatively correlated with sharecropping -- but the "fit" (never good) varies.

fitted line --
those with a
higher incidence
of sharecropping
than seems explain-
able by "risk" --
are those generally
considered least
commercialized (the
north, northwest and
southwest), while
those falling below
the line are those

Figure 3.1. Sharecropping and Risk.

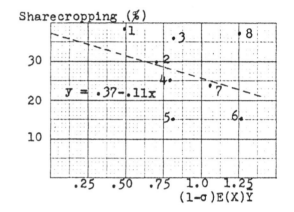

most commercialized, those where urbanization and absentee
landlordism were probably the most advanced. Some confirmation is found in the fact that the residuals are strongly
correlated with the regional averages for the percentage of
marketed crop which is sold immediately after the harvest
(Buck treats this as strongly collinear with commercialization; that would be obvious if it represented percent of all
production sold, but as it is, it might only represent the
extent of desperation of the tenant need for cash, in turn
related to the extent of cash rents, which is by definition
inversely correlated with sharecropping).[23] Unfortunately no
better index of the extent of commercialization is available
on a national basis.

Although our discussion has emphasized the risk-sharing feature of sharecropping as its fundamental raison d'etre, the apparent inability of variation in risk as measured here between localities and regions to account for more than a small proportion of variation in the incidence of this system suggests that the "conditional" factors -- commercialization, with its capital and labor intensive technologies, opportunities for off-farm labor and growth of absentee landlordism--may have been of greater importance geographically as well as intertemporally in accounting for the varying popularity of the sharecropping system.

One remaining system of land rental deserves brief mention, if only to stress the near-extinction of feudal forms of land tenure in China. This was the labor-rent system, analogous to the system of serfdom prevailing in feudal Europe. Under this system, found in a pure form in Kiangsu's Paoshan hsien and in a mixed form elsewhere, the tenant paid no crop rent, but rather performed a certain number of days of labor for the landlord (in the Paoshan case, 25-30 days per mou of land).[24] Its survival literally on the outskirts of Shanghai can probably be attributed to the difficulty of obtaining hired labor except at relatively high wages and perhaps because landowning families found off-farm employment opportunities unusually attractive and required a substitute for family labor.[25] The value of

labor involved (7-9 yüan, assuming meals were provided) was
probably a reasonable rent level for that location (1934
rents averaged about $5/mou for paddy in Kiangsu).[26]

The economic functions of two other institutional
arrangements relating to tenancy -- the so-called permanent
tenancy system and rental deposits -- deserve some discussion.
The first was prevalent only in the Southeastern provinces
of Kiangsu, Chekiang, Fukien, Kwangtung and perhaps
Kwangsi.[27] Under this system, land rights were divided
into ownership of the "subsoil" and of the "topsoil" or
surface; the first represented the usual, original claim to
landownership, including the right of sale, but exclusive of
the right of cultivation, whereas the second represented a
right of "permanent tenancy". The latter, however, could
also be sold or leased, so that in effect two distinct rents
were involved.

The economic significance of this system lies in part
in its origins and relationship to agricultural technology:
In the rice-cultivating south, the creation of fields on
the alluvial plains required dike construction and on the
hillsides, terracing. "Surface rights" were offered to
tenants by owners of wasteland in compensation for the labor
involved in such land improvement.[28] This applied also to
the restoration of land which had been abandoned and deteri-
orated to wasteland as a consequence of civil strife (such
as the T'aip'ing rebellion).[29]

Where the cultivator possessed the "topsoil rights",
rent in effect ceased to be a market-determined quantity.
To be sure, the landlord could sometimes increase rents by
manipulating the rate at which physical quantities were
converted to cash;[30] by purchasing the "topsoil rights" or
forcing the tenant to relinquish them.[31] But both custom
and law left such a tenant in a strong position, so that
unless he repeatedly defaulted on rent payments, he could
not be evicted and replaced at will by the subsoil owner.[32]

It should be kept in mind, however, that this system
was limited to a minority of peasants even in those areas
where it was most prevalent. In Chekiang, 37 percent of
tenants possessed "topsoil rights", in Kiangsu only 11 percent and in Kiangsi and Anhwei, only 9 and 5 percent
respectively. The largest proportion of peasants even in
Chekiang were under agreements specifying tenure of from one
to ten years.[33]

Under the permanent tenancy system, the sale and rental
of "topsoil rights" absorbed the pressures of supply and
demand for land, rather than the rental rate for "subsoil"
rights. Thus in areas where demand for land for use (as
opposed to investment for rental return) was low, subsoil
value (the nominal price of land) exceeded the price of
topsoil rights, whereas the converse was the case in
densely populated areas.[34] Thus, for example, in 1882 in

Kiangsu, Wu hsien, topsoil rights were valued at 60 percent
of the combined subsoil and topsoil price of land. The same
ratio prevailed on cotton land in nearby Ch'angshou hsien in
the 1930's, when subsoil rights were valued at best at 20
yüan per mou, compared to $30 for topsoil rights; for paddy
field, the rates were $30 and $60 respectively.[35]

The existence of this system complicates analysis of
rent levels in those provinces where it was prevalent (in
general, the more commercialized and often the best-surveyed
areas of South China) in that the rent paid by tenants
possessing topsoil rights bore no necessary theoretical relationship to current land productivity or demand for the
service of land. Nor can anything be said about the "equi-
tability" or "exploitation" implied by given nominal rent
levels without knowing the initial cost to the tenant or the
market value of his "surface rights", which, after all,
represented the tenant's share in the ownership of the land.
Thus, for example, "average rental shares" would not reveal
the fact that tenants without surface rights in Chekiang's
Lungch'i hsien paid rent equivalent to 55 percent of the
crop, whereas those with surface rights paid only 24 percent.[36] Nor can one be sure, as was pointed out on pp. 8-9,
how much significance to attach to an apparently greater
inequality of land distribution in these provinces when
land "ownership" was defined to include only subsoil rights.

A second institutional arrangement of interest was the rent deposit (ya-tsu) or "tenant guarantee fee" (pao-tien yin). Such a deposit was required of new tenants in 169 out of 359 counties surveyed in 1934 (47.1%), and was commonest in South China.[37] It served to establish the tenant's right to cultivate the land for a certain period and to guarantee against non-payment of rent, and as such was usually re-fundable at the end of the period of tenure. In North China it averaged $1 to $1.50 per mou, in South China about $5 per mou, though substantially higher in some areas; on the average, it represented no more than the value of a year's rent.[38]

However, in some areas rent deposits served two quite different functions and were of greater analytical interest: to equate the supply and demand for land services, probably where legal restraints or custom prevented increases in nominal rent, and to serve as a substitute for rent in localities where the rate of return to moneylending activi-ties was sufficiently higher than the rate of return to land investments to compensate for the presumably greater risk involved. In these cases the magnitude of rental deposits often exceeded that of several years' rent.[39]

The areas in which these practices seem to have occurred most frequently were those of increasing commercialization, either due to the presence of a nearby city (such as

Paoshan, K'unshan and Nant'ung <u>hsien</u> in Kiangsu and around
Ch'angsha in Hunan) or to the growth of a cash crop such as
cotton (again, K'unshan and Nant'ung, and Hupei's Tsaoyang
<u>hsien</u>); that is, either or both a demand for land driving
down its rate of return and ample opportunity for crop
speculation or lucrative investment in usurious loans to
credit-hungry cash-croppers.[40]   Thus in Paoshan, villagers
who had made money in Shanghai returned to the village and
bid up rental deposits to obtain land (according to the
gentry, "after 1918 it hadn't been easy to raise rents, and
there was no way to oppose increases in government taxes,
so the only thing remaining was to increase the rental
deposits at the time the land was rented out, and earn some
interest on the sum received).[41]   In Nant'ung, the substitution of rental deposits for rent occurred during World
War I, when the price of cotton was skyrocketing and speculation was unusually lucrative.[42]   In Chekiang, where a rent
reduction law had been imposed in the late Twenties, rental
deposits had not been banned; as a result, rental deposits
were raised to compensate, and tenants who could not pay were
forced to abandon their land and turn it over to others.[43]
Elsewhere, when tenants were too poor to pay deposits, they
were treated as loans from the landlord, tacked on as extra-
rental obligations repayable in annual installments.[44]

Where rent deposits were offered as a partial or total
substitute for rent, the amount of money involved was not

necessarily obligatory and payment brought a positive rate
of return to the tenant. In such cases, the landlord served
as a "financial intermediary", funneling the small savings
of former laborers or handicraft workers back into commercial
activities. For example, in Hopei's Tsaoyang <u>hsien</u> (1933),
a cotton-growing area with an extraordinarily large number
of peasants engaged in full-time subsidiary work,[45] the
following options were available to the tenant for varying
deposits:[46]

On 10 <u>mou</u> of land (worth 2000 ch'uan*):

Deposit	Annual Rent	Tenant's Rate of Return on Deposits
1500 <u>ch'uan</u>	none	8.0 %
500 "	70 <u>ch'uan</u>	10.0
300 "	90 "	10.0
none	120 "	--

* 8 ch'uan (string of cash) = 1 <u>yüan</u>.
  Tenant's rate of return = savings on rent/deposit.

Considerable insight can be gained from this schedule
if we examine it separately from the point of view of landlord and tenant. Only a few major points will be sketched
here, with a more rigorous theoretical analysis confined to
Appendix III-A.

The schedule may be treated as a record of the desired
investment portfolio structure of the landlord when the
choice is between financial investment of varying sums in
land, at different, near-certain rates of return, and in
loans, at higher but uncertain realized rates of return.

This approach permits us to explain why the landlord in
effect offers the tenant a lower rate of interest (in the
form of reduced rent) on a very large rental deposit than he
does on smaller deposits, a fact which at first sight appears
anomalous. This behavior turns out to be characteristic of a
risk-averter of what Tobin calls the "diversifying" sort[47]--
that is, an investor whose portfolio will generally include
a mixture of assets whose returns are certain and uncertain
and who must receive an increasing premium to be induced
to specialize in risky assets to an increasing degree. Or,
in this case, the landlord is willing to pay a higher rate
of interest on rental deposits to maintain a balance between
rental and loan income than he is if only loan income is to
be received.

From the point of view of a tenant with a certain amount
of capital, the analysis is more complicated: His choice is
among various combinations of rented and purchased land,
loans and rental deposits, given a fixed amount of capital
and labor, a "production function" involving labor and land,
and the various prices, rental costs and rates of return.
The optimum combinations for the tenant depend in part on
the rate of return to land and loans, the amount of uncertainty attached to each and the tenant's risk-aversion:
It is probably realistic to assume that, for a tenant, the
required "risk premium" is too great for him to invest in

moneylending; also the rate of return on money directly
invested in land is probably not much different from the 6
percent nominal rental rate (120/2000). Since the rate of
return on rental deposits is always greater than this,
tenants will tend to invest in deposits to the limit of their
money capital, rather than employing their money in land
purchase or direct moneylending, with respectively low
return and high risk. Or, to put it another way, landlords
were forced to offer fairly high rates of "interest" on
rental deposits most probably because so little tenant
capital was available.

Rent and the Rate of Return on Land

The level of rents can be discussed from the point of
view of either landlord or tenant. To the landlord, the
level of rent was only one of the components determining the
attractiveness of land as an investment; others included the
price of land, the level of taxation, cost of rent collection,
and various other minor current and investment expenses
associated with being a landlord. The uncertainty attached
to the return to land, though small compared with alternative investments, was nevertheless nonzero, especially so for
tenancy contracts involving sharecropping or allowing for
rent reduction in case of poor harvest (at least partially
covered by higher nominal rents or rental deposits, however).
With the spread of political consciousness among the

peasantry in the Thirties, rent default became a serious
problem, and was reflected in some areas by a fall in the
price of land.[48] In view of these costs and uncertainties,
some scholars have treated land investment as a relatively
unprofitable activity, the extent of which can only be explained on non-economic grounds.[49]

Nevertheless, two careful studies of the profitability
of land investment, based on reasonably large samples, imply
such investment offered a quite respectable net rate of
return, on the average between 9 and 10 percent (see Table
3.6.). These studies took into account all returns to the
landlord (including, in some cases, labor performed by
tenants), all expenses, and the total value of the landlord's investment (see Notes to Table 3.6.). In view of the
different time periods and the different approaches of the
surveys (the 1921-24 sample was of tenant farms; the 1934-35
of landlord holdings), the findings are remarkably consistent, although some sample differences could be expected.
It appears, first, that of landlord expenses, only taxation
was significant, at rates averaging about 1 percent of land
value in the early Twenties, rising about 20 percent by
1934-35, when it represented about 2½ percent of land value,
however, due to an apparent decline in land price. While
the tax incidence figures are confirmed by comparing Buck's
figures on tax rates with other estimates of average land

Table 3.6   Rate of Return on Investment in Land, China, 21 Localities, 1921-24 and 1934-35 (per mou)

Province	Locality	Sample Size (a)	Landlord Receipts (b)	Landlord Expenses (c)	Landlord Investment (d)	Rate of Profit (%) (e)	Rent/ Land Value (f)
1921-1923 Sample:							
Anhwei	Su hsien	57	$1.73	$ .40	$18.53	5.4	9.5
Shansi	Wu-t'ai	136	2.97	.11	16.27	17.6	22.6
Anhwei	Lai-an	51	4.83	.92	27.79	14.1	21.8
"	Lai-an	21	2.26	.81	28.24	5.1	10.0
Chekiang	Chen-hai	51	4.64	.21	50.66	8.7	9.3
Fukien	Lien-chiang	22	12.50	.36	104.29	11.6	12.0
Kiangsu	Chiang-p'u	15	3.94	.27	50.63	7.3	7.8
"	Chiang-p'u	105	2.01	.22	38.06	4.7	5.3
"	Wu-chin	43	4.94	.68	45.16	9.4	11.4
Average or Total --		501	4.43	.44	42.14	9.5	11.0
1934-1935 Sample:							
Honan	Nan-yang	20	1.39	.38	18.33	5.5	7.7
"	Huai-yang	20	1.59	.48	12.43	8.9	13.5
"	Hsin-yang	25	2.52	.21	28.19	8.2	9.4
Hupei	Hsiang-yang	28	1.75	.19	12.28	12.7	15.1
"	Chiang-ling	26	1.70	.39	5.17	25.3	33.6
"	Huang-mei	11	3.40	.84	20.98	12.2	16.3
Anhwei	Kuei-chih	27	2.89	.53	25.73	9.2	11.6
"	Wu-hu	16	1.89	.74	20.20	5.7	9.5
"	Tung-cheng	8	1.43	.31	21.63	5.2	6.8

(Table 3.6. continued)

Notes:
(a) The 1921-24 sample was of tenant holdings; 1934-35 of landlord holdings.
(b) Include crops, cash, other produce, farm work and household work performed for landlords by tenants; all but the first two of these are negligible except in regions where cropsharing tenancies are prevalent.
(c) Include taxes, repair of buildings and tools, cost of rent collection, repairing dikes, digging wells, etc. Taxes constituted about 80 percent of the total.
(d) Include land, buildings, tools, seeds, fertilizer, livestock, crops and cash loaned. All but the first two were negligible except in cropsharing tenancies. The value of land was about 95 percent of the total in both samples.
(e) Calculated as ((b) - (c))/(d), i.e. net return over investment.
(f) Rent in cash or commodities (excluding labor service) divided by investment in land only.

Sources:
1921-24 sample: Feng Ho-fa, ed., Chungkuo nungts'un chingchi tsuliao, vol. 1, pp. 118-122.
1934-35 sample: Lien-ken Yin, "Returns on Landlord's Capital Investment in Farms", Economic Facts 2, October 1936, pp. 123-132.

price on different qualities of land,[50] the qualities of land and thus their prices and rents may differ between the two survey samples rather than representing a trend (according to Buck's indices, land value in the early Thirties was only slightly different from that in the period 1921-24).[51] On the other hand, both surveys presumably recorded actually realized rather than nominal rents (note the figures for Lai-an hsien for two successive years, with no major difference in land value or expenses, but quite different per mou receipts), so that the lower average receipts and land

values of the mid-Thirties may in fact reflect the political
situation in the countryside at the latter date, as mentioned
earlier.

Yet, despite the differences in rent levels, the average
rate of return does not differ significantly between the two
samples, suggesting that land prices adjusted to the former
to maintain a rate of return determined by the supply and
demand conditions in the "money market" (that is, the
market in land and alternative investment opportunities).
Again, much of the variation in rates of return may be
"random" fluctuations due to harvest variation, whereas the
"average" rate of 9 to 10 percent may be taken as an approximation of the "expected rate of return" to the landlord.

The table also makes possible a comparison of the more
frequently cited figures on rent relative to land values
with the net rate of return. It should be noted that,
although tax rates were low, they were primarily responsible
for the spread between the two rates, and an increase in the
tax rate created a spread of 3 percentage points by 1934-35,
on the average. Variation in this spread helps account for
some anomalous patterns in the gross rate of return
frequently cited in the Chinese literature. For example, the
gross rate of return apparently varied inversely with land
"quality", as measured by its tax classification (high,
medium and low grade).[52] Since higher grade land represented

not only higher but also more stable yields, risk-averting landlords would tend to drive up its price to the point where the expected rate of return was lower (though more secure) than on lower grade land. The differential this created, however, was enlarged (in gross terms) by the differential tax incidence: With tax rates keyed to ex-pected yield, the tax rate relative to land value was lower on high grade land, so that the gross rates of return appear to differ more by land class than do the net rates of return. The following table clarifies this point, although the actual magnitudes are not reliable:

Table 3.7   Gross and Net Rates of Return on Land, by Tax
            Class.

Rate relative to land value of:	High Grade	Medium Grade	Low Grade
Gross Rent (1)	10.3 %	11.3 %	12.0 %
Taxes (2)	- 2.0	- 2.5	- 3.3
Net Rent (Approx.)	= 8.3	= 8.8	= 8.7

(1) Average rent/land value, irrigated land. Yen
     Chung-p'ing, op. cit., Table 37, p. 307. Data for
     1930.
(2) Rice region average tax/national average value per mou
     of irrigated fields. See footnote (59) for sources.
     The estimates must be considered very rough.

Our earlier analysis of the three major rental systems carried the implication that fairly consistent differentials should exist among the rates of return prevailing under each system. The proportional rent system should offer a higher rate of return to the landlord, since it requires him to bear greater risk, more closely supervise the tenant and provide some or all of the capital; the fixed commodity rent system, especially if rents were convertible into cash, differed in a more ambiguous way from cash rents, since the respective benefits to landlord and tenant varied according to the circumstances of each, and according to the direction of price trends (which was not necessarily inflationary). Moreover, Yen Chung-p'ing argues that cash rents were generally paid a year in advance;[53] if so, the effective rate of return must have been at least 10 percent higher than the nominal rate, allowing for a reasonably secure return to the investment of these funds.

Table 3.8 summarizes the available information regarding the relationship among the rates of return under each rental system. We have adjusted gross rates of return by an estimate of the tax rates; although the latter is subject to error, especially for South China (see the Notes to Table 3.8) and is probably an underestimate, it shows a moderate correlation ($r = .39$) with gross rates of return (fixed crop rents), so the adjustment should help clarify inter-provincial relationships.

The statistics suggest that the rate of return to the landlord is, as expected, highest for sharecropping. We are not as willing to generalize concerning the relation between crop and cash rent: Cash rents clearly offered only a lower

Table 3.8   Estimate of Net Rate of Return to Landlord, Three Rental
            Systems, China, 1930-1934

Province	Tax ($/mou)	Tax Rate (%)	Net Rental Rate of Return:		
			Share-Cropping	Fixed: Crop	Cash
Kansu	1.04	6.0	7.7	6.0	5.4
Shensi	.65*	2.7	9.9	10.3	7.4
Shansi	.48	1.7	4.5	4.2	4.5
Hopei	.63	1.5	6.6	6.1	5.8
Shantung	.77	2.6	18.2	16.2	13.4
Kiangsu	.72**	1.6	11.2	6.2	7.1
Anhwei	.71*	2.2	14.2	7.2	7.2
Chekiang	.26	0.6	12.6	9.7	9.3
Fukien	.72**	2.5	18.5	17.4	15.3
Kwangtung	.64**	1.6	13.8	17.4	15.4
Kiangsi	.85**	4.7	32.1	13.4	14.5
Hupei	.21**	0.5	13.1	6.3	7.8
Hunan	.41**	1.6	26.9	15.8	15.8
Szechwan	1.32**	2.7	14.2	11.8	8.7
Yünnan	.40	0.9	15.9	15.7	13.0
Kweichow	1.04**	2.8	9.3	10.6	3.4
Average	.67	2.0	13.6	11.0	9.5

*   only one or two localities included in average.
** hsien government taxes only; may underestimate total tax.
Notes: Tax figures are computed from J. L. Buck, LUC, SV, Table 7-2,
pp. 157-158; Table 8, pp. 155-156. Where possible, the average tax/mou
on medium grade land was used; where too few localities per province
were surveyed, the Table 8 figures on hsien government taxes were used
instead. Fortunately, the bulk of such instances were for S. China
provinces, where it seems that local (below county-level) taxes were
rather infrequent, but there are exceptions, such as in two localities
in Szechwan where the addition of local taxes increased the average
to $7.09 per mou. The tax figures are for 1930-1932 (generally the
latest dates for which figures were collected), while the rent statistics are for 1934. The omission of local taxes and the use of earlier
tax figures probably leads to some underestimation of the tax rate.
    Rental rates are derived from gross rents relative to average land
values by subtracting taxes. Since the same land value based was used
in calculating all three rental rates per province, whereas land value
is likely to be correlated with the type of rental system (see text),
the differences in rates among the three systems are likely to be
underestimated. The national average rates are estimated from
average rents, taxes and land values.
    Rent data from Yen Chung-p'ing (1955), Table 40, p. 309.

rate of return in those provinces where they were associated, not with commercialization, but with institutional landlords (e.g. clan, temple or government). In such circumstances tenants were often members of the owning institution, and therefore had a particularily strong bargaining position.[54] On the other hand, in provinces where cash rents were associated with commercialization (such as Hopei, Shantung, Kiangsu, Anhwei, Chekiang, Hupei, Hunan, etc.), there seems to be little or no difference between the rates of return under the two rental systems; if advance payment of cash rents was required, the latter would often offer the higher rate of return.[55]

It should be pointed out that differentials between rates of return under sharecropping and fixed rent systems as given in the table are probably underestimated, inasmuch as sharecropped land was generally of poorer quality and lower price than the latter, while the statistics given are based on a single average land value per province. It may also be the case that land values differ between the two fixed rental systems.

The regional differences in rates of return apparent in the table are not necessarily reliable, but there seems to be a tendency toward lower rates of return in the Yangtze River provinces of Kiangsu, Anhwei and Hupei and in parts of North China, with much higher returns further south. However, this was a period of intense Communist activity in Kiangsi (where some 9,000,000 peasants had been recently killed in the course of Chiang Kai-shek's campaigns against the Soviet base)[56] and parts of Fukien, Hunan and Shensi, which certainly must have depressed land prices and made rent collection difficult (!), so that the statistics on rates of return for these areas are of dubious meaning.

Useful data on the cost of renting as viewed from the tenant's side are if anything more scarce than those relating to the landlord's investment return. Table 3.9 summarizes the only large-sample information available. This indicates that relationships between rent levels under fixed and proportional rental systems are as would be expected from our previous discussion. Beyond this, however, the information is of limited value, for two reasons: First, the custom of expressing the rental rate as a fraction of the yield of the main crop only neglects the importance of second or subsidiary crops, byproducts and other farm products to tenant livelihood and the determination of rent levels; secondly, it is the absolute level of rent, rather than its proportion to farm output, which is the more interesting variable in terms of economic theory.

Table 3.10, 3.11, and 3.12 summarize the best available small-sample data on the tenant farm economy, which unfortunately overrepresents the east-central provinces of

Table 3.9 Average Rent as a Proportion of Average Value of the Main Crop, Various Provinces, 1934.

Province	Fixed Rent: Irrigated Land*	Dry Land*	Proportional Rent***
Kansu	.45**	.25**	.41
Shensi	.37	.39	.42
Shansi	.43	.41	.47
Hopei	.49	.54	.47
Shantung	.41	.48	.48
Honan	.48	.53	.47
Kiangsu	.40	.39	.43
Anhwei	.40	.44	.42
Chekiang	.44	.36	.43
Fukien	.51	.43	.46
Kwangtung	.40	.46	.45
Kiangsi	.39	.37	.43
Hupei	.43	.38	.44
Hunan	.52	.38	.47
Szechuan	.52	.46	.53
Yunnan	.37	.40	.45
Kweichou	.42	.48	.42
Average	.43	.40	.48

* average value of rent/average value of main crop, on medium grade land.
** average of Kansu, Ninghsia and Ch'inghai.
*** weighted average of modes of decile classifications; may slightly underestimate or overestimate the "true" mean.
Sources: Fixed Rent from Yen Chung-ping, op. cit., Table 34., p. 303; Proportional rent from N.A.R.B., Crop Reports, Vol. III, No. 4, April 15, 1935, p. 93.

Kiangsu, Chekiang and Anhwei. It is apparent, first, that despite nominal rental proportions running from 35 to 50% on the average, rent as a proportion of actual total farm income (narrowly defined to exclude subsidiary and off-farm activities unrelated to land rental) was between one-fifth

Table 3.10   Rent Relative to Income and Expense, Tenant Farms, Various Localities, 1926–1935

Province: County: Year: Source:	Kiangsu Wu 1933 1(p.271)	Chekiang Wu-1 1933 1(p.273)	Kwangsi Tu-lin 1933** 1(p.274)	Hupei Hwang-an 1935** 1(p.276)	Kiangsu I-hsing 1927 2(p.492)	Szechwan Cheng-tu 1926** 2(p.511)
Total Income	$271.20	$136.04	$286.90	$84.00	$100.00	$770.28
Main Crop	129.60	86.40	270.14	58.10	40.00	670.13
Other Crop	111.40	19.64			14.00	67.37
Animals	--	15.00			16.00	
Subsid. Work	25.20	15.00	13.53	25.90	20.00	27.39
Labor Earnings	5.00	--	3.24	--	10.00	5.39
Total Expense	194.80	90.00	141.50	18.82	82.00	446.59
Rent+Taxes	77.00	51.84	68.51	16.44	16.00	347.95
Fertilizer	47.10	12.00	22.78	--	18.00	25.91
Seed	6.50	3.16	19.28	1.04	--	--
Hired Labor	36.20	--	6.14	--	15.00	38.52
Animals	24.00	--	19.64	.33	--	38.78
Tools,Repairs	4.00	8.00	5.15	1.01	11.00	15.43
Other (including subsidiary industry)	--	15.00	--	--	22.00	--
Living Expense	132.00	96.72	177.72	74.74	--	--
Farm Size (mou)	14	12	?	?	2	30.1

Table 3.11   Rent Relative to Farm Income, Twelve Tenant Farms, Kiangsu, Wu-hsi, 1940

Farm	Gross Value of Product from: Rice	Wheat	Silk,Etc.	Total	Rent	Rent/ Total GVAP	Adult Equivalents	Grain Requirement	Surplus or Deficit
13	$108.00	--	--	$108.00	$48.60	45.0%	2.1	$168.00	-$60
14	72.00	14.40	8.00	94.40	29.16	30.9	2.4	192.00	- 98
33	144.00	28.80	--	172.80	38.88	22.5	2.8	224.00	- 51
57	--	--	88.50	88.50	10.00	11.3	3.8	304.00	-116
58	144.00	28.80	4.00	176.80	38.88	22.0	1.8	144.00	+ 33
59	144.00	72.00	38.00	254.00	73.08	28.8	4.7	376.00	-102
60	270.00	144.00	90.00	504.00	106.20	21.1	2.1	168.00	+342
61	241.20	144.00	--	385.20	100.80	26.2	2.6	208.00	+177
62	162.00	54.00	--	216.00	38.88	18.0	1.6	128.00	+ 88
76	288.00	126.00	100.00	514.00	118.64	23.1	2.4	192.00	+322
78	360.00	144.00	106.00	610.00	135.60	22.2	3.2	256.00	+432
80	180.00	75.60	--	255.60	77.76	30.4	2.4	192.00	+ 64

Mean Nominal Rent Percentage = 37.7 %   Mean Rent/GVAP = 26.4 %

Notes: Value of rice and wheat computed at $36/shih (Source, p. 149); male adult consumer equivalents computed according to system used in Buck, LUC, I, p. 408; grain consumption requirement computed at 2.2 shih per adult male (this figure represents average per capita -- not necessarily adult -- consumption of rice and wheat in Kiangsu, 1937, from Ch'iao Ch'i-ming, Chung-kuo nung-ts'un she-hui ching-chi hsüeh, p. 406).

Gross value of agric. product here is an underestimate to the extent of any byproducts of rice and wheat cultivation, such as the value of straw (probably about 10% of GVAP).

Source: Mantetsudo, Kōso-shō mushaku-ken nōson jittai chōsa hōkokusho (1941) (Kiangsu Province, Wuhsi County, Survey Report on Village Conditions), Statistical Appendices,

and one-third in the more commercialized regions of east-
central China, perhaps higher in the less commercialized
areas and in the north. It remained, however, the largest
single element in farm expense, perhaps about half the total
(when some actually self-supplied items are included as
expenses; closer to 75% otherwise), again probably a smaller
proportion in the commercialized east-central provinces and
larger elsewhere. It was also frequently (if not generally)
true that tenant families could not cover their consumption
requirements, however minimal, with their farm earnings net
of rent, as emerges from the samples presented in Tables
3.10 and 3.11. Tenants, at least in the localities here
sampled, were forced to supplement farm earnings with
family earnings from subsidiary enterprise or off-farm
labor; or, to put it another way, tenancy as an institution
depended in such cases on the existence of ample opportunities to supplement farm income.

We have suggested that the more commercialized regions
of east-central and south China can be distinguished from
other parts of China with respect to the proportion which
rent was of income and expense. This idea is based not only
on the limited data given above, but also on the following
line of reasoning:

Historically, the more commercialized regions have
presented greater opportunities for off-farm labor and

Table 3.12   Rent Relative to Farm Income and Direct Expense,
             Various Localities, 1921-24.

Per Mou:

Province	Locality	Gross Income	Rent	Other Expense	Rent/ Income	Rent/ Expense
Anhwei	Su hsien	$ 3.27	$ 1.73	$ .45	52.9%	79.4%
Shansi	Wu-t'ai	4.19	2.97	.31	68.5	90.5
Anhwei	Lai-an	13.28	4.86	1.79	36.6	73.1
"	Lai-an	8.34	2.26	1.27	27.1	64.0
Chekiang	Chen-hai	19.31	4.64	4.05	20.4	53.4
Fukien	Lien-chiang	37.89	12.50	2.77	33.0	81.9
Kiangsu	Chiang-p'u	20.16	3.94	2.17	19.5	64.5
"	Chiang-p'u	9.82	2.01	1.51	20.7	57.1
"	Wu-chin	20.00	4.94	6.13	24.7	45.6
Average		15.24	4.42	1.74	33.7	71.8

Note: Other Expense includes only cash expense and de-
        preciation; self-supplied production inputs are
        apparently not included.
Source: See Table 3.6.

demands for farm subsidiary products. This, combined with a
high and growing population density, has created demands for
land which have tended to drive up rents, and have led
tenants to in effect substitute capital and labor for land,
utilizing more capital and labor-intensive farming methods
on smaller tenant farms and responding to opportunities to
make use of subsidiary crops and byproducts. This in turn
has raised per _mou_ yields and farm incomes more than enough
to compensate for higher rents, _so that the proportion of
farm income taken up by rents has remained slightly lower
than outside these regions_, while on the whole rents have also

become a smaller proportion of production expense, due to greater use of inputs other than land.

While the sequence suggested in this explanation may be historically incorrect, it remains probable that the greater capital and labor intensity of tenant (and other) peasant farming in these regions explains the lower rent proportion (though higher rent level); while in some other areas (e.g. see the Szechwan data in Table 3.10) high rent proportions are compensated for by larger scale farming, in these regions subsidiary and off-farm earnings permit tenant farms of a small and uneconomical scale (uneconomical in the sense that they are unable to support a family without outside income).

Further evidence with regard to the importance of non-farm earnings will emerge in the course of subsequent discussion of the labor market.

Although the emphasis of the previous discussion has been on the entirely landless tenant, it should be pointed out that land rentals were frequently used as a means of supplementing land holdings to obtain a more optimal labor/land ratio by peasants of all classes. For example, in Kwangtung's Fan-y'u hsien (near Canton), "rich peasants" farmed 3.95 mou, but only owned 1.75 on the average, while "middle peasants" farmed 2.4 but owned only .73 mou.[57] The large numbers of partial owners (see Table 3.2) included many of the more prosperous and efficient farmers.

Land rentals were only one means of acquisition or disposal of land, albeit the most frequently used; others included outright transfer of ownership through sale, "temporary" transfer through the mortgage procedure and "forced" transfer through loan default.

A discussion of the importance of land sales must begin with the commonplace observation that Chinese social tradition placed an extraeconomic value on land which hindered the development of a high rate of voluntary land turnover.[58] This tradition was backed by potential social sanctions which, while not hindering speculative transactions by absentee landlords to whom land was purely an investment, did tend to limit the competitiveness of the land market as far as the owner-cultivator was concerned. For example, it was frequently the case that family members, fellow clansmen and/or owners of adjacent plots had a customary "right of first refusal" on land sales.[59]

Nevertheless, nonspeculative land sales did occur and, judging from fragmentary data, at a reasonably high rate (in view of the sanctions): For examples, in the Yünnan village of Luts'un (relatively uncommercialized), 2.5 percent of landholdings of local households changed hands in the course of one year;[60] in a village in Kiangsu Ch'ungming hsien, over 5 percent of the land was sold to outsiders over the period 1928-33, compared to 2 percent in Lungch'i hsien

(Fukien) (where an even greater amount was purchased from outsiders).[61] There is also evidence that land turnover had contracted by the early Thirties in some localities, perhaps due to falling land values.[62]

However, the bulk of land sales probably came from the class extremes: Either the rich, who had more land than they could work profitably and who were secure enough to accept risks and thus preferred a "balanced portfolio" of income from land and moneylending (but sometimes also to cover debts or losses); or the very poor, as the final step at the end of a process of growing indebtedness or on the death of the owner, to cover funeral expenses.[63] Other sales also came from individuals who intended to leave the village permanently, for other occupations or localities.

The reluctance to sell land of "middle peasants" may have derived as much from economic grounds as from social sanctions. For to this group the value of the marginal productivity of land was probably greater than its market price.[64] Keep in mind that indebted peasants (because of economic necessity) and the rich peasants (because of low labor/land ratios) were each willing to sell at prices below those which should appeal to middle peasants. At the same time, lack of savings among middle peasants and the extremely high rates of interest on borrowings limited demand for land from that source, whereas wealthy peasants

or landlords would offer prices based on lower economic
returns than were attainable by owner-cultivators of "middle
peasant" status. These conditions created a market imperfection such that it rarely paid the middle-peasant to sell
his land, until such time as indebtedness reduced him to
poverty. This imperfection again can be traced back to the
fundamental imperfection in the loan market created by uncertainty or risk (see the previous chapter), since in its
absence, competition would have tended to drive down the
rate of interest to the point that middle peasants would have
found it profitable to borrow to purchase additional land.

The remaining vehicles for land transfer, i.e. through
mortgages and loan defaults, are so intimately bound up with
the "money market" that they are best considered under that
heading.

Conclusions

Land in the prewar Chinese peasant economy served a dual
function as a major factor of production in agriculture and
a store of wealth offering a substantial rate of return to
the investor. From the point of view of the peasant
producer, the demand-value of land is determined at the
margin by the relative availability of complementary factors,
by the technology available, extent of uncertainty, and the
profitability of activities other than farming. From the
point of view of the landowner, the supply-value of land is

determined by its opportunity cost (value if used in production) and by rates of return on other uses of funds.
Rental values and land price are determined by the forces
of supply and demand resulting from these interactions of
multiple economic factors.

Land tenure cannot be viewed in isolation from other
aspects of the peasant economy -- this is perhaps the major
point of the discussion above. While the land market in the
Chinese peasant economy was sufficiently developed to offer
a variety of options to its participants, the choices made
by given participants were also largely determined by their
wealth and the forms in which it was held.

CHAPTER IV. THE LOAN MARKET IN PREWAR CHINA

In a developed capitalist economy, the "loan market"
(or "financial sector") serves to finance the processes of
production as well as consumption, and competes with physical assets (such as real estate) for a share of the savings
of the wealthy. In the context of an underdeveloped peasant
economy, the role of the loan market is less central: It is
most comparable to consumer credit among the poorest classes
in a developed capitalist economy, in that it is characterized by low volume, high transaction costs, small personali-
zed lending institutions engaged in "usury".

Such a loan market, however, was an active and complex
structure, tied in with the productive economy in such a
way that it was possible to use moneylending as a means of
obtaining land or labor. Moreover, since investment in land
and moneylending were alternative uses for the funds of the
wealthy, the loan market played a key role in determining
the price of land. It did not, however, serve as a major
source of finance for the expansion of agricultural production and consequently peasants were forced to depend on
their own resources for this purpose.

This chapter will attempt to explain the major institutional characteristics of the loan market in prewar China
insofar as it affected the peasants, and the interrelation-
ship between this and other factor markets. We will

attempt to account for the extent and nature of participation in this market with the aid of a crude model. We will also attempt to explain the determination of interest rates and their relationship to risk default.

As in other peasant economies, the rural loan market in China was characterized by the facts that a large proportion of the peasantry had recourse to this market (about 56 percent of all agricultural households were in debt from cash loans)[1] and that very few loans were for "productive" purposes (involving agriculture). Table 4.1 summarizes information on indebtedness derived from Buck's farm survey; given the biases towards more prosperous farms and commercialized areas, probably much less than 10 percent of farm families borrowed for farm-productive purposes (the survey did not distinguish borrowings for productive subsidiary and commercial activities, which were probably more frequent; it must be remembered also that the distinction between "productive" and "consumptive" is unclear in a family farm economy, where both purposes are served out of family income and savings).[2] Moreover, the amounts involved in such borrowings were only a fraction of the average value of consumption loans, reflecting the fact that many such loans simply covered emergency needs for small amounts of working capital.

Table 4.1 Farm Family Borrowings, Survey of 15,112 Farms, 1929-33.

Crop Region	% Borrowing for:		Average Amount for:	
	Productive Purposes	Unproductive Purposes	Productive Purposes	Unproductive Purposes
1	9	50	$ 16	$ 52
2	6	28	13	49
3	11	27	21	55
4	18	44	20	74
5	14	33	17	51
6	12	30	19	45
7	20	38	20	70
8	3	9	29	96
Average	12	33	19	61

Average Monthly Rate of Interest = 2.7%

Source: John L. Buck, LUC, Statistical Volume, Table 13., p. 403.

By contrast, for families with consumption debt, the average annual borrowings per family exceeded average per capita annual income by almost 100 percent*; with annual interest charges exceeding one-third of principal on the average, and with the cumulation of past unrepaid debt and/or interest (not presented in Buck's summary tables), many if not most debtor families could not hope to extricate themselves from their debt burden without loss of their land. It is this connection of the loan market with the

* see Appendix IV-A. for summary data on farm family in-comes.

process of pauperization which has received the main attention of many specialists in the Chinese peasant economy.[3]

Due to both the small number and low average value of
loans for productive purposes, the impact of this component
of the demand for funds can be considered negligible, as
implied by the reasonably representative results of a
sample survey of one locality displayed in Table 4.2. Most
funds, on the other hand, were absorbed either by ceremonial
expenses of a magnitude beyond the capacity of current incomes or by the ordinary living expenses of the poor (not
to mention the opium habit, which was widespread in some
regions).[4]

Table 4.2   Distribution of Loans by Purpose, Li Village,
            Tsing-tao District, Shantung, 1940.

Purpose	Percent of Value of All Loans	Average Loan Per Instance
Marriages	24.6%	$ 107.42
Funerals	16.6	96.73
Living Expenses	23.4	51.57
Medical Expenses	2.1	53.92
Home Repair	6.4	61.61
Special Tax*	8.2	64.77
Labor Animals	5.1	52.17
Mercantile Capital**	7.7	224.60
Other	5.9	
Of which "productive"***	1.6	34.40

* "bandit suppression" levy on wealthy peasants, by Japanese.
** includes one abnormally large debt ($1000) due to bank-
   ruptcy.
*** includes wage payments, land purchase and mortgage, pur-
    chases of carts, feed, etc.
Source: Mantetsu, Hokushi Jimukyoku, Chintao kinkō ni okeru
         nōson jittai chōsa hōkoku (1939), p. 103.

On the supply side, distinguishing the major sources of
supply of funds is problematic, in that there was considerable overlap in social roles (for example, a "relative",
"landlord" and "merchant" might characterize a single individual).[5] For whatever it's worth, Table 4.3 provides
survey results on sources of loans: It at least indicates
that the major sources of loans were from within the rural
sector itself, and that formal financial institutions such
as the cooperatives, modern or native banks, pawnshops, etc.
supplied only a fraction of credit extended. It was probably
also true that larger loans were somewhat more frequently
obtained from urban sources, where liquid wealth tended to
concentrate.[6]

The general forms of loan transaction, arranged in
probable order of importance, included cash and grain loans,
mortgaging, pawning and credit society (ho-hui) loans. Cash
and grain loans could also be subdivided according to
whether the guarantee of repayment was merely word-of-mouth,
involved a third-party guarantor or the title to property as
security. Grain loans were generally short-term (borrowed
at sowing time, repaid after the harvest) and involved no
guarantee; they were also more frequently sought by poor
peasants. As a result, they generally bore the highest
rates of monthly interest (6 to 7 percent per month on the
average[7]), especially where the recipients were poor.[8]

Table 4.3   Distribution of Loans by Source, 850 Counties, 22
            Provinces, 1933.

Source	Percent of Loans Grain	Cash	Percent of Value Cash*
Cooperatives	--	1.3 %	2.6 %
Friends & Relatives	10.9	8.3	**
Landlords	13.6	9.0	24.2
Rich Peasants	46.6	45.1	18.2
Merchants	11.3	17.3	25.0
Modern Banks	--	} 8.9	2.4
Native Banks	--		5.5
Shops	} 17.6	} 10.1	13.1
Pawnshops			8.8

* presumed to be cash loans only.
** this category not included; it is not certain whether it
   was too small to include or whether it has been excluded
   from the computation of percentages of value.
Source: Feng Ho-fa, op. cit., Vol. 2, pp. 790 & 806.
   Survey by Ministry of Industries, Central Agricultural
   Experiment Station.

It is difficult to generalize about longer term cash
loans, since the terms surrounding such transactions varied
greatly among localities, over time and according to circumstance. It seems to be the case, first, that small loans
among friends or relatives sometimes -- but by no means
always -- involved no definite time of repayment, guarantor
or guarantee in the form of land title; less often they
were extended on an interest free basis (more frequently for
very short periods and among wealthy families).[9] Otherwise, loans required a guarantor and/or a pledge of land
title (how often the latter was required is debatable:
Most information suggests that it was the norm rather than

the exception to require land as a guarantee, but at least
in some localities or at some times the reverse was the
case[10]). Most loans were nominally short-term (one year or
less), but were frequently extended formally or informally.
Where there was no guarantee, the lender had really no other
option; where land title was involved, it may not have been
easy to force a transfer of title. In some localities, the
pledged land was first converted to mortgaged land, with the
mortgage value applied towards the debt; only if the mortgage
was not redeemed at the appropriate time did ownership pass
into the hands of the lender.[11]

Interest rates were normally simple, not compounded,
and were paid either in cash or commodities, depending on
the terms of the loan. Repayment of interest in grain was
not uncommon, and provided a hedge against inflation (when
the principal was repaid in money, a high enough commodity
interest rate could compensate for loss of value of
principal).[12] Interest, at some times and places, was also
repayable in labor -- most frequently when short-term labor
during the harvest season was hard to come by. Where such
loans were extended primarily to ensure a labor supply, no
interest was charged and the debt was worked off at current
wage levels (in effect, the lender/hirer was paying a
higher than average wage by extending it in advance; the
arrangement was comparable to the labor rent system).[13] On

the other hand, repayment in labor was sometimes a consequence of the borrower's inability to repay in cash or
commodities, in which case the nominal interest rate was
quite high if computed in terms of nominal wages (but such
nominal wages probably did not represent equilibrium wages,
else borrowers would have been able to find employment to
obtain the cash required to repay the loan).[14] In any case,
such non-cash arrangements were confined mostly to backwards
areas and/or times of market disruption (such as under the
wartime conditions after 1937).

In contrast to the ordinary loan procedure, where the
connection between the land market and the money market was
only through the use of land as a guarantee of repayment,
the mortgage procedure constituted a direct link between the
two markets. In the most common variant, in fact, there was
little difference between this loan procedure and the rental
deposit cum rent reduction procedure discussed in the previous section. In return for a loan representing a certain
percentage of the value of a piece of land, use of the land
was given to the lender for a certain period of time, after
which the original sum had to be repaid. No interest was
involved in the transaction, the implicit interest being the
value in use of the land to the lender and the sacrificed
value in use to the borrower (these rates, of course, needn't
be the same -- see p. 121). The distinction between

mortgages and rental deposits came only in the event of default on repayment; In the former case, title then passed
into the hands of the lender, whereas in the latter there
seems to have been no such security for the tenant-lender
(unless it was a de facto right of permanent rent-free
tenancy). As Fei Hsiao-t'ung pointed out, the borrower-
mortgager was frequently a middle or rich peasant, earning a
lower rate of return on his land because of the use of hired
labor and who was in a position to lend out the loan at
higher rates of interest; the lender-mortgagee by contrast
a poor peasant with some savings, who benefited through the
differential in the rate of return on land as well as the
higher rate of return on the use of his funds (in the form
of rent-free land use).[15] That is, in such cases the
economic analysis of the respective positions of mortgager
and mortgagee is exactly analogous to that of landlord and
tenant under the rental deposit cum rent reduction system
(see pp. 99-101).

However, in many cases the lender-mortgagee was not
an owner-cultivator or poor peasant seeking land for use
but a landlord seeking less risky investment opportunity
than ordinary moneylending but a better return than could be
obtained through land purchase. In such cases the borrower-
mortgager continued to farm the land but paid rent to the

lender-mortgagee at the usual rate*, the rent in effect
representing repayment of interest. If principal and rent-
interest had not been repaid by an agreed-upon date (always
a number of years), title to the land passed to the lender-
mortgagee, and the borrower-mortgager became tenant in name
as well as in fact on his former landholding, unless the new
owner chose to farm the land himself.[16]

It should be added that the mortgage procedure was also
applied to other sorts of "property": Lacking land, in
Kwangsi it was possible to "mortgage" a child; if the loan
was defaulted, the child passed into the hands of the lender.
No interest was charged thereafter, but the child was re-
deemable only on repayment of debt.[17]

The pawnshop was an alternative source of loans for the
landless. The value of loans was (in Hopei) about one-third
the value of the property, the term 24 months and the
interest rate commonly at 3 percent per month. Although
these rates were not much different from rates on land-
secured loans, the size of loans extended was generally
trivial, reflecting the small value of the personal pos-
sessions of a poor peasant: According to one survey, about
one-third of borrowers obtained only $ .10 - .30 per article

---

*The borrower-mortgager remained liable for the land tax;
the rental rate may have been adjusted appropriately.

pawned, another third from $1 to $2, and only 3.6 percent received over $5 per article (compare this with average borrowings in Table 4.1 and 4.2).[18]

A final and most interesting source of finance was the credit association (ho-hui, ju-ch'ien hui, etc.), an organization of usually ten to twenty friends and relatives (but occasionally much larger in scale) which constituted a complete micro-market in itself. Its basic function was to assemble reasonably large (e.g. $50-200) lump sums (grain or cash) from small but regular contributions of subscribers, each of whom might receive all or part of the lump sum one or more times in the course of the existence of the association (usually five to ten years). The arrangement was so structured that the organizer received the first loan, on terms (either interest free or reduced) which compensated for his effort and cost in maintaining the participation of members, providing semiannual feasts (in some cases) and acting as guarantor. Those of the remaining members who received their loans in the first half of the term of the organization repaid them in installments in such a way that the effective interest varied in proportion to the length of time before repayment was completed; those who received sums towards the end in effect were savers, receiving interest rates which were proportionate to the "waiting time" before "withdrawal". Contributions were accepted and loans

extended biannually at times when peasant incomes were at
their height (normally after harvests).

There were three basic forms of association, giving it
considerable flexibility: In the first and simplest, the
order in which members would receive lump sums and the bi-
annual subscriptions for each member were fixed in advance,
the amount of subscriptions depending upon the order of the
member's turn to receive the loan but being fixed over the
term of the association. In the second, the collection
order was not determined in advance, and the recipient of
the loan was determined at each meeting, sometimes by lot.
Debtors -- those who had received loans -- thereafter paid a
fixed and equal sum per meeting; other subscribers (or
depositors) paid a lower and decreasing amount as time went
on. The complexity of this system was compensated for by
the fact that loan recipients were not known in advance of
meetings, thus inducing participation by members who otherwise might be reluctant to contribute their share. In both
of the above systems, the rates of return or interest were
known in advance. In a third type of society, the actual
rate of interest was variable, determined at each meeting by
auction (either the lowest bid for the sum to be collected
or the highest for rate of interest on the loan). In such
associations, the larger the number of participants, the
stiffer was the competition, with interest rates sometimes

rising above 4 percent per month.[19] More detailed descriptions of the principles of operation of this type of association are available, but it seems that they held greater appeal to the wealthy because of the prospect of a higher rate of return, and less to the poorer peasants because of the uncertainty attached to the timing and terms of loans.[20]

The above description accounts for the major forms of transaction in the loan market, though there were others of lesser importance. For example, small amounts of short-term credit often were extended by merchants or purchasing agents, with future production as security. Fei points out that this required a reasonably stable crop yield, the purchase of which was monopolized by the lending agent, else the element of risk involved was too great.[21] Consequently such credit was probably limited to areas where these conditions held. In some localities, wealthy peasants also had access to cheaper cooperative credit or to loans from modern banks, but the impact of these institutions was negligible even in areas where they existed.

The institutional form of the loan market was thus far from underdeveloped, though it was not "modern" and suffered from the general impoverishment of the peasantry and instability of agricultural production, which together created a high degree of risk and commenserately high rates of interest, ensuring in turn that outside finance would rarely be used for productive investment (in these respects, it did not differ from the loan market among the impoverished groups in developed countries).

The extent and nature of participation in this market varied with the economic situation of individual peasant families. On the demand side, the role of semi-random events (marriages, deaths, natural calamities, etc.) was the most significant determination of participation, although the ability to cope with such events without recourse to loans obviously varied with the economic status of the family. On the supply side, wealth was the most important factor: Families with large land holdings relative to family labor supply found that moneylending was more lucrative than further land investment, which would have created a need for large amounts of hired labor; comparing land and loans as mere investments, a desire for a "balanced portfolio", combined with decreasing relative risk aversion with higher incomes, meant that wealthier families would engage in more extensive lending.

A crude test of these ideas can be based on a Mantetsu survey of debt in Li village, Tsingtao, Shantung province.[22] We have chosen a subsample of the 53 largest debtors (out of 142) in the village, and the 29 largest creditors, all with sums borrowed or loaned over $100 (in some cases, net debt or lending is smaller). Table 4.4 compares some economic characteristics of the two groups, statistically, they are

Table 4.4 Economic Characteristics of Debtor and Creditor
Families, Li Village, Tsingtao, Shantung, 1939.

Characteristic	Mean: Creditors	Debtors	Median: Creditors	Debtors	T-statistic*
Land Owned (mou)	10.80	4.10	8.10	3.00	3.85
Farm Labor (f.t.e.)	1.50	1.10	1.40	1.00	1.94
Farm Labor/Land	.21	.48	.14	.30	2.02
Total Labor (f.t.e.)	2.14	1.56	1.70	1.20	2.14
Outside Income ($)	181.70	74.80	40.00	19.50	1.92
Wage Payments ($)	54.10	37.40	35.00	0.00	1.04

*test of difference between group means; at 80 d.o.f., $t_{.9}$ =
1.66 and $t_{.95}$ = 1.99.

Notes: Farm labor (male adult full-time equivalents) was
estimated from total family labor-equivalents (a
capacity measure) by subtracting off-farm labor,
estimated from employment data and treating 10 mos.
of labor as a f.t.e. Female labor is not counted in
this computation, presumably because females did not
work in the fields in this village. Outside income
and wage payments are both estimated from length of
labor multiplied by the appropriate wage rate,
except where actual income received was given.
The former includes only wages and income from self-
employment.

Source: Mantetsu, Hokushi jimukyoku, Chintao kinko ni
okeru noson jittai chosa hokoku (1939), Appendices.

significantly different in all but one of these character-

istics. Landholdings of creditor families were more than

twice as large as those of debtor families (almost half the

creditors had farms larger than 10 mou, but only one of the

debtors). At the same time their farm labor (family only)-

to-land ratio was less than half that of debtor farms,

requiring 48 percent to hire additional labor, compared to 32 percent of debtor farms. Moreover, the amount of extra income brought in by family members working off the farm was larger almost in the same proportion as were landholdings. In short, the overall wealth of creditors was greater than that of debtors, and because of the lack of family labor (compounded by a probably greater preference for leisure not reflected in potential labor supply), the rate of return on land was probably also lower, inducing greater investment in loans.

Taking this analysis a step further, we have estimated total family income, net of rent, interest and wage payments (but not excluding other costs of production), composed of income from land, labor (on and off-farm) and interest receipts.* We attempt to account for the total debt or credit outstanding (not including any back interest owed) in terms of two models: The first, a "wealth" model,

---

* Income from land estimated as follows:

Land rented out: $10/mou; Land rented in: $15/mou; Land owned and farmed: $25/mou; Land mortgaged out: $15/mou; Land mortgaged in: $25/mou if not counted in loan income, $0 otherwise. Loan income estimated at 2%/mo., as was debt repayment. These represent the local averages in 1939.

hypothesizes that loans outstanding are directly proportionate to income per consumer and, for given income per consumer, also to the number of consumers; but this only
determines total investment, which is divided between land
and loans in the "portfolio", so that these two elements
should vary inversely. The second model, more appropriate
for explaining debt, emphasizes economic need by hypothesiz-
ing that the extent of debt is inversely proportionate to
the difference between family income and the minimum income
required for subsistence. Although the "subsistence income"
is unknown (actual average consumption, according to the
survey, was about \$.30 per day or \$108 per year in market
value[23]), it can be estimated by breaking down the model as
follows: $D = a + b(Y - sC) = a + bY - bsC$, where D = debt,
Y = family income, C = no. of consumers, s = per capita
subsistence and a and b are coefficients (with $b > 0$ if debt
is treated as a negative-valued loan). For debtors the
extent of debt, for _given_ surplus or deficit of income
compared to subsistence, should vary _directly_ with land
owned, because land could be offered as security for loans
and thus permitted deeper indebtedness. Finally, we would
not expect our model to explain debt as well as it explained
credit (loans), because of the overriding importance of

semirandom, large expenses in the determination of the
former.*

Table 4.5   Results of Regressions of Value of Family Debt
(-) or Credit on Variables Reflecting Economic
Status.

Explanatory Variables	Lenders	Debtors
Intercept	31.88*	-188.49*
	(13.2)	(13.3)
Income (Total)	(n.i.)	.43*
		(.13)
Income/Consumer	1.64*	(n.i.)
	(.57)	
Consumers	23.84*	-14.66
	(10.83)	(13.30)
Land Owned	-9.83*	- 7.77
	(3.54)	(5.69)
R^2	.31	.20

* significant at the 5% level or better.

The results of the two regressions are rather interesting, considering the simplicity of the models. Signs of
coefficients are entirely in accord with our hypotheses and,
as expected, lending is better explained by the economic
variables than is borrowing (although there remains a large

---

*   the greatest weakness of both models actually is that they
    more realistically explain new borrowings or loans than
    they do the sum of unrepaid past loans or borrowings.
    There were not enough new transactions to permit the use
    of the more correct model.

unexplained residual, which may represent a combination of
specification error and errors in estimates of variables).
Moreover, the magnitudes of some coefficients are interesting: The coefficient on land should be compared (in
absolute magnitude) with the average rent level of $10 per
mou; this rent would be sufficient to repay a loan of
exactly $7.77 plus interest at 29 percent (the most frequent-
ly charged rate of interest was 30 percent per year). Thus
the coefficient of -7.77 may be taken to imply that,
ceteris paribus, peasants borrow against their land roughly
to the extent that its income (rental value) permits repayment of principal and interest. Since 12 out of the 29 net
lenders also had debts outstanding, this interpretation may
also apply to the coefficient of similar magnitude in the
other regression (but this differs from our previous, "portfolio" interpretation). Secondly, we can estimate the "subsistence income", s, as 14.66/.43 = $34 if our model is
correct; this would be about one-third of average market
value of consumption per adult (about $108),* or somewhat
more if, as is probable, total incomes have been underestimated by our computational methods, which neglect on-farm
side income. This value is reasonable enough to add

---

* this represented a guess on the part of the interviewers,
  and could be an exaggeration.

plausibility to the model. It also happens to be the mean
per consumer income of this sample of debtors. Moreover,
whereas 66 percent of the sample had incomes below the mean,
81 percent of families with new debt (i.e. borrowed within
the past year) were in this category. Some families,
because of heavy past borrowings, had reached the point
where estimated net incomes were negative, implying that they
either were in default on interest repayments or were at the
point where new loans and/or sale of assets would be necessary for survival. By contrast, the average income per
consumer of net lenders was about twice the hypothetical
"subsistence level" ($73); only four families appeared to be
"below" subsistence, of which one had extended loans to
acquire land on mortgage (see p. 55) and another was a
family with a large number of unproductive consumers (5.6
consumer-equivalents to 1.0 labor equivalent) which was
forced to depend on income from loans for its subsistence.
Half of the sample of identified major lenders (lenders who
were not heads of households could not be identified and
were therefore excluded from our sample of 29) were also
among the 10 percent of all families who possessed more than
10 mou of land.

Finally, it should be pointed out that, in this North
China sample, there is little difference between the distribution of the two sample populations by land ownership

status and that of the population as a whole (see Table 4.6).
There is, however, a tendency for the entirely landless segments of the village population to be underrepresented in
both the samples of lenders and debtors, as would follow
from our previous discussion. The propertyless classes in
North China (but not necessarily in the south) were in a
position to neither borrow nor lend large sums.

Table 4.6   Distribution of Village Families and Sampled
Families by Land Ownership Status, Li Village,
Tsingtao, 1939

Category	Percent of Village	Percent of Lenders	Percent of Debtors
Owner-Cultivators	49.6 %	55.0 %	52.8 %
Part Owners	30.5	31.0	37.7
Tenants	4.6	0	2.0
Small Landlords	3.8	3.5	0
Landlords/Cultivators	6.9	7.0	7.5
Wage Laborers	4.6	3.5	0

Discussion of the rates of interest prevailing in the
loan market is complicated by deficiencies in the data
available and the bewildering variety of factors influencing
these rates. There were in some provinces legal ceilings to
the interest rate; in such cases prevailing rates reported in
surveys may not be accurate.[24] Moreover, computation of the
true rate of interest on loans based on pawned or mortgaged
property also requires knowledge of the use-value of the
property.

The major factors influencing the rate of interest on a
particular loan were, first, the degree of risk involved,
which varied with the form of loan (commodity or cash), the
guarantee and/or guarantor, length of term, relationship
between lender and borrower, economic status of borrower
(especially the stability of his income), the size of the
loan, the price expectations of the lender, and the form of
repayment (cash, grain or labor); second, the opportunity
cost to the lender, which varied with the rate of return
and risk on alternative investments (especially land --
determined by whether the lender was an owner-cultivator or
landlord and, for the former, by the labor/land ratio) and
with the rate of time preference of the lender (i.e. the
consumption trade-off). The aggregate supply of loanable
funds, moreover, was larger near cities and in commercialized areas. Aggregate demand was determined primarily by
population density and the standard of living, but was also
larger where commercial crops (with higher-than-average
requirement of working capital) predominated or where hired
labor expense was high.

Since there was considerable interaction among factors
influencing the rate of interest, it is impossible to find
data illustrating individual relationships in isolation.
For example, normally the longer the term of a loan, the
higher the rate of interest.[25] But since short-term loans

were generally not backed by land and were more often sought
by poorer peasants, the average rate on longterm loans was
often in fact lower than for short-term loans (in Kwangsi,
2.9% per month as opposed to 3.9% for short-term).[26] Simi-
larly, the rate was generally lower on larger loans than on
smaller, because of the lower per yüan transaction cost and
the more frequent use of land as security on the former.[27]
But loans of very small size also involved lower risk of default and were frequently among friends and relatives, so
that, as is apparent in Table 4.7, the actual relationship
between rate of interest and size of loan was more complicated.
Finally, when loans are classified by the type of guarantee,
one finds that loans backed by pledged property commanded a
higher rate of interest on the average than those backed by
a guarantor only, which in turn were higher than those based
on personal trust alone -- apparently because risk and the
type of guarantee required are closely correlated, and the
guarantees in themselves were not sufficient to cover the
risk differentials.[28]

Table 4.7 Relationship Between Rate of Interest and Average
          Size of Loan, 240 Loans, Hopei.

Annual Interest:	0%	12%	20%	24%	27%	30%	36%
Average Loan ($):	59	14	51	117	78	81	65
No. of Loans:	15	30	8	127	15	15	30

Source: Feng Ho-fa, op. cit., Vol. 2, p. 835.

The relationship between interest rates and price expectations (which in turn is relevant to the relationship
between rates on cash and commodity loans) cannot be dis-
cerned on the basis of pre-1938 data, as previous to this
year there had been no particular sustained price trend of
significant magnitude (farm prices rose at about 3 - 4 percent per year in the Twenties, fell then rose again in the
Thirties[29]). However, after 1938 the rate of inflation was
well-over the annual interest rates on cash loans of the
past, and some major adjustments in the loan market could be
expected. As best as we can tell, this response came
initially in the form of a drying-up of credit at previously
prevailing rates of interest, except perhaps on commodity
loans or cash loans with interest paid in grain.[30] Grain
loans were not only inflation-proof, but were positively
advantageous as long as inflation turned the terms-of-trade
in favor of the peasantry; indeed, so were cash loans with
interest paid in grain, if not repaid for several years,
since with runaway inflation, the current money value of
interest payments soon overshadowed the face value of the
principal. For example, in Yünnan, a loan of $100 extended
in November 1938 at 40% per year (interest in grain at 50
piculs per year) would have returned to the lender $350 if
interest and principal were repaid a year later. In terms
of the previous year's purchasing power this was worth

Figure 4.1   Regional Distribution of Interest Rates,
Kiangsu, 1932?

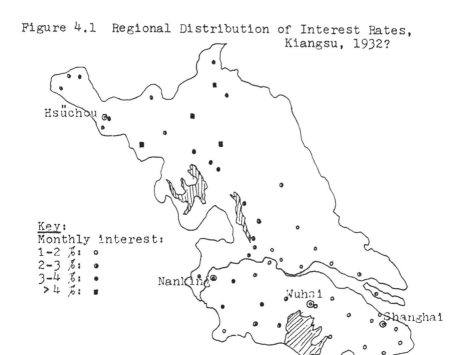

Source: Survey of most usual monthly interest rates in each
county, cited in Feng Ho-fa, <u>Chung-kuo nung-ts'un ching-
chi ts'ai-liao</u>, II, p. 893.

between $74 and $114 (the former referring to "luxury items"

and the latter to land, non-grain food items and animals), so

that at worst the lender protected most of his principal

against runaway inflation and at best earned a 14 percent

real rate of return.[31]   Moreover, interest rates cited in

terms of a fixed amount of grain per yüan borrowed proved

somewhat inflexible downward even in the face of inflation,[32]

so that after 1938-39 the Yünnan debtor could not hope to

gain through the depreciation of principal nor could the

creditor do better by merely purchasing and holding commodities for speculative gain, for the nominal interest rate
on this type of loan was now well over 100 percent at
current prices.

It is difficult to establish a predictable relationship
in theory between interest rates and commercialization,
since both the aggregate supply of and demand for loanable
funds should be greater in commercialized areas and, with
urban development, also the extent of alternative opportunities for use of funds. In the fact, however, there is no
doubt that interest rates were lower in the more commercial-
ed areas, and a higher percentage of the peasantry was in
debt.[33] This relationship is illustrated in Figure 4.1,
where it is apparent that the lowest interest rates in
Kiangsu prevailed in the Yangtze delta and Lake T'ai region
which included such commerical-industrial centers as
Shanghai, Suchou, Wuhsi and Nant'ung and was the major silk
and a major cotton-producing area, certainly the most
commercialized area in China.[34] By contrast, the highest
rates prevailed in the more backwards northern part of the
province and in the west.

Because the mortgage procedure stands in a particularily close relationship to the land market, the determination of the rate of interest on mortgages deserves special
attention. This rate is the use-value of the land divided
by the value of the loan extended, which was a fraction of

the value of the land itself. In noninflationary periods, this fraction probably averaged about 50 percent, ranging from .3 to .7 in different localities and transactions.[35] After 1937, the average may have fallen to the lower end of this range.[36] Since the use of the land was transferred to the lender but the original owner still continued to pay the land tax, the rate of return to the lender (net) was about twice the rate of return to land investment (gross of tax), which made it around 25 percent on the average, less than the average nominal interest on conventional loans of around 32 percent. As we shall see below, there are good theoretical reasons why the mortgage rate should be intermediate between the nominal rate of return on land and on loans.

Comparing investment in mortgages with investment in land, the following factors account for the higher rate of return on the former: First, with a positive rate of inflation, land tends to appreciate in value, leaving capital gains in the hands of the owner; with mortgages, this remains the mortgagee/borrower, not the lender, so a margin between the two rates of return equal to the expected rate of inflation of land values should exist. This was more than sufficient to cover the reverse margin due to the fact that the owner must in both cases pay the land tax. Secondly, the demand for mortgages (i.e. the number of persons willing to

lend against mortgages) was less than that for land. A
mortgage could not be used as security for loans; it was
less suitable as a long run store of wealth, to be passed on
to heirs, as it could be redeemed at the disgression of the
mortgagee (after a certain time had passed). Control over
the property was limited by the mortgage contract: Where
use of the land was transferred to the lender, he was
probably not able to sell or transfer that right to others;
where the mortgagee remained on the property as a tenant,
even though the mortgage itself could be sold by the
lender, the new purchaser probably could not evict the
tenant (i.e. in such cases only the subsoil right was
mortgaged).

On the other hand, mortgages were preferable to other
forms of loan in several respects: The former was a long-
term investment, which could not be redeemed by the borrower
for at least a few years, whereas other loans were repayable whenever the debtor chose to do so, to his advantage
if price fluctuations were not unidirectional. More
important, mortgages were hardly a risky investment, since
the mortgager either had the land in hand or had the same
claim to rents as a landlord. This was at least slightly
stronger a form of guarantee than where the title deed was
given to the lender as security, and obviously stronger than
loans where the guarantee was no more than a pledge of land

(which could be secretly sold or pledged as security on other loans). And since the value of property well-exceeded that of the loan, the lender was well-compensated in case of default. Thus one would expect the rates of return on mortgages to fall below those on less secure loans.

It is easy to see that mortgages would have been pre-fered by some peasants over other forms of loans because of the lower rates of interest and because the form of repayment guaranteed that the burden of debt would not multiply through default on interest payments, whereas others would avoid them if loss of land use was involved. It is not so easy to explain why peasants would prefer to mortgage their land rather than sell it, without relying on the "mystique" attached to land ownership. It was, of course, a way of getting around social restrictions on land transfer.[37] Moreover, a particular plot of land possessed qualities (including location) which the owner would probably value more highly than the market, including time-dependent know-ledge of how its yield varied with different inputs and natural conditions. This implies that there were some economic losses attached to land sale not reflected in market prices. However, again it is useful to consider the situation by classes of peasants: The rich peasant used the mortgage procedure as a vehicle for low-interest, large-scale loans, which could then be loaned out in smaller amounts at higher interest rates. By keeping land in his "portfolio", even in mortgaged form, he preserved a desired balance between risky and riskless forms of investment. The middle peasant, as we have seen above (see pp. 120-121), earned a rate of return on land well above nominal rental rates of return, and probably approaching the average rate of interest on loans (primarily because land prices were largely determined by the needs and opportunities of the rich and poor peasants). The poor peasants, finally, either had little or no land or had already pledged it as security for loans, so there was no alternative to their further use of the loan market.

Throughout this chapter, we have emphasized the role of varying degrees of risk in the determination of equilibrium returns in the peasant economy, but have provided little empirical evidence of the extent of risk involved in various investment activities. This is largely because very little evidence was collected during the prewar period: Although at least one researcher mentions (in passing) the risk involved in moneylending and points to certain limits to the lender's ability to enforce repayment,[38] including the fact that interest rates above 20 percent (by the Thirties) received no legal sanction, no efforts were made to collect information on the rate of default.

It should be pointed out that the realized rate of interest on loans is extremely sensitive to the probability of default. Suppose, for example, that a moneylender makes

ten loans of $100 each at a nominal rate of 30 percent, to
be repaid in one year. If one out of ten borrowers defaults
on repayment of principal and interest, the lender only
receives $1170, so that the effective rate falls to 17 per-
cent; if the default rate is 20 percent, the effective rate
falls to 4 percent.

What the actual default rates were is a matter of con-
jecture. If the nominal term of the loan is taken seriously,
they might seem extremely high, but it appears that creditors were forced to take a more relaxed attitude towards
collection of debt; nor is it possible to determine how
long secured loans could be in default before creditors
were able to assume title to the land. A limited amount of
relevant data is available from Mantetsu surveys of
villages near Tsingtao and Wuhsi, but its usefulness is
qualified by the possibility that either wartime dislocation
or the activity of Communist guerrillas made evasion of
repayment unusually frequent. In a 1939 survey, it was
reported that 72 percent of loans were nominally extended
for a period of one year only, but only 17 percent of outstanding debts were of no more than a year's duration,
whereas 33 percent had been outstanding for two or three
years, and some 20 percent for more than five years. Moreover, in more than one-third of the cases it was known that
one or two years' interest remained unpaid; this was true of
three-quarters of loans outstanding more than 5 years, but

also of 29 percent of those outstanding for only two or
three years. Nor did the presence or absence of pledged
land affect this rate (about the same percentage of loans
involved defaulted interest payments).[39] Similar results
were found in the Wuhsi village survey, based on a very
small sample. There the average duration of outstanding
loans was over five years, but the contractual period of
repayment was also indefinite in all cases. There were also
instances of loans with pledges of land attached which had
been outstanding since as early as 1911 and with nearly total
default on interest repayments. However, such cases
generally involved loans among friends and relatives.[40]

Since loans were generally from sources within the same
or a nearby village, often among friends, neighbors or
distant relations, it would probably be correct to say that
lenders did not press for repayment of loans (unless they
were in need themselves) so long as interest payments were
made, and borrowers in turn tried to keep their credit good
by at least making reasonably regular payments of interest.
In this context, no clear demarcation exists between a loan
of indefinite term (an annuity) and a state of default,
although we imagine that fairly frequently total default
would eventually result from the total bankruptcy and impoverishment of the borrower. In the short run, moreover,
loans were actually a much less liquid form of investment
than land or other property. That is, the difference in the

extent of risk attached to investments in loans as opposed
to land arose not so much from differences in the probabilities that interest or rent payments would be made in
full as in the differing chances of converting the investment principal (loan or land) back into cash in either the
short or long run.

We thus find that the essential nature of the money
market in the prewar Chinese peasant economy was accurately
captured by our earlier theoretical discussion (see Chapter
II.). The lower expected rate of return to moneylending,
not the nominal rates of interest, enter into decision-
making in the farm economy on alternative uses of investable
funds. This was relevant primarily to wealthy peasants or
landlords, to whom land investments brought a lower rate of
return. Poorer peasants, on the other hand, found themselves short of land relative to other factors of production,
and unable to assume substantial risks. To them, the rate
of return on land and physical capital was probably higher
than the expected return to moneylending, or at least not so
low that the risks involved in the latter were acceptable;
at the same time, the nominal rate of interest was too high
to induce borrowing for productive purposes except in small
amounts covering emergency needs. In general, then, peasants
depended on their own savings or current incomes for the
resources needed in farm production.

CHAPTER V.   THE LABOR MARKET IN PREWAR CHINA

As a result of the high and growing density of population relative to arable land, the inequality of land distribution, and the seasonality of agricultural production, many families found it necessary to supplement income from strictly farm activities with labor income from other sources.   On the other hand, many (and often the same) farms found themselves short of labor during busy seasons, and a minority supplemented family labor with hired labor on a full-time basis.   The purpose of this chapter is to explore the market arrangements which answered these needs.

The focus of the discussion is again on the variety of institutional arrangements which existed, and their interpretation as a reflection of the varied economic requirements of a peasant economy.   Moreover, since the labor market was one of the most important points of contact between the modern urban industrial and the peasant economy, a portion of the chapter is devoted to an analysis of the relationship between the two as reflected in occupational and regional wage structures.

The remaining section attempts to pull together the discussion of all factor markets for a comprehensive view of the relationship between resource endowments of the family farm and the use of the factor markets to adjust factor proportions to approach the economic optimum.

Labor Market

We have suggested above the importance to smaller
farms of opportunities to supplement farm earnings with income from other activities, and to larger farms, of opportunities to supplement family labor resources with hired
labor. By the "labor market", we mean the institutional
arrangements providing such opportunities, which, to the
non-existent "average farm" accounted for about 14 percent
of income (20 percent for small farms, 10 percent for
large), not including remittances from non-resident family
members; 23 percent of total farm family labor time.[1] From
the point of view of the employer, again considering the
"average farm", 15 percent of total farm work was done by
hired labor (compared to about 28 percent in the United
States at the same time).[2]

If we consider separately farm wage labor, home industry
(i.e. handicraft activities), and other non-farming activities, we find (see Table 5.1) that no less than one out
of seven farms received income from the first, one out of
four from the second, and a substantial segment also from
mercantile activities and non-farm forms of labor. However,
these figures include primarily slack-season, part-time
labor: Long-term laborers generally lived with their employers, and, whether or not they sent remittances to their
families, were not counted a part of their family labor

force in this survey. With an additional 17 percent of
farms hiring long-term laborers, the group dependent primarily on wage income came to some 10 percent of the rural
population (see Table 3.2).[3]

Table 5.1   Proportion of Farm Families with Income from
            Subsidiary Work, by Category of Work, 15,316
            Farms, 144 counties, 1929-33.

Type of Work	Wheat Region	Rice Region	All China
Farm Laborer	.17	.12	.14
Home Industry	.23	.21	.22
Skilled Labor	.06	.07	.07
Unskilled Labor	.13	.09	.11
Merchant or Pedlar	.21	.12	.16
Teacher	.02	.02	.02
Soldier	.01	*	*
Official	.01	.01	.01
Professional	.03	.06	.05
Other	--	*	*

* less than ½ percent.

Source: John L. Buck, LUC, Statistical Volume, Table 6.,
          p. 309.

Although contractual wage labor was the dominant form
of non-family farm labor in prewar China, a variety of
earlier institutional arrangements hung on, generally in
the more backwards areas.[4] For example, in parts of the
southwest, such as Kwangsi's Ssu-en, Ho-ch'ih and Nan-tan
hsien, slavery was still found, sometimes in a more paterna-
listic form, similar to one prevalent in Japan in the seven-
teenth century,[5] wherein a laborer was allowed to marry a

serving girl and become a permanent servant, in return for a room and some land of his own.[6]

Somewhat more common was direct exchange of labor for land or loans, a system termed "semi-feudal" because its effect was to limit freedom of contract of laborers, making their compensation non-competitively determined. The "labor rent" system, discussed earlier (see p. 95) as a rental system, was sometimes preferred by both laborers and hirers: Although the value of compensation (land and house) was at least as large as the highest money wages, the hirer was not required to provide meals during periods of slack activity, and the laborer assumed part of the risk, since his return fluctuated with his own effort and natural conditions. On the other hand, laborers with families frequently preferred this system, since they could live with their families and support them at a minimal level.[7] By greater industry, they could probably extract an income from the land greater than that of the average long-term laborer. As with rental deposits, in some cases the wage bargain was one permitting tradeoff between land use and money wages, in inverse relationship.[8] At one extreme, it shaded into a normal tenancy relationship with small labor service obligations attached to the rental terms (often in conjunction with cropsharing in "backwards areas").

A second "semi-feudal" arrangement, discussed earlier in relation to the loan market, was debt repayment in labor. At one extreme this system verged on slavery (as with the "mortgage" of children as security for debts); at another, on "labor usury", e.g. in Kwangsi's Ssu-en hsien, where the monthly labor interest was one day on each $1 borrowed (a monthly rate between 15 and 40 percent).[9] More frequently, though, this arrangement merely represented an exchange of busy season labor for small cash or commodity loans of a short-term nature, which in any case would have commanded high rates of interest.

In areas where factor markets were not well developed, or among friends, relatives and neighbors where sufficient trust existed, direct exchange of labor for tools, seed, fertilizer or animal labor was a common means of equalization of factor proportions on farms of varying endowment. For examples, in Kwangsi landlords or rich peasants sometimes rented buffaloes to poor peasants, whose obligation was to feed the animal and put in 30-40 days of plowing work for the lender during the appropriate seasons without cash compensation (in all such arrangements, meals were provided). In Szechuan and many other places, two to three days of labor exchanged for one day's use of a buffalo, depending upon local relative endowments.[10] The essence of such arrangements was that, by reducing underemployment of factors of production of <u>both</u> parties, each could gain some economies of scale.[11]

The existence of the above institutional arrangements notwithstanding, contractual wage labor remained the predominent form in the labor market. It is customary to distinguish between long-term labor (<u>ch'ang</u>-<u>kung</u>), with a period of employment of 12, 8 or 6 months (depending in part on the length of the local growing season) and short-term (<u>tuan</u>-<u>kung</u>, <u>jih</u>-<u>kung</u>, <u>yüeh</u>-<u>kung</u>), hired by the day or month. Piecework was also used on occasion for short-term labor, but largely by farmers who wished to avoid labor supervision and only at the expense of poor-quality work.[12]

Long-term laborers were generally from families with insufficient land and regarded such labor, not merely as a means of subsistence, but as a source of savings to permit marriage, acquisition of farming capital and eventually land.[13] Those who were successful in these respects could hope by age 30 to be a tenant, and by age 50 to be a full landowner.[14] Many, however, were not so "successful".[15]

Their wages were usually paid in cash (but sometimes partly or wholly in grain) but included board of at least equal money value.[16] In East Central China this was customarily supplemented with commodity "gifts" -- clothing, shoes, grain, meat, etc.[17] Terms of payment, including cash

and fringe benefits and timing of payments, varied according
to local supply and demand conditions.

Short-term labor involved larger numbers of both
employers and employees, and consequently gave rise to more
involved market institutions. Across China, some 37 percent of localities had formal market places for short term
labor, to which prospective employers went to satisfy their
needs.[18] Elsewhere the hirer either drew on neighbors
known to do this sort of work or on migrants who came singly
or in groups to the fields, the house or other markets to
make their availability known.[19] In some areas, short-term
laborers organized themselves into groups, with leaders who
served as contractors in getting jobs and setting wages.[20]
This served to give the worker greater bargaining power and
to reduce the lack of information.

Wages of short-term workers were also paid in cash
primarily (though sometimes grain or a share of the harvest),
with meals included in the great majority of cases.[21] Provision of meals was not inconvenient, because of the small
number of persons and days usually involved, and afforded
the hirer some control over the length of rest periods.
Fringe benefits were also sometimes included, in the form of
tobacco and/or wine. It also seems that food and fringe
benefits were varied more readily than the cash component in
response to labor supply and demand conditions, probably

because employers felt that the cash component was inelastic
downwards and did not wish to set precedents in times of
temporary shortage.[22]

"Professional" short-term laborers were commonly migrant
workers who, as in other countries, followed the crops. For
example, those from Honan and Shantung, after harvesting the
local crops, went to Hopei or Manchuria to assist in the
harvest there.[23] When not so employed, the landless among
them generally had side occupations during slack seasons;
some 36 percent were pedlars, 24 percent wood or manure
gatherers, 13 percent coolies and 8 percent handicraft
workers.[24]

Women and old people also were able to find farm employment: The former usually received wages averaging around
50 - 60 percent of those of males, although the rate of
compensation was much less standardized and sometimes involved nothing more than subsistence.[25] Old people
generally found employment as house servants, receiving
subsistence and care until death, but no other wage.[26]

An extensive discussion of the institutional characteristics of home or handicraft industry would require more
spadework than its importance to our theme justifies. As
was apparent from Table 5.1, more farm families (that is,
those working their own farms as owners or tenants) were
involved in home industry than in other subsidiary

occupations, but this was due largely to the fact that this was in the main a slack season activity and/or one involving women, children and old people who otherwise might have been idle. Consequently the opportunity cost of the labor required was close to zero, and earnings per unit time less than those in any full-time or busy season activity, less in some cases than even a bare subsistence.[27] This was not the case, however, for activities requiring a substantial investment of capital, which often brought in respectable rates of return.[28] A partial list of home industry activities would include spinning and weaving (cotton, silk and hemp), wine, paper, basket, rope, shoe, and beancurd making, etc., to exclude activities such as animal or silkworm raising which are more properly classed as agricultural.[29]

The significance of "other non-farm activities" is not to be minimized, for they were the bridge to wealth and social position, which were certainly not to be attained through farming.[30] For those peasants already wealthy, a substantial investment in education for their sons was required, at a total cost (including forgone farm labor and interest at 10%) of more than $5000 for each son educated through middle school.[31] However, such an investment only paid off in economic terms if the degree brought the son about $40 per month more than he could otherwise earn

(in a job with minimal skill or in farming, at about \$10
per month), since this much could be returned by investment
at a 10% annual rate of interest. Few middle school
graduates were so successful.[32] For the poor, on the other
hand, family labor was generally in excess anyway and,
even though the expense of education was prohibitive, there
were opportunities in cities and market towns for earnings
(to those who could find jobs) at least as great as those
of a farm laborer, however limited the skill of the laborer.

A sample of these opportunities, and the compensation
involved, is given in Table 5.2 for a village close enough
to a major city for off-farm activities to constitute a
major source of income.* The best paying positions were
held by villagers belonging to wealthy families: The
"official" and school principal were members of the
wealthiest family (58 mou of land), and the two managers
both heads of nuclear families, renting out their holdings
of 19.5 and 12 mou respectively. However, two of the three
schoolteachers were of only middle-peasant status, judging
by landownership. Below these high-status jobs lie the
hierarchy of opportunities open to the uneducated and un-
moneyed: Skilled industrial jobs in modern industry were

---

* though less so in 1938 than earlier -- several textile
  mills had closed following the outbreak of war.

Table 5.2 Non-Farm Earnings by Occupation, Li Village,
Tsingtao, Shantung, 1938.

Long Term	Monthly Cash Earnings	No. of Persons
Official	$ 100.	1
Company Manager	67.	1
School Principal	55.	1
Teacher (Primary)	35.	3
Manager (Railway Station)	33.	1
Railway Worker	28.	20
Servant	24.	1
Courier	20.	2
Industrial Worker (unspecif.)	15.10	12
Attendant (Government)	15.00	1
Textile Worker (Factory)	13.80	7
Commercial Employee (Urban)	12.00	10
Coolie	10.12	9
Craftsman (unspecified)	10.00	6
Merchant/Pedlar	9.25	13
Horsecart Transport	7.75	2
Farm Laborer	4.30*	6
Wine Maker	2.50	2
Beancurd Maker	1.35	2
Apprentice Factory Worker	0.	4

Short Term	Daily Earnings	No. of Persons	Average Days Worked
Cart Transport	1.37	11	57
Coolie	.47	14	86
Farm Laborer	.40**	21	93

* $13.30 counting room and board; at pre-1937 price levels,
  about $8.14 including room and board.
** $ .70 counting food provided; about $ .60 pre-1937.

Notes: Earnings are average for each occupation over months
       of employment, but in some cases where 12 months'
       employment was specified, actual work time may have
       been much shorter (this applies to merchants, horse-
       cart transport and wine and beancurd makers).
       Apprentices received room and board, but no cash
       wage to speak of. Only the number of persons for
       whom wage quotations were available were counted
       above.
Source: Mantetsu, Hokushi jimukyoku, Chintao kinkō ni okeru
        nōson jittai chōsa hōkoku (1939), Appendix Table 2.

the most lucrative, but they were limited in number and
rationed in part through the apprenticeship system (access
to which was also limited to those with "introductions").
A new recruit remained an apprentice for several years,
during which time he received only room (in the factory) and
board and no more than a yüan or two per month as spending
money.[33] Moreover, because of the scarcity of skilled labor,
frequently new factories in the interior drew upon labor
transferred from the coastal cities, limiting local peasant
sons and daughters to low-paying, unskilled jobs.[34] The
textile industry was, of course, the biggest employer, with
an important peculiarity: That it drew predominately on a
female labor force, and paid wages to women well above what
they could earn in agriculture or other industries (perhaps required to induce family heads to allow wives and
daughters to leave the home).[35]

Ranked below jobs in modern industry were jobs as
commercial employees (clerks, stockboys, etc.), coolies
for modern factories and traditional craftsmen. Although
all of the above activities were nominally full-time, it is
possible that they did not always preclude part-time or busy-
season participation in farming activities. Indeed, many
"modern" factories seem to have operated for only six to
eight months a year, especially those processing agricultural raw materials (e.g. flour-milling, rice-polishing,

oil-pressing, cigarette, leather, etc.), perhaps because
both the supply of raw materials and the labor force were
seasonal.[36] However, much of the long and short-term farm
labor in Li village was hired by families part of whose labor
force was engaged in off-farm full-time labor.

The remaining non-farm activities were generally slack-
season or part-time in nature, including a variety of
mercantile ventures on a small-scale, horsecart transportation, wine or beancurd making and coolie labor. Wine or
beancurd making, in the nature of home industry, offered
only a trivial net return.

The cash return to farm labor stands virtually at the
bottom of the list, but this is in fact deceptive since it
does not account for room and board. As best as can be
determined, most non-farm activities, including wage labor,
did not include room and board as part of the compensation,
except to apprentices. Modern factories were at best
willing to provide dormitory accomodations and mess halls
for workers at cost.[37] There were some exceptions in the
case of a few "enlightened" firms and many small, traditional
shops in particular trades. Consequently, a comparison
between wages of farm laborers and other workers must take
into account this difference. In the case of the Li village
data, this creates an apparent anomalie, since farm labor
seems to pay as well as factory labor when the value of room

and board is included, but this is probably due to the inflation which set in in 1938, to which cash wages had not yet been adjusted. If we value the non-cash component at its approximate pre-1937 value,[38] farm wages appear to be slightly below the level of wages of the least skilled urban occupations, as might be expected.

This relationship appears to hold nationally also, despite considerable regional variation in the monetary wage levels of farm laborers and industrial workers in various industries. That is to say, the entire national wage structure, including farm labor, can be described as a fairly constant set of wage relatives (ratios between wage levels in different occupations) in conjunction with regionally-defined factors which determined the absolute wage levels in each region.

To demonstrate this requires a somewhat elaborate exercise: We will first seek a numerical description of the national industrial wage structure, then show that it is closely related to the regional structure of agricultural wages. We take as data the average wage in each of 25 industries and 20 provinces, drawn from D. K. Lieu's 1932 survey of Chinese-owned factories (with at least 20 employees each and some degree of mechanization) in China proper.

Our basic model takes the form, $\bar{w} = B_I \cdot B_R + e$, where the average wage in a particular industry and region ($\bar{w}$) is equal to the product of industrial and regional wage factors, plus an error term allowing for interactions between the two factors as well as errors of observation. This model allows us to separate regional "wage levels" (determined by supply and demand conditions common to all industries in a region) from industrial "wage levels" (factors affecting the industry but independent of region, such as different mixes of skills or skill levels in the labor force of different industries, different labor supply conditions, reflecting in part work conditions, hours of labor, advancement prospects and fringe benefits affecting the laborer's offer curve). The "wage levels" are defined multiplicatively so as to permit us to specify, for a given region, the probable ratio of the average wage in industry X to that in industry Y, or for a given industry, the probable ratio of the average wage in province A to that in province B.

We must also account for the fact that female and child laborers (apprentices) were paid considerably less than adult male laborers, based on the existence of different effective supply curves and customary considerations, in addition to productivity differences. Variations in the proportion of these three types of labor among factories, industries and regions would otherwise introduce errors in the model.

Given the weighted average wage, $\dfrac{W}{N} = \dfrac{w_m M + w_f F + w_a A}{M + F + A}$

where w_m = average wage of male laborers (M);
$\quad\ \ w_f$ = average wage of female laborers (F);
$\quad\ \ w_a$ = average wage of child laborers (A), male or female;
$\quad\ \ W$ = total wage bill;
$\quad\ \ N$ = total number of laborers;

this may be rewritten as: $\dfrac{W}{M} = w_m + w_f \dfrac{F}{M} + w_a \dfrac{A}{M}.$

The parameters w_m, w_f and w_a are all functions of the industry and region (I,R). For simplification, we assume that the wage of the male laborer is the "standard-setter", and that the female and child wages (w_f, w_a) are all proportions of w_m, i.e. $w_f = b_f w_m$ and $w_a = b_a w_m$ (this assumption is not altogether innocuous: Basically we are assuming that the _average_ female and child wages are a definite fraction of the _average_ male wage, and that these _fractions_ are _independent_ of region or industry. These are hardly realistic assumptions, but any further complication would make estimation impossible). We then specify,

$w_m = F(I,R) = B_I \cdot B_R + e$, and the final model becomes:

$\dfrac{W}{M} = B_I \cdot B_R \cdot (1 + b_f \dfrac{F}{M} + b_a \dfrac{A}{M}) + u$, where u is a composite disturbance term.

Estimation of the parameters of this descriptive model is possible, using non-linear iterative least-squares regression techniques (see Appendix V-A). As the parameters

are not completely identified, estimation requires the
normalization of either the industrial or regional coefficients (we have arbitrarily chosen to restrict the
industrial factors to an average of 1.0; it may be shown
that this does not restrict the inter-industrial or interregional wage ratios, the estimation of which is our primary
objective).

Two regressions were run, the first using average
monthly wages (assuming a twelve-month work year) as dependent variable (see Table 5.3). However, the annual wage
bill data represented different numbers of work days for
different industries and regions, a result of strikes,
different customs, the seasonal nature of certain industries
and so forth. A second regression used average daily wages
as dependent variable (see Table 5.4), thus eliminating the
influence of these variations. Whereas the first regression
should produce results more representative of actual worker
earnings, the second should be more closely related to the
economic factors underlying our descriptive model. Certain
anomalous results in the first regression (notably the high
wage levels of Hunan and Fukien) led to reexamination of the
data and rejection of a few observations, so that the
results of the two regressions are not entirely comparable
to each other.

Table 5.3 Average Monthly Wage Levels: Regional and Industrial Rankings

Region	Factor	S.E.	T-Ratio	Observations	Notes
Hunan	56.65	1.12	21.0	8	
Fukien	39.75	4.86	8.0	4	
Kwangchou	34.68	3.09	10.9	14	$R^2 = .78$
Shanghai	29.26	2.30	12.7	23	
Tsingtao	25.40	2.70	9.4	13	S.E.E. = 13.32
Kwangtung	24.49	3.22	7.6	7	
Nanking	24.31	8.90	2.7	3	
Kiangsu	24.11	2.41	10.0	20	
Chekiang	23.58	1.12	21.0	15	
Kiangsi	23.17	5.75	4.0	7	$b_f = .42$
Shantung	22.21	2.96	7.5	14	(.11)
Hupei	21.45	2.51	8.5	17	(ratio of female
Anhwei	21.28	4.38	4.9	6	to male wages)
Honan	19.48	6.96	2.8	5	
Shensi	19.46	10.44	1.9	3	$b_a = -.03$
Hopei	18.95	3.37	5.6	17	(.02)
Szechuan	18.76	2.91	6.5	11	(ratio of child
Kwangsi	18.14	4.36	4.2	3	to male wages)
Peiping	12.12	4.44	2.7	5	
Shansi	11.60	3.65	3.2	8	
				203	

Industry

Industry	Factor	S.E.	T-Ratio	Observations	Notes
Water	2.56	.21	12.1	10	
Shipbuilding	2.23	.28	7.8	4	
Cement	1.85	.24	7.8	5	
R.R.Machinery	1.57	.16	10.0	12	
Flour	1.14	.18	6.3	13	
Engines	1.12	.22	5.1	6	
Cotton Spinning	1.02	.15	6.7	11	
Generators	.97	.23	4.1	6	
Paper	.95	.15	6.2	9	
Printing	.94	.14	6.9	16	
Cigarettes	.90	*	*	6	* normalization of
Matches	.90	.14	6.4	11	variables required
Spinning/Weaving	.87	.13	6.9	7	the sacrifice of one
Miscl. Machines	.87	.25	3.5	8	variable, cigarettes;
Iron & Steel	.78	.34	2.3	3	its coefficient may
Hosiery	.77	.15	5.2	5	be derived from those
Wax	.73	.23	3.2	5	of other variables,
Glassmaking	.70	.23	3.1	7	but not its standard
Cast Tools	.69	.23	3.0	6	error.
Oil Pressing	.67	.22	3.1	5	
Cotton Weaving	.65	.11	6.2	13	
Dyeing	.63	.15	4.3	9	
Rice Polishing	.56	.18	3.0	8	
Brick Making	.53	.15	3.6	10	
Leather	.40	.16	2.5	8	
				203	

Table 5.4 Average Daily Wage Levels: Regional and Industrial Rankings

Region	Factor	S.E.	T-Ratio	Observations	Notes
Kwangchou	1.30	.12	10.4	14	
Honan	1.17	.23	5.1	4	
Tsingtao	1.08	.10	10.7	13	R^2 = .73
Fukien	1.04	.20	5.3	3	
Kwangtung	1.03	.13	7.9	7	S.E.E. = .49
Shantung	1.01	.10	9.6	14	
Kiangsi	.97	.21	4.6	6	
Shanghai	.97	.09	11.3	22	
Kiangsu	.95	.09	10.5	20	b_f = .46
Hunan	.95	.28	3.4	4	(.12)
Chekiang	.86	.04	20.5	15	
Hupei	.86	.09	9.1	16	b_a = -.03
Nanking	.82	.26	3.2	3	(.02)
Anhwei	.80	.14	5.9	6	
Kwangsi	.75	.18	4.3	3	
Szechuan	.75	.11	6.8	11	
Shensi	.69	.35	2.0	3	
Hopei	.68	.12	5.7	17	
Peiping	.49	.17	2.8	5	
Shansi	.43	.11	3.8	8	
				194	

Industry	Factor	S.E.	T-Ratio	Observations	Notes
Water	2.16	.19	11.5	9	
Cement	1.79	.22	8.0	5	
Shipbuilding	1.63	.27	6.0	3	
Flour	1.52	.16	9.3	12	
R.R. Machinery	1.46	.16	9.1	11	
Cigarettes	1.14	*	*	6	*see note to Table
Paper	1.06	.15	7.1	9	5.3
Engines	1.02	.21	5.0	6	
Printing	1.02	.14	7.4	16	
Spinning/Weaving	1.01	.16	6.5	7	
Cotton Spinning	1.00	.14	7.0	10	
Iron and Steel	.92	.34	2.7	3	
Generators	.90	.21	4.3	5	
Glassmaking	.81	.21	3.8	7	
Matches	.80	.12	6.7	10	
Hosiery	.78	.14	5.6	5	
Miscl.Machinery	.76	.20	3.7	8	
Oil Pressing	.76	.21	3.6	5	
Cast Tools	.75	.22	3.4	6	
Cotton Weaving	.73	.11	6.8	13	
Wax	.69	.21	3.3	5	
Dyeing	.64	.18	3.6	8	
Brick Making	.64	.15	4.4	10	
Leather	.58	.20	3.0	8	
Rice Polishing	.42	.18	2.3	7	
				194	

While the R-squares of the two regressions are only
moderately impressive, given the number of degrees of freedom lost, the coefficients are all quite significant, though
not sufficiently so for the rank orders to be assigned any
useful degrees of confidence. Examination of the patterns
of the residuals, however, points to two erroneous assumptions
imbedded in the form of model: First, the "spread" or range
of the wage relatives by industries is not the same in all
areas. For example, the actual range for Shanghai industries
is wider than the predicted range (see Table 5.5). This is
probably because in those cities where industries were
established earliest, the work force in industries using
skilled labor was older, more experienced and thus on the
average received higher wages than their counterparts in
cities where industries had only recently been introduced.
Secondly, although the regression-estimated average ratio
of female-to-male wage levels is less than one-half, this
ratio in fact appears to differ between regions and industries. It was unusually high in the textile industry and
above the average in Shanghai in general (see Table 5.6).
Whatever the reasons for this (which we are not able to
explore here), the result is some overprediction of male and
underprediction of female wages for industries in which
females were a large proportion of the labor force.

Table 5.5 Predicted and Actual Daily Wages, Shanghai, 1933

Industry	Average, All Workers		Industry	Average, Male Workers	
	Actual*	Predicted**		Actual***	Predicted
R.R. Machinery	2.29	1.41	Shipbuilding	1.29	1.52
Cement	1.68	1.73	Printing	1.11	.99
Printing	1.38	.95	Machinery	.76	.73-1.41
Generators	1.21	.97	Tobacco	.79	1.10
Matches	.98	.53	Paper	.68	1.02
Cast Tools	.88	.71	Hosiery	.68	.75
Flour	.81	1.47	Oil Pressing	.68	.73
Miscl.Machinery	.79	.73	Cotton Weaving	.57	.71
Paper	.76	.83	Matches	.55	.77
Iron & Steel	.75	.89	Flour	.54	1.47
Glassmaking	.74	.77	Cotton Spin.	.48	.97
Leather	.68	.56			
Cotton Spinning	.67	.56			
Spinning/Weaving	.59	.55			
Cigarettes	.57	.64			
Water Supply	.56	2.09			
Oil Pressing	.50	.74			
Dyeing	.49	.61			
Cotton Weaving	.46	.50			
Brick Making	.44	.54			
Wax	.38	.49			
Rice Polishing	.28	.40			

*   calculated from D.K. Lieu survey data.
** from survey data and estimated coefficients of Table 5.4.
*** from T.Y. Tsha, "A Study of Wage Rates in Shanghai, 1930-34,"
     Nankai Social and Economic Quarterly, October 1935, pp. 506-507.

Table 5.6 Male and Female Daily Wage Rates, Shanghai, 1933*

Industry	Male	Female	Female/Male Wages
Silk Weaving	1.52	.92	.61
Printing	1.11	.45	.41
Tobacco	.79	.53	.67
Undergarments	.73	.65	.89
Hosiery	.68	.66	.97
Paper	.68	.32	.47
Wool Knitting	.63	.50	.79
Cotton Weaving	.57	.50	.88
Matches	.55	.28	.51
Cotton Spinning	.48	.45	.94

*   T. Y. Tsha (1935), pp. 506-507.

The estimated regional wage levels on the whole suggest a tendency for wages to be higher in the coastal areas than in the interior. Two of the coefficients -- those of Honan and Hunan -- both based on only a few observations, are suspiciously high and violate this pattern; we shall disregard them on the presumption of errors in the data. It is also interesting that wage levels do not seem to reflect the extent to which a province or city is industrialized: The Shanghai wage level is well below those of the less important industrial centers of Tsingtao and Kwangchou (Canton), and Kiangsu and Hupei both rank lower than would be expected. This, however, is not altogether surprising in a country where the industrial labor force represented such a small proportion of the total labor force: Regional wage levels would more probably be adjusted to the level of wages and earnings in agriculture, determining the base level of the supply curve of industrial labor.

This can be tested by comparing the regional agricultural wage levels with the rankings of provincial industrial wage levels; the former are given in Table 5.7 for both long and short-term farm labor. To the daily cash wage levels, we have added Buck's estimates of the value of meals and other commodities provided, to arrive at the full value of the daily wage. To compare the regional rankings

Table 5.7   Wages of Farm Labor by Province, 1931-32.

Province	Annual Wage	Province	Monthly Wage	Province	Daily Wage
Fukien	$72.30	Kwangtung	10.77	Kwangtung	.55
Kwangtung	69.03	Fukien	10.24	Fukien	.49
Chekiang	57.98	Chekiang	8.66	Shantung	.48
Kiangsi	57.52	Kiangsi	7.61	Chekiang	.39
Kwangsi	48.98	Shantung	6.84	Kiangsi	.37
Shantung	45.81	Kwangsi	6.68	Hupei	.35
Hopei	43.89	Hopei	5.92	Hopei	.32
Shansi	40.22	Kiangsu	5.90	Kwangsi	.31
Anhwei	39.85	Anhwei	5.38	Kiangsu	.30
Hunan	38.26	Hupei	5.13	Anhwei	.28
Kiangsu	35.35	Hunan	5.06	Shensi	.25
Hopei	34.08	Shansi	4.96	Shansi	.24
Shensi	32.57	Shensi	4.67	Hunan	.23
Honan	24.71	Honan	3.09	Honan	.19
Szechuan	23.09	Szechuan	2.79	Szechuan	.17

Notes: Data derived from responses to a government question-
naire (652 hsien responding), with follow-up and
editing to reduce errors. Does not include imputed
value of room and board, which were provided where
appropriate. Monthly and daily agricultural wages
were weighted averages of figures for busy and slack
season, on the assumption of 4 slack months per year
(see Buck, LUC, p. 296).

Source: T'ung-chi yüeh-pao (Statistical Monthly), no. 13,
Sept.-Oct. 1933, p. 100.

of these farm wages with the rankings of the regional

factors resulting from our regression on daily industrial

wages, we have computed Kendall's coefficient of rank

correlation, T = +.72, which turns out to be significant at

better than the 1% level, indicating that there is almost

zero probability that the similarity of the rankings could

arise due to chance.[39] Since the industry factor which

Table 5.8 Farm Daily Wage Levels (Including Non-Cash
Compensation) and Regional Wage Relatives
(Estimated).

Province	Cash Wage	Other	Total Wage	Rank	Regional Wage Relative*	Rank
Fukien	.49	.30	.79	1	.72	1
Kwangtung	.55	.24	.79	2	.72	2
Shantung	.48	.25	.73	3	.70	3
Chekiang	.39	.27	.66	4	.60	6
Kiangsi	.37	.25	.62	5	.67	4
Kiangsu	.30	.31	.61	6	.66	5
Hupei	.35	.26	.61	7	.60	7
Kwangsi	.31	.24	.55	8	.52	9
Hopei	.32	.23	.55	9	.47	11
Anhwei	.28	.17	.45	10	.56	8
Hunan	.23	.19	.42	**	---	**
Shensi	.25	.17	.42	11	.48	12
Shansi	.24	.17	.41	12	.30	13
Honan	.19	.19	.38	**	---	**
Szechuan	.17	.18	.35	13	.52	10

* equals the regional factors from Table 5.4 multiplied by an
industrial factor of .70, chosen so as to minimize the
mean squared difference between the levels of farm wages
and the numerical value of the regional wage relatives.
The choice of industrial factor obviously does not effect
rankings, but is merely intended to permit a comparison
of the level of farm wages with those in other industries.
** Hunan and Hupei were excluded from the rankings on the
grounds that their estimated regional factors were
implausibly high, suggesting errors in data.
Notes: Cash daily wages drawn from Table 5.7 above.
"Other" is the averages of board and other things
furnished, from Buck, LUC, Statistical Volume, p. 328.

gives a wage level most comparable to farm wages* is

* the criterion for choice of factor being to minimize the

mean squared difference between farm wages and industry

wage levels by province.

b_I = .70, between Wax and Cotton Weaving, it also can be
concluded that short-term farm labor (on the average) paid
wages below those of all but the more traditional and unskilled forms of industrial wage labor (wax making, dyeing,
brick making, leather and rice polishing), although this
statement did not hold true for every locality or region.

Whatever the explanation for the provincial differences
in average farm wages (which are shared largely by industrial wage levels), we can rule out the possibility that they
merely reflect differences in the cost-of-living. If this
were the case, one would expect to see some correlation
between average provincial grain prices in this period and
the farm wage averages (see Appendix VI.G for our estimates
of grain prices), but the rank correlation in fact turns
out to be small (about .15) and insignificant. If, then,
these variations in wage levels represent roughly corresponding variations in real income, we would expect them to
be related to farm productivity and income per unit labor,
since this in turn is closely related to the marginal
productivity of labor, which is the opportunity cost of
leaving the farm for work as either a farm laborer or

industrial worker.* We do in fact find a somewhat higher
(T = .27+) rank correlation between farm wages and land
prices by province, but the relationship is weakened by
regional variations in the ·"natural" rate of interest (re-
call that land prices are determined by both the return on
land use and the rate of return required by investors) and
the difficulty of determining an "average value" of land by
province (land value data are given separately for different types of land.)[40] A survey of 29 villages in P'an-yü
hsien, Kwangtung indicates a very close relationship between
wages and land value (r = .81), but since this county is
adjacent to the city of Kwangchou (Canton), the covariance
probably reflects the varying impact of urban demand for
both labor and land according to the proximity of the
village to the city as much as it does the relationship of
labor and land value to farm productivity.[41] It is perhaps
worthy of note that wages do not vary in the same proportion

---

* real wage and rent levels (and, for approximately fixed
  rates of return on land investment, land prices) will
  vary inversely with varying labor/land ratios and similar
  production functions, but cross-sectionally roughly
  "neutral" variation in productivity will dominate and
  should cause strong positive correlation between wage
  rates and land prices among localities.

as land values (as would be true if only price level variations were the cause); rather, the variation in wages was
between .23 and .46 of the variation in land values (at the
5% level).

As the ambiguities in the above discussion suggest,
forces underlying the determination of wage levels are too
complex for exploration of bivariate relationships to yield
much information. We therefore postpone further discussion
of this subject until the following chapters, when we can
bring together larger amounts of data in a multivariate
contex. For the moment, we are content to have established
the significant role of wage labor in a family farm economy
and to have shown that the wage level was a market-
determined variable which does not bear an obvious relation
to "subsistence".

Farm Size and Resource Utilization

What distinguished our earlier theoretical discussion
of peasant economic behavior from previous interpretations
was its emphasis on the impact of differences among peasants
in resource endowments on their resource allocations. We
must now return to that approach in order to provide empirical evidence that the prewar Chinese farm economy broadly
conformed to the model we presented. Only the fringes of the
mosaic will be laid down in this section; the more difficult
pieces will be attempted in the following chapters.

As a point of departure, it should be recalled that
two important points emerge from the theoretical conditions
regarding the behavior of producers in equilibrium in both
factor and product markets in the context of a perfectly
competitive market economy with no uncertainty: First,
producers (here, read "peasant farms") of the same product
or product mix should differ systematically in their factor
utilization only in regard to scale, and if they face the
same U-shaped marginal cost curves, as is frequently assumed,
even producer scale (here, read "farm size") should be
homogeneous. Second, there should be no systematic tendency
for producers to take either profit or loss, if all inputs
into production are accounted for as costs at their market
value (the term "systematic" is used because in the "real
world" there will be short-term profits and losses and
differences in quality of factors, including farming
ability, which should, however, be fairly randomly distributed among farms).

It is easily established that these conditions did not
obtain in the prewar Chinese peasant economy. First, a
variety of researchers have shown for the "average farm"
that, if both own-supplied and purchased factors of production (labor, land and capital services) are valued at
going market prices, and all invested capital valued at an
interest rate between 5 and 10 percent, farm producers were

generally taking a net loss in accounting terms.[42] It is not
as well known that the extent of profit or loss per mou of
land varied systematically with the size of farm, with the
level of profit (loss) rising (declining) at a decreasing
rate with increased farm size. This tendency emerges from
a study of 2866 farms by J. L. Buck; it is so consistent
among the North China farms in the sample as to hold among
as well as within localities (see Figure 5.1). There it
appears that the "break-even" point of zero profitability
is about 15-20 mou (2.5-3.3 acres), probably close to the
median size of N. China farms (Buck's Land Utilization
Survey finds 21.8 mou to be the N. China median, but this
is to be discounted due to survey biases).[43]

These variations in accounting profitability in turn
are associated with reasonably consistent differences in
factor proportions among farms of different size. There
was first a very noticeable negative relationship between
size of farm and the labor/land ratio, both within and
between localities (see Table 5.9). The latter was due in
part to a tendency for denser settlement and smaller farm
sizes in localities with longer growing seasons and easy
irrigation (note the correlation coefficients between the
labor/land ratio and double-cropping and irrigated percentages; also such land could generally absorb the energies
of a larger labor force). But this relationship remains

Figure 5.1   Scatter Diagram, Relationship of Profits/Mou
              To Average Size (in mou) of Farm,
              North China, 1921-1923

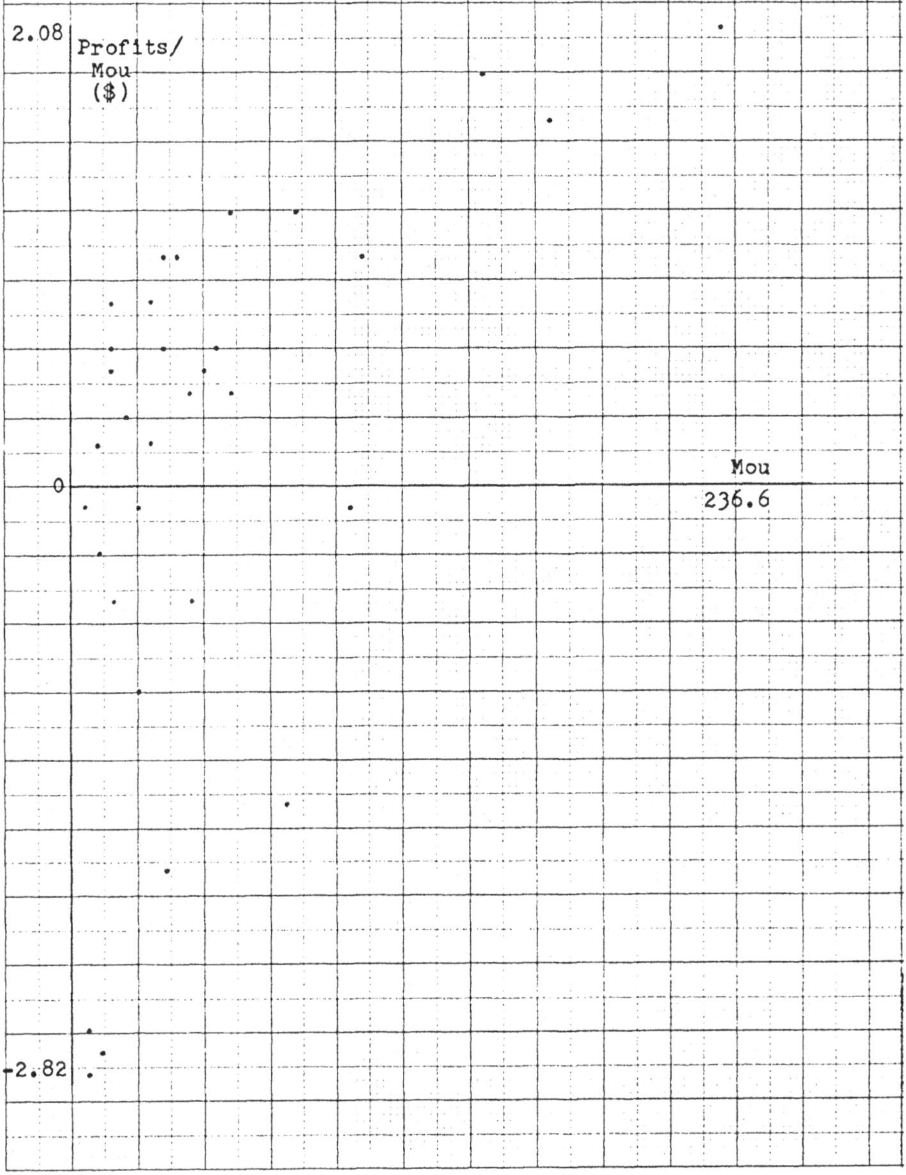

Table 5.9 Correlation Coefficients, Chinese Farm Survey
Data, 16,000 Farms, 1929-33.

Crop Region	Labor/ Land Ratio	Ferti- lizer/ Mou	Draft Animals/ Mou	Double Cropping Percent	Irrigated Land Percent	Percent of Land Rented
		Correlation with Size of Farm:				
1	-.91	-.44	-.31	-.39	-.40	-.21
2	-.79	-.29	+.36	-.24	-.24	-.13
3	-.92	-.66	+.12	-.43	-.08	+.14
4	-.83	-.38	+.28	-.31	-.12	-.07
5	-.81	-.44	+.30	-.07	-.12	-.05
6	-.87	-.59	-.01	-.28	-.16	+.28
7	-.86	-.41	+.18	+.07	+.37	+.27
8	-.94	-.54	-.37	-.32	-.07	+.01
		Correlation with Labor/Land Ratio:				
1	--	+.59	+.51	+.55	+.64	+.13
2	--	+.48	-.28	+.50	+.52	+.02
3	--	+.72	-.06	+.40	+.13	-.11
4	--	+.43	-.21	+.24	+.11	-.06
5	--	+.48	-.22	+.31	+.19	.00
6	--	+.77	+.24	+.16	+.20	-.15
7	--	+.46	-.06	-.09	-.55	-.31
8	--	+.53	+.45	+.24	+.03	-.04

Notes: All but percentage data were in logarithmic form.
Fertilizer was manure and nightsoil produced on each farm
(excludes purchased fertilizer and fertilizer of other
types); labor animals included only those owned by the
farm manager (excludes rented labor animal services).
Correlations are among averages of variables for each
farm, grouped by farm size. For fuller definitions of
variables, see Appendix VI-A.
Source: John L. Buck, Land Utilization in China, Statistical
Volume, Various tables.

significant when these factors are controlled for (partial
correlation coefficients are negative).

It is less easy to establish what the relationship is
between size of farm and use of capital services, although

it is certain to be less consistent than that of the labor/
land ratio. The constituents of this item included seeds,
fertilizer and pesticides, draft animals, tools and implements (including irrigation mechanisms), and storage buildings, of which fertilizer and labor animal services were by
far the largest expenses.

It can be shown fairly unambiguously that certain of
these constituents involved economies of scale for large
farms, so that the value of the item used per mou of land
cultivated declined with farm size. Seeds were one such
item: Use of larger amounts of seeds per mou was associated
with more labor-intensive cultivation techniques on small
farms (for one Hopei village, the correlation between value
of seeds/mou and farm size (both in logs) was -.34).[44]
Cost of storage facilities was another (r = -.24).[45]
Finally, the cost per mou of tools and implements undoubtedly declined with farm size: The correlation coefficient
derived from Buck's 1921-23 farm survey data was -.37.[46]
From the analysis of the more extensive data of the Land
Utilization survey in Appendix V-B, it seems that the cost
of this item in most regions rose only about one-half percent for every one percent increase in farm size. Since the
labor/land ratio declined at an even faster rate, there was
nevertheless some substitution of this type of capital for
labor on larger farms.

Of the remaining two components, fertilizer and labor
animals, there is little substantial evidence of differences
in the capital/land ratio related to farm size. It is
apparent from the correlation coefficients in Table 5.9
that manure and nightsoil production per mou of land was
higher on small farms than large, and these were in some
areas at least the overwhelming sources of nutrient (though
a smaller proportion of total value of fertilizer used, due
to higher costs of other types).[47] Yet these and other
types of fertilizer were highly marketable commodities, and
there is no reason to presume that small farms did not sell
or larger farms buy sufficient quantities to equalize use
per unit land. Buck's estimates of total fertilizer
applied per mou (though useless because of the aggregation
of fertilizers of different nutrient content and prices in
terms of weight) indicate little or no consistent relationship with farm size.[48] For three different small North
China samples, the correlation coefficients between value
of fertilizer used/mou and size of farm were -.14, +.11 and
+.23 respectively, which again suggests no consistent relationship.[49]

In the more commercialized parts of China, the value of
draft animals owned per mou was somewhat positively related
to farm size (see Table 5.9), but these were areas where
small farms could hire or borrow animals for plowing
purposes, so that the correlations have little significance.[50]

In the more backwards Spring wheat and Southwestern rice
regions, on the other hand, the sign of the relationship was
reversed, but this again might only mean that small farms
maintained animals in part for the rental (cum labor)
income. In any case, the correlations only represent
differences in the proportions of farms owning any labor
animals, rather than real differences in the use of such
services per unit of land.[51]

The relationship of total capital services used per mou
to farm size was no more than the sum of the relationships
discussed above, whence we consider that the average relationship was probably slightly negative, although with
considerable variance, depending on the proportions of the
individual items in the total. Drawing again on the three
Hopei localities (similar in crop mix as well as geographic
characteristics), we found overall correlations of -.36, .18
and .17 in localities where fertilizer and livestock were
around three-quarters of total cost of capital services;
where these were somewhat less important, the negativity
might be more pronounced.[52]

The relationships between size of farm and factor
proportions in farm production parallel but do not fully
reflect differences in factor endowment. For farms with
high endowments of labor relative to land owned tended to
either rent additional land and/or depend more heavily on

income from non-farm labor activities; farms with low
endowments of labor relative to land tended to either rent
out, mortgage or otherwise dispose of land and/or hired a
large proportion of their labor requirements. These adjustments preceded the correlations observed above, and thus
clearly did not represent full equalization of factor proportions among farms, although the disparity was reduced to
levels we believe consistent with "optimization conditions"
for the individual farm.

Since the most useable survey data provided only
limited information about "initial endowments" of peasant
farms, we can establish some of these points only indirectly. First, the evidence of Tables 5.10 and 5.11 shows that
small farm operators (not to mention their family members)
more frequently had side occupations than large farm operators and, because of this (and the greater importance of
remittances from family members living off the farm), a
much larger proportion of total net family income came from
off-farm labor (interest and rental income, and remittances
from non-resident family members are apparently not included in this table). Although operators of large farms
sometimes also held side-occupations, these were generally
of the more lucrative sort and their quantitative significance is out-weighed by the dependence of large farms on
hired labor to the extent of about one-third of their total
farm labor requirement (see Table 5.12).

Table 5.10   Relation of Size of Farm to Percent of Operators
             Having Side-Occupations, 2109 Farms, 1922-25.

Size of Farm:	Small	Medium	Large
Percent of operators having side-occupations	38.9%	20.3%	19.9%

Source: John L. Buck, Chinese Farm Economy, Table 49.,
         p. 49.
Note: The category of "small" farms encompasses about 75%
       of Chinese farms, judging from LUC survey results.

Table 5.11   Off-Farm Labor Income as a Percent of Total Net
             Family Income, 15,215 Farms, 1929-33.

Farm Size	Rice Region	Wheat Region	Average	Mean Farm Size
Very small	21.8 %	27.1 %	23.9 %	7.5 mou
Small	17.9	24.0	20.6	8.7
Medium	12.5	15.3	13.8	17.3
Medium large	10.5	12.1	11.2	30.0
Large	7.8	10.4	10.0	43.5
Very large	8.4	9.4	8.9	79.1
Very, very large	3.5	8.0	7.1	133.4

Note: Does not include remittances from absent family
       members.
Source: John L. Buck, Land Utilization in China, Statistical
         Volume, Table 6., p. 309.

Table 5.12   Percentage of Hired Labor Cost to Total Labor
             Cost By Size of Farm, 2866 Farms, 1921-25.

Size of Farm: Region	Small	Medium	Large
North China	4.1 %	13.0 %	31.8 %
East Central China	4.5	15.7	31.4
Average	4.3	14.3	31.6

Source: See Table 5.10 above.

Turning to land rentals, it is readily apparent both
by inspection and through calculation of correlation coefficients (which are statistically insignificant) that the
"tenancy rate" (defined as percentage of average farm area
rented, not percentage of farmers who were tenants) is
unrelated to either farm size or labor/land ratio.[53] But
this ex post result is just what one would expect if landless tenants and part-owners were renting the amounts of
land required to reach a desired optimum with respect to
size of family labor force and other considerations.

The use of the factor markets to reach a more balanced
farm labor/land ratio can best be illustrated with data
from a sample of 62 farms (Wu-hsi hsien, 1939).[54] We have
estimated the "endowed" labor/land ratio as the ratio of the
family total labor-equivalents, including members who had
left the farm for other work but were still considered part
of the family (i.e. were sending remittances), to the
number of mou of land owned. Second, we estimated the
"labor-adjusted" labor/land ratio by taking the ratio to
owned-land of the actual on-farm labor-equivalents, excluding all off-farm labor time and including hired labor.
Finally, we computed the actual ratio of farm labor to
farmed land, excluding from the denominator land rented,
mortgaged or pawned out, and including land rented in. The
frequency distributions for the three sets of ratios are
displayed as histograms in Figure 5.2.

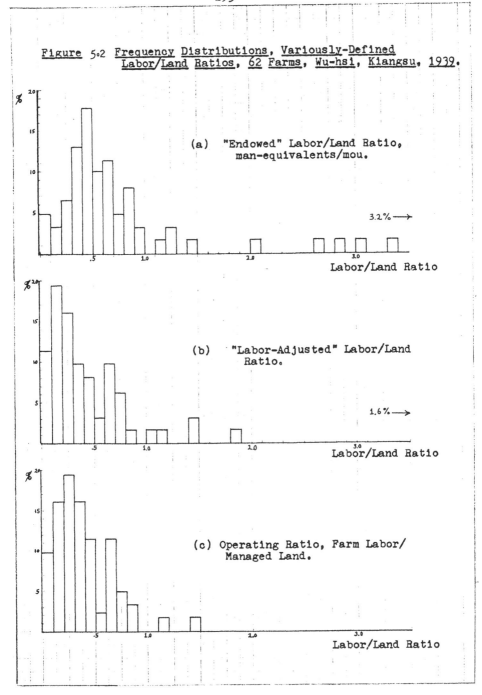

Figure 5.2 Frequency Distributions, Variously-Defined Labor/Land Ratios, 62 Farms, Wu-hsi, Kiangsu, 1939.

(a) "Endowed" Labor/Land Ratio, man-equivalents/mou.

(b) "Labor-Adjusted" Labor/Land Ratio.

(c) Operating Ratio, Farm Labor/Managed Land.

We note first that the "endowed" labor/land ratio
shows considerable variance among farms (the coefficient of
variation, $s_x/\bar{x} = 1.235$). In this densely populated locality, 52 percent of farm families in the absence of other
opportunities would have been forced to subsist with only
between 1.4 and 3.2 mou per worker (man-equivalent). The
few very large labor/land ratios represented families with
only tiny amounts of owned land, not with especially large
labor forces.

The existence of a labor market offering extensive
opportunities for wage labor in this locality permitted a
considerable reduction in the labor/land ratio, as more than
one-half of families had a member engaged in full-time non-
farm work. But this should not be viewed in isolation from
the adjustment of land holdings: Ten families rented out or
otherwise relinquished a substantial portion of their land
holdings, of whom nine were below the median "labor-
adjusted" labor/land ratio, in part because of better than
average holdings and in part because members chose to work
off the farm. Seven families rented a substantial part of
the land they worked, all above the median "labor-adjusted"
labor/land ratio and five with no family members engaged in
full-time off-farm labor. With the adjustments of the labor/
land ratios permitted by the existence of opportunities in
both labor and land markets, as revealled by the histograms,

a majority (52%) of farms were able to operate within the
more efficient range of from 2.5 to 9.1 <u>mou</u> per worker,
and few farms (3%) were to be found with less than 1 mou per
worker, compared with 20 percent so "endowed". In short,
variation in the labor/land ratio was considerably reduced
(to $s_x/\bar{x} = .75$).

Conclusion

While our Chapter II developed an analytical framework
within which any well-developed peasant economy may be
viewed, in the following chapters we have applied that
framework to an analysis of the prewar Chinese peasant
economy. Despite the shortcomings of the data used and
certain limitations on the scope of the discussion, we hope
that this approach has provided sufficient insights and
evidence to justify itself.

We have focussed on the markets in "factor services" --
labor, land and money capital -- because of their centrality
to the peasant decision-making process and the determination
of a general equilibrium. Other components of the "opportunity set" -- the choice of crops and techniques -- will be
covered in subsequent chapters using more appropriate (and
complex) analytical techniques than we wished to apply in
this chapter.

An analysis which considers only the impact of the
"peasant as decision-maker", and which moreover is based on a

limited view of peasant motivations, can at best hope to capture broad "tendencies", from which many "deviations" remain to be explained by other frameworks of analysis. The careful reader will find many points throughout the above materials deserving a non-economic approach.

Unfortunately we are dealing with historical data rather than making first-hand observations (although even the direct observers of the period often differed radically on the interpretation of what they observed), with the result that the often subtle pieces of information needed to discriminate among conflicting interpretations are frequently unavailable. For example, if we find data on a peasant family owning only a small piece of land, renting the remainder and depending in part on outside income, how does one distinguish between the following interpretations? (1) They are maximizing their income by renting additional land and simultaneously engaging in off-farm labor; (2) they have become tenants on their own land through defaulted debts and must take jobs off the farm to subsist. Both might be true (but not if we also knew that the family had not previously owned the land), or neither. The conventional answer to this question is that when a theoretical approach is clear, simple and consistent and when most available evidence can be easily interpreted within its framework, then the theoretical approach used is preferable to other approaches lacking these qualities. While the practical application of this criterion is rarely clear, we believe it is the proper basis for appraising the work of this chapter.

Our theoretical model and the "labor-surplus" model we sought to replace both took as points of departure the marginal productivity theory of distribution of conventional microeconomics. So far our discussion of the Chinese peasant economy has provided only peripheral evidence of the degree of applicability of this theory. For a frontal assault on this issue, we require proper definitions and estimates of marginal productivities of factors of production in Chinese peasant agriculture, and comparisons with their market prices. This in turn requires the use of econometric tools sufficiently complicated to handle multivariate relationships. The following two chapters will be devoted to these purposes.

CHAPTER VI.   THE AGRICULTURAL PRODUCTION FUNCTION AND FACTOR
PRODUCTIVITY IN PREWAR CHINESE AGRICULTURE

If Chinese peasant families were deploying their resources
in such a way as to even approximately maximize some (utility) function of family income, however qualified or constrained by risk aversion or other influences, the systematic relationships should exist among the marginal value
productivities of factors of production and their market
prices. We have previously described the probable nature
of these relationships, and have shown the extent to which
the Chinese institutional structure facilitated maximizing
behavior. It remains to examine the available data for
evidence of the relationships hypothesized.

The primary difficulty lies in estimating the marginal
value productivities of the various productive factors, that
is, the impact on family income of small increases or decreases
in the productive use of labor, land or capital, individually, with use of other factors held constant. We are obviously not in a position to experiment, but must deduce the
principles of change from comparisons of situations in which
many elements differ. Since we are further handicapped by
dependence on cross-sectional comparisons, we are also
generally unable to examine the situations of single farms
at more than one point in time.

Under these circumstances, we must assume that it is possible to define and mathematically describe a "production

- 198 -

function", a set of relationships between "inputs" (productive factors in use) and farm "outputs" (physical quantity or market value of products resulting), which is shared by large samples of farmers. Such a "production function" could be at best a simplified mathematical approximation of a myriad different relationships. It is a relatively easy exercise to derive such a summary measure; it is more difficult by far to ensure that it is a genuine measure of the complementarities and substitutabilities among the factors of production, of marginal productivities and returns to scale, such as pertain to individual farms. The largest proportion of the work in this and the following chapter attempts to deal with the latter problem.

There are two different (but not entirely inconsistent) ways to approach the problem of estimating production functions, which we will term the "neoclassical" and the "activity analysis" approaches. If the amount of commodity X produced is x, and the amounts of inputs A_1, A_2,....,A_n used in its production are $a_1, a_2, ..., a_n$, then the production function is the relationship $x = f(a_1, a_2, ..., a_n)$. The "neoclassical" approach assumes that this function is a continuous function of continuous variables. Moreover, if we vary the use of inputs in such a way as to hold output constant at some level x_0, and so define a hypoersurface in input space, it is assumed that in the usual case this surface will be

convex to the origin, that is, that increasing amounts of
one input are required to keep output constant in the face
of constant decreases in the use of another input (an increasing marginal rate of substitution).[1] The activity
analysis approach differs from the neoclassical in assuming
neither a continuous function nor continuously divisible
variables, although neither are necessarily ruled out.
Replacing the production function as such are sets of techniques or activities, indicating relationships between inputs
and outputs such that (1) for any particular technique,
input proportions are fixed (rather than continuously variable); (2) if more than one technique exists for producing
any type of commodity, techniques may be used in combination
to permit effective substitutability of inputs. However,
in this case the constant output surfaces are discontinuous,
composed of intersecting planar surfaces, which individually
are characterized by constant marginal rates of substitution,
and are characterized by convexity only vis à vis the location of the various planes composing the isoquant. The productive relationships here cannot be even theoretically described by a single equation,* as was the case for the neo-

---

* Although any single plane, describing the relationship among
n techniques in n factor space, may be described by a
single linear equation.

classical production function.

Since the neoclassical production function can be regarded as either a curvilinear approximation to the isoquant of activity analysis or as the limiting case of an
infinite number of techniques encompassing all permutations
of input proportions, the reader may judge the above discussion superfluous. We have, however, two reasons for
emphasizing the differences between the two approaches:
First, the activity analysis approach is in most respects
truer to the peasant's own perception of the process of
decision making in production, and is a more accurate
description of the production process in theoretical terms
in the "real world" of finite numbers of techniques available to each individual producer, for which reasons it has
been employed in our earlier theoretical discussion. Yet
the neoclassical approach is both more tractable and more
frequently employed in actual econometric estimation of
productive relationships. It is obviously important to
be aware that the latter is an approximation of the former,
often a poor approximation and sometimes totally misleading.
Second, when data are sufficiently detailed and disaggregated,
an activity analysis approach to empirical estimation may
be distinctly preferable, and will in fact be used in the
following chapter. Since the data there employed is limited
to small samples drawn from a few villages in a single region,

the large-sample, all-China analysis of this chapter should
help set a context for what follows.

Source and Form of Data

The data employed in the estimation of production functions in this chapter was derived from that published in the
Statistical Volume of John L. Buck's Land Utilization in China
(see the discussion on pp. 8 - 10 of Chapter I), representing the results of a survey conducted between 1929 and 1933
of a cross-sectional sample of about 16,000 farms. We have
taken as our basic units of observation the averages of data
for each locality at the farm level, as grouped by size of
farm. Since there were on average five size groups per
locality (with the range of farm size for each group differing from locality to locality), totalling 100 farms per
locality, this gave us a total of 750 observations.[*] This
in turn was subdivided into samples covering the eight crop
regions (see Table 6.1) determined by Buck, which have been
analyzed separately in order to reduce cross-sectional variation in agricultural technologies determined by geographical, climatic and cropping factors (which tend to coincide)

---

[*] As the data are in the form of group means, we have in
estimation corrected for heteroskedasticity by using the
square root of the number of observations in each group as
weights to unbias estimates of the covariance matrix.

TABLE 6.1 CHARACTERISTICS OF EIGHT CROP REGIONS*

Region	Mean Rainfall (mm.)	Days of Growing Season	Soil Types	Percent of Crop Area in Major Crops
1. Spring wheat	352	196	Chestnut earths and desert soils	Millets,34; Irish potatoes,10; spring wheat, 18.
2. Winter wheat-millet	430	?	Chestnut earths; podzolic soils.	Wheat,40; millet,31; cotton, 9.
3. Winter wheat-kaoliang	592	241	Calcareous alluvium, saline alluvium, Shantung brown and sha-chiang soils	Wheat,46; millet,23; kaoliang, 19; corn, 16; cotton, 9.
4. Yangtze rice-wheat	1059	293	Non-calcareous alluvium and rice paddy soils, podzolic and red soils, and saline alluvium.	Rice,58; cotton,13; wheat,31; barley, 19.
5. Rice-tea	1466	308	Podzolic and red soils	Rice,73; rapeseed, 13.
6. Szechwan rice	975	334	Purple-brown (forest) soils, non-calcareous alluvium and paddy soils, brown and gray podzolic soils.	Rice,41; wheat, 19; corn,14; rapeseed, 13; opium, 11.
7. Double-cropping rice	1742	365	Red soils	Rice,90; sweet potatoes,12; sugar, cane,6.
8. Southwestern rice	1146	360	Yellow and red soils	Rice,60; opium,19; broad beans,17; corn, 14.

* from Buck, LUC, I., Table 1., pp. 32 and 34.

TABLE 6.2 MEAN VALUES OF INPUT RATIOS BY REGION*

Region	Labor /Land (1)	Fertilizer /Land (2)	Cultivated Acreage (3)	D.C. Percent	Irrigated Percent	Tenancy Rate	Grain Yield (4)
1	0.89	8.76	1.84	.07	.36	.10	547
2	1.09	6.30	1.23	.19	.11	.17	1090
3	1.17	6.17	1.38	.43	.11	.12	1510
4	1.84	6.82	.98	.65	.64	.41	2220
5	1.76	9.88	.76	.75	.81	.46	2700
6	2.82	12.90	.68	.53	.56	.52	2930
7	2.50	12.60	.76	.77	.69	.47	3340
8	2.85	32.80	.63	.52	.82	.27	5430

* geometric means for inputs, arithmetic for percentages. As the regression
estimates are calculated for a log-linear function of the inputs, estimated coefficients are most accurate at the geometric mean of the sample
inputs. All observations are weighted by the square root of the number
of farms per observation in calculating the means.

(1) Fully-utilized man-equivalents per hectare of cultivated land.
(2) Thousands of kilograms of night-soil and manure per hectare of
     cultivated land.
(3) Hectares of cultivated land (fallow and pasture land excluded) per
     farm (1 ha. = 2.5 acres).
(4) Kilograms of grain-equivalent per hectare, assuming no destruction
     of crops through pests, drought or flood.

and to reduce the impact of variance in excluded factors of

production (such as climate and soil characteristics) which

would otherwise tend to bias estimates based on regression

analysis.

Discussion of the precise derivation of each variable used

from the Buck data is confined to Appendix VI-A. We confine ourselves here to discussion of variables actually used
in the following analysis. These variables (the means of
which are listed by region in Table 6.2) were, for the ith
observation:

Q_i = production of crops, in terms of kilograms of grain-
equivalent;

DC_i = percent of cultivated acreage double-cropped per
farm (or crop acreage divided by cultivated acreage,
minus one);

I_i = percent of cultivated acreage irrigated per farm;

T_i = tenancy rate (percent of land rented per farm);

L_i = man-equivalents of farm labor per year (with idle
time deducted);

F_i = organic fertilizer (nightsoil and manure) produced
on farm;

C_i = cultivated acreage (excluding idle or fallow land);

A_i = labor animal units (defined in terms of feed consumption, as a proxy for maintenance cost).

Discussion of the individual variables in turn follows:

(1) Q_i, the "output" variable in what follows, is a measure
of the equivalent in terms of the major local grain of all
farm produce (excluding products of animal husbandry). Equi-
valency was defined in weight in the case of other grains,
in terms of calorific equivalent in the case of legumes and
tubers, and price equivalence for all other products.[2] The

use of such a composite variable is more suitable for a subsistence than for a market economy, and can be defended (on grounds other than expediency) only insofar as relative grain prices and calorific value were similar, which is improbable.

The discussion of Appendix VI-B points up an additional problem: the production function must be assumed monotonic if we are to estimate it from observed data (excepting "random error", which is permissible). This requires that the peasant producers be actually attempting to maximize (for given input quantities) the index of aggregate output used, and that the weights used to aggregate (normally price, but here calory content and price) be the same throughout the sample. Yet if these conditions were satisfied and relative input prices were also roughly uniform throughout the sample, we would expect the observed factor proportions to show relatively little variation throughout the sample[*] creating a multicollinearity condition preventing us from distinguishing the contributions of various inputs individually. Conversely, if factor prices vary greatly (due to fragmented factor markets), we would expect commodity prices to show variance of a similar magnitude, in which case a meaningful production

---

[*] except systematic (and collinear) variations among farms of different size, as emphasized in our earlier analysis.

function cannot be defined cross-sectionally. In fact we did find multicollinearity to be our most serious problem in the estimations, as discussed below (see Table 5.9, where the correlations among the inputs are recorded).

(2) L_1, the labor input in the model, is (after removal of reported proportions of idle time) a measure of labor services used on the farm, including those of members of the farm household (with female and child labor measured at their approximate adult-male labor equivalent) and hired laborers, short and long-term. It is, however, inferior to a direct measure of labor expended in farming (and does not exclude on-farm subsidiary activities, not counted in the value of product).

(3) F_1, the total amount of nightsoil and manure produced on the farm, is estimated from the total animal and human adult-equivalents (consumption) on the farm. As it measures production rather than use, it is at least subject to error and at worst to systematic error (i.e. correlated with the magnitude of other variables) to the extent that the proportion actually used differs from the amount produced other than by a constant proportion. Moreover, it neglects use of bean cakes, compost, river mud and chemical fertilizers which in the aggregate were significant in some regions. It is also likely to be collinear with the variables labor and animal labor, from which in large part it is derived.

(4) C_1, cultivated acreage, has been deflated to exclude idle or fallow land. As a certain proportion of cultivated acreage was unharvested, presumably because of pests, drought and flood, we have also reduced this and all other physical inputs by this proportion, so that the actual magnitudes used in the regressions exclude wasted labor, fertilizer and land resulting from calamities. The objective here was to reduce estimation error due to differences in impacts of calamities among localities and farms.

The physical quantity of land cultivated is a very poor proxy for the input "land" because of the qualitative heterogeneity of this variable. More frequently in production function analysis the value of land is employed on the presumption that variations in quality (i.e. in marginal productivity units ceteris paribus) will be reflected in land price. Since we should hardly presume what we intend to test, this procedure is not altogether desireable. Moreover, with geographically fragmented land and product markets, too many influences may be introduced which affect land price, to the extent that value may be a worse index of land units of homogeneous quality than physical acreage alone. This possibility was tested in preliminary regressions using data from Buck's earlier Chinese Farm Economy survey (see Appendix VI-C), where both variables were available, and it was found that the use of land value slightly

worsened the statistical "fit" of production functions also
run with cultivated acreage, although they reduced the
multicollinearity problem (but so would the introduction of
random errors into the "land" variable!).

We attempted to account for the qualitative variations in
land by explicitly including in our specification of the
production function its major determinants -- irrigation,
double-cropping potential and inter-locality differences in
soil quality, as described below.

(5) DC_i, the percentage of land double (or triple) cropped,
together with I_i, the percentage of land irrigated, reflect
differences in climate, fertility, moisture, land situation
and crop potential which constitute a major part of variation
in land quality. I_i unfortunately was available only in the
form of averages for localities, leaving variations among
different sizes of farm indistinguishable.

Variables introduced into the production function to
account for input heterogeneity ideally should be used to
find an input index such that the numerical value assigned
should be the same wherever any two "mixes" of inputs of
different quality are perfect substitutes in production,
i.e. will produce equivalent amounts of other inputs. Thus
the weights used in aggregating land of different quality
(e.g. irrigated versus non-irrigated, single-cropped versus
double-cropped) should reflect the _relative_ marginal produc-

tivities of the components. For example, if the ratio of
the marginal product of double-cropped land to that of
single-cropped land is a constant, β, an appropriate index
would be $I_L = L_{sc} + \beta L_{dc} = L[1 + (\beta-1)DC_1]$, where L_{sc}, L_{dc}
and L represent amounts of single-cropped, double-cropped
and total land, respectively. The factor β could then be
estimated along with the other parameters of the production
function.[3]

In practice, in order to permit use of a strictly log-
linear form of production function, it was necessary to
approximate the linear scheme, $[1 + (\beta-1)]$, with the exponential form, $e^{\alpha DC_1}$. As shown in Appendix VI-C., the approximation is reasonably close for $\beta < 2$ ($\alpha < .7$), the expected
range of the coefficient. There is, however, no guarantee
that this will be the case, as differences in the extent
of double-cropping and irrigation may be closely correlated with major differences in yields and cropping patterns
among localities, so that estimated coefficients may not
represent incremental effects of increases in irrigation
or double-cropping in single localities.

(6) S_{1j}, a set of dummy variables, varied in composition
from regression to regression. The major function of these
dummies was to account for interlocality variation in land
quality and intertemporal variation in crop conditions not

accounted for by the above variables. The problem was to
reduce equation bias due to a "reverse correlation" between inputs and outputs via input quality: Poor soil and
climate require high inputs of factors such as labor, water
and fertilizer to produce even a low level of output, so
that cross-sectionally it may appear that greater amounts
of labor, irrigation and fertilizer "lead to" (are associated
with) little increase or even decrease in total product.
Since interlocality variance is generally greater than intralocality variance in Q_i, the "reverse correlation" may be
statistically stronger than the production function relationship.

There were three stages in our attempts to deal with this
problem: First, we attempted to classify localities according to their probable soil characteristics, relying on a
Chinese soil map and information given in the Statistical
Volume (Table 18., pp. 253-269). This approach was reject-
ed when dummy variables created on this basis proved to
distort rather than improve regressions, presumably because
both the accuracy of our classifications was questionable
and soil types are not in any case the primary determinants
of land fertility cross-sectionally. Second, we increased
the number of locality dummies with an eye to geography,
the data and the coefficients of determination, combining
localities in a single dummy whenever statistically signi-

ficant differences in yield unaccounted for by input intensities were not observed. Since manipulation of dummies did
affect coefficient estimates, we are not altogether happy
with the degree of subjectivity required, but this approach
did lead to the most "reasonable" results and is the basis
of coefficient estimates presented below. Finally, in a
different, nonlinear model estimated subsequently, we
decided to sacrifice all interlocality variance by using
separate dummies for each locality, leading to coefficient
estimates which reflect only intralocality relationships.
Appendix VI-D presents estimated values for the former
(multiplicative) locality dummies, where meaningful; they
may be taken as an index of relative agricultural productivity of localities which is not associated with differences
in labor or fertilizer intensity or in the extent of
double-cropping.

Intertemporal variation within the sample was accounted
for by the inclusion of dummy variables representing the
years between 1929 and 1933 in which the observations
were taken for a given locality. The intent was to account
primarily for weather conditions which were common to a
region for a particular crop season, thereby reducing the
unexplained residuals.

(7) T_1, the percentage of farm area rented, was included
to test for any qualitative differences in inputs associated

with tenancy. There is reason to expect, for example, that tenant land would have been of above-average quality.[4] T_1, like DC_1 and I_1, was included in a specification permitting an approximate estimate of the ratio of marginal productivity on rented land to that on owned land.

(8) A_1, labor animal units, is a stock rather than a flow variable. Unfortunately, as pointed out in the previous chapter, there is no justification for assuming either full or equiproportionate utilization for animal labor power on the farm of the owner, as labor animals were frequently rented to or from other producers, were sometimes jointly owned and worked, and were maintained in part because of their role in subsidiary enterprise (as a source of power and a means of transport) and as a source of fertilizer. Since, in initial regressions, A_1 proved negatively related to output and highly collinear with F_1, it was dropped from later runs.

Forms of Models Employed

The primary form of model used in estimating production functions for the eight agricultural regions was the familiar unrestricted Cobb-Douglas, in the following form:

$$Q_1 = e^{\alpha_1 + \alpha_2 I_1 + \alpha_3 DC_1 + \alpha_4 T_1 + \sum_j \alpha_{5j} S_{1j}} L_1^{\beta_1} F_1^{\beta_2} C_1^{\beta_3} A_1^{\beta_4} u$$

where all variables except u, the error term, have been previously identified. By rearranging these terms, it can be recognized that the index of land in terms of units of homogeneous quality is:

$$c_1 e^{(\alpha_1 + \alpha_2 I_1 + \alpha_3 DC_1 + \alpha_4 T_1 + \Sigma \alpha_{5j} S_{1j})/\beta_3}$$

If each component of the exponential term, for example, $e^{(\alpha_3 DC_1)/\beta_3}$, is regarded as a nonlinear approximation of the linear weighting scheme, e.g. $[1 + (\beta-1)DC_1]$ (see Appendix VI-C.), where β is an estimate of the ratio of the marginal productivity of double-cropped to that of single-cropped land (for $I_1 = T_1 = 0$), we may estimate β as $\beta^* = 1 + e^{(\alpha_3 DC_1)/\beta_3} \cdot (\alpha_3/\beta_3)$.

The choice of the above equation form was based on the ease of estimation. More complicated (and more flexible) forms generally require non-linear estimation procedures unless the applicability of the marginal productivity theory of distribution can be presumed; such methods are frequently misbehaved in the presence of multicollinearity. However, certain limitations of this model deserve mention: It restricts the production function to one involving unit elasticity of substitution, despite evidence that the elasticity is in fact higher than this in agriculture.[5] It assumes constant elasticities of outputs with respect to inputs (so that marginal productivities may not show sharp declines with increased input levels), homogeneity (so that optimal factor proportions remain the same for given factor prices regardless of the scale of production), and a particular degree of returns to scale (decreasing, constant or increasing, but not all three at different points). These constraints may be (and were) relaxed at the price of elegance by the

inclusion of interaction terms. For example, one may allow
for a decrease in the elasticity of output with respect to
labor as farm size increases by specifying $L_1^{\beta_1+\beta_2 \ln C_1}$ instead
of $L_1^{\beta_1}$. When the equation is converted to logarithmic form,
it becomes quadratic rather than linear in the logs of inputs
when interaction terms are introduced.

Neoclassical production functions (of which the Cobb-
Douglas is an archtype) impose an increasing marginal rate
of substitution along an isoquant, as pointed out previously,
whereas we considered it possible that the marginal rate of
substitution might be nearly constant over at least a certain
range if the number of available processes of production was
limited and the factor proportions required differed substantially (as, for example, with two quite different crops,
such as rice or cotton). This suggested the use of a linear
production function of the form,

$$Q_1 = \beta_1 L_1 + \beta_2 F_1 + \beta_3 C_1 (1+\delta_1 DC_1) + u \quad *$$

This equation form is linear homogeneous; to allow for returns to scale, the entire right-hand side was taken to an
exponent, λ, which serves as an estimate of returns to scale.
Moreover, for this set of regressions, it was possible to
allow for a separate scale factor for each locality, so that

---

* I_1 was excluded because it added nothing when scale factors
were separately estimated for each locality; T_1 because it
had previously proved relatively unimportant.

the form actually estimated (by a nonlinear estimation procedure) was:

$$Q_{1j} = S_{1j}[\beta_1 L_1 + \beta_2 F_1 + \beta_3 C_1 (1+\delta_1 DC_1)]^\lambda + u,$$

where λ is the measure of returns to scale, and S_{1j} is the
scale factor for the jth locality.

This equation form has the advantage that it permits a
straightforward (rather than approximate) estimate of the
parameter δ_1 of the land quality index. It presumes a constant marginal rate of substitution (at least over the range
of the data); constant marginal productivities of inputs at
any _particular_ scale of production (Q_0), whatever the input
mix (or crop mix) used to attain it; variation in marginal
productivities (in uniform proportion) over different scales
of enterprise. If returns to scale are not too significant,
this equation form is more consistent with an activity analysis
approach than the Cobb-Douglas, although it restricts one
to a single facet of an isoquant. Moreover, the appropriateness of the constant m.r.s. assumption may be tested by
including interaction or quadratic expressions within the
brackets.

Estimation Problems

Three common estimation problems afflict attempts to
derive production functions from cross-sectional data --
the simultaneous equation problem, multicollinearity and
the problem of excluded variables. The first and last can

lead to biased coefficient estimates; the second to inadequate precision of estimates.

The simultaneous equation problem (see Appendix VI-E.)
arises from the fact that if peasant producers take factor
market prices into account in their production decisions,
as asserted above, then the inputs are not exogenous variables but rather are "simultaneously" determined by a system
of relationships determined by maximization conditions. Under
these circumstances, the right-hand-side variables will not
be independent of the error term, ordinary least squares will
be an inconsistent estimator and the estimates of parameters
will be biased.[6]

This problem is less serious, however, in estimating
agricultural production functions, since it seems reasonable
to assume that the "residual element" in the production function -- those elements which are generally excluded from
the specification, such as the weather -- are treated as
stochastic by the producers, who make their decisions on
the basis of expected or anticipated output levels (given
certain inputs) in advance of any knowledge of the residual
element. Under these circumstances, there should be no
correlation between the inputs and the residual and the
problem should be minor.[7] This does not hold with regard to
exclusion of inputs which are determined simultaneously,
as discussed below.

Multicollinearity among exogenous variables, as seen above, emerges naturally from the same maximization process. By whatever measure, it seriously afflicts our data, the chief culprits unfortunately being the two major variables, labor and land.[8] However, its presence is amply reflected in the high standard errors of the parameter estimates. As the size of our samples was sufficient to provide a fair amount of independent variation in each exogenous variable, the standard errors are rarely so high that we need throw out our estimates, but they do limit our ability to place useful bounds on their confidence intervals. The reader should be warned that, while we of necessity will employ "best estimates" of model parameters in the subsequent analysis, even the best of these may differ from the "true" parameter by about 30 percent either way (at a confidence level of 95 percent). That is, a hypothetical parameter value may differ from an estimated value by as much as one-third without the difference being statistically significant. Consequently readers should treat our results with a degree of caution, even when we are tempted to do otherwise.

The problem of excluded variables arises primarily with respect to land (for which our included variable is a weak proxy) and capital. The potential impact is similar to that resulting from the simultaneous equation problem.

The "correct" specification for land in the model is:
$Q = f(L,K,C^*)$, where C^* is land measured in units of "standardized quality" per farm. Instead of C^*, we only have observations on C, actual cultivated land per farm in hectares. We have included the variables DC and I and the locality dummies, S_j, in an attempt to estimate an index of C^* simultaneously with the other parameters of the model, but this attempt is unlikely to account for all qualitative variation and indeed, through misspecification, may introduce further sources of error.

An alternative approach to the use of locality dummies is to specify an "instrumental variable" which is closely correlated with the "true" C^* but uncorrelated with the error term. The use of such an instrument makes it possible to derive consistent estimates of the parameters.[9] We sought such an instrument in the variable, P_i, the average number of persons per farm _in a locality_. Since historically relative population density should be determined largely by the extent of population which the land will support, that is, by its potential yield, P_i could be expected to be closely correlated with C^*. We found that in most regions there was a close statistical correlation between population density and the locality dummies estimated from previous regressions. Moreover there was only a moderate correlation with the variables included in the previous specification

of the production function. Since a major portion of the
residual was the qualitative variation in land which would
be accounted for by use of P_1 as an instrument, and there
was no reason to expect any particular correlation with
other components of the residual, the use of this technique
seemed justified.

In practice, instrumental variable methods brought
"reasonable" results (proper signs, high R^2) for only three
of eight crop regions. However, these results offered no
visible improvements over OLS methods in the absence of
locality dummies, nor were the directions of changes in
magnitudes of coefficients consistent among the three regions,
suggesting that the chosen "instrument" was not adequately
related to land quality. Consequently we have not included
the results of these attempts in the tables which follow.

A more serious source of bias may be the exclusion of
certain capital services -- fertilizers other than farm-
produced nightsoil and manures, seed, farm implements,
storage, and draft animal services -- which are likely to
be correlated with included variables. The following
general relationship applies: If a consistent linear
relationship, $z_t = Vx_t + u_t$, obtains between excluded
variables, z_t, and included variables, x_t, and if the
"true" specification of the model is $y_t = Bx_t + Cz_t + e_t$,
then the estimates B^* of the coefficients based on the
specification $y_y = Bx_t + w_t$ will in fact be unbiased esti-

mates of the value of $(B + VC)$, and the estimated covariance
matrix of the residuals will be a good estimate of the
combined errors, $w_t = e_t + Cu_t$.[10]

Applying this to our case, since all true coefficients
of the production function (that is, B and C) are by assumption positive, the direction of bias will be the same as the
sign of the partial correlation coefficients between the x_t
and z_t and the magnitude of bias determined by knowledge of
the dimensions of the parameters V and C.

If our earlier argument that small farms tend to be slightly more capital intensive than large farms is accepted, we
can at least specify the signs and approximate magnitudes
of the parameters V. From the analysis of Appendix V-B.,
it appears that the elasticity of the capital/labor ratio
with respect to farm size is positive but less than one-
half. This applies only to tools and implements, however,
and we would expect the magnitude for all capital services
to be even smaller. Extending this analysis further, it
emerges that the elasticity of the capital/land ratio with
respect to the labor/land ratio, holding farm size constant,
is also positive and less than unity (but with considerable
regional variation). This is in accord with the results of
a production function study of Indian data.[11] The elasticity
with respect to farm size, holding the labor/land ratio
constant, is also positive, however, and less than one-third
of the former elasticity. That is, as farm size increases

and the labor/land ratio falls, the capital/land ratio
also falls at a <u>decreasing</u> rate.[*] Thus the coefficients of
V, relating the (log of) capital/land ratio (the excluded
variable) to the (logs of) labor/land and land (two major
included variables) are both positive, the first almost
five times the size of the latter, on average (for tools
and implements only).

It should be noted that the Cobb-Douglas specification
of the production function may also be written (in the
form we actually employed in regressions):

$$Q_i/C_i = e^{(\text{terms as above})}[L_i/C_i]^{\beta_1}[F_i/C_i]^{\beta_2}C_i^{\lambda}u_i$$

where u_i includes the omitted capital-services/land ratio,
which in turn is related to the included variables:

$$K_i/C_i = (L_i/C_i)^{\gamma_1}C_i^{\gamma_2}h_i,$$ where we now know that
$0 < \gamma_2 < \gamma_1 < 1$. It follows that estimates β_1^* and λ^* of
the parameters β_1 and λ of the misspecified model will
actually be unbiased estimates of $\beta_1 + \gamma_1\beta_4$ and $\lambda + \gamma_2\beta_4$,
where β_4 is the elasticity with respect to (K_i/C_i) in the
"true" specification; $\lambda = \sum_j \beta_j - 1$ is the "scale coefficient",

---

[*] We have not given the specific numerical results, as the
methods used make them highly unreliable. Moreover, they
apply only to tools and implements: we expect that $e_{K/C, L/C}$
would be lower and $e_{K/C, C}$ higher if other components of K
were included. For tools and implements, the average estimates were .74 and .16 respectively.

from which the elasticity with respect to land may be
derived as $\beta_3 = \lambda^{+1} - \sum_1^2 \beta_j$. Since β_1 is labor's "share" of
product (though not under _our_ theoretical model) and the
second, the "scale factor", it follows that our estimates
of these parameters will be upwards-biased to an extent
depending on the magnitude of β_4. This bias will more
seriously affect β_1^* than it will the scale coefficient,
since γ_2 seems considerably smaller than γ_1.

Now there are a variety of reasons for believing that
$\beta_4 \leq .20$: First, the average of a series of elasticity
estimates for capital services or assets for various crops
in India, Japan and Taiwan is about .18, with high estimates
obtained usually for commercial crops such as sugarcane and
tea and low, zero and/or statistically insignificant estimates found for rice production.[12] Secondly, the imputed
value of interest on invested capital (excluding land) in
Chinese peasant agriculture was probably about 20 percent
of gross value of output, judging from several Mantetsu
studies.[13] Since the elasticity coefficient also represents capital's "share" of gross product _if_ producers were
behaving in accordance with neoclassical distribution theory,
whereas our previous discussion would lead us to expect
excess use of capital services (relative to what marginal
productivities would dictate under neoclassical assumptions),
20 percent, or .20, is likely to represent an upper bound

to the actual production function elasticity.[14] Thirdly,
in the last chapter, it was pointed out that in Kwangtung,
if the tenant provided all the capital, his share was 70
percent; if none, closer to 40 percent. Reducing these
figures by a factor of 1.4 to account for subsidiary crops
and byproducts not subject to rent, we have 50% and 29%
respectively, and a difference of 21% which could be attributed to capital services (again, under neoclassical assumptions).[15] Since capital intensity in Kwangtung was undoubtedly
above the levels of North China or the Southwest, this again
represents an upper bound.

On this evidence, the maximum possible bias of the elasticity with respect to labor as estimated below would be
about +.10 (assuming γ_1 = .5 overall). However, since our
regressions include an estimate of part of capital services
(fertilizer produced on farm), we are inclined to believe
the bias to be considerably smaller, perhaps between +.05
and +.07, and will operate on that assumption. On the other
hand, λ^* should be much less biased (perhaps +.02-.04),
because α_2 is much smaller than α_1. If, of course, the
reader prefers to disregard our somewhat weak evidence that
the capital/land ratio is lower on larger farms, the direction
of bias will be reversed and he will find it necessary to
inflate our elasticity estimates appropriately.

The reader who has possessed the fortitude to wade through

the foregoing pages of caviats should now be in a position
to view our empirical results with neither too much nor
too little skepticism.

Empirical Results of Regressions

The "best estimates" of the coefficients of the crop
production functions for each of the eight regions are
presented in Tables 6.3 through 6.6. Table 6.3 presents
estimates based on the constant-elasticity C-D model
with no attempt to account for interlocality dummies; for
four regions, reasonably good estimates were obtained on
the alternative assumption of constant returns to scale
(by dropping C_1 from the specification), the results of
which are also presented. Table 6.5 shows the effect of
relaxing the constant-elasticity assumption through the
use of interaction terms; the results are presented only
where statistically significant. In Tables 6.4 and 6.5,
the regressions were of yields on input intensities; consequently the coefficient on C_1 represents the scale factor (obtainable from Table 6.3 by summing the coefficients
on L_1, F_1 and C_1) and the R^2s represent the proportion of
the variance of yield "explained", not of output. Since
much of the variance in output is easily accounted for by
differences in scale of production, a high R^2 in Table 6.3
would represent only a much lower proportion of yield variance
explained.

Table 6.3   Parameter Estimates, Cobb-Douglas Equation, No Locality
Dummies

Variable:	L_i	F_i	C_i	DC_i	I_i	λ	e^{α_1}	d.o.f.	R^2
Region									
1	1.23	-.50	.79	.62	.26	1.52	0.68	66	.69
	(2.48)	(3.33)	(3.37)	(.94)	(.67)	(2.00)	(.37)		
2	.16	.08	.89	.85	.49	1.13	5.03	91	.83
	(.92)	(.67)	(6.34)	(3.16)	(1.90)	(1.47)	(3.90)		
3	.33	.13	.63	.26	.46	1.09	4.44	159	.80
	(2.24)	(1.20)	(7.64)	(1.24)	(2.92)	(1.13)	(3.96)		
4	.11	.25	.78	.87	.55	1.15	3.82	138	.78
	(.85)	(3.03)	(8.37)	(5.94)	(4.06)	(1.85)	(3.33)		
5	.28	.15	.72	.14	.68	1.15	4.67	95	.93
	(2.99)	(2.41)	(12.33)	(2.93)	(4.05)	(2.91)	(6.09)		
6	1.60	-.33	.35	-.19	-.42	1.62	0.68	17	.99
	(10.30)	(2.79)	(4.42)	(1.85)	(4.38)	(10.03)	(1.07)		
7	.34	-.02	.69	.58	.03	1.01	7.52	54	.91
	(2.61)	(.38)	(9.19)	(6.26)	(.22)	(0.14)	(4.42)		
8	.82	.30	.28	.15	.68	1.40	0.78	49	.86
	(3.65)	(3.07)	(2.50)	(.95)	(2.64)	(2.69)	(.33)		

Notes: d.o.f. = degrees of freedom. e^{α_1} is the intercept term in the equation, and a measure of "neutral" yield variations among regions. Figures in parentheses are t-statistics for the null hypothesis that the coefficient is equal to zero, except for λ, where the test is of the hypothesis of constant returns to scale ($\lambda = 1.0$). For comparison of the above equations with those which follow, it should be noted that the latter are in "yield" form (i.e. the dependent variable is yield, and independent variables are input intensities per mou of land, except DC_i and I_i) and, for example, an R^2 of .93 for an equation in normal C-D form corresponds roughly to an R^2 of .50 or less for the same equation in yield form.

Table 6.4   Production Function: Cobb-Douglas Form, Without Interactions

Variable: Region	L_i	F_i	λ	DC_i	I_i	T_i	Year	d.o.f.	R^2	No. of Dummies
1	.022 (.1)	.253 (4.6)	--	.871 (4.3)	.698 (5.7)	--	--	52	.95	4
2	.127 (1.9)	.073 (1.6)	1.059 (1.8)	.600 (5.9)	1.102 (8.5)	--	--	86	.92	5
	.056 (1.4)	.274 (5.8)	--	.816 (7.3)	.179 (1.9)	--	--	86	.91	6
3	.519 (6.9)	.344 (6.4)	1.264 (6.1)	.847 (8.6)	.633 (6.7)	--	-.433* (6.9)	150	.87	8
	.128 (3.0)	.370 (6.2)	--	.688 (6.5)	.675 (6.4)	--	-.324* (4.9)	151	.83	8
4	.449 (6.9)	.250 (4.9)	1.275 (4.8)	.633 (6.9)	-.136 (1.8)	--	.506** (9.4)	123	.94	14
5	.404 (6.8)	-.011 (0.2)	1.143 (4.1)	.044 (1.4)	.738 (6.5)	.163 (2.4)	-.153* (3.6)	90	.82	3
	.208 (3.9)	-.061 (1.0)	--	.152 (3.8)	.703 (3.4)	.156 (1.5)	--	95	.79	4
6	.556 (2.1)	-.089 (0.9)	1.299 (3.3)	.849 (3.3)	.727 (2.6)	.099 (0.7)	--	14	.96	2
7	.566 (7.5)	.109 (2.3)	1.343 (6.9)	.558 (9.6)	.269 (3.6)	--	--	50	.90	4
8	.386 (2.4)	.305 (3.2)	1.154 (1.5)	.562 (4.2)	1.350 (7.0)	.410 (2.1)	--	44	.86	4

* 1932-1933   ** 1930

Notes: Figures in parentheses are t-statistics for null hypothesis that coefficient equals zero, except for λ, where hypothesis is that $\lambda = 1.0$. d.o.f. stands for degrees of freedom. R^2 statistics are for logarithmic forms of equations, expressed in terms of yields and input intensities. Number of dummies refers to locality dummies only.

Table 6.5 Production Function: Cobb-Douglas Form, With Interactions

Variable: Region	L_i	F_i	λ***	DC_i	I_i	Interaction	Coefficient	Range of Elast.	R^2
2	.036 (0.5)	.269 (5.7)	.894 (1.5)	.733 (6.4)	.182 (1.8)	CH_i*on L_i	.033 (2.2)	.04-.38	.92
	.221 (2.8)	.246 (5.2)	1.038 (1.1)	1.968 (4.2)	.190 (1.9)	DC_i on L_i	-.447 (2.5)	.00-.39	.92
	.038 (0.5)	.203 (3.8)	.812 (2.2)	.610 (4.9)	-.860 (1.6)	CH_i*on L_i	.064 (2.8)	.05-.70	.93
						F_i**on I_i	.477 (2.0)	-.56-.91	
						C_i**on λ	-.050 (1.8)	.67-.81	
4	.492 (7.0)	.239 (5.2)	1.341 (5.1)	.667 (7.2)	-.136 (1.8)	CH_i**on L_i	-.015 (1.7)	.40-.49	.94
	.429 (6.7)	.403 (4.4)	1.244 (6.2)	.649 (7.3)	.356 (1.4)	F_i** on I_i	-.262 (2.0)	-.47-.17	.94
5	.061 (0.3)	-.012 (0.3)	1.153 (4.4)	.061 (1.9)	-.455 (0.7)	I_i on L_i	.434 (1.8)	.27-.49	.82
7	.406 (3.3)	.084 (1.5)	1.345 (7.0)	-.139 (0.3)	.234 (2.3)	DC_i on L_i	.235 (1.8)	.41-.64	.91
8	.554 (3.5)	-.611 (2.0)	1.220 (2.3)	.637 (5.2)	-2.51 (2.0)	I_i on F_i	1.157 (3.2)	.10-.55	.89

* crop hectares (in logs), i.e. total acreage cropped, equals units of cultivated area times number of crops raised per unit; thus a measure of the
effective amount of land to which a unit of labor was applied.
** measured in logs.   *** t-test is of null hypothesis, λ = 1.0.

Notes: The interaction terms were of the form, X^{a+bY}, where Y is the first
variable and X the second, b being the interaction coefficient. The "range
of elasticity" is an evaluation of a+bY for Y measured at $\pm$ two standard
deviations from its geometric mean, or its maximum or minimum, whichever
were the effective bounds; thus all but extreme observations (at most about
5% of the sample) were included within the listed range. If the interaction
term is meaningful, this range indicates the extent to which the variable
acted upon varies in its impact on output with the magnitude of the inter-
acting variable.

Table 6.6   Linear Production Function With Exponential Scale Factor
            and Unconstrained Locality Dummies

Region		L_i	C_i	F_i	DC_i	λ	d_1	R^2
2	Coefficient	1.31	4.27	21.01	17.46	1.12	5.09	.95
	Stand. Dev.	.14	.23	3.22	.61			
	Marg. Product	203	1049	29				
	% Share	15.2%	72.1%	12.7%				
4	Coefficient	1.16	7.12	1.99	5.63	1.11	1.79	.76
	Stand. Dev.	.11	.32	2.98	.43			
	Marg. Product	230	2138	4				
	% Share	18.3%	80.4%	1.3%				
8	Coefficient	2.80	12.66	14.00	5.11	1.24	1.40	.88
	Stand. Dev.	.26	1.04	1.54	1.55			
	Marg. Product	449	2138	23				
	% Share	30.8%	51.5%	17.8%				

Notes: The estimation procedures used were sequential: First a non-
linear estimation procedure was used to simultaneously estimate all
parameters; whether or not this passed a convergence test, the resulting estimates of locality dummies (one for each locality) and that
of λ were used to normalize the dependent variable and the remaining
parameters were reestimated using OLS. The standard deviations of
coefficients are thus conditional on the validity of the locality
dummies and scale coefficients, and the R^2s are not comparable to those
in preceding regressions. I_i was not included as it is redundant when
a full complement of locality dummies is employed.
    The following are definitions of variables and parameters:
a) L_i: in man-years of fully utilized labor.
b) C_i: in hectares of harvested land.
c) F_i: in 1000 kilograms of manure or nightsoil.
d) d_1: represents the ratio (on average) of the marginal productivity
            of double-cropped to single-cropped land. See text.
e)   Marginal Product: in terms of kilograms of grain-equivalent.
f)   Factor shares (%) represent the contribution to output of each
factor as measured by its marginal productivity times the amount used,
relative to the contributions of all factors together. Since increasing
returns is indicated, the total contributions in this sense exceed the
average of total product. To compare these shares with Cobb-Douglas
elasticity coefficients, the latter would have to be normalized to sum to
unity (divide by the scale factor).
g)   Marginal products and factor shares are all computed at the arithmetic
means of factor inputs and of locality dummies.

Table 6.6 presents estimates of the linear production
function for the three regions for which it was possible
to obtain convergence (of the non-linear estimation procedure). Again the R^2s are not strictly comparable with those
of previous regressions, since the dependent variables are
non-logarithmic and normalized to give yield with interlocality variation removed. Since the coefficients
in this equation form have no immediately obvious interpretation, both the marginal products and the percent
"shares" of each input (roughly comparable with the elasticity
coefficients in the Cobb-Douglas production functions) have
also been computed.

An overview of the results seems in order, before we
proceed to a more detailed analysis. First, the effects of
interlocality variation in land quality in the absence of
locality dummy variables are clearly visible in the regressions summarized in Table 6.3. Because localities with poorer land quality or climate are associated with greater use
of labor, fertilizer, etc., estimated coefficients vary
wildly among regions, some inputs display nonsensically
negative (and apparently significant!) elasticities, and
inputs other than land are often lower or less significant
than should otherwise be the case. R^2s seem high, but in
fact in general less than half of the variance in yield
(as opposed to output per farm) is accounted for. While

many individual coefficient estimates appear to be of the
"right order of magnitude," we prefer to view them only in
comparison with the following results.

A number of general results emerge from the full set of
regressions: First, the elasticity with respect to labor is
significantly different from zero in all but the two northernmost regions (some of the estimates for region 2 are also
significant, but low). Thus, for those regions more favored
by climate and availability of complementary inputs (see
Tables 6.1 and 6.2), and despite greater population density,
the marginal productivity of labor is greater than zero (this
conclusion is not affected by the small upwards-bias in this
coefficient discussed earlier).

Second, the elasticity with respect to land (for Tables
6.4 and 6.5, calculated as the difference between the scale
factor, λ, and the elasticities with respect to labor and
fertilizer) appears to be generally greater than that of
labor. This impression cannot be reinforced with statistical tests, however, as the differences in magnitude are
not statistically significant.[16]

Third, the scale coefficient, λ, is significantly greater
than unity in all but the two northernmost regions (where
again region 2 gives conflicting results). There are, then,
increasing returns to scale displayed in the sample, despite
the sample bias towards inclusion of an unrepresentative
number of larger farms.

Fourth, while the inclusion of DC_1 and I_1 in the production functions as a means of approximating differences in land quality was obviously important in reducing coefficient bias, the coefficient estimates are frequently too high to be plausible as a source of measurement of the relative marginal productivity of double-cropped or irrigated as opposed to single-cropped or unirrigated land. That is, if the estimated coefficients were taken seriously, they would imply that double-cropped or irrigated land had often more than twice the marginal productivity of ordinary land, other things (including labor and fertilizer use) remaining equal. While this may be correct cross-sectionally, this result must be due to the association of double-cropping and irrigation with quite different cropping patterns and with other excluded variables having bearing on land fertility. The estimates of δ_1, the ratio of m.p. on double-cropped land to that on single-cropped land presented in Table 6.6, are in two cases close to being "reasonable", as the use of a full complement of locality dummies in these regressions helped to reduce this source of error.

Fifth, despite the weaknesses of our proxy for fertilizer, it displays considerable significance in some regions, but not in others. The influence of this variable will be of special interest for some readers because of the presumed importance of growth in chemical fertilizer usage to post-

TABLE 6.7   MARGINAL RESPONSE OF OUTPUT TO INPUTS OF AMMONIUM SULPHATE
EQUIVALENT FROM MANURE AND NIGHTSOIL

Region	Elasticity wrt Manure	Manure per ha. (1)	Marginal Product (2)	Marginal Pro- cut per Hog (3)	Marginal Res- ponse Ratio (4)
1	.25	8.76	15.6	23	.58
2	.27	6.30	43.3	63	1.57
3	.34	6.17	83.2	121	3.02
4	.25	6.82	81.4	118	2.95
5	.00	9.88	0	0	0
6	.00	12.90	0	0	0
7	.11	12.60	29.2	42	1.05
8	.31	32.80	51.3	74	1.85

(1)   Thousands of kgs. of manure and nightsoil per hectare of cultivated land.
(2)   Per thousand kgs. of manure; in grain-equivalents.
(3)   Increase in grain-equivalent resulting from application of manure
output of additional hog, estimated at 1450 kgs. (from 8 tons
of manure/animal-equivalent; 5 hogs per animal-equivalent. As
estimated by Buck in constructing estimates of fertilizer production, in Chinese Farm Economy, p.   224.
(4)   Assuming 40 kgs. of ammonium sulphate equivalent per hog, following
Perkins (1969), p. 73. See also K. Walker, pp. 48-50 and 55-56. If
we had shosen Walker's "conservative estimate" of 30 kgs. per hog,
these response ratios would be closer to those cited in Chinese
sources. However, the latter are average, not marginal ratios,
and assuming a fairly steep drop in the marginal productivity curve
as it approaches the levels of fertilizer inputs prevalent in our
sample, there is no inconsistency between the different results.

1949 agricultural development in China. Consequently we
have computed the marginal response rates to nitrogen applications implied by our results, given in Table 6.7.   The
estimated m.r.r.s are sufficiently consistent with other

evidence to be plausible, but also lead to the surprising
implication that, given the existing crop technology, further applications of nitrogenous fertilizer in much of the
Rice Region would have been of little or no value, primarily
because the Buck data imply that current applications per
unit area were already quite high. Since this matter is of
minor importance to our theme, we have confined the extensive
discussion required to Appendix VI-F.

Finally, tenancy was associated with higher yields
(ceteris paribus) as hypothesized in at least two regions.
Whether this was because landlords had managed to accumulate
better than average quality land, or the existence of better
quality land in some way led to tenancy, or because tenants
were harder working or more efficient farmers, cannot be
determined on the basis of these results.

The use of dummies representing the time period during
which a particular locality was surveyed as a means of accounting for intertemporal variations in natural conditions
proved successful in three instances. Perhaps it is not
coincidental that the three regions where significant intertemporal variations were discovered were the same three
measuring highest on our risk index (see Chapter III). No
single calamity can be identified as the source of variation
picked up by a particular dummy, however, and it is conceivable
that the correlations were not in fact related to climatic

conditions.

The interaction terms included in the regressions the results of which are presented in Table 6.4 are intended to test the appropriateness of certain of the assumptions of our model (in Cobb-Douglas form) -- specifically, the constant elasticity assumption and the form of "land quality" index used (that is, the form in which DC_i and I_i were included). The significance of some of these terms, despite the additional collinearity introduced, implies that the log-linear form is not entirely appropriate, but the inconsistency of these results provides no basis for suggesting alternatives. Adding to the confusion is the fact that interaction terms by definition represent mutual interactions between two or more variables, which makes them hard to interpret.

The fact that so many interaction terms are significant in the region 2 regressions does suggest that the geographical boundaries of that region may be economically inappropriately defined, or that the data encompasses localities which are entirely too heterogeneous. For example, it seems that the elasticity with respect to labor is higher in localities with larger than average farm sizes, where the elasticity with respect to land and returns to scale are correspondingly lower. This region may be characterized by a geographical transition between the apparently "labor-surplus" economy of region 1 and the rural economy to the south in which labor retains considerable significance.

The modified linear production function (Table 6.6) was similarily tested for the appropriateness of the assumption that _relative_ marginal productivities of inputs remain constant regardless of scale of farm. It was found that the marginal productivity of labor rose faster with larger farm size than did the marginal products of other factors.[17] Since the Cobb-Douglas form is capable of accounting for this variation, whereas the modified linear form cannot, we have relied on the former for the analysis of factor marginal productivities which follows.

Increasing Returns to Scale

The regression results indicate that significant returns to scale existed in most agricultural regions. This statistical result arises from the fact that larger farms were managed with less intensive input ratios (per unit land), but the fall in yield which usually resulted was not at all proportionate. To put it more precisely, the data cannot be accurately described by _all_ of the following characteristics: Constant returns to scale, unit elasticity of substitution, and a substantial marginal productivity of labor. Unless the bias due to exclusion of certain inputs is much larger than we have previously argued, one or more of these characteristics does not apply to the Chinese agricultural production function.

Unfortunately, when the input data is highly collinear,
as is generally the case in an
economy in which factor markets
are well-developed, regression
techniques cannot discriminate
precisely among these attri-
butes. This point is illustra-

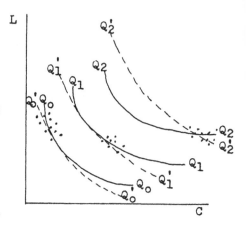

ted by the diagram at right, where the data scatter offers
little basis for choice between two quite different sets
of isoquants -- differing in returns to scale, elasticity
of substitution and relative factor marginal productivities.
It is further illustrated in Table 6.4 by comparison of
those equations for regions 2, 3 and 5 in which the scale
factor was estimated (by including C_1) with those constrained to constant returns (by omission of C_1): The elasticity
with respect to labor is reduced by the imposition of the
constant returns constraint, yet only minor impact on the
R^2s is observable.

However, we have previously provided enough theoretical
and empirical evidence of increasing returns to lend cre-
dence to our estimates. Similar results have been found for
small and disaggregated North China samples by Dittrich and
Myers.[18]

Can we account for regional differences in our estimates
of returns to scale? Perhaps: We suggested in Chapter II.
that increasing returns (in the physical sense) are due in
part to the inability to adjust factor proportions in such
a way as to achieve 100 percent utilization of capital and
labor. However, the labor variable in our regressions has
been adjusted to remove idle time; lumpy capital items
have been excluded from the roster of variables, and so
contribute to the slight upwards bias of the scale coefficients discussed earlier. A second source of increasing
returns would be the savings in labor and capital-use time
accompaning consolidation of fragmented plots or parcels
on larger farms, if parcels increase in size with increased
farm area, and even more if the number of parcels per farm
tends to decrease. Since $S_1 = F_1/N_1$, where S_1 is the average
parcel size per farm, F_1 is farm size and N_1 is number of
parcels per farm, the elasticity of parcel size with respect
to farm size would be $(dS/dF)(F/N) = 1 - (F/N)(dN/dF)$, so
that if the elasticity is positive, parcel size increases
with farm size; if greater than one, the number of parcels
per farm decreases with farm size. The impact of this
"consolidation effect" would of course be the greater, the
smaller the average size of parcels.

The empirical evidence of cross-regional association
between returns to scale and parcel size variation in the

Table 6.8   Relationship between Scale Factors and Parcel Size Elasticities

Regions (Ranked):	7	6	4	3	8	5	2	1
Scale Factor [1]	1.34	1.30	1.28	1.26	1.15	1.14	1.06	1.00
Constant Elasticity[2]	.75	.84	.76	.58	.70	.43	.39	.62
Elasticity (at mean)[3]	.83	1.11	1.10	.55	.61	.51	.44	.80
1st R^2 [4]	.48	.24	.46	.55	.60	.27	.44	.50
2nd R^2 [5]	.53	.78	.38	.60	.83	.26	.33	.35
Mean Parcel Size [6]	.24	.43	.46	.37	.27	.17	.29	.86

1) From Table 6.4. Equals the coefficient on C_i plus 1.
2) Coefficient of regression of the log of parcel size on $\ln C_i$.
3) Calculated from coefficients of a third-degree polynomial, fitted
   to the data and evaluated at the geometric mean of C_i for comparability with 2).
4) For constant elasticity (logarithmic) equation.
5) For polynomial equation.
6) Arithmetic mean, weighted by numbers of observations per group.

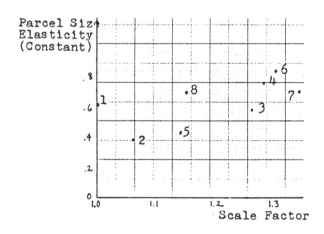

samples is presented in Table 6.8. There is in every region a significant positive relationship between parcel size and farm size; in a few regions, the number of parcels of land per farm virtually remains constant as farm size increases. There is a clearly positive association between the magnitude of the scale coefficients and the elasticities of parcel size with respect to farm size, and the deviations from this relationship are largely explained by differences in mean parcel size by region.* While there is reason to be skeptical about tests of hypotheses based upon cross-sectional relationships among estimated coefficients, rather than raw data, these results add support to Buck's emphasis on consolidation of parcels and fields as an important source of greater efficiency on larger farms.[19]

Marginal Productivities and Factor Prices

In applying the neoclassical theory of distribution to the peasant economy, we have stressed the joint impacts of uncertainty and differences in factor endowments on the equilibrium relationship between the value of the marginal

---

* If we regress the scale factor (minus 1) on the elasticity and the mean parcel size, we obtain the following results:

	Elasticity	Mean Parcel Size	R^2
Coefficient	0.596	-0.325	.74
(s.d.)	(.176)	(.131)	

The coefficients are significant at the 5% level.

productivities of the factors of production and the market
prices. Among the major implications of this analysis were
the hypotheses that small farms -- generally net sellers of
labor and renters of land -- would employ factor proportions
such that the value of the marginal productivity of labor
would be well below the nominal market wage, whereas the
marginal productivity of land would be greater than the
nominal rental cost. Conversely, large farms -- generally
net hirers of labor and rentiers -- would be found to have
marginal value productivities of labor greater than or
equal to the nominal wage and MVP of land probably close
to its nominal rental value.[*] With our regression estimates
of the agricultural production function, we are now in a
position to attempt to test these hypotheses insofar as
they applied to the Chinese peasant economy during the
Republican period.

A variety of theoretical and practical problems must
first be discussed, however. For instance, estimates of
factor marginal productivity based on regression-estimated
Cobb-Douglas production functions will be more accurate
near the (geometric) means of the data than at extremes.

---

[*] Wealthy peasants may be willing to forego some income to
escape the effort of farm management; but may require more
income to compensate for the greater uncertainty and collection costs of rental returns.

Since the equation form constrains marginal productivities
to a constant proportion of average products, the estimated
variation in marginal products by farm size is dictated as
much by choice of equation form as by the data itself. Our
confidence in our ability to measure the extent of within-
sample variations in marginal productivities should not be
high.

Which farms correspond to the "large farms" and "small
farms" specified in the hypotheses? In theory, assuming
that marginal productivities are monotonically related to
farm size (via the relationship between farm size and labor/
land ratio), we should be interested in those farms which
are, at given rental rates and wage levels, just indifferent
between hiring out or in an additional unit of labor or land
and using it in own-farm production. In practice, we have
tried to select farms which most probably hired long-term
labor on the basis of the size of their labor force (> 2.5
man-equivalents), and farms which were most probably net
rentiers or renters of land on the basis of farm size
(> 2.0 hectares assumed net rentiers; < .66 hectares assumed
net renters). The average marginal productivities for these
groups were taken to represent the situations of the
"marginal" farms, which of course may or may not be the
case.

We further required data on wages (of long-term labor),
rents and crop prices. Estimates of annual wages were

provided by Buck for (most of) the localities for which
we have estimated production functions. However, the data
are based on only three responses per locality, and could
be biased upwards, particularily in estimates of the value
of room, board and other commodities provided (inasmuch as
respondents might be inclined to exaggerate their benefi-
cence). Nonetheless, the cash component recorded does not
seem inconsistent with national survey data (presented in
Chapter V.).

Neither price nor rent data on the sample localities was
published, unfortunately. The former was required to deflate
the cash value of wages to obtain an estimate of the real
wage (in "grain equivalents"), comparable with our estimates of marginal physical product; and to value the marginal physical product of land for comparison with the
cash value of rents. Our estimates of prices of the major
grain crop (either wheat or rice) at the time the sample
was taken in each locality were derived from other data
(see Appendix VI-G) and must be viewed with some caution,
although on average they should be sufficiently accurate
to relect interregional and intertemporal price variations
in this period.

Estimates of gross rental receipts per mou of land were
indirectly derived from land value data, in the belief
that the latter bore a reasonably stable relationship to

rental receipts, as discussed in Chapter III. However, land value data (derived from another survey) were broken down by type of land (irrigated and nonirrigated; high, medium and low quality) and province (rather than crop region), and the choice of weights required to average could have biased the resulting estimates (see Notes to Table 6.10). Above all, our information on interregional variations in gross rental rates of return on land investment was too unreliable to apply anything more precise than a single average gross rental rate of return (13 percent -- see Chapter III, Table 3.8) to obtain an estimate of rent levels, injecting further error into the calculations.

Since nearly all the derived data on which the following comparisons are based are subject to unkown systematic and/or random errors, it is apparent that rigorous hypothesis testing is inconceivable (even though the law of averages may be presumed to eliminate many errors, and though the errors should generally be independent of each other). But even if our data were reliable, how testable are our hypotheses in their present form? These hypotheses concern (partial) equilibrium relationships, whereas the data are drawn from an economy in flux.

If we could show that no indentifiable disequilibriating forces were operating on the Chinese agrarian economy over the sample period, we could argue that the economy was in

either a stationary or moving equilibrium, and proceed to
test for equilibrium relationships without further ado.
Unfortunately, there is every reason to believe that the
economy was in disequilibrium in consequence of a drastic
rise in farm prices (1929-30) followed by an even more
drastic decline (1930-33), attributed by Buck to famine
conditions in North China and to the world-wide rise in
the value of silver, respectively.[20] If we examine the
relevant economic indices (in Figure VI-A), we find that
the long-term growth rates of prices, wages and land values
are not very different in the first half of the Twenties.
In the late 1920s, in North China prices rose faster than
wages in consequence of crop disasters, while in South China
prices had begun to decline relative to wages. Assuming
that the earlier trend represented a moving equilibrium,
it is probable that, in the years 1929-30, real wages fell
below their equilibrium trend in North China (but marginal
physical product would have also been lower than normal due
to adverse growing conditions). Similarily, after 1929 in
South China, and 1931 in North China, real wages may
well have been above the long-run trend, since cash wages
seem to have had a damped and lagged response to price
fluctuations. This point is confirmed by Buck: "There
is always strong social resistance to any reduction in
wages. During a period of falling commodity prices, it
is customary to hire less labor rather than to pay a lower

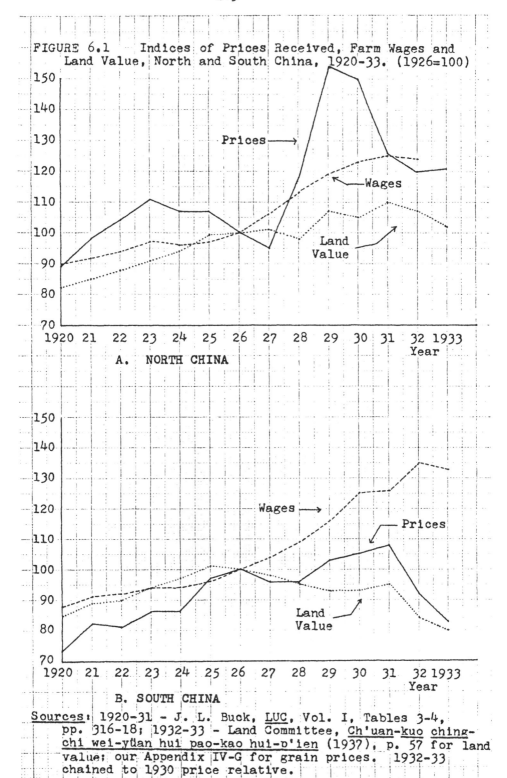

FIGURE 6.1 Indices of Prices Received, Farm Wages and Land Value, North and South China, 1920-33. (1926=100)

A. NORTH CHINA

B. SOUTH CHINA

Sources: 1920-31 - J. L. Buck, LUC, Vol. I, Tables 3-4, pp. 316-18; 1932-33 - Land Committee, Ch'uan-kuo ching-chi wei-yüan hui pao-kao hui-p'ien (1937), p. 57 for land value; our Appendix IV-G for grain prices. 1932-33 chained to 1930 price relative.

rate of wages. During the period 1931 to 1933, when prices
received by farmers were falling, there was in most areas
no corresponding fall in the wage rate of farm laborers."[21]

Since most of the samples taken in the Winter wheat-
kaoliang region (Region 3) were collected in 1929-30,
we would expect to find the real wage level below the normal
relationship with the marginal productivity of labor, if
any, for that region. Similarily, Regions 5, 7 and 8 (all
in South China) were sampled almost exclusively in 1932, when
we would expect the real wage to be higher than its long-run
trend relative to marginal productivity. For other regions,
the sampling was more intertemporally diversified, and the
biases more ambiguous, but probably in the direction of a
higher-than-normal real wage level.

As was pointed out earlier, land value from the late
Twenties ceased to follow the same upward trend as wages and
prices, instead following a slower rate of increase (in
North China) or declining (primarily in the Chiang-nan area --
Regions 4 and 5 -- of central-south China), but remaining
sensitive to price trends. This development is attributable
to either or both declining security of rent collection[22]
and increased attractiveness of commercial investment in
the growing urban areas. While this trend does not seem to
have affected the rate of return on land investment (except
via capital losses -- see Chapter III.), the level of rents

may have fallen below the marginal value product of land
in regions of high tenancy as a consequence of the political
struggle against landlordism. It should be added that the
existence of the "permanent tenancy" system in parts of
South China would also lead us to expect rent levels (on
"subsoil" rights) falling below marginal productivity.

Table 6.9 summarizes our comparison of estimates of the
real wage level for long-term laborers with estimates of
the marginal productivity of labor derived from the previous
regressions. The following general observations emerge from
these comparisons: (a) The real wage level is below the
average productivity of labor on the "average farm" in every
region. (b) The real wage is close to the average product
of labor on small farms in regions 1 and 2, but elsewhere
somewhat below average (gross) product on small farms --
it could well be equal to or greater than average product
net of rent on such farms. (c) The real wage level is not
far different from marginal product on large farms, again
with the exceptions of regions 1 and 2. (d) Since the
marginal productivity of labor is a fraction of the average
product, it is clear that the marginal product must be less
than the real wage for small farms in every region.

To devise a slightly more formal test, we may hypothesize
that the real wage is some constant fraction of average
product on small farms and of marginal product on large

Table 6.9 Real Wage, Marginal and Average Physical Product of Labor
(Kilograms of Grain-Equivalent), by Crop Region, China,
1929-1933

Region	1	2	3	4	5	6	7	8
Wage (Year Labor)[1]	$ 74	80	76	98	100	64	112	69
Grain Price[2]	$.09	.09	.10	.11	.09	.10	.13	.07
Real Wage (grain)[3]	820	887	757	895	1111	635	861	982
" " (Buck's est.)	(562)	(666)	(685)	(1187)	(1690)	(1175)	(1299)	(959)
Average Product:[4]								
Small Farms	439	824	942	1048	1242	743	1026	1226
All Farms	1038	1076	1362	1312	1624	1276	1274	1804
Marginal Product:[4]								
Large Farms	---	445	806	598	895	996	915	815
Regression Coeffi-cients:								
Real W on AP_L[5]	1.27*	.75-	.65-	.61-	.68-	.73**	.79-	.72-
Real W on MP_L[5]	5.09+	1.29*	.89*	1.30**	.93*	.57-	.74-	1.37+

* less than 1 standard deviation from unity.
** less than 2 standard deviations from unity.
- significantly less than unity (5% level).
+ significantly greater than unity (5% level).
Notes:
1) Average for localities included in our sample, from J.L. Buck,
   LUC, SV, Table   , p.
2) Our estimates, based on average provincial prices for the year
   in which each locality was sampled, per kilogram; see Appendix
   V- .
3) The wage divided by grain prices. Our estimates differ considerably
   in some instances from those of Buck (LUC, I, Table 17., p. 306),
   which represent a considerably smaller subsample, perhaps biased
   towards the end of the sample period (when prices were lower). It
   is likely that Buck divided average wages for the entire sample by
   average prices from the subsample, thus leading to a biased estimate
   of real wages.
4) Per laborer, at arithmetic means of groups. Small farms = Buck's
   small and very small farms; large farms = at least 2.5 man-equivalents of labor per farm. Marginal products derived from elasticity
   coefficients (with interaction terms, where significant) estimated
   in previous regressions, multiplied by average products.
5) Regressions of the real wage on the average product of labor (small
   farms only) and marginal product (large farms), in both cases
   suppressing the intercept term; moment matrices were weighted to
   correct for heteroskedasticity due to grouped observations. Note
   that this represents a test of the hypotheses that wages were
   constant fractions of average product (on small farms) or marginal
   product (large farms) respectively, and is not equivalent to the
   ratios of the two means.

farms, and test whether this proportion differs significantly from unity. On this count, for small farms in
6 of 8 regions, the real wage is significantly below
average product; for 4 out of 8 regions, it is not significantly different from marginal product on large farms;
for the remaining regions, the direction of difference is
not consistent.

Evidence thus tends to confirm that real wage levels were
on the average not far different from levels of marginal
product on farms large enough to (presumably) hire long-term
labor, even though wage levels at the time of this sample
probably were generally above their "equilibrium trend"
(excepting region 3, where, as predicted, real wage levels
were low relative to marginal product and to wages in other
regions at the time of the sampling).

It is also of interest that the real wage seems to
have been equivalent to about 70 percent of the gross
crop income on small farms. Since rent seems to have
accounted for about 30 percent on tenant farms (see
Tables 3.10 and 3.11), it would appear that tenants could
do as well as farm laborers (in terms of income alone) only
if subsidiary and outside income covered the cost of working
capital. Noting our earlier finding that the latter was
about 20 percent of gross crop value (see pp. 222-223) and
Buck's observation that about 20 percent of income on small
farms was derived from subsidiary work (see p. 157), there

Table 6.10 Estimated Value of Marginal Productivity of Land and Estimated Rental Value (yüan/mou), by Crop Region, China, 1929-1933

Region:	1	2	3	4	5	6	7	8
Mean Rental Value [1]	2.49	2.98	6.50	8.90	9.02	9.74	10.91	10.66
Marginal Value Product:[2]								
Small Farms	4.09	4.08	5.89	11.68	16.09	17.24	24.24	14.41
Average Farm	3.31	3.75	4.40	12.19	15.07	16.45	20.28	12.65
Large Farms	2.98	2.98	3.52	10.99	10.42	15.89	15.26	6.14
(standard deviation)	(3.01)	(1.33)	(1.41)	(8.35)	(4.32)	(8.07)	(3.83)	(1.85)
MVP Range, Large Farms:								
Lowest	0.33	1.17	1.31	0.03	4.40	7.95	10.67	4.09
Highest	11.20	7.29	6.66	34.44	20.86	32.13	25.46	9.01

1) Estimates of mean rental value of farmland were derived as follows: First, 1931 average land prices for paddy and dry fields, of high, middle and low quality respectively, were derived from 1934 prices, using separate price indices and price figures for each province (data from Land Committee, eds., Ch'uan-kuo ching-chi wei-yüan hui pao-kao hui-p'ien, 1937, Table 38., p. 55 and Table 40., p. 57). Second, on the assumption that the classification of high, middle and low quality corresponded approximately to the classifications 1, 2 and 3 - 5 used for tax assessment of productivity (given in Buck, LUC, SV, Table 9., pp. 38-39), the proportions of each type of land in each region were used to weight provincial land prices by quality category; the prices of paddy and dry field were similarily averaged, using as weights the percentages of irrigated and non-irrigated land recorded in the Buck sample. Third, the average price by region was derived by averaging prices for those pro-

may indeed have been a rough balance between these items
of income and outgo.

Turning to a comparison (in value terms) of rent levels
and the marginal value product (MVP) of land, it is readily
confirmed that the rental cost is below MVP on small farms,
allowing tenants a certain "surplus" and leaving little
inducement for small and medium farms to sell or rent out
their land. Only in region 3 does this relationship not
hold: Perhaps the high rent levels, in conjunction with
lower real wage (each relative to the respective marginal
productivities) is related to the near absence of tenancy
in this region; perhaps this is no more than a reflection
of the 1929-30 disequilibrium mentioned earlier, or a product of errors in estimates.*

The relationship between rent levels and MVP on large
farms is more ambiguous, both in theory and in the data.
For regions 1,2,4 and 5, the differences between the two
were quite insignificant. Regions 6 and 7 show rent below
MVP, just as previously wages were found to be higher than
MVP, suggesting that our regression equations might be at
fault. Region 8 has both rent and real wages above the

---

* It should be noted that Hopei rent levels were quite close
to estimated MVP for large farms in region 3; it is the high
land prices of Shantung and Honan which are responsible for
the above results.

respective marginal productivities, perhaps because of
(temporarily?) depressed prices (which were well below
levels prevailing elsewhere in China). Nevertheless, the
comparisons do not suggest that a major sacrifice of
potential land revenue ensued from renting out land previously farmed by owners, once a certain farm size had
been reached (in conjunction with declining labor intensity
of production). Rather, the evidence tends to substantiate
our argument that the land market offered an absolute
return roughly equivalent to opportunity cost to landlords,
while permitting tenants a "surplus" compensating in part
for their low marginal productivities of labor and at
the same time offered too low a rental return to induce
small owner-cultivators to abandon farming.

The Suboptimal Peasant and Wage Determination in Chinese Agriculture

A major implication of both theoretical argument and
empirical findings was that small farms derived a "surplus"
permitting survival from a land market, the prices and rents
of which were related primarily to low marginal productivity
of land on large farms. Such small farms were cursed with an
excessively high labor/land ratio, even if it was held to
a minimum by the practice of retaining only enough family
members to work the farm, the remainder generally seeking
work off the farm. Nevertheless, if peasants attempted

to maximize their expected net income and if wage levels higher than marginal productivity on small farms were in fact obtainable by those who hired themselves out as laborers, it should have been in the economic interest of these "small peasants" to rent out or sell their land (if rents and land values were determined by the marginal productivities on large or "optimizing" farms, the two actions are economically equivalent in terms of annual returns) and hire themselves out as laborers. By so doing, they should have gained the difference between the market wage and the marginal productivity of their labor on their "suboptimal" farm, minus the loss in returns to land due to the fact that the marginal productivity of their land when farmed with an economically optimal labor/land ratio must be less than when farmed with excessive labor. It is worth considering precisely how large the net gain or financial incentive for this course of action was.

Let us assume for computational convenience a two-factor, constant returns Cobb-Douglas production function, with homogeneous land and labor inputs: $Q = AL^{\alpha}C^{1-\alpha}$, or $Q = A(L/C)^{\alpha}C$. Suppose that our small peasant possesses labor and land, L_0 and C_0, so that his production per year is $Q_0 = A(L_0/C_0)^{\alpha}C_0$. Suppose that, at an exogenously given real wage, w, an amount of land C_0 should be farmed with optimal labor amount, $L_0^{*} = \theta L_0$, where θ is a fraction determined by the wage rate and the parameters of the production function. Now assume the peasant rents out his land to someone who farms it optimally (or at least pays a rent determined by the optimum factor proportions): Then the total amount of rent received will be $(1-\alpha)Q^*$, where $Q^* = A(L_o^*/C_o)^\alpha C_o$. Moreover, our peasant hires himself out, presumably to another optimizing peasant, so that the wage received is equal to the marginal product of his labor when combined with the appropriate quantity of land. Since that quantity, C_1, must be such as to maintain the same optimal labor/land ratio, L_o^*/C_o, $C_1 = L_o C_o/(\theta L_o) = C_o/\theta$ and $Q_1 = (C_1/C_o)Q^* = (1/\theta)Q^*$; the returns to his labor will be $w = \alpha(1/\theta)Q^*$. Thus by renting out both his land and his labor, the suboptimal peasant receives total returns

$$R^* = [(1-\alpha) + \alpha(1/\theta)]Q^*.$$

By contrast, if he had continued to farm suboptimally, he would have received:

$$Q_o = A(L_o/C_o)^\alpha C_o = A[L_o^*/(C_o\theta)]^\alpha C_o = (1/\theta)^\alpha Q^*$$

Therefore the ratio of his new to his old income is:

$$R^*/Q_o = [(1-\alpha) + \alpha(1/\theta)]/(1/\theta)^\alpha$$

This expression, which is a measure of the financial gain from the optimal policy (to the suboptimal peasant) or the sacrifice involved in suboptimal farming, is not very sensitive to the parameter α, which is around .3 or .4 in the Chinese case. Its sensitivity to the parameter θ, however, is more interesting, especially since $(1-\theta)$ can be interpreted as the proportion of "superfluous" labor on farms of a given

size or marginal productivity,
if the wage is taken to be
exogenous.[*]

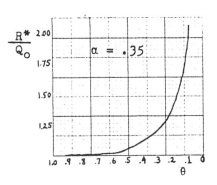

As may be seen in the graph,
more than half the labor force
on a farm must be "superfluous"
before the gain in income from
optimizing becomes greater than 6 percent. In other words,
it would take an extraordinarily inefficient labor/land
ratio before there would be sufficient incentive to compensate for the greater insecurity of wage labor, and the
loss of social benefits of life on the family farm. It
must be reiterated that this is because gains in returns
to labor are largely cancelled by losses in returns to
land, since "optimized" use of the land requires operation
at a lower labor/land ratio, thus lower yield or average
product, thus lower marginal product of land. It should
also be noted that this lack of incentive for optimization
is peculiar to family enterprises, where maximization of
the _sum_ of returns to _both_ major factors of production is
the economic objective; if labor were hired at market wages

---

* Superfluous in the sense that $(1-\theta)L$ is the amount of labor
that could be transferred from the suboptimal farm to some
other occupation or sector or farms where the marginal
productivity equals the wage, without loss to social product.

and the maximand were net returns to the landowner, the
net gain from optimized land use would be a much larger
proportion of current income.

It would be useful to translate the proportion θ into
an expression relating wage level to the marginal product
of labor. Given land C_o, the optimal L_o^* is determined by
the equation of wage with marginal product, or

$$w = \alpha A(C_o/L_o^*)^{1-\alpha}, \text{ so } L_o^*/L_o = \theta = (\alpha A/w)^{1/(1-\alpha)}(C_o/L_o)$$

Then $\theta = (MP_{L_o}/w)^{1/(1-\alpha)}$ where MP_{Lo} is the marginal product
of labor on the <u>suboptimal</u> farm.

In the Chinese case, it is apparent from Table 6.9 that,
with MP_L about .35 times average product, for the <u>average</u>
farm, the marginal product of labor was about one-half the
real wage (with considerable variation by region). With
$\alpha = .35$ and $\theta = .37$, the net gain to the average family
from abandoning family farming would have been a mere 13
percent of current gross income. For the smallest farms,
marginal product often fell to 30 or 40 percent of the
real wage, hence θ was between .15 and .25 and there was
a distinct incentive of between 25 and 50 percent potential
gain from abandoning family farming.

Although little faith can be placed in the magnitudes
of the above results, it is clearly impossible to argue
that all peasants in China, no matter how small the farms,
could be said to be near an optimum economic position with
respect to market factor prices, given their farming opera-

tions alone. About one-fourth of all Chinese farms (according to Buck) fell into the category of "small" as defined in Table 6.9, and were thus distinctly "suboptimal" in the sense used above. However, this may merely point up again the importance of subsidiary and off-farm income: If, as we presume, long-term laborers could not hope to derive such extra income (their product belonging to their hirers), the availability of such income to the peasant farmer may explain his unwillingness to abandon farming for wage labor in sufficient numbers to drive down the wage level.

If this is so, proper specification of the labor supply mechanism relating the traditional and modern sectors in the course of industrialization should emphasize, not the presumed infinite elasticity of supply at an institutionally-determine wage, but the destructive effects of industrialization on many opportunities for subsidiary income from traditional forms of production (outside of the immediate hinterland of the urban areas, where more opportunities are created than destroyed). This mode of feedback of modern industry on the agricultural sector is more likely to contribute to a growing urban labor force at relatively stable (or declining) real wage levels than, for example, movements in the terms of trade, which are likely to be in favor of the peasant, ceteris paribus.

Conclusions

The discussion of this chapter has focussed on the
estimation of an agricultural production function charac-
terizing the Chinese peasant economy, and the implications
of these estimates concerning the "equilibrium" distribution
of income within the rural economy. While I have pointed
to numerous grounds on which these results could be challenged,
and would bid the reader compare the more statistically
defensible results of the following chapter, as a whole
they sustain the argument that wage and rent levels bore
definite and predictable relationships to the values of
marginal productivities of labor and land, such as should
follow from income maximization principles, tempered by
some degree of risk aversion, in conjunction with the
maldistribution of landownership. Indeed, with the
exception of much lower overall income levels, there is
nothing in this evidence to suggest that the distribution
of income in China was governed by economic laws different
from, for example, those prevailing in the more backwards
areas of the United States today.

To deny the existence of an institutionally set "subsistence" wage is not, of course, to deny the prevalence of
bare subsistence per capita income levels for those with
little or no land. It should be obvious that neither the
real wage of a laborer nor the net surplus of crop income

of a small farm after rent payment were capable of sustaining the proverbial "five-person family" at anything near the average per capita consumption levels of about 230 kilograms of grain recorded in the early 1950s.[23] This was fundamentally a distribution problem, however, as average productivity of labor for the Chinese rural economy as a whole was technically capable of sustaining five persons per laborer at such a consumption level in the period 1929 through 1933.

Nor does the above analysis imply that the supply of labor from the rural sector would not in the long run be as elastic as maintained by the labor-surplus theorists. It is clear that a large portion of the peasant population farmed on such a small scale that only the availability of subsidiary income and part-time, non-farm earnings made farming a viable alternative to wage labor. The pool of potential wage labor could be presumed to have grown over time to the extent that the products of modern industry succeeded in displacing traditional opportunities.

CHAPTER VII. AN ACTIVITY ANALYSIS APPROACH TO PRODUC-
             TIVITY MEASUREMENT: MI-CH'ANG VILLAGE
             SAMPLE

The previous chapter was able to develop general statements regarding the relationships between factor prices
and their marginal value productivities in use in the
Chinese peasant economy on the basis of regression estimates
of the "agricultural production function". However, there
were sufficient problems with the data and the econometric
techniques employed to leave the results obtained susceptible to challenge.

South Manchurian Railway studies of small samples drawn
from farms in the Winter wheat-kaoliang region (Region 3 in
the previous chapter) produced data qualitatively superior
to that employed in the previous chapter in terms of degree
of disaggregation, completeness and accuracy.[1] This data
will be used in this chapter to provide a check on both the
methods and conclusions of the preceding chapter. Morevoer,
an alternative approach to the problem of measurement will
be developed, specifically activity analysis (or linear
programming), which we can use to establish the significance of uncertainty in peasant decision-making. While
this approach proves only partially successful, it does
provide some interesting insights into peasant behavior
regarding the choice between so-called "commercial" and
"subsistence" crops and the impact of major shifts in the

"terms of trade" (or price relatives).

Alternative Approaches to Measurement of the Relations of Production

As an introduction to and justification for the methods of analysis employed in this chapter, it behooves us to enlarge on our earlier comparison of the merits of neo-classical aggregate production functions with those of the "activity set" of linear programming analysis. To this we will add some comments on the weaknesses of the "conventional" approach to efficiency measurement, based on ordinary least-squares regression-estimates of aggregate production functions.

The most significant difference between the neoclassical and activity analysis approaches to specification of the productive opportunity set, or production function, lies in their respective methods of dealing with "gaps" in the empirical data. It has been previously stressed that the assumption of a neoclassical continuous production function is equivalent to presuming the existence of an infinite number of activities, none of which dominates another, and differing in unit resource requirements from each other in such a way that a continuous convex isoquant constitutes an adequate representation of the total unit productive opportunity set. If this assumption is justified, then

observed activities of peasants should reflect this in
their variety and form, and the activity analysis representation of their opportunity set over the range of observed factor proportions will differ from the neolcassical
only in that extrapolation between segments of an isoquant
for which actual observations do not exist will be linear
rather than curvilinear (the former having a realistic
basis in the possibility of combining or mixing activities,
the latter based only on the presumption of continuously
increasing marginal rates of substitution along an isoquant).
The difference in approach becomes a serious source of
misjudgment only on those "fringes" of the isoquant for
which no real-world observations exist: Here, activity
analysis presumes zero substitutability and marginal productivity for one or more factors of production, in the absence of empirical evidence to the contrary, whereas estimated isoquants of neoclassical form simply project the
assumed mathematical form into a statistical void. It
requires a certain faith in the mathematical symmetry of
nature to consider the latter approach preferable in theory
(although practice may be dictated by convenience), without
additional information.

There are, of course, intuitive reasons for considering
some factors of production continuously substitutable over
at least a certain range -- e.g. fertilizer, pesticides and

moisture, the prime units of which are infinitesimal in size. Moreover, continuously variable rates of substitution (and thus neoclassical production functions) would seem a more appropriate assumption for primitive agriculture than for modern industry. Yet this concerns only a given crop -- there is no intuitive reason to assume that continuously decreasing marginal rates of substitution hold where the product is a mix of crops. If there are only a limited number of crops, then even if the technology for producing each crop can be represented in neoclassical form (with constant returns to scale, say), the joint production function will have one or more linear segments where constant marginal rates of substitution and marginal products prevail (see Appendix II-A, Figure A. for an example). Over the range of factor proportions involving a crop mix, then, activity analysis is again a theoretically preferable method of representing production choices.

If the neoclassical production function has its theoretical weaknesses, tests of efficiency based on regression-estimates of particular forms of such production functions (such as the Cobb-Douglas) may compound them. If such tests are based on aggregate production functions, then they assume much of what really requires proof: It is assumed that the production function is a monotonic function of aggregate input levels. This requires (see

Appendix VI-B) that a) output be calculated as a weighted sum of different products (e.g. crops) in which the weights are the same for each producer and, b) the index of output (or its expected value) represent the actual object of maximization of the producer for given inputs. Among the assumptions sufficient to fulfill these requirements are the risk-neutrality of producers and the randomness and neutrality of productive inefficiency among producers and crops, neither of which are really justifiable.

The Cobb-Douglas function in particular has undesireable characteristics for efficiency measurement, inasmuch as it imposes an unrealistic uniformity on marginal productivity estimates (constraining them to be constant fractions of factor average productivity). Since factor marginal productivity can then only asymptotically approach zero, it provides no criteria for measurement of "surplus" resources in the sense of Lewis and Ranis and Fei, if such exist.

Finally, ordinary least squares estimates of the parameters of the Cobb-Douglas function are unbiased and consistent only if stochastic influences are confined to random and neutral influences on output unrelated to factor use (such as weather) and random errors in producer fulfillment of profit-maximizing factor-use conditions, and so long as these two influences are uncorrelated.[2] Unfortunately, one of the most common forms of producer inefficiency in

peasant agriculture is wastage of factor services (or
non-neutral technical inefficiency, to be more precise).
Combined with non-homogeneity of factors, this source of
inefficiency leads to the presence of a stochastic error
component in measured factor use values, resulting in biased
and inconsistent estimates of parameters under ordinary
least-squares regression techniques.

On the other hand, activity analysis, as an estimating
technique, has certain disadvantages compared with regression
techniques for estimating neoclassical production functions.
This is because, first, there are no conventions as to
how to go about separating "true" activity coefficients
(i.e. that matrix A of input requirements per unit output,
a_{ij}, which constitutes the locus of expected productive
opportunities) from the "noise" -- random or semi-random
deviations from the a_{ij} due to variations in efficiency,
weather, etc. Second, we are aware of no simultaneous
technique comparable to least squares for distinguishing
among a large set of a_{ij} those which are most efficient
individually or in combination. The computational process
is thus less than elegant. Again, however, regression
analysis generally assumes away the problem by presuming
that producers have already eliminated dominated (i.e.
technically inefficient) techniques, so that the remaining
stochastic element represents only more or less efficient

(allocative) use of efficient techniques (otherwise there
would be no grounds for assuming that the stochastic element
is neutral and has a zero expected value).[3]

Finally, the technique of linear programming presumes
constant returns to scale (although programming frameworks
exist which can accomodate non-linear objective functions).
It will lead to erroneous depiction of production opportunities if this assumption is seriously violated. It is, of
course, possible to approximate mild forms of non-constant
returns by grouping the a_{ij} by enterprise size ranges.

The Nature of the Data

The data employed in this chapter were drawn from a
S.M.R.R. survey of 20 farms in Mi-ch'ang village, Feng-jun
county, Hopei province over the years 1937-39.[4] Thirteen of
the farms were studied in each of three years, and the remainder for two or less, so that the sample offers an opportunity
to observe peasant behavior both cross-sectionally and
over time.

Since an excellent description of both the economy of
this region and locality and the survey data may be readily
found in an article by Dittrich and Myers based on the same
data[5], we will confine our comments to those aspects of
specific relevance to our study.

The village in question was somewhat unusually commercia-

lized, due to its proximity to the railroad, and consequently
an exporter of an industrial crop, cotton, and net importer
of foodgrains, although most producers also engaged in some
production of corn and kaoliang (sorghum) largely for self-
consumption. The sample was intended to represent a cross-
section of farm types, and therefore includes several
atypically large farms (more than 40 acres), small farms
(less than 3 acres), as well as the more frequent "middle-
sized" farms. Tenant or partial-tenant farms were also
well-represented in the sample.

As pointed out by Dittrich and Myers, the unique value
of this data is that the Japanese field workers obtained
for each farm estimates of input use by type of crop, using
market prices for computing input value whether purchased
or self-supplied. In addition, information on physical
units of inputs of land, labor and animal labor were obtained.

The computations in this chapter concentrate on the three
major crops, corn, cotton and kaoliang, and the inputs used
in their production. We chose to class the latter as labor,
land, animal labor, fertilizer and other capital (the last
including seeds, depreciation and maintenance costs for
farm tools and storage facilities). Where possible we
have employed physical rather than value units: For the
first three inputs, value was imputed by the researchers

to the physical units, at uniform rates in the cases of
human and animal labor, and in an unknown manner (which
is not systematically related to farm, time or productivity
in any discernible way) to land (although the average per
mou valuation used did not differ substantially from reported average rent levels).

Where value units had to be used, it was necessary to
adjust the data for price changes to permit a pooled sample.
The magnitude of adjustment required may be seen in Table
7.1, where actual and estimated price indices are presented.
Of the various forms of capital services, depreciation and
maintenance costs were apparently not adjusted upwards by
the survey field workers to reflect the inflation of replacement cost, and so required no deflation.

Some comments are required on the changes in crop prices
over the sample period to put them in perspective: The
farm price of cotton in Mi-ch'ang retained throughout the
period a fairly stable relationship to Shanghai wholesale
prices* (the farm price being about 40 percent of the latter).
This was not the case for foodgrains, on the importation of
which Mi-ch'ang was dependent for most of its consumption
requirements: Although Shanghai prices for corn did increase (from 1936 to 1939) at a somewhat faster rate than

---

* The nearest major market was Tientsin, for which we have
no price series, however.

Table 7.1   Product and Factor Prices and Indices, Mi-ch'ang
             Village, 1937-39.   (prices in yuan)

	1937	1938	1939
Farm Prices:			
Corn (per tou)	1.00	1.44	4.28
Index	100	144	428
Cotton (per 100 chin)	15.9	17.8	31.5
Index	100	112	198
Kaoliang (per tou)	1.00	1.28	4.30
Index	100	128	430
Factor Prices:			
Labor (per man day)[a]·	.45	.55	.70
Index . . . . ·.	100	122	156
Cash Rent (per mou)[b]·	3.80	4.00	7.00
Index	100	105	184
Animal Labor (per day)	.80	1.00	1.20
Index . . . . . . ·.	100	125	150
Seed Price Indices:[c]·			
Corn.	100	136	210
Cotton.	100	100	170
Kaoliang. . . . .[d]. . . .	100	128	223
Fertilizer Price Index[d]·.	100	140	178

Notes:
a. Probably represents average cash payment, not including
    food supplied, valued at about $.23 in 1930-31 (see
    Table 5.8) and probably comparable in value in 1937
    (grain prices had just about reached 1930 levels again
    by 1937, according to Shanghai and Nankai price
    materials).
b. But average imputed rental value for 14 farms in 1937 was
    $4.50. A less. frequent rental standard was one-half of
    the value of all crops (not including byproducts). This
    would have been more than $4.50 in most cases.
c. Estimated on the assumption of no overall changes in the
    density of seed use per mou. These indices correspond
    roughly to changes in crop prices (given the time lag
    between seeding and marketing).
d. Based on average of year-to-year increases in value of
    fertilizer used/mou for each crop, where an increase
    (rather than a decrease) occured. Since most farmers
    were decreasing fertilizer use over this time span, it
    was in effect assumed that any apparent increases re-
    flected only price rises. Since the resulting index
    does not differ much from the overall rate of inflation,
    it is not likely that our assumption was far from the
    mark.

cotton prices, the shift in the grain/cotton price relatives in Mi-ch'ang was much more pronounced, due perhaps
to disruption of the transport network or the diversion of
supplies to military use. If price relatives in Mi-ch'ang
shifted in accordance with national trends previous to
1937, then 1935 marked the end of a period during which
the "terms of trade" were exceptionally favorable to peasant
production of cotton (from 1931-1934) and began to shift in
favor of grain production (in comparison with the relatives
prevailing throughout the 1920s).[6] This perspective will be
of relevance when we consider peasant crop allocation changes
over this period.

However an aggregate production function is estimated,
one important assumption must be that substitutability
among crops is feasible. Relevant information was supplied
by the survey report: In this village, cotton was usually
grown on higher ground, corn on lower, apparently because
cotton required better drainage. This implies that there
is only a limited possibility of replacing existing corn
acreage with cotton (but not vice versa), and in itself
could account for the reported unwillingness to completely
specialize in cotton (which, however, need not be presumed
economically superior, as we shall see below). This will
not prove to be a meaningful constraint, however, inasmuch
as any question of optimal shifts in crop allocation turns

out below to involve rather the replacement of cotton by
corn.*

A more serious problem arises from the common practice
of interspersing beans with kaoliang. Properly speaking,
this combination should be treated as a joint product, with
no attempt made to separate the inputs into the production
of each crop. However, while full information was provided
in the survey on the production and input requirements for
kaoliang, none was provided on the interspersed beans. We
suspect that the recorded input requirements are those for
kaoliang and beans taken together, and that the recorded
value of kaoliang produced does not reflect the full productive value of the recorded inputs. As a result, kaoliang
production (at 1937 prices) appears to involve a negative
profit, which may not have been the case if the value of
the subsidiary product could be taken into account.

A Regression-Estimate of the Aggregate Production Function

To provide a basis for comparison with the results of
the previous chapter and the activity analysis which follows,
we have fitted a Cobb-Douglas production function to the
pooled, aggregate production data. Land, labor and animal

---

* Corn and kaoliang are also harvested subsequent to the cotton
harvest, permitting spreading of peak labor requirements over
a longer period and reducing wage costs.

Table 7.2   Cobb-Douglas Aggregate Production Functions,
Mi-ch'ang Village Sample, 1937 Prices

Elasticity coefficients with respect to:

Labor	Land	Animal Lab.	Fertilizer	Other K	
.52	.40	-.05*	.11*	.19	R^2=.93
(.17)	(.14)	(.06)	(.09)	(.09)	

Labor	Land	All Capital	
.50	.44	.20	R^2=.93
(.18)	(.13)	(.11)	

* not statistically significant at the 10% level or better.
Note: Standard deviations of coefficients in parentheses.

labor were aggregated in physical units; crop output and
other factors of production, at 1937 prices. Aggregate
capital services was computed as the sum of the 1937 values
of animal labor, fertilizer and other capital services.
The results of two regressions, with aggregated and disaggregated capital services respectively, are displayed
in Table 7.2.

The elasticity coefficients for labor and land in this
locality turn out to be precisely the same as those estimated for region 3 (Winter wheat-kaoliang) as a whole
(in Table 6.4). The disaggregated capital services display mixed results: Only "other capital" -- farm tools,
seeds and storage costs -- is statistically significant;
animal labor is again perverse in sign (which was the cause
of its exclusion from the regressions in the previous chapter), even though it represents here, not capacity, but

Table 7.3 Estimates of Factor Marginal Value Product at
1937 Prices, Based on Cobb-Douglas Equation

	MVP of Labor	MVP of Land	MVP of Capital
Mean, All Farms	.71 (.19)	5.92 (1.60)	1.14 (.33)
Mean, Large Farms	.79 (.19)	6.51 (1.37)	1.18 (.42)
Mean, Small Farms	.59 (.22)	5.51 (2.23)	.99 (.39)

Notes: MVP estimates computed as constant proportion of
the arithmetic mean of average products on each farm,
equivalent to taking the mean of estimates of MVP computed
separately for each farm. This permits comparability with
estimates derived from activity analysis, but differs
slightly from estimates based on the geometric means of
inputs. Large farms: over 45 mou (7.6 acres); small
farms: less than 20 mou (3.3 acres). Standard deviations
of individual farm estimates around their means given in
parentheses.

actual days of use. The marginal response rate to fertilizer
does not appear at all near as high as elsewhere in the
region (perhaps because of unusually heavy use -- cost per
mou for cotton was often as great or greater than rental
cost). Aggregated capital services displays an elasticity
coefficient of "reasonable" magnitude (although weak
significance); the sum of the elasticities is 1.14, indicating
mild returns to scale.[*]

[*] Although there is as usual considerable multicollinearity
among variables, it is most severe between labor and land,
and does not in itself account for weak capital significance.

The estimated marginal value products of the factors of
production are of interest, calculated in Table 7.3 as
a constant proportion of average productivity. On the
average, the MVP of labor is slightly above the daily wage
of hired labor (estimated at $.68, including $.23 non-cash
component -- see Table 7.1, note a.). The MVP of land is
well above the average level of cash rent ($3.80), and
with an average land price of $45 per mou and tax of $1.80
(the latter in 1939), offered a rate of return (at 1937
prices) of 9.2 percent after tax. However, about 20 percent
of tenants were on the crop-sharing system, with rent
being a 50% share of all crops, excluding byproducts. With
the value of byproducts about 10 percent of total value of
crop output, this represents about 45% of total output,
close to the elasticity with respect to land estimated in
Table 7.2. As suggested in an earlier chapter, therefore,
the high rate of return to land obtained even by large
owner-cultivators in this North China village left little
incentive for landlordism.

Although the low statistical significance of the capital
services elasticity coefficient indicates considerable
variability among farms (and/or years) in the rate of
return on that investment, that rate averages about 14
percent, roughly the same as the before tax rate of return
on land investment.(not including any capital gains due

to inflation). It is therefore in that range where it does
not generally pay to borrow (at nominal rates over 30 percent)
for productive purposes, but may be at about the same level
as that expected return on lending which compensates for
the additional risk of default (which rate is of course
unknown and subjective).

Although we have computed separately the mean MVPs for
large and small farms in the sample, the differences between them reflect only returns to scale and the constant
elasticity assumption; moreover the difference is significant only for the MVP of labor. However, small farms
do appear to have a slight excess of both labor and capital
relative to market valuations, and a slight deficit of
land -- again in accord with theoretical expectations
(see Chapter II).

Thus, while Dietrich and Myers found that allocation
of the factors of production among crops was reasonably
efficient at 1937 prices (a point which we will reconsider
below), our regression estimates of the Cobb-Douglas
production function indicate that adjustment with respect
to factor markets, given allocations among crops, was
efficient, on the average and in the face of uncertainty.
These results are in accord with our findings for the
Winter wheat-kaoliang region as a whole in the previous
chapter, despite the poor quality data on which the latter was
based.

An Alternative Approach to Efficiency Measurement

The weaknesses of the regression approach to efficiency measurement have already been pointed out above. We now intend to develop an approach which differs in two respects: a) the use of activity analysis; b) the attempt to distinguish a true "production possibilities frontier," or to discard the assumption that measured input data are in terms of equivalent "efficiency units".

Assuming constant returns to scale, we define an activity as any method of producing a unit output of a particular crop, characterized by a set of unit resource requirements, a_{ij} for $j = 1,...,m$ resources. Further define a "frontier activity", a_i^* as any activity for which $a_{ij}^* < a_{kj}$, for at least one j and all possible k. That is, a "frontier activity" is one which is not dominated by any other activity.

Now, taking the a_{ij} to represent the measured unit resource requirements for a particular crop on a particular farm at a particular time, there are two reasons why this may differ from some corresponding a_{ij}^*: First, growing conditions may be less than optimal at that time, so that proportionately more of each resource will be required to produce a unit output; second, some part of one or more measured resource requirement may represent "wastage" or "underemployment" or "technical inefficiency" -- that is, the measured a_{ij} and the a_{ij}^* are not in terms of the same

"efficiency units" of resource utilization. Thus for each
farm, crop and time, there is some a_{ij}^* such that

$$a_{ij} = c_{it}e_{ijt}a_{ij}^*$$

where c_{it} is a random variable with $E(c) > 1$ representing
deviation from the frontier due to less than optimal growing conditions, and $e_{ijt} \geq 1$ is a measure of the inefficiency
of factor use, or alternatively a factor converting the
standard of "efficiency units" at the frontier to the actual
units of measurement of the a_{ij}.

So defined, the problem of specifying a common locus
of productive opportunities for all farms and times becomes
that of determining the a_{ij}^*, or alternatively $E(c_{it})a_{ij}^*$.
Since most farms will exhibit some degree of inefficiency
in factor use, that is most e_{ijt} will be greater than unity,
and this inefficiency is unlikely to be random and independent with respect to crop, resource, farm or time, ordinary
least squares estimation methods will not be appropriate.
However, under certain assumptions a much simpler approach
will suffice.

First, we must assume that some farms in the sample display close to maximum efficiency of factor utilization for
a given crop -- that is, $e_{ijt} = 1$ holds approximately for
a given i and t and all resources j (actually uniformity
of the e_{ijt} over all j is more important than that they be
close to unity, so that observed factor proportions corres-

pond to frontier factor proportions). Obviously, the larger
the sample size, the more likely it is that such a set of
observations can be found.

Second, for the same set of observed a_{ij}, some e_{ijt}
must equal unity, to permit us to distinguish between the
c_{it} and e_{ijt}. Now, of all the factors of production, it
is hardest to conceive of "wastage" or "underemployment"
of land, when it is measured as actually cultivated acreage.
Examples of underutilization of land generally refer to
differences in intensity of cultivation, which are reflected
in insufficient use of other complementary inputs and really
constitute different techniques. That is, variations in
the land requirement per unit output (the inverse of yield)
may be attributed entirely to choice of technique reflected
in use of complementary factors and to varying efficiency
in the use of those factors.* It therefore seems reasonable
to assume that $a_{ij} = c_{it}a_{ij}^{*}$ for $j = 1$ (land), and measure
$E(c_{it}) = a_{ij}^{*-1}E(a_{ij})$ for any i and $j = 1$.

Third, there must be no other sources of error in the
observed data, or at least not in the subset from which the
frontier techniques are estimated, and not in the input
proportions. Obviously a technique of estimation which
depends on the extreme observations among the data will be

---

* One (important) exception arises from variations in the
quality of land not reflected in the index of land employed.
The technique used will invariably exclude such observations
from the frontier.

unusually sensitive
to errors in the un-
derlying data.

Figure 7.1

If these assump-
tions are acceptable,
the following techni-
que may be used (illus-
trated in Figure 7.1
for the two-factor
case):

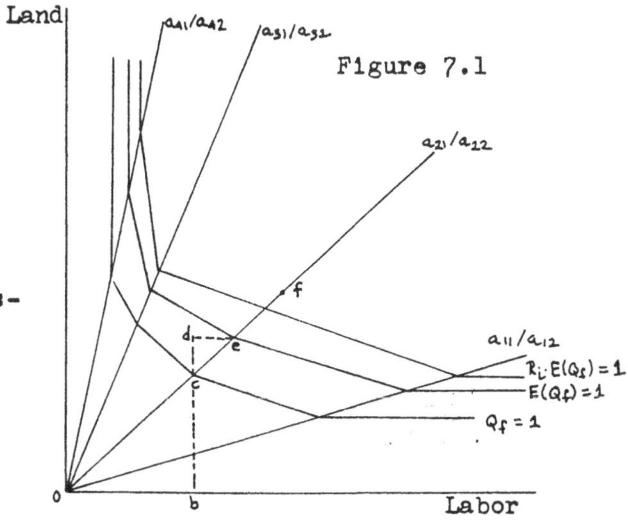

From the observed
matrix A of techniques, a_{ijt}, choose as the "frontier set"
those activities which individually or in combination form
an inner envelope to all other observed techniques, i.e.
dominate them (the isoquant, $Q_f=1$, in Figure 7.1). Then
for each activity (e.g. a_{21}/a_{22}), determine

$E(c_{1t}) = a_{ij}^{*-1}E(a_{ijt})$, where j is the land input: Since
there will be no obvious way of distinguishing which a_{ij}^{*}
each observed a_{ijt} corresponds to, $E(a_{ijt})$ may be approximated by grouping the observed activities according to
crop, or ranges of factor proportions, for example, and
taking group means. Applying $E(c_{1t})$ (the ratio of cd to
cb for technique a_{21}/a_{22}, for example) to all a_{ij}^{*} of type
i (giving point e for example), one arrives at a new set
of activities, $E(c_{1t})a_{ij}^{*}$, which we may term the "expected
efficiency frontier" (in Fig. 7.1, at $E(Q_f) = 1$), which

represents the expected (long-run) input requirements per
unit output when all inputs are utilized at peak efficiency
(minimal slack or underemployment).[7]

What relationship does this "expected efficiency frontier" (which we will call the EEF) have to the optimization
of peasant production? It is in fact the "true" production
function faced by the peasant farm; if all farms were
entirely efficient in the technical sense of minimal slack
or misuse of input services, then observed input utilization
per unit output, which is stochastic, should be distributed
symmetrically around the EEF along rays from the origin
(in the absence of changes in product or factor price
relatives). Moreover, given such efficiency, the OLS
regression-estimated production function would then give
a good (unbiased) approximation to the EEF.

Suppose that activities have been defined in terms of
units of market value of output, and that the EEF has
been estimated: For given farm factor availability or
market prices, could the EEF be used to determine the
efficiency of factor allocation among alternative activities
and/or with respect to the market? If peasants possess a
healthy degree of risk aversion, it could not, since
different activities involve a stochastic element (risk)
of varying magnitude which will affect their allocative
decisions. Supposing that this element can be expressed

as a "risk premium" (more properly, a discount) associated
with each activity (not necessarily a constant), the peasant
will subjectively "revalue" output of activities in such a way
that he may be viewed as acting on the basis of a subjective,
"risk-weighted" EEF (in Figure 7.1, for example, $R_1 E(Q_f)=1$),
where R_1 is a variable risk discount) in determining his
allocation of resources among activities and his factor
market activity. In general, this frontier will lie further
from the origin the more risky the activity, will differ
in marginal rates of substitution from the ordinary EEF,
and may even eliminate certain activities from consideration
because of the risk involved (e.g. point f on ray a_{21}/a_{22} in
Fig. 7.1). The economic efficiency of the peasant surely
must be measured with reference to the "risk-weighted"
EEF if it can be in some way estimated, or at least the
probable impact of varying risk on peasant decision making
should be taken into account.

The approach outlined above gives us a new theoretical
basis for efficiency measurement. The remaining details
will be explained below in the course of the application of
this approach to the Mi-ch'ang data. Whether our perhaps
excessive attention to theoretical and econometric "niceties"
proves to be a mountain or molehill, it should be of interest
to view quantitative alternative results.

Farm Efficiency in Mi-ch'ang Village

As discussed above, the first step in forming a basis for measurement of efficiency of farm production in the Mi-ch'ang village sample is the isolation of a set of frontier techniques from among the 145 observed sets of unit input requirements for crops produced on the sampled farms. Inspection revealed that returns to scale only became significant among farms over 45 mou in size, so the sample was divided into the set of 17 observations (on 7 farms) for large farms, and 34 observations (on 13 farms) for medium or small farms, with a separate set of frontier techniques, characterized by constant returns to scale, assumed for each.

Isolation of each frontier set was accomplished by the simple expedient of elimination (by inspection) of observed techniques which were dominated by other observed techniques for producing the same crop. Attention was paid to the possibility of errors in data making certain techniques appear spuriously superior. C. P. Timmer, in another frontier-oriented efficiency study, dealt with this problem by arbitrarily excluding that 5 percent of observations which appeared most efficient.[8] Since this method involves a high probability of "throwing the baby out with the bath-water" and since our sample was small and permitted inter-temporal comparison of data pertaining to the same farms, we did not choose to take this approach. However, we did

find that using the survey valuation of land in computing
coefficients introduced improbable inconsistencies in factor
proportions, and therefore we chose to use physical measures
of inputs (mou for land, days for human and animal labor)
wherever possible. On this basis, we found no grounds for
rejecting any of the observed "techniques", although there
is enough variation in observed use of various capital
services to suggest that errors might exist in that component.

To further eliminate observed techniques which were
dominated by combinations of other techniques, we took
the actual allocation of resources among crops on each farm
as given, and solved (a series of linear programming problems)
for the optimum combinations of crop techniques for each crop
and farm. Techniques which did not appear in any such
solution (and could thus be presumed suboptimal for any
combination of resources actually observed in the sample)
were eliminated from further consideration.

The remaining techniques constitute the frontier production opportunity set -- the minimum resource requirements
per unit output, given optimal growing conditions and
the highest efficiency of input use observed in the sample.
The technical coefficients (unit resource requirements) of
this set, for large and non-large farms, are given in Table
7.4 by crop. These techniques were almost exclusively among
those observed in 1938 and 1939: Inspection of the residuals

Table 7.4. Frontier Techniques, Mi-ch'ang Village Sample.
Requirement per y̎an of output of:

	Land	Labor	Animal Labor	Ferti- lizer	Other Capital	Total Capital
Large Farms:						
Corn:	.041	.363	.033	.096	.019	.141
	.053	.222	.022	.041	.041	.100
	.049	.483	.051	--	.012	.053
	.039	.329	.033	.086	.021	.133
	.143	.518	--	--	.089	.089
Kaoliang:	.076	.420	.041	.002	.044	.079
	.081	.675	.060	--	.033	.081
	.075	.727	.055	.092	.030	.166
Cotton:	.048	.716	.016	.097	.020	.130
	.039	.532	.019	.066	.030	.111
	.043	.563	.004	.122	.021	.146
	.038	.499	.004	.117	.032	.152
	.046	.491	.027	.127	.017	.166
Non-Large Farms:						
Corn:	.143	.518	--	--	.089	.089
	.091	.460	.032	.003	.015	.044
	.109	.651	.004	.070	.030	.103
	.136	.446	.003	.014	.077	.093
	.074	.450	.010	.081	.038	.127
	.075	.290	.046	--	.023	.060
	.033	1.040	.033	.026	.014	.066
	.072	.932	.012	--	.047	.057
	.070	.271	.004	.004	.078	.085
	.049	.445	.037	.036	.056	.122
Kaoliang:	.108	.929	.016	.027	.025	.065
	.153	.668	.048	--	.014	.052
	.082	.567	.011	--	.031	.040
	.074	4.441	.132	--	.021	.127
	.106	.231	.042	--	.079	.113
Cotton:	.041	.600	.017	.134	.018	.166
	.040	.741	.056	.162	.016	.223
	.041	.592	.023	.162	.033	.213
	.041	.903	.018	.080	.022	.116
	.043	.663	.013	.120	.017	.147
	.034	.613	.015	.085	.019	.116
	.047	.776	.014	.112	.042	.165

(Table 7.4 Continued)

Notes: Units of measurement for inputs are: Land -- mou;
labor -- days; animal labor -- days; all others -- yüan
at 1937 prices. Animal labor is aggregated in total
capital at its average 1937 price (.80 per day).
Large farms: Over 45 mou.

of the previously estimated Cobb-Douglas production function left no doubt that 1937 was a year of exceptionally
poor growing conditions for all crops and all but a few
farms; 1939 seems also to have been better than 1938 for
most crops and farms, although not as consistently so.

Inspection of the input requirements in the table reveals
the economic characteristics of each crop, at least under
optimal conditions: Cotton tends to be the highest yielding
crop, though at the expense of heavy labor and capital
requirements. Corn saves on both labor and capital at the
expense of a lower yield, although on large farms it at
best entirely dominates cotton techniques. Kaoliang has
only the virtue of being capital-saving, especially of
fertilizer, and is generally inferior to corn techniques
under optimal growing conditions (at least given our lack
of information on intercropped beans). Finally, although all
crops permit some degree of flexibility in factor proportions,
cotton is the most rigid in its requirements and corn the
least.

This production frontier is not, of course, the "expected
efficiency frontier" described earlier inasmuch as we have

not yet accounted for variation in growing conditions and
their impact on different crops. Rather than defining an
EEF, it is convenient to take this into account in terms
of the "objective function" -- the object of maximization
-- of the hypothetical optimizing peasant farm, so that we
can simultaneously account for the impact of risk aversion.
Let us define y_f as the income derivable under optimal
growing conditions through the use of some combination of
frontier activities by a given farm, and let z be the
deviation of actual income, y, from frontier income due
to suboptimal growing conditions, so that $y = y_f + z$,
with $E(z) < 0$ and $\sigma_y^2 = \sigma_z^2 > 0$, the growing conditions being
treated as stochastic. If peasants were risk neutral, and
took the frontier activity set of Table 7.4 as their production opportunity set, then a suitable expression of
their objective function would be:

$$E(y) = y_f + E(z) = \sum_i w_i a_{i1}^* E(a_{i1}^{-1}) A_i^* \qquad (7.1)$$

where A_i^* represents the level of use (in yüan) of the ith
frontier activity; a_{i1}^* represents the land requirement per
unit use level of that activity; w_i is a price-weight,
equal to unity unless the crop is partially or wholly
self-consumed, in which case it will be somewhat higher
to reflect the wholesale to retail price conversion;
$E(a_{i1}^{-1})$ is the mean yield (yüan per mou) for a particular
crop (more precisely, activity). Thus the objective
function is the weighted sum of frontier activity levels,

but the weights include a discount to reflect the deviation
of "normal" from "frontier" yields.

Since peasants are presumably risk-averters, however,
we must deal directly with the tradeoff between risk and
return through explicit assumptions about the form of
"utility function" (see Chapter II). We take as the object
of maximization of the peasant:

$$E[U(y)] = U(y_f - \bar{z} - \bar{\pi}) \tag{7.2}$$

where $\bar{z} = E(z)$ and $\bar{\pi} = E(\pi)$ is a mean "risk premium",
$\bar{\pi} > 0$. If $\sigma_y^2 = \sigma_z^2$ is large relative to $E(|z-\bar{z}|^3)$, we may
approximate:[9]

$$\bar{\pi} = [\sigma^2/2(y_f+\bar{z})]R(y_f+\bar{z}) \tag{7.3}$$

The magnitude of $R(y_f+\bar{z})$, and thus of the risk premium
required to induce acceptance of a given level of risk,
depends on the utility function. A computationally convenient
choice is the form, $U = \alpha + \beta lny$, which displays decreasing
absolute risk aversion with increased income ($-U''/U' = \beta/y$)
but constant relative risk aversion of a magnitude depending
on β (here we must disregard our earlier insistence that
peasants are characterized by decreasing relative risk
aversion as well). With this utility function, $R(y_f+\bar{z}) = 1$
so that:

$$E[U(y)] = U[y_f + \bar{z} - \sigma^2/2(y_f+\bar{z})] \tag{7.4}$$

and expected utility is maximized by maximizing the
expression:

$$y' = y_f + z - \sigma^2/2(y_f + \bar{z}) \tag{7.4A}$$

Now let L be the vector consisting of the products, $w_1 A_1^* a_{11}^*$, as previously defined, for each frontier activity; let V be the variance-covariance matrix of the actual crop yields (a_{11}^{-1}) and V_1 its ith row. Then:

$$\sigma_y^2 = \text{var}[\textstyle\sum_1 w_1 A_1^* a_{11}^* a_{11t}^{-1}] = L'VL \tag{7.5}$$

Letting E represent the vector $E(a_{11}^{-1})$, we have:

$$y' = L'E - (2L'E)^{-1}L'VL \tag{7.6}$$

This expression is non-linear in the activity levels, A_1^* (unlike the objective function of a risk-neutral peasant), as can be seen by taking partial derivative with respect to the A_1^*:

$$
\begin{aligned}
\delta y'/\delta A_1^* &= w_1 a_{11}^* E(a_{11}^{-1}) - (L'E)^{-1} w_1 a_{11}^* V_1 L \\
&\qquad + (2L'E)^{-2} 2 w_1 a_{11}^* E(a_{11}^{-1}) L'VL \\
&= w_1 a_{11}^* E(a_{11}^{-1}) \Big[1 - \frac{V_1 L}{E(a_{11}^{-1})L'E} + \frac{L'VL}{2(L'E)^2} \Big]
\end{aligned} \tag{7.7}
$$

Although this expression seems formidable, its interpretation is simple: The expression to the left of the brackets is the same set of weights described as appropriate for a risk-neutral peasant in equation 7.1. The expression within the brackets is a further discount factor accounting for the contribution to the variance of income of an additional unit of an activity, corrected for the increased income it adds.

The expression 7.7 appears to create insoluble computa-

tional problems, inasmuch as the weights on the basis of
which an optimal set of activities and allocation of
resources among them are supposed to be found are now
dependent on the optimal solution itself. However, we
can bypass this problem with some simplifying assumptions:
First, we use $E(a_{11}^{*})$ instead of a_{11}^{*}, that is we use the
mean input requirement of land for that set of frontier
activities for producing a single crop known to appear
frequently in solutions (from previous approximately-
weighted trials) rather than the actual requirement for
each frontier activity, in computing the discount for the
difference between frontier and mean actual yield for
each crop. Secondly, we chose to use the actual land
planted in each crop in computing the additional discount
for yield variability. Thus this discount factor will be
strictly correct only if the farm was actually producing
at the optimal allocative position. However, it emerged
from the calculations that the risk discount factor for
each crop was relatively constant in magnitude over the
range of observed variation in land allocation among crops,
so we ended up using the same discounts for all farms.

Finally, we treated yield variance as pertaining to
crops rather than activities. Although one technique for
producing, e.g. corn, may involve greater yield variance
than another, the major differences in variance were cer-

tainly between crops. We excluded observed yields on large
farms from our computation of variance and covariance to
prevent bias due to returns to scale.

These assumptions permitted the computation of a set of
weights which were roughly constant for each crop. The
weights and some of the data on which they are based are
given in Table 7.5. This information adds to the insights
concerning the economic characteristics of each crop derived
from the frontier activity coefficients.

We have previously pointed out the advantages of corn
relative to kaoliang, and the ambiguous superiority of
cotton over corn, under optimal growing conditions. It now
appears that, accounting for expected yields under average
growing conditions and discounting for differential risks,
the relative advantages of cotton and, to some extent, kao-
ling increase relative to corn. For corn, yield on the
average is much less than yield under optimal conditions,
whereas for cotton, yield on the average does not differ so
much over time from "best yields". This is reflected also
in the respective coefficients of variation of yield, and
thus in the variance-covariance matrix. Kaoliang fares
somewhat better than corn, inasmuch as its coefficient of
variation in yield is lower, it doesn't covary much with
cotton (thus providing some insurance effect), and, for
non-large farms, does not involve very high yielding

Table 7.5. Weighting Scheme for Objective Function.

	Corn	Kaoliang	Cotton
Large Farms:			
a. Mean Yield (yüan/mou)	13.42	8.50	20.83
b. $E(a_{I1}^{*})$	.049	.076	.044
c. Discount for deviation from frontier (a. x b.)	.66	.65	.92
Non-large Farms:			
a. Mean Yield (yüan/mou)	10.89	7.89	19.52
b. $E(a_{I1}^{*})$	.059	.106	.040
c. Discount for deviation from frontier (a. x b.)	.64	.84	.78
Variance/Covariance of Yields:			
Corn	31.51	13.35	11.86
Kaoliang		7.72	3.70
Cotton			19.78
Coefficient of Variation:	.52	.35	.23
Mean Risk Discount:	.93	.97	.98
Crop Weights:			
Large Farms (1937 prices)	.62	.63	.90
Non-large Farms:			
1937 prices	.60	.81	.76
1938 prices	.86	1.04	.86
1939 prices	2.56	3.48	1.51

Notes: For computational formula and methods, see text, equation 7.7 and the following discussion. The w_i were assumed to equal 1.0 for 1937; for 1938-39, to be larger in accordance with the crop price indicies in terms of 1937 prices (in which all other coefficients were computed). The crop weights are the products of the discounts for deviation from the frontier and the mean risk discounts, times the appropriate w_i.

frontier techniques, so that expected deviation from the
frontier is low.*

On the whole, the introduction of risk-aversion into the
objective function does not have much impact, the maximum
risk premium being 7 percent of the value of expected corn
production. The risk discount, however, depends on the choice
of utility function; it may be that the form assumed is not
appropriate, but the results obtained below do not suggest
that a greater degree of risk aversion is necessarily required to account for observed behavior.

The problem of choice of price-weights, w_i, remains:
In the absence of knowledge of what margin if any exists
between farm prices and local retail prices of self-consumed
grain crops (corn and kaoliang), we have not given these
crops the additional weight in the objective function theoretically proper (since farmers must pay retail prices to
obtain grain if they do not self-produce it). A more
important issue, though, is the formation of peasant price
expectations in advance of the harvest. For the sample

---

* We are still unsure of the impact of the joint product,
beans; also, the discount used for kaoliang for large
farms may be inappropriate, especially in view of the
fact that no kaoliang production appears in optimal
solutions for large farms.

years of rapid inflation (1938 and 1939), actually realized
absolute or relative prices would certainly have deviated
substantially from a priori expectations. The weights in
the objective function, on the other hand, should reflect
the latter. Were peasant expectations determined by the
previous year's harvest prices, or by some weighted average
of past prices? If the latter, with how much relative
weight given to price changes in recent years? The relevance of this matter should be apparent from Figure 7-2: If
current or one-year lagged prices were the basis for formation of expectations, a strong and accelerating shift away
from cotton production and towards grain crops should appear
over the sample years, 1937-39; if long-run experience were
weighted more heavily by the peasants, then the shift might
be less pronounced or even nonexistent. Observation of
actual changes in crop allocation over this period does not
resolve the problem (see Table 7.6): There is indeed a
shift away from cotton and into corn and kaoliang in 1937-
38, but between 1938 and 1939, only a slight shift, from
corn into kaoliang. The direction of the shifts is consistent with contemporaneous relative price changes, but
not the magnitudes. It is possible that peasants were unable to discern shifts in relative prices amidst the
general hyperinflation; it is equally possible that they

were reacting to shifts in price relatives with as much as a
three year lag.

With no firm evidence to go on, we tried all three sets
of prices (1937, 38 and 39) and found that, if peasants were
optimizing on the basis of current or the previous year's
prices alone, then the shift out of cotton and into corn production should have been much more pronounced than was in
fact the case. 1937 prices, however, led to optimal solutions for crop allocation which were on the average quite
close to actual proportions in 1938 and 1939, with some

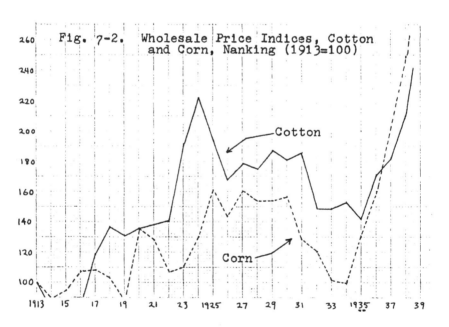

Fig. 7-2. Wholesale Price Indices, Cotton
and Corn, Nanking (1913=100)

Source: Nan-ching ta-hsüeh ching-chi yen-chiu so (eds.),
Nan-kai chih-shu tsu-liao hui-p'ien, 1913 - 1952, pp. 70-74.

underprediction of cotton production in 1937, which would
follow from the higher relative price of cotton previous to
1937. Lacking knowledge of pre-1937 farm prices in Mi-ch'ang,
we chose to disregard post-1937 inflation and assume that the
1937 relative prices reflected fairly well peasant relative
price expectations over the period.

Table 7-6. Shifts in Land Allocation Among Crops, 1937-39,
Mi-ch'ang Village Sample.

Percent of land in cotton:	Percent of farms:		
	1937	1938	1939
80+	14.3	11.1	10.5
70-79	7.1	5.6	0
60-69	35.7	11.1	21.1
50-59	28.6	33.3	26.3
40-49	14.3	22.2	31.6
< 40	0	16.7	10.5
. . . .			
Mean percent of acreage in:			
Corn	11.1	14.5	13.6
Kaoliang	23.8	29.8	31.4
Cotton	65.1	55.7	55.0
Indices of Price Relatives:			
Cotton/kaoliang	100	87	46
Corn/kaoliang	100	112	100

Elasticity of mean acreage with respect to price relatives:		
	1937-38	1938-39
Cotton	1.11	.03
Corn	2.55	.56

With the methodological problems behind us, we may turn
to the final set of calculations. The model of peasant production behavior embodied in our combination of objective

function and frontier activities assumes that peasants attempted to approach the "best local practice" in efficiency of factor use, and allocated factors among activities so as to maximize expected income, discounted appropriately for differential risks. Although the computational method treats overall factor proportions on each farm as fixed, it is rather assumed that they may be varied through use of the factor market: At an optimal allocative solution for a given set of resources, the correspondance between the market and "shadow prices" of these resources indicates how successfully the market opportunities for readjustment of factor proportions have been utilized.

Since our approach is only as valid as the assumptions on which it is based, we must first show that observed behavior does not deviate substantially from hypothetically optimal behavior on the average. This will involve a comparison of actual gross incomes with maximum potential incomes, taking into account the stochastic element in yields. A more stringent test requires the comparison of actual with "optimal" crop proportions.

With the approach established as valid, we may then turn again to the issue of systematic differences in the economic behavior of large and small farms resulting from their different situations with respect to factor markets.

Discussion of Results of Activity Analysis

Taking the observed aggregate use of each input as a fixed resource constraint, we computed for each farm the set of activities and allocation of inputs among them giving maximum expected output, discounted for risk. Since actual output is stochastic, it may be well above or below maximum expected output at any point in time, so that direct comparison is not appropriate. To compare optimal with actual output, we need a measure of expected output at given levels of inefficiency (of input utilization and crop allocation). The best measure available is perhaps the predicted output based on our estimate of the Cobb-Douglas production function above, which, however biased, does approximate well the average relationship between actual output and measured inputs.

The three sets of output data for all farms -- observed, Cobb-Douglas predicted, and allocative-optimal -- are given in Table 7.7, along with identifying information. One possible summary measure of inefficiency in resource use and factor allocation is the average percent of output foregone, measured as the mean difference between allocative-optimal and Cobb-Douglas predicted output levels taken as a percentage of mean output. As given in Table 7.8, this measure indicates a loss of only 5.6% of potential output for large farms, and 4.7% for small. However, the Cobb-Douglas

function was fit over both large and small farms jointly,
and the larger residuals for large farms tended to inordinately influence the estimated parameter values under the
least squares procedure, leading on the average to underprediction for small farms.* In fact, the estimates of
allocative-optimal output for non-large farms come closer to
minimizing the sum of squares of the residuals of observed
minus predicted output than do the "least-squares" Cobb-
Douglas estimates, as should be apparent from comparison of
the respective standard errors of prediction. Thus in fact
the loss of potential output on non-large farms is less than
4.7% on the average.

Table 7.7.   Observed, Cobb-Douglas Predicted, and Allocative-
Optimal Output in 1937 Prices, Mi-ch'ang Sample.

Farm		Observed Output	C-D Predicted Output	Alloc.-Optimal Output
1	1937	1768	1715	1738
2	1939	1619	1739	1732
3	1937	1607	1672	1711
	1938	1420	1769	1780
	1939	1859	1578	1679
4	1937	749	1024	1161
	1938	894	896	1046
	1939	1015	912	903

* probably because the increasing returns to scale observable
in the sample is not continuous as farm size varies, but
really only becomes significant on the 7 largest farms
(over 45 mou) in the sample.

(Table 7.7. continued)

5	1937	865	1019	1167
	1938	972	940	1160
	1939	1202	932	1118
6	1937	1017	1116	1025
	1938	953	961	1163
	1939	1088	956	984
7	1937	917	941	1102
	1938	761	768	883
	1939	729	688	669
8	1937	306	438	452
	1938	553	556	563
	1939	506	523	552
9	1938	473	418	401
	1939	475	398	374
10	1937	487	525	523
	1938	552	564	579
	1939	516	408	447
11	1938	544	447	452
	1939	480	442	472
12	1938	430	406	417
	1939	433	365	422
13	1938	478	439	433
	1939	556	442	448
14	1938	468	416	465
	1939	458	455	473
15	1937	101	212	235
	1938	155	179	197
	1939	125	187	178
16	1937	227	217	257
	1938	205	169	204
	1939	204	226	251
17	1937	230	286	305
	1938	245	254	259
	1939	257	199	215
18	1937	187	268	180
	1938	404	251	312
	1939	339	260	293
19	1937	83	79	93
	1938	107	90	112
	1939	143	127	133
20	1937	92	130	175
	1938	133	97	116
	1939	91	129	142

(Table 7.7. continued)

Notes: Allocative-optimal output estimated separately for
        large and non-large farms (sample division represent-
        ed by dotted line), using separate frontier technique
        sets and weights. It occasionally falls below the
        C-D predicted output, due in part to the more tight-
        ly bounded surface in factor space which is the
        isoquant of activity analysis (positive marginal
        productivity is assigned to all factors by the C-D
        function no matter how imbalanced the factor pro-
        portions, whereas activity analysis treats some
        resources as "slack" when factor proportions are
        imbalanced).

Table 7.8.   Summary Measures of Sub-Optimality of Production.

	Large Farms	Non-Large Farms
Mean, Observed Output	1143	325
Mean, C-D Predicted Output. . . .	1154	312
Mean, Allocative-Optimal Output	1219	327
Mean Deviation of Alloc.-Optimal from C-D Predicted, % of Observed	5.6 %	4.7%
Standard Error of Prediction: Observed Minus:		
C-D Predicted	164.9	65.0
Percent of Mean Observed. .	14.4 %	25.0 %
Allocative Optimal	198.8	60.9
Percent of Mean Observed. .	17.4 %	18.8 %

Loss due to allocative errors and factor underemployment does not include the additional losses due to maladjust-
ment with respect to the factor market, implied by slack
existing in some variables at the allocative optimum and
considerable variation among factor shadow prices on

different farms. Supposing it were possible to redistribute all resources equally among farms in the sample, and for each farm to concentrate on the one activity most profitable at existing factor prices (a cotton-producing technique), we can obtain a measure of the maximum possible improvement in output value. This turns out to be less than 15 percent of current average farm output value, adding about 10 percent to output foregone due to allocative inefficiency. More of course could be gained by consolidating existing farms into an average size sufficient to take advantage of returns to scale -- specifically, as much as an additional 25 percent of existing total output.

Therefore, given the existing institutional arrangements and size distribution of farms, given the existing allocation of factors among farms, given only the best local practices as the standard of existing technology, and given our assumption that most of the observed intertemporal variation in yields was beyond the control of peasants, then peasant agriculture in Mi-ch'ang was highly efficient, as measured by the less than 5 percent of potential output lost. More substantial gains, but still limited to at most 10 percent more, could follow from redistribution of land, labor power and capital among farms and complete specialization. More spectacular gains could only come from improved factor utilization on large farms, or from changes beyond our purview.

A second test of our assumption of peasant attempts to "optimize" and of our characterization of their production opportunities can be based on a comparison of actual with hypothetically optimal land allocation among crops. Inspection of Table 7.9. and of the data on which the "optimal" solutions were based suggest that errors remain in our model. A first problem is the failure of the model to find any kaoliang production desirable for large farms: This is due to a combination of a relatively high discount for this crop in the objective function of large farms (which differ from non-large farms in this respect) and a relative scarcity of labor. It may be, as previously suggested, that the lack of inclusion of the joint product, beans, in the value of output for kaoliang is to blame (and that the higher weight given to kaoliang for non-large farms unintentionally accounts for the missing value); it may also be that the apparently low average yields for kaoliang represent three straight years of poor harvests for that crop.

Table 7.9. Comparison of Actual and "Optimal" Land Allocation Among Crops, Mi-ch'ang Village Sample.

Farm	Year	Corn (%) Actual	Corn (%) Optimal	Kaoliang (%) Actual	Kaoliang (%) Optimal	Cotton (%) Actual	Cotton (%) Optimal
1	1937	13.9	17.0	36.2	0	49.9	83.0
2	1939	13.3	53.7	37.8	0	48.9	46.3
3	1937	7.6	11.2	35.9	0	56.6	88.8
	1938	9.4	35.1	35.2	0	55.4	64.9
	1939	12.0	56.1	33.2	0	54.9	43.9
4	1937	10.8	0	34.6	0	54.6	100.0

(Table 7.9. continued)

4	1938	7.1	30.9	38.2	0	54.7	69.1
	1939	8.4	40.3	43.8	0	47.9	59.7
5	1937	4.2	3.0	20.4	0	75.4	97.0
	1938	12.0	4.2	34.4	0	53.6	95.8
	1939	9.9	21.1	32.2	0	57.9	78.9
6	1937	0	0	13.1	0	86.9	100.0
	1938	10.4	0	7.3	0	82.3	100.0
	1939	0	2.2	12.5	0	87.5	97.8
7	1937	5.1	15.5	34.8	0	60.1	84.5
	1938	22.9	27.4	35.7	0	41.4	72.6
	1939	14.9	45.4	45.2	0	40.0	54.6
8	1937	15.2	37.0	31.4	16.2	53.4	46.9
	1938	20.4	49.8	30.4	12.0	49.2	38.2
	1939	16.5	41.6	41.9	26.0	41.6	32.4
9	1938	23.6	0	18.5	51.3	57.9	48.6
	1939	17.8	4.7	47.6	59.9	34.5	35.5
10	1937	7.9	27.7	27.4	17.3	64.7	55.0
	1938	21.4	8.8	19.6	24.2	59.0	67.0
	1939	14.4	40.8	25.3	17.0	60.3	42.2
11	1938	21.5	5.2	31.0	16.9	47.5	77.9
	1939	12.7	50.0	30.8	0	56.5	50.0
12	1938	20.0	0.3	45.9	44.5	34.1	55.3
	1939	14.2	37.6	28.5	13.2	57.2	49.2
13	1938	27.6	16.8	20.7	35.9	51.7	47.3
	1939	15.6	0	34.4	57.0	50.0	43.0
14	1938	15.8	0.3	19.2	44.6	65.1	55.1
	1939	14.2	0	18.9	43.4	66.9	56.6
15	1937	3.3	0	34.8	79.5	61.9	20.5
	1938	1.9	0	74.2	80.5	23.9	19.5
	1939	0	0	76.2	62.7	23.8	37.3
16	1937	27.4	0.5	23.8	45.1	48.8	54.3
	1938	15.7	69.0	50.6	0	33.7	31.0
	1939	27.0	0	30.1	46.9	42.9	53.1
17	1937	19.9	0	2.9	0	69.9	100.0
	1938	24.8	4.0	1.3	0	73.8	96.0
	1939	32.1	0	3.6	20.8	64.3	79.2
18	1937	0	33.8	0	21.4	100.0	44.8
	1938	3.3	5.2	10.0	8.8	86.7	86.0
	1939	12.2	9.9	6.8	0	81.1	90.1
19	1937	36.4	14.2	0	51.1	63.6	34.7
	1938	30.8	32.9	0	2.9	69.2	64.2
	1939	20.0	42.1	15.0	21.9	65.0	36.0
20	1937	0	1.5	50.0	32.4	50.0	66.1
	1938	8.2	0	51.0	71.5	40.8	28.5
	1939	9.6	4.9	42.2	40.2	48.2	54.9

(Table 7.9. continued)

Means:

Large Farm	9.5	21.4	31.2	0	59.3	78.6
Small Farm	17.9	15.8	26.3	31.3	55.8	52.8

While for non-large farms, our estimates of optimal crop acreages are on the average close to actual acreages planted, this is not very consoling if estimates for individual farms are far off. This does not seem to be the case in general with either cotton or kaoliang: Correlation coefficients between optimal and actual percentages are .53 and .58, respectively, for these crops. But for corn, optimal and actual percentages are in fact negatively correlated, though insignificant. The source of error lies in the frontier coefficients: Cotton and kaoliang techniques appearing in optimal solutions involve rather stable factor proportions, whereas frontier corn producing techniques show wide variation in factor proportions. By excluding from the frontier all "dominated" techniques, we may have eliminated some cotton and/or kaoliang producing techniques involving unusual factor proportions which might in fact appear efficient if the yield in the year in which they were observed or the quality of land on which they were raised had not been unusually poor. Consequently, whenever farm factor proportions deviate from a certain range, the linear-programming solutions require corn production to take up the slack. The error stems from insufficient data, particularily the too short time series.

Of course, not all deviations of optimal from actual crop acreage distributions represent errors in the model. For example, large farms on the average devote a higher proportion of their land to cotton and a smaller proportion to corn than do smaller farms, yet their factor proportions should dictate the reverse, both because the relative abundance of land on large farms favors land-intensive, labor-saving crops (such as corn) and because returns to scale are much more significant for corn than for either cotton or kaoliang (compare the yield figures in Table 7.5.). The optimal solutions pick up correctly the desireability of this shift in land allocation, and raise the question of why large farms specialized so heavily in cotton. One answer may be that non-large farms weighted corn more heavily than large farms because the former consumed it and the latter either did not or did so only to a lesser extent. If this is correct, then our neglect of the farm versus retail price distinction in our weighting scheme is at fault, as discussed earlier.

Thus, although for non-large farms, our model of production optimization frequently and on the average leads to accurate prediction of peasant behavior (how well the Cobb-Douglas production function approach would stand up under an

equally stringent test we leave an open question), we do find
that many deficiencies and ambiguities remain, largely
stemming from (the usual) inadequacies of the data on which
it was based.

Solution of the "duals" of the optimization problems for
each farm for the "shadow prices" of the factors of production reveals that the same weaknesses of data and/or
model which caused substantial misprediction of crop allocations results in improbably high variance in shadow prices.
These shadow prices should accurately represent the marginal
value productivities of the factors of production at the
existing input proportions on each farm.

As the Cobb-Douglas approach imposes an artificially
high degree of uniformity on factor MVPs, resulting from the
constant elasticity assumption, we expected the activity
analysis approach to yield greater variation among farms and
over time. The extent of variation attained for the shadow
prices of labor and land (see Table 7.10.) seems plausible,
with the possible exception of the high percentage of sample
observations with zero shadow prices for these resources.
The latter phenomenon does not in fact imply much "slack" in
these resources: Only 6.8% of total land and 2.8% of total
labor were treated as "surplus" at the optimum for each farm.

However, the distributions of the estimated shadow
prices of the various capital services are bimodal, generally

Table 7.10. Frequency Distributions and Means of Shadow
            Prices of Land and Labor, At Allocative
            Optimum.

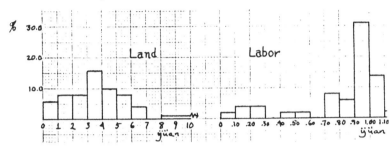

Means:	All Farms	Small Farms	Large Farms
Shadow Price of:			
Land	3.73	5.04	4.24
Labor.	.65	.44	.70
Percent of farms			
with zero shadow			
prices:			
Land	27 %	22 %	53 %
Labor.	22 %	33 %	29 %

either implausibly high or zero. This occurs because the

"frontier production techniques", as estimated, allow

considerably less variation in the proportions in which

capital services are used than is characteristic of the

sample. Thus, for most farms, one or two capital services

(frequently animal labor or tools, seeds and storage) appear

to have been serious "bottlenecks" (with shadow prices

several times larger than market values), while others were

substantially slack (i.e. surplus).

    While our inclination in seeking greater regularity in

the sample is to attribute these puzzling results to our

omission of an adequate variety of techniques from the estimated production frontier, it should be remembered that the
Cobb-Douglas approach to these data produced equally weak
results with respect to capital services (see Table 7.2).
What under activity analysis appears as a strange variation
in shadow prices there appears as insignificant elasticity
coefficients. Therefore the problem most probably lies in
the data: Either there were serious errors of measurement of
individual capital services*, or there was indeed a serious
maldistribution of capital among farms which was not
sufficiently alleviated by institutions of market or nonmarket exchange.

Supposing that the latter was the case, what was the
nature of this "maldistribution"? For the category of
"Other Capital Services", primarily tools and implements and
storage, an overall scarcity seems to have existed. Although
3.4 % of total "other capital" in the sample was computed to
be "slack", this quantity is more than balanced by the
shortages on other farms implied by high shadow prices
(frequently $20 per $1 market value). Moreover, a "surplus"

---

* or lack of homogeneity in land, which would cause low
   yields to be associated with high inputs of capital
   services in some cases.

of this type of capital existed only on the smallest farms, and the scarcity was greatest on large farms. No consistent patterns of scarcity or surplus emerge for animal labor or fertilizer.

Keeping in mind that errors in the analysis reflected in implausible shadow prices for capital services also affect the computed shadow prices of labor and land, we can return to consideration of the latter. Comparing the mean shadow prices for labor and land with the marginal value products computed from the Cobb-Douglas equation (Table 7.3), we find that the activity analysis approach gives generally lower estimates (because of the higher average shadow prices of some capital services). The difference is greatest for land: Most probably, the regression approach, with no consistent relationship between capital services and output, led to an upwards-bias in the elasticity with respect to land. The mean shadow prices (discounted implicitly for risk) for all farms are almost precisely equal to the average level of cash rent ($3.80) and total wage per day (about $.68). Comparing the means (in which zero shadow prices are included) with the modes of the distributions,* little difference is apparent for land, whereas about half of the sample have shadow prices of labor over $.90.

---

* from which the percentages of zero shadow prices have been omitted.

Dividing the sample into large (over 45 mou), small
(under 20 mou and primarily tenants) and medium-sized farms
(owners and part-tenants), some interesting differences in
shadow prices are apparent: Large farms on the average have
shadow prices of both land and labor not far different from
market rates, not surprisingly since these farms participate
in both markets, as net rentiers and hirers of labor. Small
farms (here, one owner-cultivator, one part-tenant, and
four tenants) maintain shadow prices of land well above the
average market rent level, but of labor, well below the
average wage level. The distribution of "slack" resources,
as signalled by zero shadow prices, follows the same
pattern. Moreover, the activity analysis, contrary to the
results of the Cobb-Douglas approach, suggests that the
shadow price of land on small farms is higher than on large
farms, as we have consistently asserted.

However, the "medium-sized" farms (20-45 mou) are quite
maladjusted with respect to the factor market: Their
labor/land ratio is apparently too low, as the shadow price
of labor ($.83) is well above and of land ($2.23) well below
market levels. Yet this group of farms not only hire a
substantial part of their labor force, but also rent much of
their land! We find this result impossible to explain.

These measurements of shadow prices of course hold good
only if producers are actually operating at the allocative

optimum as estimated. Since individual producers, as seen above, did frequently deviate from the optimal crop allocations, individual sets of shadow prices may well misrepresent the true scarcities of inputs at the observed allocative pattern. However, since on the average our model is not far from the mark in predicting either allocation or average output, we are of the opinion that the activity analysis estimated marginal value productivities (shadow prices), when grouped and averaged, better approximate true factor scarcities than do the Cobb-Douglas estimates.

Conclusions

The activity analysis approach to efficiency measurement, developed as an alternative to the neoclassical approach of estimating aggregate production functions through ordinary least squares regression techniques, is a viable response to some of the caviats we have raised concerning the latter method. Viewing productive relationships as a disaggregated set of activities rather than as manifestations of an all-embracing aggregate production function forces more explicit consideration of various types of inefficiency, the impact of risk and the nature of peasant perceptions of their production opportunities. If this leads to unresolved problems, it still adds greater realism and plausibility to the analysis.

On the other hand, one of the greatest strengths of
activity analysis efficiency measurement may also be its
greatest weakness: In the absence of information to the
contrary, it presumes no marginal relationship between inputs and outputs (that is, treats a given resource as "slack"
or surplus), assumes the "null hypothesis", so to speak.
The conventional approach tends to assume what requires
proof, and in the process to "homogenize" estimates of
factor marginal productivity. However, while extreme
variation in factor marginal productivities, bounded only by
zero and the average product, may be a truer representation
of real-world productive processes than near-homogeneity,
the human inclination is to find similarity more plausible
than difference. To compete with the ability of the Cobb-
Douglas and similar neoclassical production functions to
extrapolate into the voids of factor space, the activity
analysis approach requires a much larger quantity of data,
in which extreme factor proportions are well-represented.

It should also be reassuring to supporters of the
regression approach, and to readers of our previous chapter,
that although the alternative approaches yield somewhat
different results, especially as we move away from the mean
of the data, the differences are explainable and not so great
as to refute the conclusions which may be drawn from either
approach. In particular, both approaches show, in the context of a particular North China village, that peasants are

not on the average particularily inefficient in either their allocative decisions or their use of the factor market. As the analysis of differences between optimal and actual output values suggested, such inefficiency as exists has no great quantitative significance, <u>within</u> <u>the</u> <u>context</u> of existing institutions and inequality of distribution.

CHAPTER VIII.   SUMMARY AND CONCLUSIONS

The fundamental theme of this dissertation is that the basic decision-making unit of the peasant economy is in essence a family firm, with assets (family labor and capital) fixed in the short run.   The objective function of such an enterprise requires the maximization of some function of expected net income and its variance, subject to the limitations of these assets and to the opportunities for exchange offered by existing factor markets.   The peasant economy is further distinguished from a developed, agricultural economy largely by the characteristics of technology, the low levels of firm assets, and the strong influence of uncertainty which results therefrom.   Differences in economic behavior among enterprises are primarily a product of differences in asset levels and structures, as in modernized economies, rather than being a result of qualitative differences in motivations.

If we explore the nature of partial equilibrium relationships in the peasant microeconomy following the above approach, theoretical contortions are not required to explain observed characteristics of that economy.   By contrast, previous approaches have strained credulity in their reliance on alleged motivation or behavior of economic classes of decision-makers which is at variance with individual or family self-interest.

Much of the discussion above has focussed on the partial equilibrium relationship between the value of the marginal productivity of labor on farms of different size and the wage rate for farm labor. Since it was quite apparent that labor intensity in production varies inversely with farm size in peasant economies, and on strict neoclassical assumptions about the nature of the "production function", the marginal product of labor could be presumed to decline with increased labor intensity, there were grounds to suspect that the wage level was above the MVP of small farms and/or below that of large farms.

We have tried to show that this conclusion need not be correct, although strictly speaking we only wished to establish that considerable variation in labor intensity could occur without _much_ effect on labor's marginal productivity. For example, if greater labor intensity (relative to land) is also associated with greater capital intensity, the fall in the marginal product of labor need not be great. Moreover, some crops are significantly more favorable to labor than others, and by varying the proportions of each crop produced, it might be possible to maintain fairly stable marginal productivities over a wide range of factor proportions.

In looking for evidence on these points from the Chinese example, we were able to show that at least labor intensity

was not consistently negatively correlated with capital intensity: The overall relationship may have varied from
locality to locality, depending in part on the relative
importance of different types of capital services, but seems
to us to have been slightly positive on the average. For the
sample used in Chapter VII., small farms were both more
labor and more capital intensive, even though they were on
the average no more specialized in cotton (the labor-and
capital-using crop) than larger farms.

It is more difficult to establish that the elasticity of
substitution between labor and land is very high: Since
almost all production data involves high collinearity between labor/land ratios and size of farm, it is impossible to
assemble data exhibiting sufficient variation in the former
at a roughly constant output level to permit accurate
specification of the curvature of individual isoquants. As
we have indicated previously, econometric estimates of the
Cobb-Douglas production function (which "forces" a unit
elasticity of substitution) cannot distinguish between a
high elasticity of substitution and increasing returns to

scale.* Since our estimates of the Chinese agricultural

production function consistently indicate increasing

returns, they were at least consistent with a "true" high

elasticity of substitution. More direct evidence may be

drawn from the activity analysis of the Mi-ch'ang data:

Although the elasticity of substitution over the full range

of factor proportions was by no means infinite, due in good

part to constraints on some capital elements, still about 60

percent of farms were characterized by shadow prices of

labor between $.70 and 1.10, within which range the labor/

land ratio varied from 7.2 to 11.6 man-days/mou. In this

North China village, much greater labor intensity than this

was associated with an apparent labor surplus, although, as

we have pointed out above, this result may be a product of

our inability to find among the data _efficient_ techniques

---

* As an afterthought, we generated an artificial data set

   based on the specification, $Q_i = (\alpha L_i + \beta K_i)^\lambda$, where

   $\lambda = 1.15$ is a scale coefficient, then fit a C-D pro-

   duction function to the data. The resulting fit was very

   close, and with returns to scale equal to 1.39. Since

   the input data was generated to be collinear, the C-D

   function was able to approximate constant marginal pro-

   ductivity ratios with the aid of an exaggerated scale

   coefficient.

with such labor intensity (only two farms operated with labor intensity beyond this range).

Such variation in marginal productivities as does occur we have sought to explain largely in terms of the effects of increasing returns to scale and uncertainty on input utilization. For example, factor indivisibility and market imperfections could account for considerable deviation from marginal optimality conditions in a world of tiny economic units. In the absence of part-time labor opportunities at appropriate times, family labor may remain underutilized ("slack") except during the busiest seasons. This in fact may account for our finding such low marginal productivities for fertilizer in both the Buck and Mi-ch'ang studies: Fertilizer was generally collected by family labor during slack seasons, when the opportunity cost of labor was close to zero, hence it might have been economically optimal to apply it to the point where response rates fell to near-zero. This also accounts for the persistence of low-paid handicrafts like wine and beancurd-making.

The problem of scale is undoubtedly greater for "lumpy" capital services, however. Although for Mi-ch'ang we found an average gross rate of return of about 14% on investments in both land and capital services, the return on the latter was frequently either extremely high or zero, as would follow from indivisibility problems. We also found small farms to have a slight surplus (slack) of tools and equipment, but a serious deficit on large farms. Unfortunately, the Buck data did not adequately cover capital services, so our analysis of this item is sketchy.

We argued that the inferior quality of hired labor would lead larger (hiring) farms to keep labor intensity below the levels which estimated marginal productivity per laborer would seem to warrant (if labor were homogeneous). No confirmation of this point was found in our analysis of the Buck data, where, however, the many possibilities of error weaken the conclusions. Nor, in the Mi-ch'ang analysis, were the shadow prices of labor on large farms significantly above the wage level. There thus seems to be little or no quantitative significance to this effect.

One of the theoretical bases for expecting increasing returns lay in the expectation that farm fragmentation would decrease with farm size. We were able to verify from the Buck data that both average number of plots decreased and average size of plot increased with farm size. Moreover, the regional differences in estimated returns to scale proved significantly related to the extent of consolidation as farm size increased. This happened to be a conveniently measureable factor, however; the existence of one meaningful explanatory factor does not rule out the importance of others which could not be measured.

The implications of uncertainty, or generalized risk,
for partial equilibrium relationships in the productive
sphere is of particular interest in the study of peasant
economies because a) output levels in agriculture are more
subject to random influences than is true of industry; b) the
low level of peasant agricultural technology does little to
mitigate the impact of random factors; c) the absence of
well-lubricated market structures may amplify random disturbances*; d) income levels are close enough to subsistence
that random disturbances frequently threaten survival;
e) production units based on the family will be sensitive
to uncertainty in all factor markets which generate family
income. If the existence of uncertainty causes divergence
from optimal marginality conditions in theory, then the
quantitative significance of this effect would surely be
greatest in peasant economies.

In the absence of adequate time-series data, it is
difficult to measure the extent of uncertainty, unless we
choose to assume that some types of observed cross-sectional
variation are actually the product of random intertemporal

---

* if random influences are not geographically uniform,
market arbitrage can serve to reduce fluctuations in
supply and demand.

variation. This problem has limited our ability to test the importance of uncertainty on the basis of Chinese data.

However, the divergencies between values of marginal productivity of the factors of production and nominal market prices predicted to result from the presence of risk are amply confirmed in the Chinese case. It seems clear from our analysis that farms which were most probably net renters of land (i.e. small farms) kept the expected MVP of land well above market rent levels. Similarily net sellers of labor (again, small farms) used more labor on their own farms than nominal wage levels would justify in the absence of un- certainty. Again, wealthier peasants (i.e. large farms) utilize both labor and land in proportions closer to those which would follow from risk-neutrality and maximization of expected net incomes, which could be attributed to decreasing risk aversion with increased income.

However, correlation does not indicate causation; the theoretical argument would be more convincing had we been able to provide tests of higher power.

Unfortunately, our two attempts to quantify uncertainty do not constitute convincing evidence of its pervasive influence. We had expected to find some clear correlation between measures of the risk of agricultural calamity and the geographical incidence of the sharecropping system. We found only weak correlation, though we are more inclined to

doubt the accuracy of our measures or of the implied ceteris
paribus condition than to reject our hypothesis. We had
expected that differences in riskiness could account in good
part for choice of crop mix in Mi-ch'ang, although there
was no reason why this factor should have been more important
than others. In the event we discovered that complicated
risk-discount expressions in hypothetical peasant objective
functions reduced in evaluation to minor quantitative magnitudes. While these results do not bear directly on the major
partial equilibrium relationships we were interested in,
they surely suggest a need for further quantitative investigation of the influence of uncertainty.

An important part of such investigation must be devoted
to the relationship between nominal and actual expected rates
of return in the "loan market" in peasant economies. It is
obvious that nominal rates were quite high; we have produced
substantial evidence, from rent and land price data and from
production function studies, that the return on productive
investment in agriculture was reasonably high on the average,
but not sufficient to justify borrowing for productive
purposes (except at sub-market rates of interest), nor
sufficient to explain why most peasants preferred to keep a
large part of their assets in land and productive capital, in
the absence of high risks attached to moneylending. It would
be useful, for analytical and policy purposes, to be able to

verify that expected rates of return in moneylending were higher than expected rates of return on productive investments only to an extent justifiable by differences in risk.

As the above discussion indicates, we have attempted throughout the empirical chapters of this dissertation to test, using Chinese data, the implications of our theoretical explanation of the salient characteristics of the peasant economy. In our judgment, theory and data have proved sufficiently consistent to demonstrate that, with appropriate modifications to account for the peculiar conditions faced in peasant economies, the neoclassical theory of the distribution of income, relying heavily on the theory of production, is indeed relevant.

APPENDIX II-A. PROOF OF RELATION BETWEEN NUMBER OF CONS_STRAINTS AND NUMBER OF TECHNIQUES*

Assume n production techniques for a single good, $F_i(X_j, V_k)$, where X_j is a vector of r factors of production available on the market at prices w_j; and V_k is a vector of (m - r) factors with which the firm is initially endowed in fixed amounts $\bar{V}_k$.

The problem is to maximize $p\sum_i F_i - \sum_i\sum_j x_{ij}w_j$ subject to $\sum_i v_{ik} = \bar{V}_k$.

Maximization requires, first, that $\delta F_i/\delta x_{ij} = w_j/p$ for each i and j; this gives us (n x r) equations, allowing us to solve for the (n x r) x_{ij} in terms of the v_{ij}. These solutions permit us to express the maximand (the net revenue function) in terms of the v_{ij} alone.

Since the F_i are, by assumption, first-degree homogeneous and the first derivatives thus zero-degree homogeneous, the above maximization conditions imply that a proportional increase in the v_{ij} requires an equi-proportional increase in the x_{ij}, so the net revenue function $R(V_k)$ itself will be first-degree homogeneous in the v_{ij} when the x_{ij} are used in optimal amounts. Furthermore, a set of isorevenue surfaces for any _particular_ F_i will be convex to the origin.

The remainder of the proof is best sketched graphically for a case in which there are only two v_j, say capital and land. The isorevenue curves for two techniques are sketched

* The directions of this proof were suggested by Chulsoon Khang.

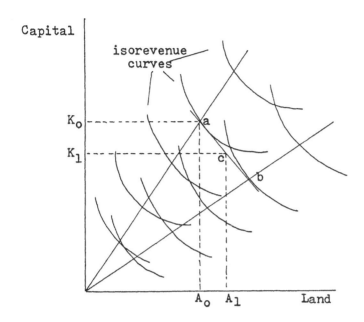

in the figure, along with different constraints for the
v_j (e.g. $[K_o, A_o]$, $[K_1, A_1]$). A linear combination of any
two production activities which will produce equivalent
net revenues can be depicted as a line tangent to two isorevenue curves offering the same net revenues (thus any
additional production functions with higher isorevenue
curves will be dominated by two such functions which offer
equal net revenues with lower use of the two fixed resources).

It should be obvious that maximum net revenue, given the
two constraints, will be reached at the point where one such
tangent line goes through the point formed by the intersection of the two constraint lines; that this may involve the

use of only one production function (as at a) or a combination of two (as at c), depending on the factor endowments.
For two constraints, no more than two production functions
will be used.

It follows that, even with constant returns production
functions, in an economy in which there is more than one
non-marketable factor of production with which firms are
unequally endowed, considerable difference in technique
and in factor ratios may be observed.

If the underlying production functions are homogeneous
of other than the first degree, these results must be qualified somewhat: With diminishing returns, the tangent line
between two isorevenue curves is replaced by a line convex
to the origin, representing mixed use of production functions
offering equal net revenues; the conclusions are unaltered,
except that a single fixed asset, tradable on the market for
other factors (i.e. equivalent to a budget constraint), will
then lead to uniform use of mixed production processes but
at uniform factor proportions.

With increasing returns, on the other hand, it pays to
specialize, even with two factors, provided that the gains
from specialization are not outweighed by the possible gains
from the greater factor substitutibility allowed by mixing
(graphically, the line a-b becomes concave to the origin, and
may or may not be dominated, at a particular factor endowment, by the isorevenue curve from either production func-

tion used alone). Increasing returns thus serve to narrow the range of fixed factor proportions within which technique mixing will be optimal. The greater the elasticity of substitution for either production technique and the smaller the difference in factor "favorability" (as previously defined), the more likely it is that specialization will occur. Moreover, the increased substitutibility resulting from a factor market will in this case lead to a breakdown of diversified production.

APPENDIX II-B. FACTOR ALLOCATION IN THE PRESENCE OF UNCERTAINTY[*]

Assume that the producer operates with a production function, $F(L)$, characterized by diminishing returns to the one
variable, marketable input, L; that the producer is also
aware that his realized production, $\gamma F(L)$, is affected by a
stochastic scale factor, γ, which, for simplicity of analysis
we may also assume is decomposable into an expression:

$\gamma = \alpha(L)\theta + \beta$, where θ is the random variate. Define a
"small increase in risk as a 'stretching' of the probability
distribution around a constant mena."[**] We thus wish to vary
α and β in such a way that $\delta\beta/\delta\alpha = -E[\theta]$, or

$\delta\gamma/\delta\alpha = \theta + \delta\beta/\delta a = \theta - E[\theta]$.

We also choose to assume that γ is not independent of the factor L, but rather an increase in L tends to decrease the
extent of risk, or $\delta\alpha/\delta L < 0$; that the producer has a utility
function of his net income, $U(C)$, characterized by risk-aversion, i.e. $U'(C) > 0$ and $U''(C) < 0$; that he attempts to
maximize the expected utility of his net income,

$U(C) = U[\gamma F(L) - wL]$, letting the price of output be a
numeraire and letting w represent the market price of input L.

The first-order conditions for the producer's interior
maximum are:[***]

---

[*] The approach is borrowed from Bardhan and Srinivasan,
"Cropsharing Tenancy in Agriculture: A Theoretical and Empiri-

$$E\left\{U'(C)[\gamma F' + F(\delta\gamma/\delta L) - w]\right\} = 0$$

Rearranging and noting that

$$\delta\gamma/\delta L = [\theta + \delta\beta/\delta\alpha](\delta\alpha/\delta L) = (\theta - E[\theta])(\delta\alpha/\delta L), \text{ we have:}$$

$$E[U'(C)\gamma F'] + E\left\{U'(C)F[\theta - E(\theta)](\delta\alpha/\delta L)\right\} = E[U'(C)w]$$

Subtracting $E[U'(C)E(\gamma)F']$ from both sides of this expression gives:

$$E\left\{U'(C)F'[\gamma - E(\gamma)]\right\} + E\left\{U'(C)F[\theta - E(\theta)](\delta\alpha/\delta L)\right\}$$
$$= E[U'(C)][w - E(\gamma)F'] \qquad (1)$$

Now let $\pi_1(\gamma) = U'(C)F'$ and $\pi_2(\gamma) = U'(C)F$ in the expression above; by strict concavity, we have $\pi_1'(\gamma) < 0$ and $\pi_2'(\gamma) < 0$ and it must hold that $E[\pi(\gamma)] < \pi[E(\gamma)]$ for both π_1 and π_2. Therefore:

$$E\left\{U'(C)F'[\gamma - E(\gamma)]\right\} < U'[E(C)]F'E[\gamma - E(\gamma)] = 0 \qquad (2)$$

and

$$E\left\{U'(C)F[\theta - E(\theta)]\right\} < U'[E(C)]FE[\theta - E(\theta)] = 0 \qquad (3)$$

Since $\delta\alpha/\delta L < 0$ and since the sign of $[\gamma - E(\gamma)]$ is the same as that of $[\theta - E(\theta)]$ for $\alpha > 0$, results (2) and (3)

---

cal Approach," <u>AER</u>, March 1971, pp. 62-63; A. Sandmo, "On the Theory of the Competitive Firm under Price Uncertainty," in the same issue, pp. 66-68.

** Sandmo, <u>op</u>. <u>cit</u>., p. 67.

*** The second-order conditions do <u>not</u> restrict the firm to increasing marginal cost at the maximum point.

together establish that the signs of the first two terms in
equation (1) are respectively negative and positive. We
We may describe these as the effect of pure uncertainty and
the insurance effect of inputs respectively. Since
$E[U'(C)] > 0$, it is apparent that the sign of $[w - E(\gamma)F']$
depends on the relative importance of these two effects.
That is, the effect of pure uncertainty in itself is to
induce the producer to use less of the input (and produce
less output) than would be necessary if the expected value of
the marginal product of the factor were to be equated with
its price (the rule in the absence of uncertainty and/or
risk aversion). This is because the higher the output, the
greater the variance (since the uncertainty parameter enters
multiplicatively), and the risk-averting producer will keep
the expected marginal value productivity of an input high
enough to compensate for the variability of marginal returns.

On the other hand, if increased use of the input can also
reduce the degree of variance -- e.g. protecting the peasant
against the weather variation, pestilence, etc. -- this
"insurance effect" will induce him to increase his input beyond
the level dictated by "pure uncertainty", conceivably beyond
the certainty-equivalent level (some inputs may have little
effect on average yields, but may significantly reduce the
variation in yields, although it is difficult to think of
significant examples of inputs which reduce the "spread"
of the distribution without simultaneously skewing it.

Organizational arrangements, such as choice of crops or
seed types and deliberate fragmentation of holdings, more
frequently decrease variance while often _decreasing_ expected yield).

APPENDIX III-A. CHOICE-THEORETIC APPROACHES TO RENTAL DEPOSITS

Landlord Optimization:

We make the following assumptions and definitions:

i' = nominal rate of interest on loans;

i = actual realized rate of return on loans, a random variable such that $E(i) = \bar{i}$ and $\sigma_i > 0$;

A_1 = proportion of money invested in land;

$A_2 = 1 - A_1$ = proportion of money invested in loans;

r = rental rate of return on land value, assumed to be certain -- that is, no risk is involved in land investment.

Let:

$i' = \bar{i} + k$, where $k > 0$ is a constant defined as the difference between the nominal rate of interest and $E(i)$;

$W = rA_1 + i'A_2 = r + (i'-r)A_2$ is the nominal or "apparent" portfolio rate of return, a weighted average of the certain rate of return on land investment and the nominal rate of return on loans;

$R = rA_1 + iA_2 = r + (i-r)A_2$ is the actual, realized rate of return on portfolio.

Then:

$$E(R) = r + (\bar{i}-r)A_2 = r + (i'-k-r)A_2 = W - kA_2 \qquad (1)$$

$$\sigma_R = A_2\sigma_i \text{ or } A_2 = \sigma_R/\sigma_i \qquad (2)$$

where σ_R is a measure of portfolio risk.

In portfolio analysis, it is frequently assumed that the

investor's satisfaction is a function of both the expected
return and the uncertainty or risk involved, i.e.

$U = U[E(R), \sigma_R]$ where $U_1 > 0$ and $U_2 < 0$, if the investor is
a "risk averter". This implies that the slope of the indifference curves between $E(R)$ and σ_R is positive, since
$\delta E(R)/\delta \sigma_R = -U_2/U_1$ along an indifference curve. Tobin[*] further
distinguishes two subtypes of risk averters: plungers and
diversifiers. A plunger is an investor whose utility function has the characteristics, $U_{12} > 0$ and $U_{22} > 0$, that is,
the more risk he accepts in his portfolio, the less reluctant he is to accept further risks and the more easily he is
compensated by increased expected return. The more "normal"
investor's psychology is presumably that of the diversifier,
with $U_{12} < 0$ and $U_{22} < 0$; he is more likely to end up with a
balanced portfolio if an appropriate tradeoff between risk and
return is offered him. The diversifying risk averter has an
indifference relationship between $E(R)$ and σ_R with an
increasingly steep slope; vice versa for the plunger. This
may be seen by examining the sign of the change in the slope
of the indifference curve with respect to σ_R:

$U_{12}U_2/U_1^2 - U_{22}/U_1 > 0$ for diversifier; < 0 for plunger.

Now we can also employ equations (1) and (2) to express
the tradeoff between $E(R)$ and σ_R in the landlord's portfolio

---

[*] J. Tobin, "Liquidity Preference as Behavior Towards Risk,"
Rev. of Economic Studies 26 (1958), pp. 65-86.

as defined above, transformed into more accessible components
and allowing r to vary with the proportion of portfolio in
land investment:

$$\delta E(R)/\delta\sigma_R = (\delta W/\delta A_2)\sigma_i^{-1} - k\sigma_i^{-1}$$
$$= (i' - r - A_2\delta r/\delta A_2)\sigma_i^{-1} - k\sigma_i^{-1} \quad (3)$$

In the following analysis, we intend to employ (3) to
show that the "revealed preferences" of a group of landlords
between various combinations of rental and loan income at
varying rental rates on land value were such as to imply that
these landlords were "diversifying risk averters." While this
is not a surprising result, it helps account for the relationship between land and money markets in peasant China in choice-
theoretic terms.

The landlords of Hupei's Tsaoyang county (1933) offered
their tenants a choice among the following combinations of
rental deposits and annual rents on land valued at 2000
ch'uan; we consider it reasonable to assume that the magnitudes chosen were such that landlords were "indifferent" as
to which combinations were actually chosen:

Although the landlord's funds
were nominally tied up in land,
the rental deposits permitted
him to convert part of his total

Deposit	Annual Rent
1500 ch'uan	none
500	70 ch'uan
300	90
none	120

investment (proportion A_2) into loans at a nominal rate of
interest i', probably about 24 percent per year or more;

but in so doing, he earned a lower rate of return (r) on
the remainder of his investment $(A_1 = 1 - A_2)$, which we
may calculate by dividing the remaining rent by the difference between the value of land and the deposit (for 10 mow,
land value = 2000 ch'uan). We may thus construct the
following table, containing elements of equations (1) and (3):

W	A_2	r	i'	dr/dA_2	$A_2 dr/dA_2$
.180	.75	0	.24	0	0
.095	.25	.047	.24	-.093	-.023
.081	.15	.053	.24	-.063	-.009
.060	0	.060	.24	-.047	0

Now, using equations (2) and (3), the following represents the slope of the landlord's indifference curve
between $E(R)$ and σ_R for constant but unknown $E(i)$ and σ_i
at four different observations on r and A_2:

$$R = \qquad 0 \qquad .15\sigma_i \qquad .25\sigma_i \qquad .75\sigma_i$$
$$\delta E(R)/\delta\sigma_R = (.18-k)/\sigma_i \quad (.20-k)/\sigma_i \quad (.22-k)/\sigma_i \quad (.24-k)/\sigma_i$$

The sign(s) of $\delta E(R)/\delta\sigma_R$ depend on the magnitude of k,
that is on the spread between nominal loan interest rate
i' and the expected realized rate, $E(i)$. We can only
establish a range for this constant if we assume that landlords are at least not risk-seekers -- that is, they will
never prefer a risky asset to a riskless one if the expected
rates of return are the same. In this case it can be deduced
that, with the rate of return on a relatively riskless asset,
land, = 120/2000 = .06, that the expected rate of return on

the risky asset (loans), $E(i) = \bar{i}$ must be greater than
120/1500 = .08, the rate of return which would bring
the landlord exactly the same annual income as he obtains
from rentals with no deposits. Thus $k \leq .24 - .08 = .16$
follows from the assumption that landlords could not be
indifferent between no deposits and a rental return on
investment of .06 and a situation where no rental income
is received, but an equivalent income on the average and
over the long run is received from loaning out rental
deposits.

With $k \leq .16$, the slope of the indifference curve is
positive and increasing, so that the landlords display risk
aversion of the "diversifying" sort. That is, the observed
tradeoffs between rental deposits and rent in Tsao-yang
county are thoroughly consistent with normal investor
behavior when the difference in risk between land investment
and loans is taken into account.

Tenant Optimization

Definitions and assumptions:

K_o, L_o = money capital and labor stocks of prospective
tenants;

A_2 = proportion of K_o invested in rental deposits;

A_3 = proportion of K_o invested in land purchase;

$1 - A_2 - A_3 = A_1$ = proportion of K_o loaned out;

$Q(L,Z)$ = production function (Z = land);

$Z = Z_1 + Z_2$ = land rented + land purchased;

$r(h)$ = rental rate on land value, as determined by

$h = A_2 K_0 / p_z Z_1$, the proportion of land value advanced as rental deposits, where $r'(h) < 0$ and $0 < h < .75$;

$i' = E(i) + c$, where i' is the "certainty equivalent" rate of return, i.e. the rate of return on a riskless invest-ment which a tenant would be willing to pay to escape the risk ($c < 0$). We do not intend to make use of this expression, except to point out that the absolute magnitude of c is likely to be quite high for the average tenant and i' rather low, so that tenants are unlikely to engage in direct lending without the insurance which a financial intermediary provides;

p, p_z = commodity and land prices, respectively.

We take as the object of tenant's maximization his annual net income, Y_T, defined as follows; we neglect physi-cal capital as an element in production costs and investment and off-farm wage income as an alternative opportunity (these complicate but do not improve the analysis):

$$Y_T = i'K_0(1-A_2-A_3) + pQ[L_0, Z_1+Z_2] - r(h)p_z Z_1$$
$$= i'K_0(1-A_2-A_3) + pQ[L_0, Z_1+A_3 K_0/p_z] - r(A_2 K_0/p_z Z_1)p_z Z_1$$

Maximizing with respect to A_2, A_3 and Z_1, we have:

$$\delta Y_T/\delta A_2 = -i'K_0 - (\delta r/\delta h)(\delta h/\delta A_2)p_z Z_1$$
$$= -i'K_0 - K_0 \delta r/\delta h = 0 \tag{a}$$
$$\delta Y_T/\delta A_3 = -i'K_0 + p(\delta Q/\delta Z)K_0/p_z = 0 \tag{b}$$

$$\delta Y_T/\delta Z_1 = p\delta Q/\delta Z - (\delta r/\delta h)(\delta h/\delta Z_1)p_z Z_1 - r(h)p_z$$

$$= p\delta Q/\delta Z + (\delta r/\delta h)A_2 K_0/Z_1 - r(h)p_z = 0 \qquad (c)$$

Dividing equations (a) and (b) by K_0 and (c) by p_z and rearranging, we find that the tenant should, if feasible, allocate his funds K_0 between land purchase, loans and rental deposits, and allocate his total land use (purchased and rented), such that the following are all equal to each other:

(1) i': the "certainty equivalent" rate of return on loans

(2) $-\delta r/\delta h$: the incremental effect of increased rental deposits on rent, expressed as a rate relative to land value;

(3) $(p/p_z)(\delta Q/\delta Z)$: the marginal productivity of land per unit of land value (the "natural rate of return");

(4) $r - h\delta r/\delta h = (R - A_2 K_0 \delta r/\delta h)(1/p_z Z_1)$: the "opportunity cost" of renting an additional unit of land, measured as the sum of the rent (post-deposits, if any) and the total return to investment in rental deposits, measured at the margin, relative to the value of land rented (R = total rent post-deposits).

These maximization conditions are very confusing to analyze, because so many interrelationships are involved. However, it appears that, given the Shao-yang schedule, it is impossible for all maximization conditions to be satisfied. We have, first, the following givens:

h	r	$-\delta r/\delta h$	$r-h\delta r/\delta h$
0	.060	.10	.060
.15	.045	.10	.060
.25	.035	.07	.053
.75	0	0	0

Since $-\delta r/\delta h$ is always larger than $r-h\delta r/\delta h$ (except at h = .75, where all variables go to zero), clearly they cannot be equated whatever the allocations selected by the tenant. Secondly, since i' includes a large negative risk premium, it is likely to be too small for the tenants to put any funds into direct loans. The tenant will, moreover, only invest in land purchase if (3), the rate of return on land investment (or the "natural rate"), is greater than $-\delta r/\delta h$. Evidence provided in the text (Chapter III) suggests that the former (net of taxes) is close to 10% on the average, so the two rates of return are quite comparable. Therefore it would seem that the tenant might simultaneously purchase and rent land and invest in rental deposits; as long as the "natural rate" (3) was greater than the "real rental rate" (4), the tenant would desire to rent more land, in turn raising $-\delta r/\delta h$ and inducing further investment in rental deposits. It is likely, given constraint K_o, that the tenant would run out of capital before $-\delta r/\delta h$ fell far, leaving him at an equilibrium where (2) = (3) > (4). That is, the overall poverty of tenants created on the one hand lucrative opportunities in moneylending for whatever capital landlords could mobilize, and on the other constrained the supply of savings which could be mobilized via rental deposits. The landlords were in this instance serving as financial intermediaries between tenant lenders and tenant borrowers, absorbing risks too high for smaller lenders and reaping high returns as rewards. Since the main near-riskless alternative for small lenders was land investment, landlords were forced to offer net rates of return on rental deposits of roughly equal magnitude to induce tenant lending.

APPENDIX IV-A. AVERAGE FAMILY INCOMES AND THE DISTRIBUTION
OF INCOME IN THE CHINESE PEASANT ECONOMY

The available data on farm family average incomes and
expenditures in the prewar period (primarily in the early
1920s) is summarized in Table A. The "typicality" of many
of the areas studied is open to question: For instance,
comparison with postwar materials suggests that the villages
sampled in Lien-chiang <u>hsien</u> in Fukien were as relatively
prosperous for that county as the county was compared to
others in Fukien.[a.] The income distribution in Su <u>hsien</u>,
Anhwei, was exceptionally skewed towards higher income groups,
resulting in high average incomes (see Table C.). Moreover,
variation in incomes between samples within a single <u>hsien</u>
is sometimes enormous (witness the three Chiang-ning sample
income averages). Considering these facts, it seems most
probable that mean family income in rural China in the early
1920s must have been between 100 and 200 yüan and, with an
average family size of about 5 persons, per capita income
probably between 30 and 35 yüan (or 25-30 yüan if largely
imputed items like rent and fuel are excluded). Since prices
received and paid by farmers (including material inputs and
labor) rose uniformily by about 35 percent between 1922 and
1930[b.], current yüan per capita rural income by the latter
date must have approached from 33 to 40 yüan.

The average income is by no means the whole story, however.
Table B. and Graph 1. summarize the available information on

TABLE A. SAMPLE SURVEY RESULTS FOR NET FARM FAMILY INCOME AND CONSUMP-
TION, VARIOUS LOCALITIES, CHINA, 1922-1934

Locality	Date	Source	Family Income	Family Expenditure	Savings/ Dissavings	Per Caput Income	Net of Rent;Fuel
Hopei:							
Pinghsiang	1923	(1)	137.1	88.6	+48.5	30.9	26.2
Yenshan	1922	(1)	144.4	113.1	+31.3	27.0	21.7
Yenshan	1923	(1)	122.4	155.2	-32.8	23.7	16.9
Ting hsien	1928-9	(2)	281.1	242.6	+38.5	46.4	40.2
Peiping vi- cinity	1927	(2,3)	217.0	235.2	-18.2	36.2	30.0
" "	1926	(2,3)	180.8	164.0	+16.8	44.5	39.4
" "	1923	(3)	--	135.0	--	--	--
Honan:							
Hsincheng	1923	(1)	348.6	258.6	+90.0	50.0	44.7
Kaifeng	1923	(1)	405.8	349.7	+56.1	51.8	47.5
Shansi:							
Wuhsiang	1922	(1)	160.7	115.3	+45.4	35.6	30.0
Kiangsu:							
Chiangning	1923	(1)	517.9	338.8	+179.1	89.7	80.8
"	1923	(1)	200.6	251.3	-50.7	30.3	23.7
Wuchin	1924	(1)	275.4	293.3	-17.9	56.5	47.4
Chiangning	1934	(2)	191.6	228.2	-36.6	34.6	30.1
Nanking vicinity	1930	(4)	--	--	--	62.0***	--
Anhwei:							
Huaiyüan	1924	(1)	171.7	185.2	-13.5	33.0	28.0
Su hsien	1923	(1)	254.6	259.3	+4.7	82.3	78.3
Lai-an	1922	(1)	366.0	223.1	+142.9	64.0	54.0
Hupien	1924	(3)	--	157.1	--	31.4	26.4
Chekiang:							
Linan	1930	(4)	--	113.7**	--	--	--
Fukien:							
Lienchiang	1922	(1)	499.0	336.7	+162.3	99.5	90.5
Szechwan:							
Mt. Omei	1926	(5)	122.1*	--	--	--	19.1

* excluding imputed home rent and fuel. ** 26.2% is house rent and fuel.
*** consumption expense.
Notes: Savings/dissavings is the residual between income and expenditure;
the form was not given. The (largely imputed) costs of rent and fuel are
removed from per capita income in the final column for better comparability
with postwar statistics on rural incomes, which would generally not include
such items.

Sources:
(1) John L. Buck, Chinese Farm Economy, p. 385.
(2) Chiao Ch'i-ming, Chung-kuo nung-ts'un she-hui ching-chi hsüeh,
       pp. 382-384.
(3) H.D. Lamson, "The People's Livelihood as Revealed by Family Budget
       Studies," Chinese Economic Journal, Vol. VIII, No. 5, May 1931,
       pp. 455-56.

(TABLE A. CONTINUED)

(4) Feng Ho-fa (ed.), Chung-kuo nung-ts'un ching-chi tzu-liao, pp. 464-465 and p. 642.
(5) Harold D. Brown, "A Survey of 25 Farms on Mt. Omei," Chinese Economic Journal, Vol. I, No. 12, December 1927, p. 1071.

the distribution of income in China at the time, compared with distributions for other underdeveloped and developed countries ("composite" distributions for these are given in the graph). Even if we dismiss the distributions for Anhwei (Su hsien) and Chihli (one of the villages sampled had a disproportionately large number of resident families with substantial incomes drawn from urban investments) as "atypical", it is apparent that rural China had an income distribution sharing the worst features of those distributions characteristic of the agricultural sectors of underdeveloped countries and the industrial sectors of both underdeveloped and developed countries -- that is, the relatively high share of the top 5 percent of families characteristic of the former and the relatively low share of the bottom two quintiles characteristic of the latter.[c.] The result is a concentration ratio (see the note to Table B. for definition) higher than is observed in the agricultural sector elsewhere in the underdeveloped or developed world. The explanation would seem to be that the Chinese "rich peasant" or kulak and middle peasant were better off relative to the "poor peasant" than is the case elsewhere.

The distribution of income is intrinsically more revealing

TABLE B. SHARES IN TOTAL INCOME OF ORDINAL GROUPS, CHINA (1920s) AND SELECTED OTHER COUNTRIES

	0-20%	21-40%	41-60%	0-60%	61-80%	81-90%	91-95%	Top 5%	Concentration Ratio
Rural China, 1920s*									
1. Chekiang	3.9	7.0	12.5	23.4	20.0	15.4	13.5	28.3	.52
2. Kiangsu	4.1	7.6	11.9	23.6	19.8	15.4	13.5	28.3	.52
3. Anhwei	2.5	4.6	9.5	16.6	15.3	15.1	8.6	45.4	.65
4. Chihli	--	--	--	7.4	10.4	13.1	11.6	57.5	.79
India, 1950*									
1. Rural	8.8	10.3	12.5	31.3	17.1	12.8	9.6	28.9	.40
2. Urban	3.6	4.4	5.8	13.8	9.2	8.2	7.3	61.5	.69
Ceylon, 1952/53**									
1. Agriculture, hunting, fishing	5.5	9.8	13.5	28.8	18.4	13.5	9.4	29.9	.45
2. Other	3.4	7.7	12.1	23.2	19.0	14.6	10.4	32.8	.52
Poland, 1929*									
1. Agriculture	5.4	12.5	17.6	35.5	23.2	13.8	9.7	17.8	.35
2. Other	4.6	7.9	12.0	24.5	18.8	15.2	10.3	31.2	.50
Italy, 1948*									
1. Agriculture	6.1	10.4	14.2	30.7	20.3	14.9	10.7	23.4	.41
2. Other	6.2	10.7	14.8	31.7	20.2	14.0	7.6	24.5	.40
United States, 1929*									
1. Farm	4.1	9.3	14.7	28.1	23.4	17.5	11.9	19.1	.43
2. Other (incl. capital gains)	3.9	9.1	11.9	24.9	16.9	12.7	9.2	36.3	.51
United States, 1950-53									
1. Farm	4.7	10.0	15.3	30.0	22.5	16.1	10.7	20.7	.41
2. Non-farm	7.2	12.7	16.5	36.4	21.2	13.8	9.1	19.5	.34

Graph A. Lorenz Curves, China, 1920s, Comapred with
"Typical" Distributions for DCs and UDCs

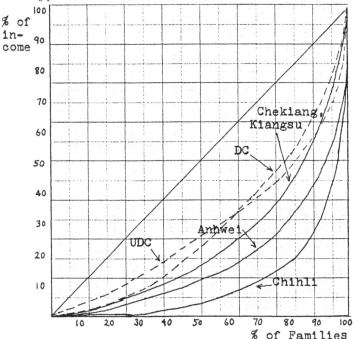

Note: "Typical" distributions for underdeveloped (UDC) and
developed (DC) countries from Simon Kuznets, _Economic Growth
and Structure_, p. 289. Distributions for China from Table B.

than the statistics on mean incomes, because of the extent to

which the latter are influenced by extremely high incomes at

the upper end of the distribution: For instance, it is appa-

rent from the four Chinese samples that about 75 - 80 percent

of the families had incomes below the mean (the points may be

determined by drawing tangents to the Lorenz curves parallel

to the diagonal). In the Chekiang and Kiangsu samples, al-

though the mean income was something over 150 yüan (roughly

30 yüan per capita), the median family income was about
100 yüan.

The potential appeal to the masses of a program of income
redistribution is apparent in the possibility that 75 to 80
percent of peasant families could benefit from such a policy
(although a lesser percentage of individuals, since family
size was larger at the upper end of the distribution). Income,
however, flows not from some abstract cornucopia but from
ownership of assets and the provision of labor at varying
rates of return. An unequal distribution of land ownership
of course was the key source of income inequality, as Table
D. implies. But it follows from the facts that income was
less than unit-proportional to land holdings and that perhaps
90 percent of families owned less than the mean value of
property holdings (including land and other assets; see
Table D.) that the inequality of asset distribution was
"alleviated" by a greater proportion of income from subsidiary occupations accruing to the landless and small-holding
peasants. For example, in I-hsing hsien, Kiangsu, it was
estimated that roughly 46 percent of the income of a peasant
with 2 mou of land came from non-crop sources, of which 20
percent was from side occupations and the remainder from
animal husbandry.[d] Properly interpreted, this means that
the distribution of income and leisure combined (with leisure
valued at its opportunity cost) was more unequal than that
of income alone; and that a redistribution of assets would

TABLE C. RELATIONSHIP BETWEEN LAND HOLDING AND FAMILY INCOME, VARIOUS
LOCALITIES, 1920s CHINA

Locality	Item	Landholdings: (mow) None	Under 3	3-5	6-10	11-25	26-50	Over 50
Chekiang	% of Families	28.6	11.4	9.5	14.7	20.4	11.7	3.8
	Mean Income	63	96	110	151	219	383	924
Kiangsu	% of Families	3.6	11.4	24.1	29.1	21.8	5.8	2.8
	Mean Income	28	40	81	141	241	539	1535
Anhwei	% of Families	18.3	7.6	12.6	14.4	17.7	10.1	21.0
	Mean Income	111	60	73	90	131	160	800
Chihli	% of Families	16.8	10.7	16.4	17.2	17.3	9.6	12.0
	Mean Income	18	14	24	38	71	185	831

Source: Feng Ho-fa, Chung-kuo nung-ts'un ching-chi tzu-liao, p. 30. See
notes to preceding table for description of data.

TABLE D. DISTRIBUTION OF PROPERTY, LAND OWNERSHIP AND CULTIVATION AMONG
AGRICULTURAL FAMILIES IN LIN-AN COUNTY, CHEKIANG, 1920s

Value of Property (yüan)	Percent of Families	Land Owned (mow)	Percent of Families	Land Cultivated (mow)	Percent of Families	Percent of Land
Below 100	24.4	None	42.3	1- 5	31.0	7.0
100 - 499	43.5	1- 50	56.6	6- 10	17.1	6.1
500 - 999	15.6	51-100	4.1	11- 50	40.8	8.7
1000-1999	7.3	101-200	2.4	51-100	6.4	26.0
2000-2999	3.6	201-300	0.3	101-200	3.8	30.5
3000-3999	2.3	301-500	0.2	201-500	0.7	13.0
4000-9999	2.0	Over 500	*	Over 500	0.2	8.7
10-29000	1.1					
30-49000	0.2					
50-99000	0.1		* less than 0.1 percent			
Over 100000	*					

Mean Value: 1984 yüan

Notes: The data in this table pertains to 18,281 agricultural families in
the county. No information was given on the methods by which the information
was obtained or estimated, and it should not be taken as too reliable.
Source: Feng Ho-fa, Chung-kuo nung-ts'un ching-chi tzu-liao, pp. 588-590.

imply equalization of leisure as well as income.

Notes to Appendix IV-A:

a. See C. S. Chen and C. P. Ridley (eds.), Rural People's Communes in Lienchiang, p. 24 and p. 37.

b. J. L. Buck, LUC, Statistical Volume, pp. 149-151.

c. See Simon Kuznets, Economic Growth and Structure, p. 289.

d. Feng Ho-fa, op. cit., p. 484.

APPENDIX V-A. ESTIMATION PROCEDURE FOR INDUSTRIAL WAGE
STRUCTURE MODEL

The model presented in Chapter V. may be expressed in
terms more suitable for estimation purposes as follows:

Defining the observed value of the dependent variable
$(\bar{w}N/M)$ for the kth observation as y_k, and neglecting the error term, the model for the kth observation may be expressed
as:

$$y_k = (\sum_{i=1}^{m} b_i x_{ki})(\sum_{m+1}^{n} b_i x_{ki})[1 + b_{n+1}F/M + b_{n+2}A/M]$$

where the first m coefficients b_i represent the locational
coefficients; those between m+1 and n are the vector of
industry coefficients respectively, as defined in the text.
The observational vector X consist of dummies: If the kth
observation represents the lth location and the rth industry,
then x_l and x_{m+r} both equal one, all other components of
the vector being zero-valued. If the expression is simplified by eliminating the zero-valued components, it reduces
to the formulation given in the text.

However, as this stands, the industrial and locational
coefficients are not absolutely identified, i.e. although
the relative magnitudes within each set can be estimated,
the absolute magnitudes within a set are defined only relative to any member of the other set. Consequently an infinite
number of solutions to the normal equations is possible,
and an estimation procedure will not converge on a particular solution. This problem may be solved by any form of

normalization which does not constrain the _relative_ magnitudes of either set; we chose to restrict the _average_ value of the industrial coefficients to 1.0. As there are a total of 25 industrial coefficients, this is equivalent to the expression: $\Sigma_{m+1}^n b_1 = 25$ or $b_n = 25 - \Sigma_{m+1}^{n-1} b_1$, where b_n is an arbitrarily chosen component of the coefficient vector (in our case, the coefficient for the tobacco industry). This equation may be used to eliminate b_n from the above model, yielding an estimable model:

$$y_k = [25x_{kn} + \Sigma_{m+1}^{n-1} b_1(x_{k1} - x_{kn})][\Sigma_1^m b_1 x_{k1}][Sum_k]$$

where Sum_k is the final term in the first model.

The above model, which is nonlinear in form, may be estimated using an iterative technique requiring first a linear approximation by means of a Taylor-series expansion. Representing the model in general terms by the expression

$$y_k = F[b_1, \ldots, b_n; x_{k1}, \ldots, x_{kn}] + u_k,$$ the Taylor series expansion, dropping the second-order and higher terms, is:

$$y_k \approx F[b_1^o, \ldots, b_n^o; x_{k1}, \ldots, x_{kn}] + \Sigma_1^n db_1^o dF/db_1$$

where the first term represents an initial evaluation of the function on the basis of a trial set of parameters; db_1^o is an error term representing the difference between the initial estimates b_1^o and the true parameters b_1 for each of the n coefficients.

Estimation proceeds using ordinary least-squares techniques, with the difference between y_k and the approximation to it, $F[B^o, X^o]$ as dependent variable, the n derivatives,

dF/db_1, as independent variables and the terms db_i^o as the estimated coefficients. In iterative fashion, estimated values of db_i^o are combined with previous estimates of b_i^o to derive a new estimated $F(B^o, X^o)$ until repeated estimates of the error terms converge on sufficiently small values. It may be shown that the standard errors of the estimated error terms for each coefficient are in fact the standard errors of the coefficients themselves.[*]

---

[*] For further discussion of the technique, see N. Draper and H. Smith, Applied Regression Analysis (New York, 1966); for another application, see Robert J. Gordon, "The Incidence of the Corporation Income Tax in U.S. Manufacturing, 1925-62," American Economic Review, Vol. LVII, No. 4, September, 1967, pp. 731-758.

APPENDIX V-B. RELATIONSHIP BETWEEN CAPITAL/LAND RATIO AND
SIZE OF FARM

Information on ownership of farm implements was collected
by Buck for a subsample of about 8 percent, chosen to represent small, medium and large farms for each locality. If
we take Buck's averages by crop region (subject to some con-
ceptual error, because of the lack of uniformity of farm-size
classifications) and the corresponding weighted averages of
farm sizes (grouped into three instead of eight classes),
it is possible to get a rough idea of the relationship between the capital service/land ratio and farm size (i.e.
cultivated hectares, C_1 in the model). We have chosen five
major items -- plows, hoes, sickles and animal and human-
driven irrigation pumps -- as representing these services,
and aggregated these at their annual depreciation value.*
The relationship between the logs of capital services/hectare
and farm size (hectares) for each region is depicted in the
scatter diagram below (Graph A.); the slopes of the relationship between $\ln(K/C)$ and $\ln(C)$ (the coefficient V
relating the excluded exogenous variable "capital" to the
included variable, "land") are to be found in Table A..

Aside from the often near-perfect log-linearity of the

---

* Calculated as the difference between present value and
original cost, divided by years of use, from a survey reported
in Pan Hong-sheng and O. King, "Preliminary Note on an Economic
Study of Farm Implements," Economic Facts, No. 3, November 1936.

TABLE A. RELATIONSHIP BETWEEN CAPITAL/LAND RATIO AND LAND, EIGHT CROP REGIONS, CHINA, 1930s

Region	Farm Size	Total Capital[1]	Crop Hectares	Log (K/C)	Log C	dln(K/C) /dlnC [2]
	S	.34	1.11	-1.17	0.10	
1	M	.54	2.80	-1.66	1.03	-.59
	L	.77	7.80	-2.30	2.05	
	S	.37	.60	-0.48	-0.51	
2	M	.72	1.37	-0.63	0.31	-.46
	L	.84	3.69	-1.27	1.31	
	S	.30	.67	-0.80	-0.40	
3	M	.47	1.62	-1.24	0.48	-.46*
	L	.84	3.69*	-1.47*	1.31*	
	S	.45	.55	-0.20	-0.60	
4	M	.95	1.47	-0.43	0.39	-.22
	L	1.57	2.73	-0.54	1.00	
	S	.60	.39	0.43	-0.94	
5	M	1.10	.96	0.14	-0.04	-.39
	L	1.67	2.15	-0.25	0.77	
	S	.44	.50	-0.13	-0.69	
6	M	1.25	1.20	0.04	0.18	-.05
	L	2.40	2.97	-0.21	1.09	
	S	.55	.41	0.29	-0.89	
7	M	.89	.90	-0.01	-0.11	-.19
	L	2.01	2.07	-0.03	0.73	
	S	.58	.38	0.43	-0.97	
8	M	.92	1.01	-0.09	0.01	-.52
	L	1.46	2.77	-0.63	1.02	

* We have replaced the average farm size for the "large" grouping in Region 3 with that estimated for Region 2. The former seemed excessive, due perhaps to sampling error. However, we have used only the S and M observations in estimating the slope for this region.
(1) As evaluated at annual rate of depreciation, in yüan; rates for items included are as follows: Plows, .17; hoes, .055; irrigation pumps, human-powered, .39; animal-powered, 1.01; sickles, .05. Data on average number of farm implements of each type per farm from Buck, LUC, Statistical Volume.
(2) The slope of the linear relationship between the two items, as estimated from scatter diagrams in Graph A.

GRAPH A. RELATIONSHIP BETWEEN CAPITAL/LAND RATIO AND LAND, 8 REGIONS.

* third observation is hypothetical:
  see Table A.

TABLE B. ELASTICITY OF CAPITAL/LABOR RATIO WITH RESPECT TO CHANGES IN CULTIVATED AREA (CROSS-SECTIONALLY)*

Region	$r_{L,C}$	s_C	s_L	$B^*_{L,C}$	$e_{K/L}$
1	-.91	1.09	.79	-.66	.07
2	-.79	.80	.53	-.52	.06
3	-.92	1.03	.68	-.61	.15
4	-.83	.89	.57	-.53	.31
5	-.81	.76	.50	-.60	.21
6	-.87	.90	.49	-.47	.42
7	-.86	.73	.53	-.62	.43
8	-.94	.81	.55	-.64	.12

* $e_{K/L} = V - B^*_{L,C}$, where V is the vector $d\ln(K/C)/d\ln C$ from Table A. and $B^*_{L,C}$ is the slope of the linear relationship between the log of the labor/land ratio and the log of C; the latter may be estimated as $r_{L,C}(s_L/s_C)$ where $r_{L,C}$ is the correlation coefficient between labor and land and the remaining terms are the standard deviations of the two variables.

of the relationships manifested, the most stiking conclusion is that the correlation between the capital service/land ratio and land is distinctly negative; large landowners worked their farms with less capital investment per hectare than did small farmers (at least insofar as tools and implements were concerned; since rental of capital services by small farms could be expected to be higher than those of large farms, the conclusion is not altered by inclusion of rented capital services).

This should not be taken to imply that large farms were less capital intensive than small farms, if the capital/labor ratio is taken as the index of capital intensity, for the labor-land ratio (and indeed virtually all of the input

ratios) also fell as the size of farm increased, and at an
even more rapid rate. If we subtract from the slope of
the regression of ln(K/C) on lnC the corresponding coefficient of ln(L/C) on lnL, the result is the elasticity of
the capital/labor ratio with respect to farm size. As may
be seen in Table B., it is consistently positive and moderately substantial except for the (relatively capital-poor)
regions 1, 2 and 8.

It has been our thesis that the decline in capital/land
ratio with farm size, presumed to be valid for capital
services as a whole, is a consequence of not only increasing
returns to scale but also a combination of lesser availability
of financial capital/ acre on large farms and differing
attitudes towards the alternative uses of such finance
capital due to the relationship between risk aversion and
income.

APPENDIX VI-A. NOTES ON DATA DERIVED FROM JOHN L. BUCK,
    LAND UTILIZATION IN CHINA, STATISTICAL VOLUME.

The selection and compilation of data from the Statistical Volume of Buck's Land Utilization in China was influenced by the objective of empirically estimating the
productive relationships between inputs and outputs at the
farm level. The breakdown of data had to be finer than
averages for a locality, so as to reflect differences between
farms of different size in a single locality. Consequently
only data broken down by size of farm in the SV were used;
where important data were only available in the form of
averages for localities, it was assumed that the same
average pertained to each farm size category. It was
possible to use only the data pertaining to the 142 hsien
and 150 localities which appear in all tables broken down by
farm size. Thus the total number of observations obtained
was 740, subdivided into eight segments corresponding to the
eight crop regions as defined by Buck (segments ranging from
30 to 172 observations each). As each observation represented a mean value for a group of farms, and the number of
farms represented varied, in regressions it was necessary to
correct for heteroskedasticity by weighting by the inverse of
the square root of the number of observations per grouped
observation.

The variables used in production function estimation were
derived from other variables given in the SV, occasionally
in more than one way. Since the former represent in many
cases ratios or products of grouped averages (which may
differ from averages of ratios or products), errors may have
been introduced (in part due to rounding in the original
data). Where variables could be derived from the published
data in more than one way, the alternative methods were used
and the data checked for inconsistencies and errors (this
pertains primarily to C_i and F_i, land and fertilizer, for
each of which three separate estimates could be derived).

The method by which each variable was computed is given
below, in terms of the original data from the SV:

   a) Q_i = QPMExMANEQ/(100x(1-UNHAR)xCULT). To eliminate the error introduced by land to which
inputs were applied, but which could not be
harvested due to pests, disease, flood, etc.,
we _inflated_ output on the assumption that
yields on unharvested land would have otherwise been the same as on harvested land.
Q_i = yields/mou.

   b) L_i = MANEQx(1 - IDLEFxIDLE/12)x10/CULT. Labor
time, as reported, included idle time, which
we removed. 10 is a scale factor. L_i =
labor/mou.

c) F_i = FERTxHECT/1000xCULT. 1000 is a scale factor.
    F_i = fertilizer produced/mou (manure and
    nightsoil only).

d) C_i = CHPMExMANEQx(1-LIDLE)x100/DCIND. Idle
    (fallow) land has been deducted from total
    crop area (i.e. cultivated acreage). The
    latter may also be computed as PPFRM/PPCUL or
    LANDxPRDPC (the last with modification to
    remove productive but non-cropped land).
    Either the first or the second method was
    generally chosen (as the mode of the three
    alternatives).

e) DC_i = (DCIND-100)/100.

f) T_i = TENCY.

g) A_i = ANIMLxHECT/CULT.

h) I_i = IRRIG/100. It was assumed (in the absence of
    a more detailed breakdown) that the same
    percentage of crop area was irrigated for
    each farm size group in a locality.

i) Year = WETA, WETB, WETC, WETD, as described below.
The variables provided by Buck and the location in the
Statistical Volume from which they were drawn are as follows:

(1) UNITS: Number of farms sampled per farm size
    group (SV, p. 289). Used for weighting
    purposes.

(2) LAND: Average size of farm area in hectares (SV, p. 291). Not equal to cultivated area.

(3) DCIND: Index of double-cropping (SV, p. 296). Equals (crop hectares/crop area)x100.

(4) MANEQ: Number of man-equivalents per farm (SV, p. 297). Man-time on farm, including idle time, which is attributed to on-farm and subsidiary labor time in the same proportions as actual labor.

(5) CHPME: Crop hectares per man-equivalent (SV, p. 298). Crop hectares = crop area x double-cropping index/100.

(6) ANIML: Labor animal units per crop hectare (SV, p. 299). Accuracy is questionable; at least differs systematically from LAUME for smaller farms, with ANIML always greater. Perhaps ANIML refers to use, LAUME to ownership, although this is not stated anywhere. FERTL was estimated by Buck from LAUME, not ANIML, as was apparent from consistency checks.

(7) PPFRM: Size of household (persons per farm) (SV, p. 300).

(8) QPME: Quantity of production in kilograms of grain-equivalent per man-equivalent (SV, p. 302).

(9)   IDLE: Number of idle months per able-bodied man
(SV, p. 307). Presumably refers to all idle
time.

(10) IDLEF: My estimate of percentage of IDLE attributed by Buck to MANEQ. Equals the percentage which man-equivalents in farm work is
of total man-equivalents, an average for each
locality (not broken down by size of farm).

(11) PPCUL: Persons per hectare of crop area (SV,
p. 425).

(12) PRDPC: Percent of farm area in productive uses
(SV, p. 65).

(13) CULT: Crop acreage per farm. Calculated from
other variables (see discussion of C_i above).

(14) UNHAR: Percentage of crop area unharvested (SV,
p. 43). Assumed the same for each farm size.

(15) LIDLE: Percent of crop area idle (see UNHAR).

(16) TENCY: Percentage of farm area rented (SV,
p. 55).

(17) IRRIG: Percentage of crop area irrigated in a
locality (SV, p. 214). Assumed the same for
all farms.

(18) LAUME: Labor animal units per man-equivalent
(SV, p. 135). See ANIML above.

(19) FERTL: Animal manure and night soil per crop

hectare (kgs.) (<u>SV</u>, p. 137). Estimated by
Buck from total animal-equivalents and total
human adult-equivalents per household.

(20) WETA-WETD: Dummy variables identifying the time
period over which each sample was taken.
These represented the years 1929, 1930, 1931
and 1932-33. If the typically 12-mo. sample
period fell within one of these years, the
value of the dummy for that year and locality
was 1.0. If the period overlaps two years,
the value of the dummy is in proportion to
the number of months falling within each
year. (<u>SV</u>, pp. 464-472.)

(21) PARSZ: Average crop area per parcel of land
(<u>SV</u>, p. 63).

APPENDIX VI-B. WEIGHTED OUTPUT DATA AND THE ESTIMATION OF
AN AGGREGATE PRODUCTION FUNCTION.

A key assumption (or condition) behind the empirical estimation of aggregate production functions is that the "true"
function be monotonic -- i.e. that a given set of values of
(exogenous) inputs corresponds to one and only one value of
the dependent variable, normally a weighted combination of
individual physical outputs. If the data used for estimation
are such that there are structural reasons (not related to
errors of measurement) why the relationship cannot be considered monotonic, the probability of identification of the
parameters and indeed their meaning is greatly reduced.

As our study will utilize physical units (rather than
values) of inputs, with a fairly high degree of uniformity,
we limit ourselves here to discussion of how this problem
relates to the choice of output measure, which in our case
is dictated by the data available.

Assume a two-commodity aggregate production function:
$Q = w_1 q_1 + w_2 q_2 = w_1 F_1(x_1^1,\ldots,x_n^1) + w_2 F_2(x_1^2,\ldots,x_n^2)$, where Q
constitutes an output index composed of the weighted quanti-
ties of individual outputs, q_1 and q_2, each of which is the
product of an individual production function, F_1 or F_2, with
inputs of each type split among the two production processes
so that $x_i = x_i^1 + x_i^2$.

Now, in estimating an aggregate production function, we
are working from data which gives us no knowledge of either
the allocation of the inputs between activities F_1 and F_2 or
the individual outputs, q_1 and q_2. We are, rather, estimating
a joint relationship between Q and the total of each type of
input. But the production function as expressed above does
not define a unique, monotonic relationship of this sort:
Clearly the same set of inputs, $x_1 \ldots x_n$, can by virtue of
different allocation among activities, can produce different
values of Q (and, vice versa, a particular value of Q may
correspond to an infinity of different sets of inputs). If
the model is to be presumed monotonic, some additional condition must be imposed, such as: The producers' behavior
must be such as to maximize Q given fixed input supplies.
By adding appropriate Lagrangian expressions representing
input constraints, differentiating with respect to the
individual inputs to each activity, setting derivatives
equal to zero and solving the resulting set of equations, it
may be shown that unique solutions for the individual inputs
are obtained, implying a unique Q-maximum corresponding to
any overall values of the inputs (given the usual conditions
on the forms of the functions F_1 and F_2).

It will also be noted, however, that if these equations
are solved for Q-maximum in terms of the inputs $x_1 \ldots x_n$, the
parameters of the resulting function will involve the weights

w_1 and w_2. _It is thus necessary that these weights be_ _constant over all observations within the sample_ if a single set of parameters are to be estimated.

The two assumptions italicized above define the conditions which the output index Q should satisfy to a high degree if a meaningful estimate of an aggregate production function is to be possible. The weights which combine individual products should be such that they are constant from observation to observation and the aggregate index should in fact represent the object of maximization of the producer. Any errors in these assumptions should at least be random rather than systematic.

Obviously the most natural weights to choose for such an index are the prices of the products received by the producer: The aggregate index then represents gross receipts, a likely object of maximization (when fixed inputs are assumed). In general, in a perfectly competitive market in homogeneous products, the price-weights will differ from observation to observation (in cross-sectional analysis) only because of transportation cost.

In the context of the Chinese peasant economy, however, this argument is not very reassuring. First, the isolation of rural local markets (and the absence of a smooth flow of agricultural commodities from area to area in response to supply and demand conditions) implies that price-weights

would show considerable cross-sectional variance, which may
also be expected to influence input allocations (and thus not
be strictly random). Second, w_1, w_2, F_1 and F_2 must be
considered intertemporally random variables, with different
variances and expected values different from observed values
at given points in time. Producers, undoubtedly risk-
averse, must be expected to have taken this into account in
their decision-making, and in a manner which will differ
from producer to producer (probably systematically with
scale of farming). Under these circumstances, weights would
not be in fact constant from farm to farm, nor would observed prices correspond to subjective, risk-discounted
weights. Finally, producers may differ systematically in
efficiency, not only with respect to how successfully they
maximize, but in how hard they try to maximize. While
varying success in maximization can be treated as a stochastic error attached to allocation of inputs, lack of
motivation will directly affect the relations F_1 and F_2 in a
manner which is not statistically independent of input
levels or proportions.

For these reasons, the assumptions guaranteeing mono-
tonicity break down in a peasant economy and estimation
procedures are apt to lead to biased estimates of ill-
defined functions.

The actual quantity index employed in Chapter VI defined in terms of "grain-equivalents", improves on this situation in only one respect: The weights employed are more constant cross-sectionally than price-weights. These weights are as follows: Foodgrains (in kilograms) are combined with a weight of 1.0 (food value assumed to be approximately equal); tubers, oilseeds and legumes (staple foods and substitutes for grain) are converted according to approximate calorific value; fruits and vegetables are combined using their nationally-averaged prices relative to grain; other non-food crops were converted on the basis of local prices, where available. The object of measurement was clearly the calorific value of production (with kgs. of grain being the standard unit), on the assumption that output of other than staple foods could be converted to the latter at market prices.

If such an index is used in estimating a production function, the implicit assumption must be that peasants were indifferent between different food grains and their calorific equivalent in terms of other food crops, and measured cash crops by their rate of conversion into foodgrains at market prices. While this assumption might be semi-realistic for a truly subsistence agrarian economy, it is a weak approximation for a semi-market oriented economy such as we are considering here.

Our only excuse for employing such an index is that it was
impossible to disaggregate and reweight the data as given.
However, some consolation may be found in the facts that
about 90% of the index represents foodgrains; within a
single crop region (for which a production function was
estimated), rarely were more than two or three foodgrains
raised in quantities sufficient to distort the index. Nevertheless, the inconsistency of these weights with the unknown
weighting scheme presumably employed by peasant-maximizers
certainly provides statistical grounds for questioning
estimates of the parameters of an aggregate production
function. It is therefore important to compare the results
of Chapter VII, where a better output index and an alternative method of estimation are employed.

APPENDIX VI-C.   SPECIFICATION OF LAND IN PRODUCTION FUNC-
                 TION ESTIMATION

Production function studies generally take either the
acreage of cropland or the value of cropland (evaluated as
rental value or as a potential return on land investment at
market rates of interest) as the proper measure of the input
of land in the production process. The former approach leads
to possible errors resulting from the non-homogeneity of
land measured in physical terms (compounded by the correlation of land quality with quantities of other inputs required
per unit output). The latter, on the other hand, is based
on an assumption which is at best a testable hypothesis:
that variations in land value reflect variations in the
marginal productivity of the different qualities of land.
This assumption is probably more questionable for land than
for any other factor of production (land is neither geographically mobile nor reproducible); it is especially implausible
in the context of peasant economies, except for geographically localized samples. Nor, of course, is it in accord
with the current belief in the inapplicability of marginal
productivity distribution theory to peasant economies which
is here being challenged.

If sufficient additional information reflecting the sources
of qualitative variation in land is available, it is possible
to take the alternative approach of estimating an index of

land in quality-equivalents as a concomitant of the complete
production function estimate. The objective is to find an
appropriate specification for an index which combines land
of different qualities in such a way that components which
are perfect substitutes will have equivalent values. That
is, if one acre of type A land is substitutable for two
of type B, type A land should receive a weight double that
of type B in the index.

Suppose, for example, that the extent of double-cropping
is the only factor affecting land quality (or, more properly,
reflecting it). Suppose that there are two kinds of land,
C_{sc} and C_{dc}, and $C = C_{sc} + C_{dc}$, where C = 'total land',
C_{sc} and C_{dc} are single and double-cropped land respectively.
Suppose further that the ratio of the marginal productivity
on double-cropped land to that on single-cropped land
(ceteris paribus) is equal to a constant, β. Then the proper
index combining the two types of land should be:

$I_C = C_{sc} + \beta C_{dc} = C[1 + (\beta-1)DC]$, where DC is the percentage of land double-cropped (C_{dc}/C). Then, in a constant-
elasticity Cobb-Douglas production function with capital
and labor as the other inputs, land could be entered as
follows:

$Q_1 = AL_1^{\alpha 1}K_1^{\alpha 2}\{C_1[1+(\beta-1)DC_1]\}^{\alpha 3}$, where the parameters A,
α_1 to α_3 and β would have to be estimated iteratively.
However, since $1 < \beta < 2$ in this instance, we may approximate

the linear form, $S = 1 + (\beta-1)DC_1$, with a nonlinear form,
$S' = e^{\alpha DC_1}$ for greater convenience in estimation. As may
be seen in Figure A., for the ranges $0 < DC_1 < 1$ and
$1 < \beta < 2$, this exponential form does not deviate substantially from the linear form. Moreover, we may now
write $Q_1 = Ae^{\theta DC_1}L^{\alpha_1}K^{\alpha_2}C^{\alpha_3}$, where $\theta = \alpha_3\alpha$. This equation

form is linear in logs and
may be estimated using OLS
techniques. From estimates
of θ and α_3, we may derive
an estimate of β:

$$\beta^* = 1 + \alpha^*e^{(\theta^*/\alpha_3^*)DC_1}$$

where $\alpha^* = \theta^*/\alpha_3^*$ and DC_1 is
taken at the mean. The accu-
racy of this estimate will
probably be greatest if the
data includes considerable

Figure A. Evaluation of
$S = 1 + (\beta-1)DC_1$ and
$S' = e^{\alpha DC_1}$ at varying
values of β and α

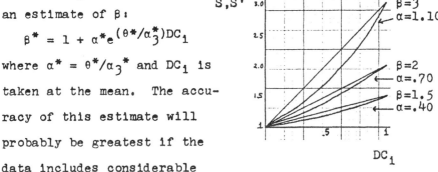

variation in the proportion of land double-cropped, with
the mean percentage greater than or equal to 50 percent.

If more than one qualitative factor is associated with
variance in land quality, the approach is greatly complicated, since there is no reason to assume that the impacts
of, for examples, double-cropping, irrigation, soil type,
etc. are either additive or multiplicative. Ideally, the
index should assign a different 'relative productivity'
weight to each possible combination of characteristics.

This is impractical because of the loss of degrees of freedom which would result. To simplify, we must assume that any additional characteristic, such as irrigation, enters the index in the form, $C_1[1 + (\beta_1 - 1)DC_1][1 + (\beta_2 - 1)I_1]$, etc. (where I_1 is the percentage of land irrigated), and further approximate this by a multivariate, multiplicative exponential function, $C_1(e^{\alpha_1 DC_1})(e^{\alpha_2 I_1})$, etc. Such simplifications introduce specification error, but nevertheless permit us to account for qualitative variation in factors without prejudging the impact of that variation entirely.

It is possible to compare the approach outlined above to the more conventional practice of using the rental value of land as the index of land input, on the basis of the sample farm data assembled by John L. Buck in The Chinese Farm Economy. We have grouped this data, which pertains to 2866 farms, into subsamples covering respectively North and South China, and have estimated Cobb-Douglas production functions following both approaches. The model employed was: $Q_1 = Ae^{\theta DC_1}L_1^{\alpha_1}K_1^{\alpha_2}C_1^{\alpha_3}u$, where:

Q = value of production (in yüan);
DC = percent of land double-cropped;
L = man-equivalents of labor;
K = value of variable capital and interest on fixed capital;
C = hectares of land (crop area);
u = error term.

C_1 was also replaced with C_1', the rental value of land, whence we would expect DC_1 to become insignificant, and was in one regression dropped entirely (equivalent to assuming constant returns to scale).

The results, summarized in Table A., are on the whole typical of studies of this type, in that the R^2s are high, indicating a statistically good "fit"; signs and magnitudes of coefficients change spectacularily when the specification is modified. This is evidence of strong multicollinearity among the independent variables, here especially between labor and land inputs. A plot of the labor observations against the crop area observations for the same producers (North China subsample) in Figure B. provides striking evidence of how little independent variation there is in these two variables.

Equations 1 and 4 included physical inputs of land, equations 3 and 6 the rental value of land: Although the variation in land values within the samples does apparently reflect to some extent the qualitative differences in land (note that the coefficient for DC_1 for the North China data becomes statistically insignificant when the value of land replaces acreage as the unit of measure of the land input), it does not do so quite as well as the combination of acreage units and the double-cropping percentage, as the R^2s for the latter equations are both slightly higher than for the former. Although the standard errors are not shown, the t-statistics for land in value units are also substan-

Table A. Regression Estimates of Elasticities of Output
with Respect to Various Inputs, N. and S. China

Equation	Elasticity with respect to:				
	L_1	K_1	C_1	DC_1	R^2
North China:					
1	-1.16**	-.06	2.00**	.63*	.915
2	.75**	.15	--	.10	.828
3***	.32*	-.10	.70**	.17	.901
South China:					
4	-.21	.49**	.58*	-.09	.894
5	.44**	.46**	--	-.13	.867
6***	.46**	.48**	-.05	-.12	.867

* Significant at the 5% level. ** Significant at the 1% level.
*** Replacing physical with value units of land.
Note: Based on observations grouped by size of farm, 36
for North China subsample, 31 for S. China. Data from
J.L. Buck, Chinese Farm Economy, Appendix I., Tables
1 to 17. Capital computed as total farm capital less
value of land and buildings.

tially lower than those for land in acreage. Clearly,
using value units injects greater error into the land
variable than it accounts for qualitative variation, at
least in comparison with an equation where the extent of
double-cropping is included to more accurately reflect
the latter.

Despite the effects of multicollinearity on the estimate
of the elasticity with respect to land, the estimate of
β^*, the ratio of marginal value product on double-cropped
land to that on single-cropped land, ceteris paribus, based
on equation 1, is 1.36 (when value units of land are used,
as in equation 3, this only falls to 1.27, indicating that

Figure B. Plot of Labor Input (logs) against Crop Area (logs of hectares), North China Data

the rental value of land does not adequately account for higher productivity in areas of high double-cropping). Surprisingly, no impact is found for the South China subsample, a result we are at loss to explain, unless due to errors in data.

APPENDIX VI-D. LOCALITY INTERCEPTS

Table A. lists the locality intercepts of the Cobb-
Douglas production functions fit to the Buck <u>Land</u> <u>Utiliza-</u>
<u>tion</u> <u>in</u> <u>China</u> survey data for the eight crop regions. These
intercepts constitute a cardinal index of variation in yield
(in terms of grain-equivalents/<u>mou</u>) between localities which
could <u>not</u> be accounted for by differences in labor or fertilizer intensity, scale of farming, or extent of irrigation
and double-cropping.* Although their values reflect in part
differences in land productivity created by <u>past</u> human
effort, they reflect more closely variations in <u>natural</u>
conditions (excepting those permitting irrigation and
multiple-cropping) than would an index of yields, for
example. This explains the fact that the intercepts do not
appear noticeably higher in regions 7 and 8 (southeast and
southwest China) than in the far north of China (the much
higher yields of regions 7 and 8 are attributed by the regressions to greater labor and fertilizer intensity, and
higher irrigation and double-cropping percentages).

A potential use for such an index is in studying the
spatial distribution of the Chinese population. For those
parts of China where irrigation and double-cropping are

---

* the intercepts are multiplicative; e.g. an intercept of
2.0 indicates twice as high a yield as one of 1.0.

virtually non-existent, the intercepts show a high correlation with population density (for hectares per capita, the
correlation with the intercepts is -.50 in regions one and
two)*. Elsewhere it is necessary to account also for the
extent of irrigation and double-cropping. When this was
done (for the intercepts of the linear production functions,
which were less aggregated than those given in Table A.), we
found similarily high correlations in other regions (between
intercepts and logs of population densities): r = .57 in
region 5; r = .70 in region 3 for examples. Keeping in mind
that the intercepts also reflect random intertemporal
fluctuations in yield, these correlations suggest a certain
degree of equilibrium between the population density and the
capacity of the land to support man, at least cross-
sectionally, due, one imagines, to interregional migration.

---

* using the intercepts of the linear regressions, the
correlation is .93 with the logs of population densities
in region one alone.

Table A. Values of Locality Intercept Terms, Cobb-Douglas
          Production Functions Estimated From J. L. Buck,
          Land Utilization in China, Survey Data.

Region	Province	Locality	Intercept	T-statistic*
1	Kansu	Wuwei	1.0	5.2
	Shansi	Ningwu	3.9	8.4
	Suiyuan	Kweisui	"	"
	Shensi	Tingpien	0.3	14.3
	Suiyuan	Paotow	--	--
	Chinghai	Sining	2.7	2.5
	Kansu	Kaolan	2.0	5.8
	Ninghsia	Ninghsia	"	"
	Shansi	Tatung	"	"
	"	Tsinglo	"	"
	Shensi	Yulin	"	"
	Shensi	Kweisui	"	"
	Chinghai	Hwangyuan	"	"
2	Shansi	Pingting	4.3	1.6
	"	Taiku	"	"
	Shensi	Sunyi	"	"
	Hopei	Fowping	5.8	5.5
	Shansi	Showyang	"	"
	"	Wuhsiang	"	"
	Shensi	Shang	"	"
	Shansi	Sin	20.3	19.1
	"	Lin	6.6	4.6
	Shensi	Weinan	3.0	6.4
	Kansu	Pingliang	3.3	4.5
	"	Tienshui	"	"
	Honan	Lingpao	4.6	9.1
	"	Loyang	"	"
	"	Tsiyuan	"	"
	Shansi	Anyi	"	"
	"	Tsincheng	"	"
	"	Tsingyuan	"	"
	Shensi	Chenan	"	"
	"	Chowchih	"	"
3	Honan	Hiangcheng	2.0	10.0
	Hopei	Kiaoho	"	"
	"	Tsing	"	"
	"	Tung	"	"
	Liaoning	Liaochung	"	"
	Shantung	Ankiu	"	"
	"	En	"	"
	"	Laiyang	"	"
	"	Tangyi	"	"
	Anhwei	Fowyang	1.2	2.0
	"	Su	"	"

(Table A. Continued)

	Kiangsu	Kwanyun	1.2	2.0
	Shantung	Showkwang	2.3	9.0
	"	Wei	"	"
	"	Ningyang	0.9	4.5
	"	Taian	0.5	10.8
	Hopei	Chengting	0.9	3.4
	Honan	Kaifeng	0.7	10.0
	"	Shangkiu	"	"
	Hopei	Nankung	3.1	8.4
	Honan	Chi	1.3	1.5
	"	Linchang	"	"
	"	Nanyang	"	"
	"	Tsinyang	"	"
	"	Yencheng	"	"
	Hopei	Changli	"	"
	"	Sushui	"	"
	"	Tsang	"	"
	Shantung	Fushan	"	"
	"	Huimin	"	"
	"	Tsimo	"	"
	"	Tsining	"	"
	"	Yi	"	"
4	Anhwei	Fengyang	2.5	9.2
	"	Ho - 1	"	"
	"	Ho - 2	4.3	14.4
	"	Hofei	3.2	11.6
	"	Tungcheng	"	"
	"	Liuan	3.1	12.5
	"	Taihu	"	"
	"	Wuhu	3.2	12.5
	Chekiang	Kahsing	"	"
	"	Tehtsing	1.0	2.6
	"	Yuyao	3.0	7.6
	Hupei	Kishui	3.4	9.1
	"	Yingcheng	4.8	17.1
	"	Yunmeng	"	"
	Kiangsi	Pengtseh	2.7	8.1
	Kiangsu	Changshu	3.2	10.8
	"	Kunshan	"	"
	"	Kiangtu	1.1	1.3
	"	Wutsin	4.4	15.1
	"	Yencheng - 3	2.5	6.7
	"	Yencheng - 1	1.3	1.3
	"	" - 2	"	"
	"	" - 4	"	"
	Honan	Sinyang	"	"
	Hupei	Chungsiang	"	"
	"	Tsoyang	"	"

(Table A. Continued)

	Kiangsu	Fowning	1.3	1.3
	"	Huaiyin	"	"
	"	Tai	"	"
5	Chekiang	Tungyang	5.3	1.6
	"	Tangki	8.5	10.1
	Hunan	Wukang	"	"
	Chekiang	Yungkia	6.6	4.5
	Anhwei	Siuning	4.7	9.7
	Chekiang	Fenghwa	"	"
	"	Linhai	"	"
	"	Lishui	"	"
	"	Shun-an	"	"
	"	Tunglu	"	"
	Fukien	Nanping	"	"
	Hunan	Changteh	"	"
	"	Chen	"	"
	"	Sinhwa	"	"
	"	Yiyang	"	"
	Kiangsi	Fowliang	"	"
	"	Nanchang	"	"
	"	Teh-an	"	"
	"	Tuchang	"	"
	Fukien	Minhow	--	--
6	Szechuan	Fowling	8.0	4.2
	"	Mienyang	1.5	3.2
	"	Neikiang	2.8	2.0
	"	Ta	"	"
	Shensi	Mien	"	"
	Szechuan	Suining	--	--
7	Fukien	Hweian	3.9	5.6
	"	Putien	"	"
	Kwangsi	Jung	1.9	6.3
	Kwangtung	Kukong	"	"
	"	Namyung	"	"
	"	Koyiu	1.8	7.0
	"	Mowming	"	"
	"	Chungshan	2.4	1.4
	Fukien	Lungki	2.7	3.9
	Kwangsi	Yungning	"	"
	Kwangtung	Chaoan	"	"
	"	Kityang	"	"
	"	Kukong	"	"
8	Kweichou	Tushan	1.3	5.6
	Yunnan	Iliang	1.8	3.3
	"	Yuki	"	"
	"	Yungjen	"	"
	"	Mengtze	1.2	7.1
	"	Pinchwan	"	"

(Table A. Continued)

Yunnan	Yuankiang	1.0	4.9
Kweichou	Anshun	2.5	1.3
"	Pan	"	"
"	Tingfan	"	"
"	Tsunyi	"	"
Yunnan	Tsuyung	"	"

* for any region, the t-statistic for the last intercept given is a test of the hypothesis that the intercept is 1.0 (i.e. its log is zero); for the preceding intercepts, it is a test of the hypothesis that they are equal to the last intercept (i.e. that the log of the ratio of that intercept to the last intercept is zero).

APPENDIX VI-E. THE SIMULTANEOUS EQUATION PROBLEM IN THE
  ESTIMATION OF THE CHINESE AGRICULTURAL PRODUCTION FUNCTION.

A major statistical problem commonly arises in the estimation of production functions, called the "simultaneous
equation problem." Its origin is as follows:

A production function is defined as a relationship between output (or a mix of outputs) and a set of inputs,
which are assumed to determine the former. To employ
ordinary least-squares regression techniques to estimate
such a function, one must assume that these inputs are exogenous, i.e. are determined independently of the expected
level of output, lest the explanatory variables be correlated with the error term. But in the normal economic model,
it is in fact assumed that the inputs are determined simultaneously with the outputs, via a set of relations defining
profit-maximizing conditions. In this instance, OLS will
be inconsistent as an estimator, and the estimates of
parameters will be biased.*

In cross-sectional estimation of production functions for
the industrial sector, there is no satisfactory way to avoid
this problem. Consequently, estimation techniques for
simultaneous equations are often employed, the entire system

---

* see E. Malinvaud, Statistical Methods of Econometrics,
  pp. 517-519.

of relationships being specified, or various econometric
tricks are used, such as the combination of time-series with
cross-sectional data with dummy variables to remove correlations of the explanatory variables with the residuals. In
some cases, however, econometricians have chosen simply to
ignore the problem, as data permitting full estimation of
the system is often lacking.

In the agricultural sector, there are more grounds for
optimism. This is because the behavior of producers is
necessarily somewhat different from that of producers in
the industrial sector. In particular, it may be realistic
to consider that the residual in the production function --
the influence of factors influencing production which are
not normally included in that function -- is considered a
stochastic element by the producers, who make their decisions
on the basis of expected or anticipated output levels,
given certain inputs, in advance of any knowledge of the
residual element. The effect of weather is one such element
in the residual which is not predictable before choice of
most inputs is made in agriculture. If this can be safely
assumed, there should be no correlation between the inputs

and the residual and OLS techniques will be consistent and
unbiased.*

However, even if weather constitutes the major portion
of residual influences, there are still likely to be other
differences between producers not directly accounted for in
the production function, but affecting the choice of inputs.
For example, if "efficiency" is something other than a
random variable, producers with higher efficiency should be
aware that they are likely to get higher output from given
inputs; and under profit maximization conditions, more
efficient producers will utilize more of any given input.
While such sources of bias may not be quantitatively important, inclusion of as many such "hidden influences" as
possible in the model will tend to minimize correlation with
the error term, and thus reduce bias.

There is, of course, additional cause for optimism in the
very "backwardness" of Chinese peasant agriculture: Even
though the thrust of our argument is that factor markets
were used in peasant China with a reasonably degree of

---

* see Irving Hoch, "Estimation of Production Function Parameters Combining Time-Series and Cross-Section Data,"
Econometrica, January 1962, pp. 37-38; Zellner, Kmenta and
Dreze, "Specification and Estimation of Cobb-Douglas Production Function Models," Econometrica, October, 1966,
pp. 784-795.

efficiency, these markets _were_ less developed than in industrialized economies, and farms _were_ more dependent on
their own assets. Moreover, we have argued that the peasant
producer's "liquidity" was low, preventing any rapid expansion of scale of operation in response to incentives such as
would be reflected in a correlation between input levels and
the residuals.

For all of the above reasons, there seems no reason to
expect serious bias from the use of OLS estimation techniques
to estimate a Chinese agricultural production function.

APPENDIX VI-F. RESPONSE TO FERTILIZER APPLICATIONS AND
TECHNOLOGICAL CHANGE IN CHINA.

Among the findings of our study of the aggregate production function in prewar Chinese agriculture were the implications that, at existing levels of application of organic
fertilizers, the response rate to additional applications of
nitrogenous fertilizer (measured in ammonium sulphate equivalent) only reached the level of 3 units of additional output
per unit of additional fertilizer input in two crop regions,
specifically the Winter wheat-kaoliang and Yangtze rice-
wheat regions, whereas in the major rice producing areas, it
fell to 1.0 or less. While this result could well be in
error (and in any case probably disguises considerable
variation in response rates within crop regions), it does
conflict with the assumption of Kenneth Walker and Liu
Jung-chao that the marginal response ratios (for ammonium
sulphate) averaged as high as 3.0 in postwar China.[1] Moreover, the Buck data suggests that applications of organic
fertilizers (in terms of nitrogen equivalent) were on the
average much higher than has been previously assumed,
although consistent with postwar Chinese estimates.

If these findings are correct, a case can be made that
the "conventional wisdom" regarding postwar Chinese agricultural policy and performance is incorrect in its assertions
that (1) productivity change in Chinese agriculture during

the Fifties was on the whole non-existent or negative; (2) a
major policy weakness during the period 1952-59 was the
failure to devote sufficient resources to expansion of
chemical fertilizer production. Rather, we will argue below
that the primary bottlenecks to productivity expansion lay
elsewhere, in the need to first develop improved seeds and
increase the depth of plowing, while raising the overall
standard of husbandry, which measures alone would tend to
raise the response rate to fertilizer application, justi-
fying a rapid expansion of fertilizer production. We will
also show that, if the existing level of fertilizer application is taken into account, productivity improvement in the
Fifties was substantial, and may be roughly attributed to
the spread of existing improved seed types, as well as to
increased double-cropping and irrigation.

We will attempt below, first, to show that previous work
on the response rate to fertilizer applications has been
misleading and inaccurate; second, that if the interrelation-
ship of response rate and other technical factors and the
experience in other countries are taken into account, quite
different conclusions emerge. Finally, we shall explore the
consequence of these conclusions in reassessing the nature of
productivity change in the Fifties in Chinese agriculture.

Inadequacies of Existing Estimates of Response Rates

Walker and Liu, in separately concluding that the overall response rate to nitrogen (in terms of ammonium sulphate equivalent) was about 3.0 in Chinese agriculture in the Fifties, share two errors: First, the information on the basis of which their computations were made included almost exclusively average response data -- i.e. the effect of a certain application of fertilizer in comparison with the yield when no fertilizer at all is applied.[2] Given diminishing returns, marginal response rates are of course below average response rates, and can be only estimated from the latter if factors such as soil quality, seed type and levels of other inputs are held constant for each observation. Liu is aware of this problem, and on the basis of scanty data, does attempt to compute marginal yields at different levels of applications. However, examining the data (based on only two experiments) from which his computations are derived, one finds contradictory results: The marginal response rates for rice, at applications of between 15 and 30 kgs./ha., were given as 2.4 and 1.9 respectively; between 30 and 60-75 kgs./ha., fell to 2.3 and .5 respectively. Such differences in response are not too surprising, in view of the fact that the experiments took place 15 years apart and presumably with different seeds, soil, etc. Neither, however, support a response rate approaching 3.0.

Second, Liu and Walker both underestimate the importance
of organic fertilizers -- including manures, nightsoil and
green fertilizers -- in Chinese grain production. Walker
dwells only on manure from pigs; Liu mentions the use of
manures, then proceeds to neglect it in choosing his marginal
response ratios -- or rather, he accounts for it in reverse,
estimating total fertilizer applications from known grain
yields, using an inappropriate formula (see below). Thus he
concludes that the average application of nutrient per
hectare was about 25 kilograms (Perkins raises this to 30 on
the basis of hog production alone).[3]

However, if Buck's estimates of the animal population per
farm in the early Thirties are not too far off, then potential fertilizer consumption from manure and nightsoil
alone was at that time above 30 kgs./ha. in every region of
China, and in the rice-producing regions, ranged from 34 to
164 kgs./ha. of nutrient (the last figure may be unreliable
-- compare Tables 12. and 13., Ch. VIII, LUC, I). A conservative estimate for total organic nitrogen applications
per hectare in 1957, based on Chinese government estimates
of total production of compost and manure, was 58 kgs./ha.
(but 73 kgs./ha. in 1956, as a result of a campaign in that
year; see Note subsequent to this Appendix).

Liu buttresses his argument with a formula estimated
by Williams and Couston[4] from cross-country data, which

represents <u>aggregate</u> yields of <u>all</u> grains as a function of
average fertilizer applications, but with no attempt to hold
constant the differences in soil, seed, technology or type of
grain. Aside from the unreliability of such a formula, its
implications are abused by successively Liu and Perkins.
First, Liu has simply miscalculated the marginal yields
implied by the formula (in his Table 7.3, p. 114): For
instance, at applications of 30 kgs./ha. of nutrient, the
formula implies a marginal response rate of 2.5, not 3.0
(Liu has calculated arc slopes instead of point slopes, at a
point where marginal responses are falling rapidly according
to the formula). Nor do "yield responses eventually level
off" at 3.0, as Perkins asserts: Response rates fall below
2.0 for applications of nutrient above 50 kgs., and eventually to the asymptote of 0.4.

However, the Williams and Couston formula is based on a
particularily inappropriate equation form ($Y=778.5 + .39X
+ 134X^{\frac{1}{2}}$), which <u>assumes</u> marginal response is infinite at zero
levels of application and falls at a <u>decreasing</u> rate to an
asymptote above zero. This inappropriateness is perhaps
reflected in the low R^2 (.75) obtained by Williams and
Couston in their regression on cross-country data.

Such estimates of response rates as have been presented
in the literature, then, rest on flimsy foundations. Nor,
Judging from the evidence presented, do these foundations

justify the assumption of a response rate at the margin
approaching 3.0. As we shall see below, the evidence is
much more consistent with the hypothesis that the response
rate in the Fifties was close to zero, at least for rice, and
in any case insufficient to justify large-scale production of
chemical fertilizer.

Table A.   Average Nutrient (N) Produced Per Hectare, in
           Kilograms, Eight Crop Regions, China 1929-33.

Crop Region	Manure/Hectare	Nutrient/Ha.
Spring wheat	8760	43.8
Winter wheat-millet	6300	31.5
Winter-wheat kaoliang	6170	30.9
Yangtze rice-wheat	6820	34.1
Rice-tea	9880	49.4
Szechuan rice	12900	64.5
Double-cropping rice	12600	63.0
Southwestern rice	32800	164.0

Note: Average of manure/ha. per farm, from J. L. Buck,
        Land Utilization in China, Statistical Volume, p.
        137.   Converted to nutrient assuming 0.5% nitrogen
        by weight (see note 84).   Green manure excluded, as
        were other types of fertilizer.

Sources of Yield Improvements: The Case of Rice

Fertilizer is only one of a variety of sources of yield
improvement in the context of labor-intensive agriculture.
Moreover, the utility of additional fertilizer applications
depends heavily on its interaction with other improvements.
These interactions may be seen clearly in the context of the
agro-technical program for the communes in China, introduced

in September 1958 by Chairman Mao Tse-tung himself in the form of the "Eight-Character Charter" (Pa-tsu hsien-fa).[5] The technical reforms promulgated were an outgrowth of Soviet and Chinese experience (and had been advocated before 1958), and took soil improvement (particularily deep plowing) as their base, heavy applications of fertilizer, irrigation, drainage improvement and the selection of seeds as prerequisites, and scientific close planting as the main theme, supported by plant protection from blight and harmful insects, careful field work, and improvement of farming tools.[6] As the wording suggests, it represented an integrated program of labor-intensive farming; it was illegitimate and often counterproductive in either theory or practice to isolate and selectively implement one or a few of the reforms advocated without implementing the others.

A number of the interrelationships among the individual improvements may be sketched with reference to foodgrains: Close planting, which means a greater density of seedlings per unit area, if undertaken as an isolated practice, invariably results in lower yields after a certain point, due to loss of some percentage of seedlings, insufficient tillering (sprouting from the main stalk), fewer grains per head, and lower weight per grain. If it is to successfully increase yields, the practice requires first the selection of proper seeds (for example, see Table B.); because roots

Table B. Relationship between Type of Seed, Density of
         Planting and Yield, Two Types of Rice.

Density: Seedlings/Mou (000's)	240	300	360	450	480	600
Huangmei Early 20 Day Variety:						
Tillers per Mou (000's)	276	310	372	440	440	555
Grains per Tiller	86	87	63	61	47	36
Weight of 1000 Grains (gms.)	23	22	22	22	22	22
No. of Sterile Grains	16	24	17	18	18	22
Yield (chin/mou)	1000	938	950	869	819	763
Kuei-hua ch'ou Variety:						
Tillers per Mou (000's)	356	360	404	445	472	570
Grains per Tiller	60	56	49	45	37	39
Weight of 1000 Grains (gms.)	26	26	26	26	26	25
No. of Sterile Grains	11	8	12	14	13	10
Yield (chin/mou)	1036	1075	1138	1038	1017	950

Notes: Tillers are the grain-bearing sprouts from the main
        stalk of the plant. "Grains per Tiller" actually
        refers to the number of florets, which, if not
        sterile, produce a single grain. Weight of 1000
        grains presumably refers to non-sterile or realized
        grains. Note that at these densities, either the
        survival rate of seedlings or the tillering rate is
        very low, as only about one tiller per seedling
        results. At lower densities, there are generally
        more tillers per plant, but with less grain per
        head. Source: Ting Ying, Chung-kuo shui-tao
        tzai-p'ei hsueh (A Study of Chinese Paddy Rice
        Cultivation), Table 13-1, p. 348.

must grow downwards rather than sideways, deep plowing is
necessary, which in turn requires better plows; to guarantee
sufficient fertility to support more plants in an increased
volume of soil, heavy use of fertilizer is essential, which
in turn requires deep plowing, etc. (selection of proper

seed varieties is, moreover, important in ensuring response to fertilizer applications); high density decreases resistance to certain types of blight, requiring increased plant protection work.[7] Obviously such rather complicated interrelationships do not fit the simplified framework of, say, the Cobb-Douglas production function, with neutral technological change and inputs whose influences can be independently evaluated. It appears also that either inadequate understanding of or inability to deal with these interrelationships contributed to the failure of the Great Leap in agriculture.[8]

Seed Selection and Fertilizer Response

Of the interrelationships among the eight types of technical improvement mentioned above, that between seed selection and fertilizer response is the easiest to document because of its importance in the Japanese experience. This experience is of interest particularily because the extensive use of chemical fertilizer in Japanese agriculture is often cited as evidence that marginal response ratios (or the marginal productivity per unit of fertilizer applied) in China must be high.[9] Such a comparison is dubious primarily because it ignores the overwhelming importance of the development of new seed types, deep plowing and crop diversification in increasing the use of fertilizers in Japan.

The initial "take-off" in fertilizer consumption in Japan occured in 1888-92, subsequent to and consequent upon the development of the "shinriki" strain of rice, characterized by high responsiveness to fertilizer.[10] This was accompanied by the introduction of new types of plow: "The traditional plows were not capable of cultivating deeply enough to permit the rice plant to make use of heavier applications of fertilizer."[11] Diversification of crops was also important in increasing fertilizer demand, because non-grain crops generally required or proved responsive to much larger applications of fertilizers.[12]

Some Japanese authors are quite explicit in crediting these and subsequent innovations with "making the slope of the marginal productivity curve of fertilizer less steep in successive periods."[13] For those convinced that even without development of new seeds, response to fertilizer was high, it was necessary to explain the disconcerting fact that, despite an approximately 200 percent increase in per acre fertilizer consumption in rice cultivation from 1908-12 to 1933-37, rice yields increased only 17 percent.[14] Nakamura used this observation to argue that yields in the early Meiji period were underestimated (i.e. he could not reconcile the much higher increases in yields before 1903-07 with the rapid increases in fertilizer utilization after that date).[15] Ogura sought an answer in the presumed but unproven decrease in the intensity of family labor in the latter period[16] (why wouldn't intensity changes follow changes in nominal employment, which decreased more rapidly in the earlier period?). Hayami and Yamada, however, provide convincing evidence that a decrease in the rate of development and spread of new seed types was entirely responsible for this phenomenon: They constructed a "seed improvement index" based upon experimental yields for various rice types and the percentages of total crop area sown to each type; they regressed a series of rice yields from 1893-1937 on this index and total per acre fertilizer input (using a log-linear regression), obtaining a good fit (R^2 = .98) and finding that the seed improvement index was definitely more significant than fertilizer application levels, accounting in particular for the lower rate of growth of yields in the Twenties; an elasticity of response to fertilizer applications of .14 was estimated, close to our prewar estimates for Region 7 (Double-Cropping Rice).[17] The three indices are summarized in Table C.

It should be noted that increased response ratios for fertilizer applications to paddy were not the only or necessarily the major reason for continual and rapid increases in fertilizer utilization in the Twentieth Century. Of great significance was the rapid fall after 1920 of the ratio of fertilizer prices to output prices, which made

Table C.   Indices of Rice Yield, Seed Improvement and
            Fertilizer Input Per Acre, Five Year Averages,
            1893-1937, Japan*

Period	Indices of:	Rice Yields	Seed Improvement	Fertilizer Input
1893-1897		100	100	100
98-1902		106	101	104
1903- 07		114	103	110
08- 12		121	104	125
13- 17		129	105	136
18- 22		135	105	148
23- 27		132	105	165
28- 32		134	105	187
33- 37		141	107	210

* From Yūjīrō Hayami and Saburō Yamada, "Agricultural
  Productivity at the Beginning of Industrialization,"
  Table 3., in Ohkawa, Johnston and Kaneda, Agriculture
  and Economic Growth, p. 114. We have converted his
  figures to an 1893-97 base and rounded.

greater applications profitable despite declining physical
response ratios.[18] Thus improved seeds and declining ratios
of output to fertilizer prices have apparently enabled
Japanese agriculture to constantly increase fertilizer
applications while operating at low marginal response
ratios.[19] In fact, production function studies for postwar Japan have found no significant marginal effects for
fertilizer applications, a finding which has been ascribed
to excessive fertilizer use.[20]

It is impossible to generalize on the basis of the
Japanese experience that marginal response ratios to fertilizer applications in Chinese rice production (and probably

other foodgrains) were high at the beginning of the Fifties.
For one thing, Japanese fertilizer use in rice cultivation
only surpassed that of China in the Fifties, although this
fact is often overlooked by Western economists, who have
generally neglected or underestimated the significance of
Chinese organic fertilizer usage.[21] Japanese fertilizer use
in paddy rice cultivation averaged 65 kilograms/hectare
of nitrogen in 1950, rising to 90 kgs./ha. in 1960.[22] We
have estimated that about 58 kgs./ha. were applied on the
average to all crops in 1952; in the prewar period, Buck's
data suggest manure applications of from 54 to 180 killo-
grams/hectare in the rice-growing south.[23]

More important, however, the Chinese were only beginning
to establish in the Fifties the preconditions which permitted
Japanese fertilizer usage to "take off" in the late Meiji.
One such precondition was the extension of deep plowing.
Previous to the 1958 autumn crop, it is reported that plowing was commonly done to a depth of only 3 - 4 inches,
comparable to the practice in Japan prior to the introduction of improved plows in the late Meiji.[24] Although a
major effort had been devoted to producing improved plows,
culminating in 1956, these plows proved too heavy for paddy
cultivation.[25] Consequently, despite particular emphasis on
deep plowing after the promulgation of the "Eight-Character
Charter" in late 1958, increases in depth of only 1 inch on

the average were reportedly attained, probably because traditional implements were still being used, though with greater labor intensity.[26] A major and generally adopted reform in plowing practices, one may assume, awaited the increased emphasis upon supply of capital goods to agriculture of the post-Leap period.

The second precondition was the development of seeds which are responsive to increased fertilizer applications. It has generally been argued by Western economists that existing seeds were responsive, based on the Japanese experience, assumed low levels of fertilizer application in China, and figures on average response resulting from Chinese experimental work. The weaknesses of these arguments have been discussed above. The Japanese experience in particular, even if properly interpreted, is irrelevant insofar as rice is concerned: Rice seed in South China was of the Indica variety; by comparison with the Japonica types developed since the late Meiji, with this type "there is no or little increase in yield by applying nitrogen."[27]

While this statement is somewhat exaggerated, it is true that Indica varieties found in India and Southeast Asia cease to be responsive to nitrogenous fertilizer at relatively low levels of application (by Japanese standards).*

---

* Actually, leaves and stalks are responsive, but grain yields are not.

Diagram 1. Marginal Response of Rice Yields to
Applications of Nitrogen, India, Japan and
China

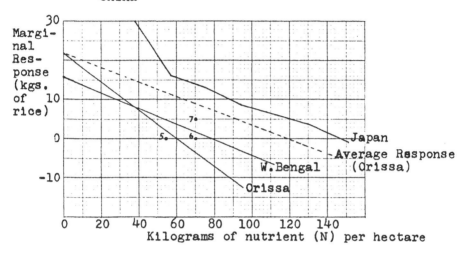

Kilograms of nutrient (N) per hectare

Notes: The marginal response equations for Orissa and W.
Bengal were, respectively:

$$\delta y / \delta x = 21.8 - .3638x \qquad \text{(Orissa)}$$
$$\delta y / \delta x = 16.5 - .2108x \qquad \text{(W. Bengal)}$$

The points number 5, 6 and 7 indicate our estimates based on
Cobb-Douglas production functions for regions 5, 6 and 7
at the geometric mean of existing levels of application
of nitrogen from manure and nightsoil.

Sources: Equations for Orissa and W. Bengal from Robert W.
Herdt and John W. Mellor, "The Contrasting Response of Rice
to Nitrogen: India and the United States," _Journal of
Farm Economics_, 46, Febryary 1965, pp. 150-160.
    Data for Japan derived from Seiichi Tōbata and Kazushi
Ohkawa, eds., _Nihon no keizai to nogyō_ (Japanese Economy
and Agriculture), Vol. 2, Table 5.12, p. 230.

Herdt and Mellor have estimated response curves from the results of experiments in Orissa and West Bengal*, restricting the data to results for commonly grown varieties of lowland rice under irrigation; recent data covering repeated applications of fertilizer over a number of crop years; only inorganic fertilizers applied; and a constant level of P_2O_5 applications.[28] The equations fitted were as follows:

Orissa: $Y = 2156 + 21.8X - .1819X^2$ ($R^2 = .978$)
West Bengal: $Y = 1910 + 16.54X - .1054X^2$ ($R^2 = .949$)

The data clearly indicated that marginal productivity of fertilizer turned negative at levels of application well within the limits of the data (in Orissa, the equation indicates maximum yield and zero marginal response at 60 kgs./ha. of nutrient; in W. Bengal, at 78.5 kgs/ha.). The marginal response curves for nutrient are plotted in Diagram 1., along with a similar curve for a _Japonica_ variety (these may be translated into response to ammonium sulphate by dividing the response ratios and multiplying the nutrient level by 5.).

While the _Indica_ varieties in China and India have evolved separately from common origins and thus do not necessarily have similar response curves, the weight of the evidence

* Orissa and W. Bengal are in the same range of latitude as parts of S. China.

suggests little difference. For one thing, our prewar
estimates of fertilizer response in Regions 5, 6 and 7 fall
fairly near the Orissa and W. Bengal marginal curves (see
Diagram 2.). An experiment in the 1930's gave an average
response of 2.06 for applications of fertilizer to rice of
300 kgs./ha. At this level (60 kgs. of nutrient), the
Orissa equation gives a zero marginal response and an
average response of 2.02! At a nutrient level of up to
74 kgs./ha., a 1962 Chinese source gives an average response
of 2.0 for "foodgrains in general";[29] the Orissa formula
gives 1.6, with a marginal response of - 1.0. Finally,
Walker notes that when central pressure to collect fertilizer was let up, "the Kwangtung authorities did not organ-
ize a fertilizer-collecting campaign as they had done the
previous winter (1956), partly because it was widely
believed that additional fertilizer applications would have
no effect -- the maximum output having already been attained."[30] Fertilizer applications in Kwangtung in 1957 were
reported to be approximately 80 kgs./ha. of nutrient,
implying that marginal response was believed to fall to
zero at or somewhat above this level, a figure which
accords well with the W. Bengal equation but might also
reflect some improvements in seeds by that date.[31] Liu
cites studies showing that, for two rice varieties in
common use, marginal response rates became negative at

applications between 30 and 60 kgs./ha.; for two others, at
much higher applications (some of the varieties used were
recently developed seed types). Moreover, he points out,
"the problem of crop decline as a result of excessive
application of fertilizer has been cited in China as one of
the gravest agricultural problems."[32] There is thus substantial evidence that negative response rates were being
discovered at existing levels of fertilizer use.

It can be concluded that response ratios for fertilizer
applications to paddy rice in China were low, perhaps close
to zero or negative in the early Fifties (this does not
apply to other crops: Our analysis of the Buck data indicates that response ratios in North China remained reasonably high and application levels relatively low; moreover,
vegetables, fruits, and many commercial crops can absorb
much higher levels of nitrogenous fertilizer[33]). Thus the
lack of chemical fertilizers in the Fifties was not as
important a constraint on foodgrains (or at least rice)
production as the unresponsiveness of the seeds employed;
without development and extension of cultivation using
improved seeds, even the incentive for expanded collection
of domestic fertilizers was slight (the fact that only
average rather than marginal response ratios are available
in Chinese materials suggests that Chinese agronomists themselves may have been unaware of this problem).

It is often observed that technical progress in Japanese agriculture during the Meiji period was able to draw on a backlog of improved techniques already built up in certain advanced areas;[34] also that the development and spread of these techniques was attributable largely to the initiative of individual farmers, though with strong official encouragement and support in the diffusion process.[35] Much the same comments apply to seed selection and development in China in the Fifties. The development of an extensive network of agricultural technical stations in China was late in coming, being very much the product of the cooperative movement (their number almost doubled between 1955 and 1956, reaching the level of about one per eight-thousand households[36]). At the same time, new schools and courses were opened to give rapid, short-term training in agricultural technology.[37] The rapidity of development of these institutions undoubtedly meant inexperienced and ill-trained staff; centralized direction and organization for these institutions only seems to have been formalized in 1957, with the formation of the Academy of Agricultural Sciences in Peking under the Ministry of Agriculture.[38]

Given these circumstances and the number of years required to fully develop a new seed type (at one or two generations per year), adapt a breed to suit local conditions and produce sufficient seed, it is not surprising that

seed improvement in the Fifties drew heavily on a backlog of
improved types developed previously, either by experimental
stations under the previous regime or selected by individual
farmers. A tabulation of the origins of improved seed types
(rice) available by the end of the decade is given in Table
D.

Table D. Origins of Improved Rice Varieties by Region of
Cultivation.

Origin Region:	South	Central	North	North-East	South-west
Experimental (Pre-1949)	4	11			1
Experimental (Post-1949)	6	9	1	8	4
Farmer Selection	22	18	3		18
Japan				2	2
Korea				1	3
Taiwan	2				
Total No. of Types	34	38	7	13	23

Source: Ting Ying, *Chung-kuo shui-tao tzai-p'ei hsüeh* (A
Study of Chinese Paddy Rice Cultivation), pp. 257-
61, 269-74, 277-78, 282-84, and 288-90.

What the tabulation doesn't show, moreover, is that about
half of the farmer-selected and imported seeds were a
product of the pre-1949 period (the time element is not
always clear for these categories). The materials from which
these figures are drawn also give the areas of cultivation or

expansion of many of these varieties at different dates; it
is noteworthy that, relative to seeds of other origins, few
figures on cultivated area were given for varieties developed
experimentally post 1949 and all of these were for 1958
(figures for others give dates ranging from 1955 to 1959).
The inference to be drawn is that the spread of new seed
types, at least in rice cultivation, through 1957 (by which
time 55 percent of all crop area employed "improved" seeds)
depended almost exclusively on types developed or selected
in the prewar period and/or by individual peasants. The
benefits of seed development and selection arising from the
greater investment in agricultural research and extension
after the formation of the APC's -- and these benefits
potentially included not only greater responsiveness to
fertilizer, but greater resistance to drought, lodging, flood,
and plant diseases, shorter growing seasons, better adapta-
tions to local conditions, etc. -- could only begin to manifest themselves during and after the Great Leap.

Dense Planting: The "Main Theme"

Of all the agricultural practices recommended by the
"Eight-Character Charter", the only one which represented a
break with trends in technique elsewhere in Asia was dense
planting. For instance, the traditional planting density of
rice in Kwangtung was less than 100 thousand seedlings/mou,[39]
and probably differed little from standards elsewhere in Asia

(density in the Phillipines was traditionally 88 kgs./ha. of seed, or about 88 thousand seedlings per mou).[40] But by 1958, this density had been increased by about 50 percent, and, with the enuciation of the "Eight-Character Charter" and the Great Leap in time for the fall planting, density reached 400-500 thousand seedlings per mou on the average, higher for some hsien. Nor did this end the matter, for the Kwangtung CP Central Committee advocated an increase to 800 thousand to a million seedlings per mou for 1959.[41]

By contrast, in Japan "there has been a gradual tendency for the density of planting rice .. to decrease as the quantity of fertilizers used has increased and as rice varieties of a more prolific type have become common."[42] That is, seed selection emphasized development of plants bearing a maximum number of tillers (grain-bearing offshoots of the main stalk) per seedling. This trend had the particular advantage of saving labor expended in transplanting.[43] Thus, by the Fifties, standard density in Japanese agriculture was down to only 56 thousand seedlings per mou.[44] Improved row planting methods in the Phillipines were said to reduce density to 66 thousand/mou; experiments with the newly developed IR-8 seed in West Pakistan found that a relatively "high" density of 50.8 thousand/mou gave highest yields, though traditional varieties were best at lower densities.[45]

The contrast between the two approaches leads one to wonder whether emphasis on the advantages of dense planting (which was applied to virtually all crops) in fact constituted a productivity-raising innovation or merely another one of those technically-misguided and politically-directed blunders so often cited in the Western literature on Communist Chinese agricultural policy.

The answer, as usual, seems to lie in between the two extremes. There is, for instance, no doubt that planting densities were increased blindly, by administrative fiat, and with little or no regard for local conditions.[46] It is apparent, also, from the volume of propaganda refuting local opinions regarding the practice, that it was introduced over the strong objections of many peasants, although this might be true of any radical reform in agricultural practice.[47] Finally, it seems to have been concluded by non-technically trained authorities that, because increases in density up to those attained in 1958 (500 thousand/mou) had increased yield, that further increases in density would have similar results. It can be assumed that the resultant "leap" contributed substantially to agricultural disaster in 1959-60.

Judging from a debate on the subject in 1961, the initial mistake seems to have arisen from neglect of the economic costs of the increased yields from denser planting.

According to Ma Chien-yu, it was true that an increase from
150 to 500 thousand seedlings/mou increased yield, but
(according to experiments) only by 24 chin (150,000 seedlings resulted in 190,000 effective ears, at 64.24 grains/ear;
500,000 seedlings led to 390,000 ears, but grains/ear decreased to 32.58 and weight per grain also decreased by
about 10 percent). But the increased density required
increased seed to the extent of 20 chin/mow, virtually
cancelling the gain in yield. Moreover, additional land had
to be reserved for seedbeds (at a sacrifice of grain from
both the preceding and following crops, since the growth of
seedlings overlapped the previous harvest and the succeeding
field preparation), additional labor was required for their
preparation, transplanting and care, and heavier applications of fertilizer were needed. An economic loss would
inevitably result from such high densities.[48]

Although the high densities prevailing during the Great
Leap were adjudged by Chinese agronomists themselves ex-
cesses rather than improvements, they nevertheless concluded
that agriculturists should "look for a reasonable range of
density." This range was determined to be 150 to 250
thousand seedlings per mou for rice, or three to five times
as high as recommended in Japan.[49]

The accuracy of the belief on the part of Chinese agronomists that a "reasonable" but increased density of planting

would constitute an economic improvement can be assessed on
the basis of representative experimental materials assembled
in Table E. As is clear from Tables E-2 and E-3, the significance of dense planting lies not only in its yield-
increasing ability at constant levels of other inputs, but
also in its effect on the marginal response to increased
fertilizer applications. As Table E-1. suggests, the latter
was quite low in the early Fifties -- less than one kilogram of grain could be added by an increase of one kilogram
of ammonium sulphate equivalent (note that to obtain an
MRR(N) approaching 5.0 required chemical fertilizer, applied
as top dressing, in amounts not widely available at the
time; organic fertilizers were too bulky to apply as top
dressings). Even though improvements in responsiveness were
obtained experimentally by 1956, probably through use of
better seeds, the marginal response to ammonium sulphate was
still scarcely over 1.5. At such response ratios, it was in
fact not profitable to increase fertilizer applications:
The farm purchase price of rice in 1956 was about .073 yüan
per chin; of ammonium sulphate, about .17 yüan; the wholesale price of bean cakes, something over JMP .34 per chin of
ammonium sulphate-equivalent.[50] It follows that a response
to ammonium sulphate of over 2.3 (to nitrogen of over 11.7)
was required for increased chemical fertilizer applications
to be profitable; of 4.8 or more for increased beancake

applications to be attractive. Even given the distortions
of "competitive" patterns involved in these price ratios, it
is possible that heavy government investment in chemical
fertilizer production was not socially optimal given the
response ratios prevailing in the mid-Fifties.

Table E. Results of Chinese Experiments Indicating Effects
of Varying Densities and Fertilizer Application
Levels on Yields of Rice and Marginal Response
Ratios for Nitrogen (MRR(N)).

1. Effects of Organic and Chemical Fertilizers on Yield,
    Early Experiments.

Year	N/Ha.	Base Application[1] Yield	MRR(N)	Including Top Dressing[2] Yield	MRR(N)	Mixed Base[3] Yield	MRR(N)
1954	60	4270		4280		4670	
			2.9		4.8		5.2
	105	4400		4490		4910	
1956	60	4515		4740		4970	
			6.4		2.9		8.2
	105	4810		4870		5260	

Notes: All application and yield figures are in kilograms per
       hectare. Nitrogen levels given directly in source.
1 -- 3/4 organic; $\frac{1}{4}$ ammonium sulphate; no top dressing.
     "Base application" means application during field
     preparation.
2 -- top dressing of ammonium sulphate, accounting for $\frac{1}{4}$ of
     nitrogen applied. "Top dressing" means application
     after transplanting. Base exclusively organic ferti-
     lizer.
3 -- top dressing as in 2; base 1/5 ammonium sulphate, 4/5
     organic fertilizer.

(Table E. continued)

2. <u>Effects of Increased Seedlings Density on Gains in Yield</u>
   <u>from Increased Nitrogen Application (78 kgs./ha.) in</u>
   <u>Conjunction with Deep Plowing (6-7 inches)</u> [initial
   <u>application level: 80 kgs./ha.; plowing: 3-4 inches.</u>]
   Heilungkiang, 1958

Density (thousands/mou)	Initial Yield*	Marginal Yield**	MRR(N)
68	6550	427	5.5
100	6900	652	8.4
132	7070	652	8.4
160	7140	825	10.6

* kilograms/hectare.
** to additional fertilizer applications (N = 78 kgs./ha.)
Notes: Fertilizer applied included stable manure, ammonium
       sulphate (200 kgs. at initial level; 300 at
       increased level), and ashes. The nitrogen content
       of stable manure was estimated at .3 percent (earth
       applied as fertilizer contains roughly .15 percent
       N; animal manure, .5 percent). The ashes were
       assumed to be free of nitrogen.

3. <u>Effects of Increased Seedlings Density on Gains in Yield</u>
   <u>from Increased Nitrogen Application (1958 Chekiang</u>
   <u>experiments)</u>.

Density Level (000's):	100		200	
Nutrient Applied (kgs./ha.)	Yield	MRR(N)	Yield	MRR(N)
75.0	4540		4680	
		7.0		9.2
112.5	4800		5010	
		2.1		5.1
240.0	5060		5660	

Notes: First two levels of application include primarily
       animal manures, assumed to have .5 percent nitro-
       gen content. Third level includes 100 <u>tan</u>/<u>mow</u> of
       mud (assumed to have same nitrogen content as earth
       (<u>t'u-fai</u>) used as fertilizer, or .15%; 10 <u>chin</u>/<u>mow</u>
       of ammonium sulphate.

(Table E. continued)

Source: Ting Ying, <u>Chung-kuo shui-tao tzai-p'ei hsueh</u> (A
    Study of Chinese Paddy Rice Cultivation), p. 384,
    p. 369 and p. 372 respectively.

Consequently the fact that a "reasonable" degree of close
planting, as advocated in the Sixties, could roughly double
the response to additional applications of nitrogen provides
an additional economic justification for the practice. This
is true despite the suggestion that, considered independently
of fertilizer usage, density increases above 150 thousand
seedlings/<u>mow</u> were not economically justifiable: For
instance, at the nutrient application level of 75. kgs./ha.,
Table E-3. implies that a doubling of density increases
yield by only 140 kgs., while seed requirement alone would be
about 100 kgs. But the yield increase resulting from a
combination of increased density and fertilizer is greater
than the sum of the increases resulting from either undertaken independently, and, at a slightly higher ratio of
grain to fertilizer prices than prevailed in 1956, the former
might have been profitable to the commune as well as the
state even though neither density nor fertilizer increase
was in itself profitable.

The probable reasons why dense planting in rice cultivation has not been encouraged in Japan (except during the war,
when it was officially encouraged because of the <u>shortage</u> of

fertilizer[51]) can now be sketched: Of primary importance is
the fact that it wasn't necessary, given the price policies
of the Japanese government: Since the war, the latter has
followed policies aimed at maintaining artificially high
grain purchase prices and low fertilizer prices, through
price regulation for both commodities and heavily subsidized
investment in the fertilizer industry (which, moreover, has
been in existence long enough to have passed the initial
high-cost stage).[52] By 1960, these policies had lowered
the marginal response ratio for ammonium sulphate necessary
to make increased consumption profitable to about .33,
compared to 2.3 for China in 1956.[53] Secondly, the trend in
the real wage rate in Japanese agriculture has been sharply
upwards since World War II, while the agricultural labor
supply has been decreasing;[54] thus relative price changes
dictated labor-saving rather than labor-using innovations
such as dense planting. Thirdly, the whole evolution of
Japanese seed types has apparently been in the direction of
increasing tillers per stalk and grains per tiller; while
this may have been economically sensible, given the above,
it constitutes an evolutionary path differing from the
yield-per-unit-land emphasis of seed development oriented
around dense planting, and might be "irreversible" (i.e.
Japanese seed types might not respond well to dense planting).
Finally, Chinese rice culture by the late Fifties, combining

substantial amounts of nitrogen from organic sources with
growing supplies of chemical fertilizers, was poised at the
brink of a "leap" into a fertilizer-consuming technology
which could take it well beyond the 81 kilograms/hectare
recommended nitrogen consumption of Japanese rice farmers[55]
(note the application levels involved in the experiments in
Table E.); the situation was thus unprecedented in Japanese
agricultural experience.

On the basis of the above discussion, it seems to us that
the formula for a technical revolution in agriculture expressed in the "Eight-Character Charter" is well-founded and
scientific. Its prescription of a technology taking land as
the primary scarce resource and treating labor as virtually
unlimited differs from the Japanese approach -- but then it
is accepted that Japan no longer possesses the extremely
elastic supply of labor characteristic of the Fei-Ranis/
Lewis type economy,[56] whereas China does. It is not, however, a prescription to be applied blindly, as it often was
previous to and during the Great Leap, since it is clear
that local and seasonal shortages of labor and other resources are not infrequent. Finally, it is a prescription
which, while labor intensive, requires heavy support from
the industrial sector, since organic fertilizers probably
could not be expanded much beyond the levels reached in the
Fifties, seasonal and local bottlenecks in labor and animal

power required labor-releasing mechanization, and improved
implements and increased pesticides and other agricultural
chemicals were necessary to sustain a technique based on
dense planting.

Productivity Change in Chinese Agriculture in the Fifties

The method most commonly used to provide a "quantitative" measurement of technological change over a period of
time assumes that the production process can be described by
a linear homogeneous production function (the Cobb-Douglas
form is normally assumed) and that technological change
operates in a "neutral" fashion, i.e. raises the level of
output by a uniform factor or percentage, regardless of the
level of inputs of labor, land or capital. Under these
circumstances, if an index of gross output is available,
the contribution of technological change to changes in output can be derived by subtracting from the output index an
index of inputs weighted by the appropriate parameters in
the production function (in the Cobb-Douglas form, the
elasticity coefficients).

Whatever the justification for application of this
method to measurement of technological change in advanced
Western countries (simplicity is no doubt the primary one),
the assumptions on which it is based are of questionable
relevance to the agricultural sector of an underdeveloped
country like China. Significant technological change over

a long period is clearly not "neutral", as may be seen by
comparing value-shares of inputs in the advanced countries
with those in underdeveloped countries (for example, the
share of labor in Japanese agriculture increased from about
one-sixth in the late Meiji to about one-half by the onset of
the Depression).[57] Consideration of the types of innovations which were spreading rapidly by the late Fifties in
Chinese agriculture (e.g. new seed types, deep plowing,
close planting) suggests some shifts in the parameters of
the production function by that time. Thus one must assume
technological change wasn't very significant in Chinese
agriculture before one can measure it on neutrality assumptions.

Nevertheless, for those who would discount the above
objections or for whom "this kind of aggregate economics
appeals" (to quote Solow, its foremost exponent[58]), we will
attempt such a measurement of technical change as a "residual". It has been done previously for Chinese agriculture
(Anthony Tang, in A. Eckstein et al., 1968) as well as for
the Japanese case (Shūjirō Sawada, in K. Ohkawa et al.,
1970), and there is positive value in correcting the misleading conclusions drawn from the former and in having a
basis of comparison in the latter. We are able, moreover, to
draw on our study of the prewar agricultural production
function instead of relying entirely on value-shares of

inputs, and make good use of the greater information on fertilizer usage and productivity which we have derived.

The details of our criticism of Professor Tang's previous attempt to construct an index of factor inputs and the precise derivation of our own weighting scheme are left to a concluding Note. In sum, Tang derives an index which suggests a very rapid rate of growth of inputs, following entirely from an unwarranted weight given to the rapid growth from insignificant levels in 1952 of chemical fertilizers and insecticides.[59] Similarily, the lower growth rate of our indices (see Table F.) follows exclusively from the downward revision of these weights; we have in addition taken explicit account of fertilizer produced within the agricultural sector (which Tang implicitly accounts for in the high value-share weight given to labor in his index -- a procedure which makes sense only in a perfectly competitive context). The separate inclusion of farm-produced fertilizers is consistent with our physical-input approach to the prewar production function, makes clear the relative insignificance of chemical fertilizer production, and makes the weighting scheme more comparable with those derived for Japan and Taiwan, where purchased fertilizer is predominant.

Both the Tang and our input indices share a number of weaknesses which taken together probably lead to an underestimate of changes in inputs: Changes in the rate of

Table F. Output, Input and Productivity Indices, 1952-1957 (1952=100)

Type of Index Year:	1952	1953	1954	1955	1956	1957
Output Index (Official)	100.0	103.1	106.6	114.8	120.5	124.7
Output Index (Tang Adjusted)	100.0	101.5	103.3	109.5	113.2	117.2
Input Index (Cultivated Land)	100.0	101.9	104.4	106.0	111.9	109.6
Input Index (Sown Acreage)	100.0	102.3	105.5	107.4	114.7	111.8
Productivity Index (Offic./Cult.)	100.0	101.2	102.2	108.8	108.6	115.1
Productivity Index (Offic./Sown)	100.0	100.8	101.1	107.4	105.8	112.9
Productivity Index (Tang/Cult.)	100.0	99.6	98.9	103.5	101.3	107.6
Productivity Index (Tang/Sown)	100.0	99.2	97.8	102.1	98.5	105.4

Notes: The official output index is derived from the gross value of agricultural product in 1952 prices. The Tang adjustment is based on the
assumption that output was underreported by 6% in 1952, the extent of
underreporting declining linearly until 1956. Both indices are cited
in A. Tang, "Policy and Performance in Agriculture," in Eckstein (1968),
p. 489. The two input indices are derived in the Note following this
appendix, using, respectively, cultivated and sown land as the land inputs.
The productivity indices are residuals from the output and input indices,
with different permutations thereof.

utilization of the potential labor force, and of the ratios
of seed and traditional fertilizer to sown acreage (except
1956-57 for the latter) are assumed away, despite evidence
that these were on the increase through the period (after
all, such mobilization of resources and increased intensity
of cultivation were major aims of the cooperativization of
the countryside). Farm implements are assumed to have
followed the same growth path as livestock and feed. It is
to be expected, then, that a residual productivity index,
based on such an input index, will exaggerate the influence
of changes in "productivity", unless that concept is defined
rather broadly to include improved rates of utilization.

There remain the questions of the reliability of the
official output series and of whether the input series
ought to be based on cultivated or sown acreage. Tang
accepts the basic reliability of the official series, but
assumes an underreporting of 6 percent in 1952, decreasing
to zero by 1956.[60] The existence of overall underreporting, decreasing over time, is at least debatable: For
instance, if 1952 gross value of agricultural product in
1933 prices had reached the 1931-37 level, then Dwight
Perkins' recent reestimation of 1931-37 and 1957 GVAP gives
an index value of about 124.4 for 1957 over a prewar base,
comparable to the official index at 124.7, over a 1952
base.[61] Ignoring changes in price relatives between 1933

and 1952, this undercuts the Liu-Yeh argument for underreporting, based in part on the assumption of recovery to
prewar levels by 1952.[62] Moreover, underreporting of output
would surely extend also to inputs, since the major source of
underreporting would certainly be misestimates of cultivated
or sown area, upon estimates of which in turn are based the
indices of seed and traditional fertilizer;[63] animal production, moveover, appears both in the GVAP and as an input
to production under capital. If outputs and inputs were
assumed to have been underreported in the same proportions,
the productivity index resulting would be less impressive
than that derived from the official index (see Table F.),
but certainly more so than that based on the Tang revised
output index.

The question as to whether an input index based on cultivated or sown acreage would be more proper is more difficult
to resolve. Sown acreage of course takes into account to a
greater extent the expansion of irrigation facilities and a
higher rate of utilization of potential factor supplies;
yet acreage in a second crop should not be given the same
weight as an expansion of single-cropped land by the same
proportion, from which one would normally expect higher
marginal yields.[64] An appropriate input index thus would
probably be something in between those given in Table 1. for
cultivated and sown acreage.

The residual productivity indices of course reflect not only the inadequacies of the input and output indices, but also the unquantifiable effects of varying natural conditions, particularily weather. One way of dealing with this problem is to assume with Tang that official reports of harvest conditions ("good", "bad" and "average") reflect only natural conditions and that these can be treated as random variations around a linear productivity trend.[65] These assumptions seem hard to justify for a command economy undergoing rapid year-to-year changes in organization and inputs, but they do imply a trend consistent with official assessment of harvest conditions (see Figure 2.).

Figure 2. Productivity Index and Harvest Conditions

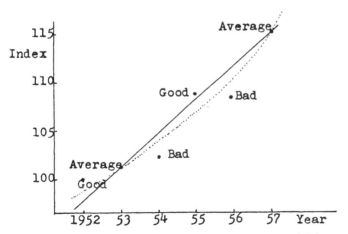

Note: Technique due to Tang, Fig. 1, p. 486. Lines fitted through average years (1953 and 1957).

Such a linear trend implies an annual rate of growth of productivity of between 2.7 and 3.4 percent (using the official
indices; the Tang indices lower this to slightly less than 1
percent). But the productivity index and reported harvest
conditions are equally, or perhaps even more consistent with
an accelerating productivity trend, with a rather low rate of
growth in the first few years but approaching 5 percent per
year by 1956-57.

Starting from roughly the same basic data as Professor
Tang, but revising the weights given to the commercial
portion of current inputs to properly account for their
relative insignificance in the early Fifties, we thus
arrive at a conclusion quite the opposite of his: That
changes in "productivity" (within which we must include
changes in utilization of inputs, in irrigation and double-
cropping, etc., not reflected in our aggregate input index)
were responsible for more than half (in the late Fifties) of
the changes in the value of output in Chinese agriculture,
1952-57. This conclusion is, of course, more in accordance
with official claims of innovation, mobilization and capital
improvements than it is with the overemphasis on the lack of
"adequate regional experimentation" and "price signals" of
most American China-watchers.[66]

Before taking a closer look at the sources of input and
productivity growth, it may be instructive to compare these

results with similar estimates for the agricultural sector
in Japan (due to Shūjirō Sawada[67]). The Sawada estimates
are also based on the assumptions of a production function
homogeneous of degree one, and value-share weights, but
since the period analyzed is lengthy, five-year period
average changes are estimated and shifts in weights between
periods are permitted to relax the neutrality assumption.
Our previous objections to the value-share weighting approach
apply equally to Sawada's attempt (at least for the prewar
period[68]), but the current inputs index and its weight
(about 20 percent of gross value in the prewar period) seem
in order.[69] As Sawada's index is based on value added in
agriculture, we have revised his productivity index to a
gross value basis for comparability with our own.

If our estimate of 2.7 - 3.4 percent for the annual trend
of productivity growth in Chinese agriculture for 1952-57
is acceptable, it evidently surpassed the rates of growth of
productivity in Japan for all periods but 1953-56. Nor did
Japanese gross output at any time in the prewar period
display as high a growth rate as those suggested by either
the official or the Tang-adjusted indices for China.
Technological change was, of course, not an insignificant
source of growth in agriculture in Japan -- indeed, if
Sawada's indices are to be believed, it was the major source
of growth of value added and more than held its own as a

Table G. Five-Year Growth Rates of Value Added (V) and
          Current Inputs (K); One-Year Growth Rates of
          "Technical Change", Estimated from Value Added
          Index (F) and Gross Value Index (F'): 1883-1963.

Period	Five-Year Rates:	$\frac{\dot{V}}{V}$	$\frac{\dot{K}}{K}$	One-Year Rates: (percent)	$\frac{\dot{F}}{F}$	$\frac{\dot{F'}}{F'}$
1883-87		0.099	0.067		1.5	1.3
88-92		0.018	0.083		1.3	1.0
93-97		0.129	0.058		1.9	1.4
98-02		0.091	0.207		1.3	1.1
1903-07		0.097	0.121		1.1	0.9
08-12		0.127	0.121		1.9	1.6
13-17		0.044	0.128		0.4	0.4
18-22		-0.014	0.113		-0.3	-0.3
23-27		0.056	0.073		0.9	0.8
28-32		0.050	0.110		0.8	0.7
	One-Year Rates:					
1953-55		0.095	0.060		9.4	6.5
54-56		0.082	0.074		8.3	5.7
55-57		-0.004	0.053		0.8	0.6
56-58		0.037	0.084		4.4	3.0
57-59		0.019	0.095		2.7	1.9
58-60		0.006	0.088		0.9	0.6
59-60		0.002	0.058		0.5	0.3

Notes: The first three columns are taken directly from
        Shūjirō Sawada, "Technological Change in Japanese
        Agriculture: A Long-Term Analysis", in K. Ohkawa
        et al., eds., Agriculture and Economic Growth
        (Princeton, 1970), Table 1., p. 143. The fourth
        column converts the rates of technological change
        based on the value-added index V/V and an aggre-
        gate inputs index giving only one-year interest
        value weight to current inputs K/K to rates based
        on a gross value of output index and an input
        index giving full value proportion weight to
        current inputs. The conversion was based on data
        and information given in the same table and on
        pp. 140-141. It may be shown that the apparent
        rate of technological change based on a value-
        added approach is always greater than that based on
        a gross-output approach. Readers should refer to
        the above reference for further information on the
        components of the input index and the weights used.

share of growth in gross product, compensating for a declining labor force and only slowly increasing acreage. But it would seem that China compressed into five years productivity changes taking between two and three times as long in Japan. Before accepting such a conclusion, however, it would be advisable to examine more closely the sources of such changes in both countries.

Three major elements contributing to productivity can be "quantified": The formation of the APC's saw substantial increases in the area sown with "improved" seeds, irrigated and, to a lesser extent, double-cropped. The growth in the percentages of total cultivated area having these improvements is displayed in the first three columns of Table H. To obtain at least a vague idea of their overall effects on production, we shall make several "simplifying" (and ultimately indefensible) assumptions: (1) That these factors separately affect the "production function" in a neutral, independent and multiplicative fashion (as we have assumed for "technological change"); (2) "improved" seeds are assumed to increase yield uniformly by 15 percent (an impressionistic but conservative figure, based on gains to improved rice varieties, as given in Ting Ying, A Study of Chinese Paddy Cultivation, pp. 257-290); irrigation is assumed to improve yields by 30 percent (based on figures given in Table 14, p. 223 of John L. Buck, Land Utilization in China, Statistical

Table H.   Hypothetical Effects of Improved Seed Utilization,
Irrigated and Doubled-Cropped Area on the
Production Function, 1952-57.

Year:	1952	1953	1954	1955	1956	1957
Percent of Cultivated Area:						
Sown to Improved Seeds	4.7%	7.4%	14.9%	20.6%	36.4%	55.2%
Irrigated	19.8	20.3	21.3	22.4	28.7	31.1
Multiple-Cropped	30.9	32.7	35.3	37.2	42.3	40.6
Indices of Productivity Improvement Due to:						
Improved Seeds	100.0	100.6	101.7	102.7	104.9	107.8
Increased Irrigation	100.0	100.1	100.3	100.7	102.3	103.1
Increased Multiple Cropping	100.0	100.7	101.7	102.1	103.7	103.2
Index of Productivity Increase Due to Above Factors	100.0	101.3	103.7	105.3	111.2	114.9
Residual Index of Productivity (from Table 1., column 5)	100.0	101.2	102.2	108.8	108.6	115.1

Notes: The basic data are derived from Nai-ruenn Chen,
Chinese Economic Statistics, Tables 5.3 (p. 288),
5.4 (p. 289), and 5.1 (pp. 284-85). The percent of
area sown to improved seeds is for foodgrains only.
The indices of productivity improvement are based on
weighted averages of yields on "ordinary" land and
yields on land sown to improved seeds, irrigated or
double cropped. It is assumed that improved seeds
offer gains in yields of 15 percent; irrigation, of
30 percent; each additional crop on the same land,
of 35 percent. The overall index is a multiplicative composite of the separate indices (since each
factor is assumed to affect the production
function independently and multiplicatively).

Volume); double-cropping by about 35 percent (Kenneth Walker cites figures suggesting a 43 percent gain for double-cropped rice; we have reduced this arbitrarily to account for the fact that yields of second crops other than rice were probably a lower percentage of the first-crop yield[70]). It is apparent from the indices of productivity increases derived from these sources (see Table 4.) that the major gains were all made after collectivization. Moreover, the composite index of productivity gains from these sources is strikingly close in magnitudes to the previously derived residual index based on the official index and cultivated land (see Table F.). Indeed, the differences between the two indices in different years are in the directions suggested by Communist assessments of "harvest conditions" (refer to Figure 1.). If our weights are not exaggerated (and even though our "independence" and "neutrality" assumptions deserve rejection), we may tentatively conclude that virtually all net gains in productivity through increased collectivization in the Fifties may be attributed to these three elements, with other positive and negative influences

roughly cancelling out*; of these three elements, the spread
of improved seeds brought the greatest gains in productivity
in the 1955-57 period, underlining Vogel's assertion that
"with the new organization, new knowledge and new techniques
could be diffused by political directives."[71]

Our emphasis on the importance of improved seeds is, we
believe, unique in the literature on postwar Chinese agricultural development.[72] This is probably because of the
difficulty of quantifying this and similar "qualitative"
changes. Nevertheless, in view of the facts that Chinese
efforts to step up the rate of discovery and adoption of
such qualitative changes increased rapidly after 1955 and
were "institutionalized" in the Sixties; that reassessment
of the sources of growth in Japanese agriculture shows such
factors (and particularily seed selection) to have been of
key importance; that recently developed rice, wheat and corn
hybrids have been shown to have a potentially revolutionary
impact on the agricultural production functions of countries
adopting them, outweighing by far the effects of growth in
traditional inputs,[73] it would be advisable to examine more

---

* This does not mean that other positive elements were negligible; strictly speaking, the most that can be asserted
   is that other sources of productivity gains did not in
   the aggregate outweigh negative influences.

closely the potential and actual impact of qualitative
technical change in postwar Chinese agriculture.

NOTE: DERIVATION OF INPUT INDEX FOR CHINESE AGRICULTURE,
       1952-57.

It is the purpose of this appendix to attempt to reconstruct an index of changes in productive inputs to the
agricultural sector in post-war China which will reflect,
through an appropriate weighting scheme, the relative contributions of each type of input to changes in gross output,
and thereby, on the assumption that technological change was
"neutral", permit us to deduce the impact of technological
change as a residual.[74] We use the word "reconstruct"
because such an attempt has already been made by Prof.
Anthony M. Tang, who purported to show that technological
change was uniformly negative over the period 1952-57.*
To justify a new attempt, it is our first task to show that
Prof. Tang's work is based on inaccurate and inappropriate
assumptions.

Professor Tang's aggregate input index and its separate
components are summarized in Table H. These components
include labor (defined as the labor force potentially available for agricultural work, with no attempt to account for
changes in the rate of utilization of that labor force over
time, e.g. through more labor days per year or increased

---

* Anthony M. Tang, "Policy and Performance in Agriculture",
   in A. Eckstein et al., eds., Economic Trends in Communist
   China.

female participation in production); cultivated acreage
(Index I) or sown acreage (Index II); capital (theoretically animals and farm implements, but in fact reflecting
only changes in total livestock and feed); and current inputs. The last includes seed, chemical fertilizer, traditional fertilizer and insecticides (see Table B., which
breaks down that index); but Prof. Tang, lacking knowledge
of changes in seed and traditional fertilizer use over time,
in fact employed the index for sown area as a substitute
for both, implying (unjustifiably) constant per sown
hectare utilization of both inputs over time (in actuality
it is probable that both increased towards the end of the
period[75]). There is then, because of underrepresentation
of changes in labor, seed and traditional fertilizer utilized, some downward bias to the individual indices. Yet
the overall input indices both indicate a substantial increase in input levels between 1952 and 1957, higher in fact
that even official Chinese indices of output (whence the
negative technological change conclusion). It is apparent
at a glance that this effect is almost entirely traceable to
the weighted effect of the current input index. It is
incumbent on us, then, to examine the weighting scheme
employed.

The ideal weights for the separate indices of agricultural
inputs would be the elasticity coefficients of the production

function if known. By contrast, Prof. Tang employs the
common alternative of using the total values of each input
(as a percentage of output) as relative weights. This is
justifiable only if inputs in Chinese agriculture were employed in such a way as to equate the value of marginal
product of each input with its price, in which case the two
methods are equivalent. That this was the case in post-war
Chinese agriculture is at least questionable on two grounds:
First, we have already shown in our analysis of prewar farming that the value of marginal product was not equal to the
price of labor or land on the majority of farms (this, of
course, is the whole thrust of the Fei-Ranis/Lewis theories
of labor-surplus peasant societies). Secondly, it is well
known that the Chinese Communists often employed rationing
rather than let prices adjust to excess demand; and that
agricultural inputs such as chemical fertilizers and insecticides were in effect rationed commodities in the early
Fifties at least. Therefore the use of value shares as
proxies for elasticities may considerably overestimate the
effect of labor inputs, and underestimate that of land and
any inputs for which excess demand exists.

However, the above objections are insignificant in comparison with the distorting effects of the specific weights
chosen in aggregating the current input index. The weights
chosen by Prof. Tang are borrowed from Liu and Yeh[76] and

represent the percentage of gross value of plant products taken up by seed (4.4%), purchased fertilizers (5.0%) and agricultural chemicals (.9%).[77] However, (1) the gross value of plant products represents only part of the gross value of agricultural output (from which the output index is derived) and the input weights should be adjusted downwards to account for this; (2) Tang claimed that the 5.0% weight for purchased fertilizers pertained to all fertilizers, when in fact Liu explicitly states that this represents only purchased fertilizers (according to Liu's data, all fertilizers were valued at about 22.2% of plant output in the mid-Fifties); Tang splits this 5% into traditional fertilizer and chemical fertilizer (the former given twice the weight of the latter for reasons not made explicit: Liu implies the weights should be three to one for purchased traditional fertilizers versus chemical fertilizers); (3) the Liu-Yeh weights for these items pertain to mid to end-of-period (Liu-Yeh's figures for seed pertain to 1954; for other items, they represent averages of three figures, one for a single county in Chekiang, 1953-56, the others for Liaoning and Kiangsu both in 1957; the variance of these figures is tremendous, moreover), whereas 1952 weights should be used, else rapidly growing inputs receive much too great a weight. The overall effect of all these errors is to give chemical fertilizers and insecticides an unjustified weight in the index, totally out of line with either their value percentage or their effect on output in 1952.

To reconstruct the input index, we begin with the index of current inputs. From our work on the prewar agricultural production function, we know that the elasticity with respect to fertilizer was roughly 15-25 percent, which compares favorably with the Liu-Yeh estimate of 22.2 percent for all fertilizers as a percent of gross value of plant output. This would suggest that at least in the mid-Fifties Communist valuation of fertilizers was such that price was approximately equal to the value of marginal product (the 1955 price of chemical fertilizer was about .17 yüan per chin; with paddy rice priced at about 6.00 yüan per picul to the farmer, marginal value product pricing would imply a marginal response ratio for chemical fertilizers of about 3.0, which is consistent with the findings of other scholars, however questionable they may be).[78] The price of chemical fertilizer in 1952 was about .19 yüan/chin,[79] implying that total production was valued at about 212 million yuan, .25 percent of 1952 GVAP.[80] Estimated total production of compost and manure in 1956 was 2500 million tons, in 1957 2000 million tons.[81] Since 1956 may have seen an exceptional effort to collect native fertilizers,[82] we shall assume that the 1955 production was the same as the lower 1957 level, and, in

the absence of other knowledge, derive the 1952-55 figures
(following Tang) on the assumption that they grew only as
fast as sown acreage. Assuming a rate of utilization of 65
percent[83] and since both green fertilizer and manure contain
approximately .5 percent nitrogen or 2.5 percent ammonium
sulphate equivalent,[84] we derive a chemical fertilizer
equivalent for total compost and manure production using a
conversion factor of .01625 (the resulting estimates may be
conservative, since the utilization figure is applicable to
potential, not actual production and moreover we have
neglected nutrients other than nitrogen, which by contrast
are accounted for in the chemical fertilizer production
figures; on the other hand, the reliability of the Communist
estimates of manure and compost production are probably
not very high). The estimated 1952 total production of
domestic fertilizers of 30,400 million metric tons implies
an application level of 288.4 kgs./ha. of ammonium sulphate
equivalent, which is certainly not to be viewed as an overestimate in comparison with prewar estimates based on
Buck's figures on manure production alone. It also implies
that for every 100. units of chemical fertilizer-equivalent
from organic sources, 1.05 units of chemical fertilizer were
applied. Using these proportions to estimate the percentage
weight for changes in organic fertilizer utilization from
the .25 percent weight estimated for chemical fertilizers,

we derive a weight of 23.8 percent for traditional fertilizers, or roughly 24.0 for all fertilizers, which compares
well with the 22.2% average for the Liu-Yeh figures, the
19% estimate for Taiwan given by Tang, and our prewar estimates (all based only on crop output, however).

Turning to insecticides, the Liu-Yeh figures were 0.3, 0
and 2.3 percent, all for mid or end-of-period. The price of
the commonest insecticide ("666") was about .25 yüan/chin
in 1955, and .68 yüan/chin in 1952.[85] Taking the latter
price (even though it may be high relative to value of
marginal product), total value of insecticide production in
1952 was about 20,400 thousand yüan, or .042 percent of GVAP.
Note that production increased about ten times over the
period while GVAP increased less than 20 percent, so that
towards the end of the 1952-57 period insecticide would
constitute about .35 percent of GVAP in 1952 prices, or
about .5% of gross value of plant output, a figure within
the range of the Liu-Yeh figures, though less than the
average of .9% which both they and Prof. Tang employ (the
average is inordinately effected by the 1957 figure for
Liaoning, a province which could hardly be said to be
typical of Chinese agricultural production patterns).

We accept the Liu-Yeh estimates for value of seeds as a
percent of gross value of plant output (based on a nationwide

survey); adjusting these by the 1954 percentage of GVPO to
GVAP[86] gives a weight of 3.2 percent.*

The sum of the weights for the components of the current
input index gives us the overall weight of that index as
27.3 percent (compared to Tang's 11.0 percent). It remains
to derive the weights for other inputs: In the absence of
other information and because of its consistency with
Japanese and Taiwan value shares, we accept Tang's estimate
of .09 for the share of capital. Judging from our work on
the prewar production function, labor's share may be closer
to 35 percent than to 55 percent as Tang assumes; land is
derived as a residual at 29 percent (if prewar rents were
about 45 percent of the main crop; and this represented
about 80% of all crop output; and GVAP is about 1.38 times
the value of all crop output: then the land rent share of
GVAP would be about 26 percent).

While the relative weights given to the main subordinate
indices may be individually off by a margin of plus or minus
five or ten percent, the effect on our derivation of an
index of productivity will not be sufficient to reverse the

---

* GVAP includes, in addition to GVPO, the gross values of
animal, forest, fishery and miscellaneous products, to
none of which are seeds, fertilizers and insecticides
relevant inputs.

conclusion that productivity change in postwar Chinese
agriculture was positive. This follows entirely from our
downgrading of the weights assigned to chemical fertilizers
and insecticides and upgrading of the significance of traditional fertilizers; those who wish to dispute our conclusions
must be prepared to show that such a revision was not
appropriate.

Table H.   Tang Aggregate Input Index, China, 1952-57.

Year	Labor	Land Cultivated	Sown	Capital	Current Inputs	Aggregate Inputs I	Inputs II
1952	100%	100.0%	100%	100%	100%	100.0%	100.0%
1953	101	100.6	102	107	115	103.1	103.5
1954	103	101.3	105	113	138	107.3	108.2
1955	105	102.0	107	109	172	112.0	113.2
1956	107	103.6	113	108	243	121.3	123.6
1957	109	103.6	111	120	249	124.2	126.0

Source: Anthony M. Tang, "Policy and Performance in Agriculture," in A. Eckstein, W. Galenson and T. C.
Liu (eds.), Economic Trends in Communist China,
p. 482.

Notes: Indices I and II correspond to the use of cultivated
and sown land indices as components, respectively.
Weights employed were: Labor .55; land .25;
capital .09; current inputs .11. See text for
discussion of components and weighting scheme.

Table I. Tang Current Inputs Index and Its Constituents.

Year	Seed	Chemical Fertilizer	Traditional Fertilizer	Insecticide	Aggregate Index
1952	100	100	100	100	100
1953	102	186	102	127	115
1954	105	252	105	272	138
1955	107	395	107	447	172
1956	113	505	113	1060	243
1957	111	611	111	994	249

Source: Anthony M. Tang, op. cit., p. 481.
Notes: Weights employed were: Seed 42.7%; chemical fertilizer 12.2%; traditional fertilizer 36.4%;
insecticides 8.7%.

Table J. Reconstructed Current Inputs Index and Aggregate
Indices.

Year: Indices	1952	1953	1954	1955	1956	1957
Traditional Fertilizer	100	102	105	107	125	107
Current Inputs	100.0	102.7	106.5	110.2	128.5	113.6
Aggregate Input Index I	100.0	101.9	104.4	106.0	111.9	109.6
Aggregate Input Index II	100.0	102.3	105.5	107.4	114.7	111.8

Notes: All component indices not listed in this table are the
same as those in Tables H. and I. Weights employed
in aggregating current inputs index were: Seed
11.7%; chemical fertilizer .916%; traditional
fertilizer 87.2%; insecticide .154%. Aggregate
indices I and II correspond to cultivated and sown
acreage respectively. See text for weights.

APPENDIX VI-F: NOTES

1. See K. Walker (1965); Liu Jung-chao (1970).

2. K. Walker (1965), p. 49fn.; Liu (1970), Appendix C-7, pp. 154-155.

3. Liu (1970), p. 114; Perkins (1969), p. 73, fn. 34.

4. See M.S. Williams and J. W. Couston (1962).

5. S. Burki (1969), p. 4 and Asakawa Kenji (1961), translated in JPRS 9209, p. 42.

6. Asakawa Kenji (1961), in JPRS 9209, pp. 41-43.

7. See "Kuang-tung-sheng ti shui-tao mi-chih ch'ing-k'uang," in Ministry of Agriculture (1961), pp. 5-11; also Ting Ying (1961), pp. 363-396.

8. Discussion in Ministry of Agriculture (1961) argues that crop failures under dense planting could always be attributed to neglect of these interrelationships. An article by Ma Chin-yu, dated March 23, 1961 (JPRS 9398), stresses neglect of economic costs of related requirements by advocates of extremely high planting densities. The labor cost was particularily serious.

9. Perkins (1969), p. 76.

10. Takekazu Ogura (1967), pp. 14 and 370.

11. Ibid., p. 645.

12. Vegetables, for instance, can take levels of application twice as high as paddy rice. See the recommended application levels in Table 5.11 of Tōbata and Ohkawa (1964), Vol. 2, p. 229.

13. Shūjirō Sawada, "Innovation in Japanese Agriculture, 1880-1935," in W. W. Lockwood (1965), pp. 345-347.

14. Ogura (1967), pp. 34-35; Tōbata and Ohkawa (1964), Table 5.7, p. 214.

15. James I. Nakamura, "Growth of Japanese Agriculture, 1875-1920," in Lockwood (1965), pp. 292-293 and 295.

16. Ogura (1967), pp. 33-35 and 38.

17. Hayami and Yamada in Ohkawa (1970), pp. 114-116.

18. See Tōbata and Ohkawa (1964), Graph 5.2, p. 214.

19. Ibid., pp. 228-230.

20. Heady and Dillon (1961), p. 625.

21. See our discussion of Tang's input index in the Note following this appendix, as well as our earlier criticisms of Walker and Liu's approaches.

22. Ogura (1967), Table 19-8, p. 386.

23. See Table A. of this appendix.

24. The figures for China are reported in Ministry of Agriculture (1961), p. 9 (Kwangtung) and p. 25 (Kiangsu); for Japan, in Ogura (1967), p. 370.

25. K. Walker, "Organization of Agricultural Production," in Eckstein, Galenson and Liu (1968), p. 420.

26. Ministry of Agriculture (1961), pp. 9 and 25.

27. Ogura (1967), p. 604.

28. Herdt and Mellor (1965), pp. 150-160.

29. Quoted in K. Walker (1965), Table XIII, p. 49.

30. K. Walker, in Eckstein, Galenson and Liu (1968), p. 435.

31. Total supplies of traditional fertilizer, including green manures, approximated 2100 chin/mou in Kwangtung in 1957 (in Hopei, almost twice this level), according to Sun Hsing-tung (1962), p. 315. Green manures and animal manures have about the same yields of nitrogen (Ibid., p. 316); animal manure yields nitrogren equivalent to about .5 % of its weight (see note 84.). We have used this figure for conversion, even though certain other types of traditional fertilizer included in this figure have lower nitrogen content; but 1957 applications of traditional fertilizers were reported 20 % lower than 1956 nationally. Finally, one additional kg./ha. of nitrogren was added to reflect available chemical fertilizer supplies (Perkins, 1969, p. 74).

32. Liu Jung-chao (1970), p. 115.

33. Tōbata and Ohkawa (1964), Table 5.11, p. 229.

34. Perkins (1969), p. 53.

35. Bruce F. Johnston, "The Japanese 'Model' of Agricultural Development: Its Relevance to Developing Nations," in Ohkawa (1970), pp. 61 and 94.

36. Nai-ruenn Chen (1967), Table 5.101, p. 369 and Table 5.104, p. 370.

37. Ezra Vogel (1969), p. 151.

38. S. Burki (1969), p. 48.

39. Ministry of Agriculture (1961), p. 5.

40. From unpublished materials of the I.R.R.I. in the Phillipines. Data given by Ma Chin-yu (JPRS 9398) implies that .66 kgs. of seed produce 10,000 seedlings.

41. See note 39.

42. Takane Matsuo (1959), p. 127.

43. Ibid., p. 127.

44. Ibid., p. 164.

45. The Phillipines datum is from unpublished IRRI materials (1968); the Pakistan data from Government of West Pakistan, Agricultural Department, Annual Report on Accelerated Rice Research Program (1966), Table 7., p. 31.

46. K.Walker in Eckstein, Galenson and Liu (1968), p. 421.

47. Many such materials are to be found in Ministry of Agriculture (1961).

48. Ma Chien-yu (JPRS 9398). It is interesting that the subject was still controversial as late as 1961.

49. Ting Ying (1961), p. 353.

50. Rice purchase price for Kwangtung, cited in K. Walker in Eckstein, Galenson and Liu (1968), Note 16., p. 432; ammonium sulphate retail price to cooperatives for 1955, from Government of India (1959), p. 126; price of bean cakes given in N. R. Chen (1967), p. 419; according to Sun Hsing-tung (1962), p. 316, 1000 chin of green manure is equivalent to something over 100 chin of oilseed cakes,

implying that the latter contain less than 5 parts per
hundred of nitrogen.

51. Takane Matsuo (1959), p. 128.

52. Ogura (1967), pp. 208-209 and 227-230.

53. The wholesale prices of rice and ammonium sulphate
in 1960 were 76.4 yen and 21 yen per kilogram respectively.
We have assumed a 10 percent margin between grain farm
purchase and wholesale prices, and fertilizer wholesale
and retail prices. Statistics from Oriental Economist,
Japan Economic Yearbook, 1961, p. 178.

54. See Ryōshin Minami, "The Supply of Farm Labor and
the 'Turning Point' in the Japanese Economy," in Ohkawa
(1970), p. 276 (Fig. 1) and p. 283.

55. As of 1956. Walker (1965), p..48. Actual utilization
in Japan, of course, had gone well beyond this figure by
the Sixties.

56. There remains some dispute about when the 'turning
point' was reached (whether after World War I or II). See
Ryōshin Minami in Ohkawa (1970), pp. 286-291.

57. See Shūjirō Sawada, "Technological Change in
Japanese Agriculture: A Long-Term Analysis," in Ohkawa (1970),
Table 1., p. 143.

58. Robert M. Solow (1957), p. 312.

59. Anthony M. Tang, "Policy and Performance in Agriculture," in Eckstein, Galenson and Liu (1968), pp 481-483.

60. Ibid., pp. 485-487.

61. Perkins (1969), p. 30.

62. Liu and Yeh (1965), p. 414.

63. Crop output was estimated from yield and sown area data. See N. R. Chen (1967), pp. 61-62.

64. See Table 7, p. 423 of K. Walker, "Organization of Agricultural Production," in Eckstein, Galenson and Liu (1968), pp. 397-458.

65. A. Tang, in Ibid., pp. 485-487.

66. Ibid., p. 490.

67. Shūjirō Sawada, in Ohkawa (1970), pp. 136-154.

68. See Keizō Tsuchiya, "Economics of Mechanization in Small-Scale Agriculture," in Ohkawa (1970), pp. 155-169, for evidence that labor hours and use of machinery were optimal with respect to relative prices in the period 1957-1964 in Japan.

69. For time series of commercial and traditional fertilizer inputs, see Yūjirō Hayami and Saburō Yamada, "Agricultural Productivity at the Beginning of Industrialization," in Ohkawa (1970), p. 114.

70. Walker in Eckstein, Galenson and Liu (1968), Table 7, p. 423.

71. E. Vogel (1969), p. 173.

72. Perkins (1969), pp. 38-41 and p. 52, gives the subject more discussion than most, but treats it as of uncertain importance.

73. See Lester Brown (1970) for further discussion.

74. See Robert Solow (1957), pp. 312-320 for discussion of the methodology.

75. Both dense planting (requiring more seeds per hectare) and collection of manure and planting of green manure crops were being strongly advocated by the mid-Fifties. See Government of India (1959), p. 146 and pp. 159-160.

76. Liu and Yeh (1965), Appendix, Tables E-9 and E-10, p. 414.

77. Ibid., p. 414.

78. See Walker (1965). Note also our criticisms of his findings as related to the prewar response to fertilizer applications.

79. Government of India (1959), p. 126 for 1955 prices; N.R. Chen (1967), p. 410 for price index.

80. Volume of fertilizer production from Tang in Eckstein, Galenson and Liu (1968), p. 481; 1952 GVAP from N. R. Chen (1967), p. 139.

81. From Asakawa Kenji, "Four Reforms in Agriculture," (JPRS 9209), p. 61.

82. Walker in Eckstein, Galenson and Liu (1968), pp. 423-424.

83. Government of India (1959), p. 146 gives the utilization of night soil as 70 percent of potential production and of stable manure as 60 percent. It is uncertain whether

the government figures on manure and compost represent
potential or actual applications or something in between,
but we have assumed the former to remain on the conservative side.

84. Ibid., p. 147. Fresh nightsoil contains about .85%
nitrogen; fermented (diluted with water) about .5%. Dried
manure cakes, as used in North China, contain about 1.7%
nitrogen. The following information may be found in
Bulletins Nos. 3 and 4 of the Imperial College of Agriculture
and Dendrology, Tokyo, November 1888 and March 1889:
Composition of nightsoil includes from .55 to .59% nitrogen;
dried bean cakes about 4.3%; astralagalus lotoides (a typical
green manure) about .48% in its fresh state, previous to
plowing under.

85. Government of India (1959), p. 126 and N. R. Chen
(1967), p. 410 give 1955 price and price index respectively.
We have interpolated the price index to derive 1955 from
1954 and 1956 price index numbers.

86. Liu and Yeh (1965), p. 400 and p. 412.

APPENDIX VI-G. GRAIN PRICES IN PREWAR CHINA: DATA AND SOURCES

This appendix summarizes the primary statistical materials
used in deriving regional grain prices for 1929-32 China. It
is hoped that these materials will be of use to other scholars.

The first set of materials (Table A.) is a list of conversion factors intended to permit standardization of local
market prices of rice and wheat given in prewar sources for
units of volume and weight differing from the national
standards. This standard, beginning from the early Thirties, was supposed to be the "shih" or market system (according to which, 1 shih shih = 10 tou = 100 sheng was equivalent to 100 litres; 1 shih tan (picul) = 100 shih chin
(catties) was equivalent to 110 pounds or 50 kilograms).
However, the system most prevalent as late as 1935 (and,
according to source (2)*, through 1949 in many areas) was
the old Ch'ing system, with 1 chin = .597 kilograms and
1 shih = 1.035 hundred litres. Yet, lacking any serious
government efforts to standardize, even this system was
honored more in the breach than in the observance. This
was in large part because use of non-standard weights and
measures permitted merchants to increase their profit mar-
gins in both buying and selling. As will be seen from
Table A., standardization even relatively speaking extended
only to the picul, and not at all to the shih. As grain
prices and volumes of production were most frequently quoted

in <u>shih</u>, conversion to standard piculs presents a problem
to any scholar interested in comparing prices, yield or
total production in different areas. It is hoped that
Table A. will facilitate such conversion for data on rice
and wheat, although its geographical coverage remains
spotty (note that the conversion factors given do not apply
to other crops, for which totally different measures were
often used).

The number of <u>shih</u> catties of husked rice per <u>shih</u> <u>shih</u>
has been placed at 150 (Perkins, 1969, p. 314; the Shanghai
standard according to source (18) was 156 shih <u>chin</u>); by
the old standard, then, 129 <u>chin</u> of rice is equivalent to
1 Ch'ing <u>shih</u>. This figure agrees well with source materials
permitting calculation of the conversion rate. It also
appears to be the case that the weight of one <u>shih</u> of wheat
was not substantially different from that of a <u>shih</u> of rice.
Consequently we have taken this as the standard for conversion of local units of grain volume to weight equivalents
in Ch'ing <u>chin</u> where direct equivalents were not given.

Table B. gives price data for wheat and rice for 1935,
drawing on source (7). Conversion to prices in Ch'ing standard piculs was based on the data provided in Table A. The
methods and assumptions used are summarized in the note
preceding that table.

Both Table A. and Table B. include map keys, giving the

coordinates for the appropriate provincial map in Chang
Ch'i-yün's (National War College) <u>Atlases of North and South</u>
<u>China</u> (Taipei, 1961-62); these should be helpful in locating
particular <u>hsien</u>.

Table C. constitutes an attempt to link the 1935 prices
to those of the years 1929-1933 by means of price indices.
The weakest links in the chain are the years 1929-1930, for
which we had to rely on Buck's limited sample and other
piecemeal data. A number of interpolations for these years
were unavoidable because of gaps in the published data.

On the basis of the average provincial prices for 1935
(from Table B.) and the indices of Table C., Table D. gives
the average provincial prices for each kilogram of rice or
wheat in the years 1929-1933. These are the prices used in
the text in the conversion of money to real wages, etc.

---

* Sources given by number refer to the bibliography of
source materials on weights and measures and prices given
at the end of the appendix.

TABLE A. CONVERSION FACTORS: LOCAL SHIH AND CHIN TO CH'ING OFFICIAL CHIN*

Province	Locality	Map Key	Chin to Local shih	Chin to Local chin	Comments
Hopei	Peking		129	1.00	
	Tientsin		129	1.00	
	Hulu	F3	185	.93	
	Cheng-ting	F3	191	.95	
	Ch'ing-yüan	G3	129	1.00	
	Hsing-t'ai	F4	252	.96	
	Ts'ang	H3	183	.93	
	Yenshan	I3	409	1.01	
	Chi-tse	F5	214	.93	
Shantung	T'eng	C4	150	1.00	tou used instead of shih
	Chi-nan	C3	180-260	.88	
	Tsing-tao	F3		1.00	
	Fu-shan	G2	350-400	1.00	underlined for rice
	Lin-i	D4		.94	
	Ch'ing-ch'eng	C2	223	.91	
	T'ai-an	C3		1.01	
	Li-chin	D2	216	.96	
	Hui-min	C2	268	.86	
	Chi-ning	B4		1.00	
	Ch'ang-shan	C3		1.00	
	Wei	E3		1.00	
	Tzu-yang	B4	1000	1.00	1 tou = 100 chin (wheat)
	Ch'ang-lo	D3	220		
Honan	K'ai-feng	E4	310	.86	rice (special ta-tou)
	"		180	.86	wheat (special ta-tou)
	Cheng	D4	375	.86	
	Hsü-ch'ang	D4	267	.89	
	Yen-ch'eng	E5	287	.96	
	Shang-shui	E5	263	.94	rice
	"		282	.94	wheat
	An-yang	E2	287	.96	
	Nan-yang	C6	195	.88	
	Lo-yang	C4	242	.86	wheat
	Ch'üeh-shan	E6		.89	
	Hsin-yang	E6	366	1.00	
	Huang-ch'uan	F6	226	.94	

* One Ch'ing shih of rice = 129 Ch'ing chin.

(TABLE A.CONTINUED)

Shansi	Reported to have converted to shih system (1 shih = 125 Ch'ing chin)				
Shensi	Sian	E7	161	1.00	other source 270 chin
	San-yüan	E7	218	.99	
	Li-ch'üan	E7	202	.96	
	T'ung-kuan	G7	222	.98	
	Ch'ien; Pin	E7	214	.98	
	Feng-hsiang	D7	201	.98	
	Nan-ch'eng	D8	218	.79	
	Liao-yang	C8	315	.97	
	Yen-an	F5		1.03	
	Kan-ch'üan	F5		1.03	
	Fu	F5		1.03	
	Sui-te; Wu-pao	G4	151	.93	
	Pao-ch'i	D7	260		
	Liu-pa	C8	300		
	An-k'ang	F9	200		
	Tso-shui	F8	320		
Kansu	Lan-chou	D7	365	.98	
	P'ing-liang	G8	320	.98	
	Ku-yüan	G7	530	.98	
	Ching-ch'üan	H8	353	.98	
	Ching-yüan	E7	375	.99	
	Ting-hsi	E8	314	.96	
	Hsi-ho	F9	375	.99	
	Ch'eng	F10	325	.98	
	Li	F9	376	1.00	
	Hui	G10	1000	1.00	wheat 1 tou = 100 chin
Ninghsia	Ning-hsia		350	.98	(Yin-ch'üan hsien)
Kiangsu	Nanking		125	1.00	wheat
	Shanghai		~130	1.00	
	Wu	G4	129	1.00	
	Wu-hsi	G4	116	1.05	
	Chiang-p'u	E3	119	.96	
	Kuan-yün	F1	245	.88	also Kan-yü, Tung-hai
	"		(210)	.88	barley
	Hsiao	C1	146	1.00	
	T'ung-shan	D1	179		

(TABLE A. CONTINUED)

Province	Place	Code	Value	Ratio	Notes
Chekiang	Hang-chou		126	1.04	by "ordinary" standards
	Yin	D4	126	.96	
	Yung-chia	C5	126	.88	
	Feng-hua	D4	147	.98	
	Lin-hai	D5		1.02	
	Chin-hua	B4	139	.97	
	Lan-chi	B4	139	1.05	
	Ch'ang-shan	A5	168	.99	
	Li-shui	B5	187	.96	
	Chien-te	B4	137	.98	
	Huang-yen	D5	140		
	Wen-ling	D5	140		
	Lo-ching	C5	140		
	Chia-shan;	C3	150		
	Wu-i	B5	"		
	T'ien-t'ai	D4	100		
	I-wu	C4	100		
	Hsüan-p'ing	B5	100		
	Chiang-shan	A5	180		
Anhwei	Huai-ning	D5	134	1.00	
	Wu-hu	E4	124-130	1.00	
	Hsi	E6	79	1.00	
	Hsiu-ning	E6	79	1.00	
	Ch'i-men	D6	130	1.09	
	Hofei	D4	124	1.00	
	Feng-yang	D3		.94-1.00	
	Shou	C3	222	1.03	
	Ch'u	E3	181	.98	
Kiangsi	Nan-ch'ang	C3	147	1.00	
	Chiu-chiang	D2	160	1.00	
	Ch'ing-chiang	C3	140	1.00	wholesale (retail = 125)
	Fu-liang	E2	142	1.01	
	Shang-jao	E3	127	1.00	
	Lin-ch'üan	D3	108	1.01	
	P'ing-hsiang	A4	112	1.00	
	Chi-an	B4	127	.98	
	Kan-chou	B6	136	1.00	"other grains" = 140
	Jui-chin	C6	112	.98	
Hupei	Hankow		134	*	*varies with origins of merchants

(TABLE A. CONTINUED)

	Chiang-ling	E4	112	.98	
	I-ch'ang	D4	143	1.20	
	Chung-hsiang	E3	177	.98	common along Han River
	Mien-yang	F4	130	.99	
	Ching-men	E3	177	.98	
	Hsiang-yang	E2	177	.96	
	I-ch'eng	E3	191	1.00	(also called Tzu-chung)
	Kuang-hua	D2	108	1.00	see also Chung-hsiang
	An-lu	F3	218?	1.00	tou = 2.5 chin by definition
	Tzu-kuei	C4	270	.96-.99	
Hunan	Ch'ang-sha	D3	119	.83	
	Yüeh-yang	E2	135	.98	
	Li-ling	E4	124	1.02	also Ch'ing tou
	Li	C2	128	1.00	
	Heng-yang	D4	157	.96	
	Ch'ang-te	C2	144		
	Yüan-ling	B3	169	.95	
	Chih-chiang	A4	170	.96	
	Huei-t'ung	A5	147	.88	
Szechuan	Ch'eng-tu	D4	300	.94-1.00	
	Feng-chieh	I3	388	.94	
	Chung-ching	F5	300	1.01	
	Wan	H4	487	.98	
	Lo-shan	C5	600		others also used
	I-pin	D6	300	1.00	
	Nan-ch'ung	F4	310	>1.00	possibly ≤ 370
Sikang	Ya-an	C4	320	1.00	Szechuan map key
	K'ang-ting	A4	258	1.00	
Fukien	Fuchou	D3	163	1.00	
	Hsia-men	C5	124	.96	
	Ning-te	D3	117	1.00	
	Ku-t'ien	C3	147	.92	
	Chien-ning	A3	81	.97	
	Nan-p'ing	C3	120	1.10	

(TABLE A. CONTINUED)

	Shun-ch'ang	B3	260	.94	
	Ch'ang-ting	A4	119	.85	
	Shao-wu	B2	119	.96	
	Lung-ch'i	B5	137	1.24	
Kwangtung	Kuang-chou		129	1.01	
	Swatow			1.01	
	Ho-p'u	C5	188	.94	
Kwangsi	Kuei-lin	G2		≈1.00	
	Ts'ang-wu	H4	117	.94	
	Yung-ning	E5	≈200	1.00	
Yunnan	Hsiang-yün	G4	105		
	Ma-kuan	K7		1.01	
	Meng-tzu	J6	83	1.01	other grains ≈ 60
	Huitze	J3	58		other grains ≈ 65
	Chao-t'ung	J2	58		other grains ≈ 65
Kweichow	Kuei-yang	D3	179	≈1.00	
	Kuei-ting	E3	224	≈1.00	
	Ssu-nan	F2	530	.83	
	Chen-yüan	F2	342	.99	
	Ta-ting	C2	474	≈ .80	
	Pi-chieh	C2	320	≈ .89	

TABLE 8.   NOTES ON SOURCES AND METHODS OF EXTRAPOLATION

All price data are drawn from source (7); these prices are given
therein as the range of (monthly?) prices for one or more markets
per hsien, covering hsien exporting the products for which prices are
given (therefore hsien without marketed surpluses or in which the
relevant product was not marketed outside the hsien will not have
price quotations.) Where these ranges are reasonably narrow, it is
to be expected that an average of extremes, as taken here, will not
differ greatly from a weighted mean of monthly price averages. It is
apparent from the Forward that quotations are for 1935, when the
survey was carried out.

Prices of grains are quoted for units of either weight or volume,
without any mention of the local variations in the size of these
units compared with national standards, creating a conversion problem
(in the case of Szechuan and Yünnan, compounded by a currency conversion
problem.) We have drawn on Table A. for weights and measures
information by hsien; but, as the hsien for which such data was available
were considerably fewer than those for which prices were quoted, it
was necessary to guess at the system used in many cases, largely on
the basis of geographical contiguity to localities for which the system
was known. As an aid in assessing the reliability of the resulting
price figures, a "Degree of Confidence" rating has been given for such
"guesstimated" hsien (an 'H' refers to adjacent localities, likely to
share markets and systems of weights and measures; an 'M' to hsien
separated from the "known" hsien by one or two counties, yet likely to
share external markets; an 'L' refers to estimates strongly subject to
error in weights and measures.) Hsien which were obviously on a
different system (e.g. price averages based on likely measures were
clearly too high or too low) or on a system not likely to be related to
any particular known system have simply been excluded from our listings.
Where price quotations were based on piculs, however, we have assumed
in the absence of other information that official weights were used,
as the variation in weights across China was generally within ten percent
of the official standard. The conversion factors actually used in each
calculation have been underlined. Where confidence ratings are not
given, weights and measures data were available for the specific hsien.
Additional notes are given where further caviats are required.

As a final warning, it should be remembered that the variation in
units of volume between even adjacent hsien can be very great. Thus
where extreme variations in prices between nearby hsien are recorded
in Table 8., it is as likely as not that it is our use of inappropriate
conversion factors that is responsible. For example, for Lan-chou,
Kansu, our 1934 source gives a catty equivalent of 365 for wheat,
whereas a 1927 source gives 1200. For two hsien (Yu-chung and Ning-
ting) in the immediate vicinity of Lan-chou, examination of prices

suggested that one might be using the first and the other the second
system, and it was on this assumption that the conversions were made.
But it is certainly possible that each locality might have used systems
totally different from either of those applied.

Given these caviats (which apply only to data originally in terms of
units of volume), however, the price estimates given seem considerably
more consistent than use of uniform conversion factors would imply,
and probably reflect well not only variations in price between provinces,
but between smaller agricultural regions as well.

TABLE B. PRICES OF WHEAT AND RICE BY COUNTY, CHINA, 1935

Province	Locality	Map Key	Conversion Factors Volume	Weight	Confidence	Prices Wheat	Rice
Hopei	Tientsin	I2	129	1.00			11.30
	Ning-ho	I2	129	1.00	H	7.50	9.50
	Fu-ning	K2	129	1.00	L		10.45
	Ho-chien	H3	183	.93	m	9.68	
	Ku-ch'eng	H4	183	.93	L	6.30	
	Ch'ing	H3	183	.93	H	11.30	
	Ch'ing-hai	H3	129	1.00	H	4.10	
	Peking	H2	129	1.00		7.10	9.50
	Ta-hsing	H2	129	1.00	H	5.35	10.45
	Tung	H2	129	1.00	H	6.75	
	Shun-i	H1	129	1.00	m	8.15	9.70
	Huai-jou	H1	129	1.00	H	7.35	8.15
	Cho	G2	129	1.00	H	8.95	13.00
	Wen-an	H3	129	1.00	m		8.10
	Man-ch'eng	G3	129	1.00	H	5.25	
	Hsin-ch'eng	H2	129	1.00	H	4.45	
	Jung-ch'eng	G2	129	1.00	H	5.50	
	Hsiung	H3	183	1.00	L	9.25(?)	
	Jen-chiu	H3	129	1.00	m	4.45	
	Huai-lu	F3	185	.93		4.05	4.60
	Luan-ch'eng	F4	191	.95	m	3.90	
	Lung-p'ing	F4	191	.95	L	3.00	
	Chu-lu	G4	214	.93	m	2.34	
	Yao-shan	F4	214	.93	L	2.58	
	Nei-chiu	F4	252	.96	H	3.10	
	Yung-nien	F5	214	.93	H	4.05	
	Ch'eng-an	F5	214	.93	m	4.30	
	Tung-ming	G6		1.00(?)	L	8.00(?)	
	Pu-yang	G6	180		L	5.25	
	Ch'ang-yüan	F5		1.00(?)	L	5.00	
	Mean (per shih chin)					5.78 (4.84)	9.49 (7.95)
Shantung*	Chu-ch'eng	E3		1.00	H	9.65	
	Huan-t'ai	C3		.93	L	4.10	
	Te	B2	183		L	4.10	
	Te-p'ing	B2	268	.86	H	4.50	
	P'ing-yüan	B2	183		L	5.05	
	Ch'ü-fu	B4	1000	1.00	H	3.65	
	Teng	C4	150	1.00		2.90	
	I	C5	150	1.00	H	2.75	

* Some hsien data has been excluded because of obviously high and
  unknown local standards of volume.

(TABLE B. CONTINUED)

	Wen-shang	B4	1000	1.00	H	2.75	
	P'u	A4		1.00	L	3.50	
	Fan	A4		1.00	L	4.10	
	Kuan-ch'eng	A4		1.00	L	2.85	
	Ch'ang-lo	D3	220	1.00	H	9.75	
	Kao-mi	E3	220	1.00	M	7.95	
	Mean (per shih chin)					4.45 (4.00)	
Honan	Chi	E4	180	.86	M	5.55	
	Yen-ling	E4	267	.89	H	4.50	
	Huai-yang**	E5	282	.94	H	8.00	
	Shang-shui	E5	282	.94		4.05	
	Hsi-hua	E5	282	.94	H	3.20	
	T'ai-kang	E4	282	.94	L	4.80	
	Fu-k'ou	E4	267	.89	M	3.10	
	Yen-ch'eng	E5	287	.96		3.84	
	Shang-chiu	F4	282	.94	L	4.35	
	Ning-ling	F4	282	.94	L	4.80	
	Sui	F4		.86	L	2.80	
	Nei-huang**	E3	287	.96	H	4.35	
	Chi	E3	180		L	4.10	
	Ch'i	E3		.96	L	7.30	
	Hsiu-wu	D3	375	.86	L	7.55	2.55(?)
	Yang-wu	D3	375	.86	L	5.80	
	Mien-chih	B4	242	.86	L	5.60	
	Nan-yang	C5	185	.88		5.15	
	T'ang-ho**	C6	185	.88	H	8.10	
	Fang-ch'eng**	C5	185	.88	H	10.30	
	Wu-yang	D5	287	.96	H	4.00	
	Shang-ts'ai	E5	287	.96	M	5.05	
	Sui-p'ing	E5	287	.96	M	7.30	
	Hsin-yang	E6	366	1.00		3.75	2.90
	Ku-shih	F6	226	.94	H		4.00
	I-chuan	C4	242	.86	H	8.65	
	Mean (per shih chin)					5.44 (4.56)	3.15 (2.64)
Shansi***	Tai-yüan	D4	129	1.00			7.75
	Yu-tzu	D4	129	1.00		4.50	3.15
	Hsin	D3	129	1.00			3.10

** large difference between maximum and minimum price implies average
   of the two may diverge widely from annual average price.
*** Shansi reported to be universally using the Ch'ing official
    standards; in fact this apparently was not true in some cases.

(TABLE B. CONTINUED)

	Fen-hsi	C5	<u>129</u>	1.00		2.70	
	Yu-hsiang	B7	<u>129</u>	1.00		3.20	
	Chieh	B7	<u>129</u>	1.00		3.50	
	Hsi	B5	<u>129</u>	<u>1.00</u>		3.50	3.50
	Yung-ho	B5	<u>129</u>	1.00		4.25	
	Tun-liu	D5	129	<u>1.00</u>		2.70	
	Chin	D5	129	<u>1.00</u>		2.40	
	Ho-shun	E4	129	<u>1.00</u>		2.90	
	Shuo	D2	129	<u>1.00</u>			1.28(?)
	Mean (per <u>shih chin</u>)					3.25 (2.72)	3.76 (3.15)
Shensi	Kao-ling	F7	<u>218</u>	1.00	H	6.20	
	Chou-chih	E7	<u>161</u>	1.00	M		7.00
	Ho-yang	G6	200	.98	M	7.88	
	Mei	D7	<u>260</u>	.98	H	5.75	8.85
	Han-yin	E9	<u>200</u>	1.00	M		6.00
	Mean (per <u>shih chin</u>)					6.61 (5.53)	7.28 (6.09)
Kansu	Yu-hung	E8	<u>1200</u>	.98	H	4.60	
	Ning-t'ing	D8	<u>365</u>	.98	M	3.70	
	P'ing-liang	G8	<u>320</u>	.98		4.85	7.65
	Lung-te	G8	320	.98	M	2.80	
	Chuang-liang	F8	<u>320</u>	.98	M	4.05	
	Ting-hsi	E8	<u>314</u>	.98		10.80	
	Hui-ning	F8	<u>314</u>	.98	H	6.35	
	T'ung-wei	F8	<u>314</u>	.98	M	9.55	
	Hui	G10	<u>1000</u>	1.00		2.75	5.50
	Ching-yang	H7	<u>129</u>(?)		L	4.85	3.10*
	Ho-shui	H7	<u>129</u>(?)		L	3.50	2.30*
	Hu-an	H7	<u>129</u>(?)		L	3.10	2.30*
	Cheng-ning	I8	<u>129</u>(?)		L	3.50	2.70*
	Ning	I7	<u>129</u>(?)		L	3.90	2.70*
	Mean (per <u>shih chin</u>)					4.52 (3.79)	6.58 (5.51)
Suiyuan	Lin-ho	D4	<u>350</u>	.98	L	2.30	
Kiangsu	Nanking	E3	125	1.00		5.75	6.25
	Chen-chiang	F3	125	<u>1.00</u>	H	4.96	6.63
	Chiang-ning	E4	125	<u>1.00</u>	H	5.75	7.75

* "yellow rice" -- price not included in average for Kansu.

(TABLE B. CONTINUED)

Li-shui	E4	125	1.00	H		5.50
Chiang-p'u	E3	119	.96			5.50
Liu-ho	E3	125	1.00	H	2.20	6.40
Kao-ch'ün	E4	125	1.00	M	4.90	4.00
Wu	G4	129	1.00		5.25	6.55
Wu-chiang	G4	129	1.00	H		7.42
Wu-chin	F4	116	1.05	H	4.35	7.08
Wu-hsi	G4	116	1.05		4.27	6.10
Chiang-yin	G4	116	1.05	M	3.80	6.60
I-hsing	F4		1.00	L	3.75	6.45
Ch'ing-chiang	G3	116	1.05	M	4.43	
T'ang-yang	F4	125	1.00	H	4.36	
Chin-t'an	F4	116	1.05	L	4.35	
Li-yang	F4		1.00	L	4.75	
Huai-an	F2		1.00	L	4.75	
Fo-ning	F2		1.00	L	5.50	
Yen-ch'eng	G2		1.00	L	5.25	7.50
Kuan-yün	F1	220	.88		3.70	
Ch'iang-tu	F3	125	1.00	H	5.40	7.15
I-ch'eng	F3	125	1.00	H	4.20	
Kao-yu	F3	125	1.00	M	6.87	8.50
Hsing-hua	F3		1.00	L	4.40	
Pao-ying	F2		1.00	L	5.00	
T'ai	F3	125	1.00	M	4.65	7.43
Tung-t'ai	G3		1.00	L	5.75	6.80
Yang-chung	F3	125	1.00	L	3.50	
Nan-t'ung	G3	130	1.00	L	2.70	
T'ai-hsing	G3	116	1.05	L	4.02	
T'ung-shan	D1	179	1.00		3.60	
T'ang-shan	C1	179	1.00	M	2.15	
Feng	C1	179	1.00	M	3.20	
P'ei	C1	179	1.00	M	4.78	
Su-chien	E2		1.00	L	3.58	
Sui-ning	D2		1.00	L	3.95	
Shanghai*	H4	130	1.00		3.00	10.50(?)
Kunshan	G4	130	1.00	H	4.05	6.00
Sung-chiang	H4	130	1.00	H	5.50	7.93
Feng-hsien	H5	130	1.00	H	6.00	
Chin-shan	H5	130	1.00	L		7.25
Nan-hui	H4	130	1.00	H	3.63	8.45
Ch'ing-p'u	H4	130	1.00	H		5.68
T'ai-ts'ang	H4	130	1.00	H	3.85	
Ch'ung-ming	H4	130	1.00	H	3.70	
Ch'i-tung	H4	130	1.00	H	4.50	
Chia-ting	H4	130	1.00	H	4.75	7.65

* suburbs.

(TABLE B. CONTINUED)

	Hai-men	H4	130	<u>1.00</u>	H	5.50	
	Mean (per <u>shih chin</u>)					4.42 (3.70)	6.92 (5.80)
Chekiang	Hai-ning	C3	126	1.04	H	4.46	
	Lin-an	B3	126	<u>1.04</u>	H	4.80	6.25
	Chia-hsing	C3	150	<u>1.00</u>(?)	L		6.38
	Chia-shan	C3	150	<u>1.00</u>(?)			6.35
	T'ung-hsiang	C3	126	<u>1.00</u>(?)	L		5.50
	Wu-hsing	C3	126	<u>1.00</u>(?)	L		6.40
	An-chi	B3	126	<u>1.00</u>(?)	L		6.00
	Tz'u-ch'i	D4	126	<u>.96</u>	H		5.74
	Hsiang-shan	D4	147	<u>.98</u>	M		6.90
	Lin-hai	D5	140(?)	<u>1.02</u>			8.30
	Huang-yen	D5	140	<u>1.02</u>	M		5.90
	Wen-ling	D5	140	<u>1.02</u>	M		7.10
	Lan-ch'i	B4	139	<u>1.05</u>		4.30	4.30
	Wu-i	B5	150	<u>.97</u>	M		3.50
	Lo-ch'ing	C5	140	<u>.88</u>	M	6.50	
	P'ing-yang	C6		<u>.88</u>	L		8.20
	Mean (per <u>shih chin</u>)					5.02 (4.20)	6.20 (5.19)
Anhwei	Huai-ning	D5	134	<u>1.00</u>		3.75	4.50
	T'ung- ch'eng**	C4	134	<u>1.00</u>	H		6.00
	Wang-chiang	C5	134	<u>1.00</u>	H	2.85	
	I	D6	130	<u>1.09</u>	H	4.15	
	Hsüan-ch'eng	E5	130	<u>1.00</u>	M	1.30(?)	4.20
	T'ai-p'ing	E5	130	<u>1.00</u>	L		9.00(?)
	Ching-te	E5	130	<u>1.00</u>	L		4.75
	Nan-ling	E5	130	<u>1.00</u>	M		4.50
	Tang-t'u	E4	146	<u>1.00</u>			7.50
	Fan-ch'ang	E4	130	<u>1.00</u>	H		5.50
	Ho-fei	D4	124	<u>1.00</u>			4.97
	Lu-chiang	D4	130	<u>1.00</u>	M		5.00
	Shu-ch'eng	C4	124	<u>1.00</u>	M		7.50**
	Ch'ao	D4	130	<u>1.00</u>	M		5.20
	Feng-yang	D3	222	<u>1.00</u>		5.85	
	Shou	C3	222	<u>1.03</u>		4.75	8.00**
	Feng-t'ai	C3	222	<u>1.03</u>	H	2.75	
	Su	C2		<u>1.00</u>(?)	L	3.75	
	Ying-shang	C3	222	<u>1.03</u>	M	4.30	

** large difference between maximum and minimum price implies average
   of the two may diverge widely from annual average price.

(TABLE 8. CONTINUED)

	Wo-yang	C2		1.00(?)	L	3.20	
	T'ai-ho	B2		1.00(?)	L	7.50	
	Meng-ch'eng	C2		1.00(?)	L	2.85	
	Lang-ch'i	F4		1.00(?)	L		5.25
	Ch'u	E3	181	.98		2.75	4.15
	Lai-an	E3	181	.98	H	3.45	3.05(?)
	Ho	E4	130	1.00	m		4.95
	Han-shan	E4	130	1.00	L	3.50	4.50
	Chia-shan	E3	181	.98	H	2.50	3.90
	T'ien-ch'ang	E3		1.00(?)	L	4.00	4.00
	Mean (per shih chin)					3.85 (3.22)	5.00 (4.19)
Kiangsi	Nan-ch'ang	C3	147	1.00		4.65	
	Chin-hsien	D3	108	1.01	H	3.70	
	Feng-hsin	C3	147	1.00	m		5.50
	Ching-an	C3	147	1.00	m		3.50
	Yü-kan	D3	108	1.01	L	3.00	6.45
	Yü-chiang	D3	108	1.01	L		5.70
	I-yang	E3	127	1.00	m		4.60
	Tu-ch'ang	D2	160	1.00	L	3.90	
	Yung-hsiu	C2	147	1.00	m		6.50
	Nan-feng	D4	108	1.01	L		6.00
	Lin-ch'uan	D3	108	1.01			6.25
	Chin-ch'i	D4	108	1.01	H		6.45
	Ch'ung-jen	C4	108	1.01	H		7.70
	Tung-hsiang	D3	108	1.01	H	4.45	
	Hsin-kan	C4	140	1.00	H		5.50
	Hsin-yü	B4	140	1.00	H		5.90
	Kao-an	C3	140	1.00	M-H	3.00	
	Fen-i	B4	140	1.00	L		6.00
	Lien-hua	A4	112	1.00	L	6.00	
	T'ai-ho	B5	127	.98	H	5.10	
	Huei-ch'ang	C6	112	.98	H		7.75
	Hsün-wu	C7	112	.98	L		12.75
	Mean (per shih chin)					4.23 (3.54)	6.44 (5.39)
Hupei	O-ch'eng	G4	134	1.00(?)	H	3.80	
	P'u-ch'i	F5	134	1.00	L		6.00
	T'ung-ch'eng	F5	134	1.00	m		3.55
	Hsiao-kan	F4	134	1.00	H	2.55	
	Huang-p'o	G4	134	1.00	H	4.50	4.65
	Mien-yang	F4	130	.99		3.45	5.00
	Chung-hsiang	E3	177	.98		3.65	3.65

(TABLE B. CONTINUED)

	Ching-shan	F3	<u>134</u>	1.00	L		3.33
	T'ien-men	F4	<u>177</u>	.98	M		7.65
	Tang-yang	D4	<u>143</u>	<u>1.20</u>	H	4.90	
	I-ch'eng	D4	<u>143</u>	1.20		3.25	
	Kuang-hua	D2	<u>108</u>	1.00		5.55	
	Ying-shan	F3	<u>134</u>	1.00	L		5.60
	Huang-kang	G4	<u>134</u>	1.00	H	4.00	7.00
	Hsi-shui	H4	<u>134</u>	<u>1.00</u>	H	2.40	6.10
	Ch'i-ch'un	H4	<u>134</u>	1.00	H		4.10
	Kuang-chi	H4	<u>134</u>	1.00	H		5.77
	Chiang-ling	E4	<u>112</u>	.98		3.55	4.85
	Sung-tzu	D4	<u>112</u>	.98	H	6.65	7.65
	Mean					4.02	5.27
	(per <u>shih chin</u>)					(3.37)	(4.41)

Hunan	Ch'ang-sha	D3	<u>119</u>	.83			6.00*
	Hsiang-yin	D3	<u>119</u>	.83	M		4.92*
	Ning-hsiang	D3	<u>119</u>	.83	H		3.70*
	I-yang	D3	<u>119</u>	.83	M		5.13*
	Hsiang-hsiang	D4	<u>119</u>	.83	M	2.30	
	Li	C2	<u>128</u>	1.00		2.75	
	Wu-kang	85	<u>147</u>	.88	L		1.53(?)
	Lei-yang	D5	<u>157</u>	.96		4.70	
	Lan-shan	D6	<u>157</u>	.96	L		3.50
	Chia-ho	D6	<u>157</u>	.96	L	4.70	
	T'ao-yuan	C3	144		H		2.78
	Hsü-p'u	84	<u>169</u>	.95	M	3.90	3.38
	Ling-ling	C5	<u>157</u>	.96	M		3.82
	Tung-an	C5		.96	L	3.10	
	Nan	C2	135	.98	M		3.65
	Mean					3.58	3.84
	(per <u>shih chin</u>)					(3.00)	(3.22)

Szechuan**	Shuang-liu	C4	<u>300</u>		H	3.10	4.05
	Hsin-fan	D4	<u>300</u>		H	3.90	3.90
	Hsin-tu	D4	<u>300</u>		H	3.90	3.90
	Chien-yang	D4	<u>300</u>		H	2.80	4.90
	Kuang-han	D4	<u>112</u>		H		5.25
	Mien-yang	D3	<u>300</u>		M	3.80	

* If .83 is too low, an artificial price disparity has been created
by its use as a conversion factor.
** All Szechuan prices multiplied by .894 (1935 Chungkiang dollar
equivalent of one National dollar).

(TABLE B. CONTINUED)

	An	D3	300		M	4.05	4.45
	I-pin	D6	300	1.00			6.25*
	Fu-shun	D5	300	1.00	H	5.65	4.90
	Nan-ch'i	D6	300	1.00	H		4.55
	Ch'ang-ning	D6	300	1.00	H		3.70
	P'ing-wu	D2	300(?)		L		7.75(?)
	Chiang-yu	D3	300		L	2.65	3.45
	An-yüeh	E4	300		L		6.10
	Mei-shan	C4	300	.94-1.00			6.25*
	Chien-wei	C5	300	1.00	M	4.30	6.45
	P'u-chiang	C4	300		M	2.55	3.00*
	Chiang-chin	F5	300	1.01	H	2.45	9.05*
	Yung-ch'uan	E5	300	1.01	M		7.30
	T'ung-liang	F5	300	1.01	H		7.30
	Ta-tsu	E6	300	1.01	M	3.20	5.85
	Chung	G4	300	1.01	M		2.20
	Hsüan-han	G3	487	.98	M	5.30	7.05
	T'ung-nan	E4	300	1.01	M		6.15
	P'eng-an	F3	310		H	6.60	
	Ying-shan	F3	310		H		6.10
	Yüeh-ch'ih	F4	310		H		6.50
	Mean					3.88	5.33
	(per shih chin)					(3.24)	(4.56)
Fukien	Min-hou	D3	163	1.00			6.00**
	Lien-chiang	D3	163	1.00	H		9.50
	Fu-ch'ing	D4	163	1.00	M	5.50	
	Chin-men	C5	124	.96	H	1.15(?)	
	Chien-yang	C2	120	1.10	M		6.35
	P'u-ch'eng	C2	120	1.10	L		7.25
	Shun-ch'ang	B3	260	.94		7.20	
	Ming-ch'i	B3	120	1.10	L		3.65
	Chien-ning	A3	81	.97			8.00
	Lung-ch'i	B5	137	1.24			5.85
	Yün-hsiao	B5	124	.96	L		7.05
	Chang-p'u	B5	124	.96	L		6.25
	Hai-ch'eng	B5	124	.96	H		6.75
	Kuang-tse	B2	119	.96	H		6.75
	Mean					6.35	6.65
	(per shih chin)					(5.32)	(5.57)

* large difference between maximum and minimum prices implies average
  of the two may diverge widely from annual average price.
** minimum only?

(TABLE B. CONTINUED)

Kuangtung	Fan-yü	G3	129	1.01	H		8.40
	Ts'ung-hua	G3	129	1.01	H		4.95
	Lung-meng	H3	129	1.01	L	4.95	7.90
	Chung-shan	G4	129	1.01	M		7.25
	Yün-fo	F4	129	1.01	L		4.60
	Fo-kang	G3	129	1.01	L	3.45	4.45
	Yang-shan	F2		1.01	L	4.70	
	Ying-te	G2	129	1.01	M		6.65
	Hui-yang	H3	129	1.01	M		9.90
	Lung-ch'uan	I2		1.00	L		5.75
	P'ing-yüan	I2		1.00	L		6.50
	Ling-shan	C4	188	.94	M		7.30
	Lien-chiang	D5	188	.94	L		8.00
	Mean (per _shih chin_)					4.37 (3.66)	6.80 (5.70)
Kuangsi	Hsing-an	G2		1.00		5.50	5.50
	Liu-chiang	F3		1.00			6.00
	Liu-chiang	F3		1.00		4.30	6.75
	I-shan	E3		1.00		3.70	5.50
	En-lung	D4		1.00			3.75
	Ho	H3		.94	M		7.65
	Li-p'u	G3		1.00			7.00
	Hsiu-jen	G3		1.00			6.00
	Meng-shan	G3		.94	L		8.00
	Yü-lin	G5		.94	L		7.70
	Po-pai	G5		.94	L		8.50
	Pei-liu	G5		.94	L		8.75
	Lu-ch'uan	G5		.94	L		9.60
	Hsing-yeh	F5		.94	L		5.05
	Kuei-p'ing	F4		.94	L		10.60
	Kuei	F4		.94	L		9.55
	Heng	F5		1.00	L		6.50
	Shang-ssu	E5		1.00	M		5.50
	Ssu-lo	D5		1.00	L		5.50
	Chen-chieh	D4		1.00	L		4.00
	Mean (per _shih chin_)					4.50 (3.77)	6.87 (5.75)
Kweichou	Lung-li	D3	179	1.00	H		3.90
	Hui-shui	D3	179	1.00	M	5.85	5.85
	Ch'ang-shun	D3	179	1.00	M		6.00
	San-sui	F3	342	.99	H		4.50
	Yü-p'ing	F2	342	.99	H	2.20	
	T'ien-chu	G3	342	.99	M		3.50
	Huang-p'ing	E3		1.00	L		3.00

(TABLE B.CONTINUED)

	Ma-chiang	E3	1.00	H		3.50
	Lu-shan	E3	1.00	H		3.50
	Mei-t'an	E2	.89	L		5.05
	Sui-yang	E2	.89	L		5.05
	Mean				4.03	4.39
	(per shih chin)				(3.38)	(3.68)
Yunnan*	An-ning	I5	1.00	L		5.50
	Feng-i	G4	1.00	L		4.00
	Pin-ch'uan	G4	1.00	L		4.00
	Yao-an	B4	1.00	L		5.50
	Ta-yao	H4	1.00	L		5.50
	Yang-pi	F4	1.00	L	2.50	4.00
	Mean				2.50	4.75
	(per shih chin)				(2.09)	(3.98)

* further price data is available, but the information on weights
  and measures and/or currency which would permit its translation
  into national standards is not.

TABLE C. PRICE INDICES, WHEAT OR RICE, 1935 = 100

Province	Crop	1929	1930	1931	1932	1933	Estimated Price* 1929	1931
Hopei	W	113	108	105	107	96	5.47	5.08
Shansi	W	134	186	131	131	107	3.64	(4.80)
				(176)	(173)	(117)		
Shantung	W	136	134	121	101	91	5.44	4.84
Honan	W	132	109	101	121	105	6.02	4.58
Shensi	W			167	153	146	4.72^a	5.37^a
Kansu	W	153	176	119	110	107	5.80	4.52
Kiangsu	R	134	148	125	115	79	7.77	7.25
Anhwei	R	109	141	102	90	72	4.56	4.27
	W	113	147	107	109	82	2.64	3.44
Chekiang	R	127	115	111	97	76	6.60	5.76
Kiangsi	R	88$_b$	96$_b$	96	87	74	4.75$_b$	5.18
Fukien	R	109$_b$	123$_b$	99	102	111	6.07$_b$	5.50
Kwangtung	R	117^b	131	106	110	104	6.67	6.05
Kwangsi	R	100	101$_c$	101	110	109	5.75$_c$	5.80
Hupei	R	103^c	132$_c$	96	97	74	4.55$_c$	4.23
Hunan	R	120^c	154$_c$	112	113	74	3.88^c	3.60
Kweichow	R	91^d	91$_d$	91	95	110	3.32^d	3.35
Yunnan	R	50	56	81	88	101		
		(55)	(62)	(84)	(95)	(92)	(3.34)	(2.18)
Szechuan	R			108	128	98	4.55^e	4.92

---

* in yüan per shih piculs.

a) 1929 and 1931 prices assumed same as average of Shansi and Kansu.
b) 1930/1931 and 1929/1930 ratios assumed same as average of Kiangsu
   and Chekiang.
c) 1930/1931 and 1929/1930 assumed same as Anhwei.
d) 1929/1931 assumed same as Kwangsi.
e) 1929 price assumed same as Hupei and Anhwei.
Notes: Parenthetical indices are averages for hsien for which 1935
   actual prices were available but probably atypical. Indices from
   1931 and 1935 are based on unweighted averages of hsien prices
   relatives for wheat or rice, from N.A.R.B. Crop Reports, 1937-38.
   1929-1931 indices are, unless otherwise stated, averages of locality
   indices of prices received by farmers, as given in John L. Buck,
   Land Utilization in China, Statistical Volume, Table 2.1, p. 149.
   This represented a quite limited sampling.

TABLE D. ESTIMATED PRICE PER KILOGRAM OF GRAIN (WHEAT OR RICE), 1929-35

Province	Crop	1929	1930	1931	1932	1933	1935
Hopei	W	.108	.103	.100	.102	.092	.096
Shansi	W	.072	.100	.095	.093	.063	.054
Shantung	W	.100	.099	.089	.074	.067	.074
Honan	W	.120	.099	.091	.110	.095	.091
Shensi*	W	.093	.116	.090	.079	.074	.051
Kansu	W	.114	.132	.089	.082	.080	.075
Kiangsu	R	.154	.170	.143	.132	.090	.115
Anhwei	R	.090	.117	.084	.074	.059	.083
	W	.077	.101	.073	.075	.056	.062
Chekiang	R	.130	.118	.114	.099	.078	.103
Kiangsi	R	.094	.102	.102	.093	.079	.107
Fukien	R	.120	.136	.109	.113	.123	.111
Kwangtung	R	.132	.148	.119	.124	.117	.113
Kwangsi	R	.115	.116	.116	.126	.125	.115
Hupei	R	.090	.116	.084	.085	.065	.088
Hunan	R	.076	.098	.071	.072	.047	.064
Kweichow	R	.066	.066	.066	.069	.080	.073
Yunnan	R	.043	.048	.066	.069	.072	.079
Szechuan	R	.090	.116	.098	.116	.089	.091

(TABLE D. CONTINUED)

* Shensi 1932 prices known from survey; 1931 derived on assumption
   that 1931/1932 wheat price ratio for Shensi as a whole was
   identical to that in Sian (1.13). 1929 and 1930 prices are
   averages of Shansi and Kansu. 1932 prices from Shensi shih-yeh
   k'ao-ch'a t'uan ed., Shensi shih-yeh k'ao-ch'a (Shanghai,
   1933), pp. 345-346 and p. 430. 1933 and 1935 prices derived
   from 1932 price and wheat price index from N.A.R.B. Crop Reports.

Notes: All prices except Shensi derived from 1935 price average
   (from Table B.) and price indices (from Table C.).
      As a rough check on the overall accuracy of the estimated
   price figures, the following is of value: John L. Buck, Land
   Utilization in China, Atlas, Ch. 9, Map 2., p. 125 presents a
   table showing the average for each crop region of the amounts
   or rice or wheat which a year's wage (of farm laborers) could
   purchase, calculated at farm prices. It is possible to get an
   idea of the approximate level of these prices by dividing the
   kilograms of grain purchasable by the average wage for the region
   (the resulting figure of course reflects not only variations
   in price between localities and the years from 1929 to 1932,
   but also the effects of wage variations between localities and
   over time). The 'grain prices' for each region are listed
   below. They are very close to our estimates for North, Northwest
   and Southwest China, but lower than ours for Central and South
   China, where our weights and measures and 1935 price data is
   strongest but our 1929-1930 links are weakest. However, the
   distinction might be between husked and unhusked rice (our
   prices are for husked, Buck's may be for unhusked).

Region	"Price"
Spring Wheat	.13
Winter Wheat-millet	.12
Winter Wheat-kaoliang	.11
Yangtze Rice-wheat	.07-.075 (wheat-rice)
Rice-tea	.06
Szechuan Rice	.05
Double-cropping Rice	.08
Southwestern Rice	.07

SOURCE MATERIALS ON WEIGHTS AND MEASURES AND PRICES

Weights and Measures:

1. Ch'en Chieh and Lin Kuang-wei, Chung-kuo tu-liang-heng (Chinese
   Weights and Measures), Shanghai, Commercial Press, 1934.

2. Wu Ch'eng-lo, Chung-kuo tu-liang-heng shih (A History of Chinese
   Weights and Measures), Shanghai, Commercial Press, 1957.

3. Tu Siu-chang,"Chekiang sheng mi-chia pien-tung chih yen-chiu" (A
   Study of the Price Changes of Rice in Chekiang Province), Agriculture Sinica, 1: 2(1934), p. 67.

4. P'ing-han yen-hsien nung-ts'un ching-chi tiao-ch'a (P'ing-han
   Railway Village Economy Survey), Shanghai, Chung-hua Press,
   1936. Communications University Research Institute, Social Economy
   Department, Monograph No. 4. Appendix, Table 2.

5. Ministry of Industry and Commerce, Ch'üan-kuo wu-chia t'ung-chi
   piao, 1926-1927 (All-China Price Statistics), Nanking, 1928.
   Forward.

6. John Lossing Buck, Land Utilization in China, Statistical Volume,
   Chapter 12, Table 2., p. 473.

(Further scattered information may be found in sources 8, 10 and 16).

Prices:

7. Postal Administration, Ministry of Communications, Chung-kuo
   t'ung-yu ti-fang wu-ch'an chih (A Record of Products of the
   Chinese Postal Areas), Shanghai, Commercial Press, 1937.

8. Hua-yüan shih-yeh tiao-ch'a t'uan eds., Shensi nung-k'en tiao-
   ch'a pao-kao (Report of the Survey of Agricultural Cultivation
   in Shensi), Nanking, 1933.

9. Committee for the Study of Silver Values and Commodity Prices,
   Silver and Prices in China, Shanghai, Commercial Press, 1935.

10. Wan-chung keng-mi ch'an-hsiao chih tiao-ch'a (Survey of Rice
    Marketing in Central Anhwei), Shanghai, 1936. Communications
    University Research Institute, Social Economy Department,
    Monograph No. 2.

11. Chung nung ching-chi (Chinese Farm Economy), 1: 3(October, 1940).

12. Shih-yeh yüeh-k'an (Industrial Monthly), 1936, various numbers.

13. Chinese Agriculturalist's Bank, Szechuan Village Economic Survey Committee, Survey Report, No.4, Chungking, 1941, p. 77.

14. Wu Pao-san and Chang Chih-i, Fu-chien sheng liang-shih chih yün-hsiao (Foodgrains Marketing in Fukien), Shanghai, Commercial Press, 1938. Academia Sinica Social Science Research Institute Series, No. 11, pp. 63, 64.

15. John L. Buck, Land Utilization in China, Statistical Volume, Chapter 5, Table 2-1, p. 149.

16. Shensi shih-yeh k'ao-ch'a t'uan eds., Shensi shih-yeh k'ao-ch'a (Investigation of Shensi Industries), Shanghai, 1933, pp. 435, 436, 430.

17. N. A. R. B., Crop Reports, 1937-1938.

18. Shanghai chieh-fang ch'ien-hou wu-chia tzu-liao hui-pien, 1921-1957 (Materials on the Prices in Shanghai before and after Liberation), Shanghai, 1958.

(Prices for 1920-1927 may be found in source 5 above and Chung-kuo lao-tung nien-chien /China Labor Annual_7, no. 1, Peiping, 1928, pp. 66-139, but only for major cities.)

NOTES

Abreviations:

CFE: Chinese Farm Economy (Chicago, 1930)

JPRS: U. S. Government, Joint Publications Research Service

LUC, SV: Land Utilization in China, Statistical Volume
(Nanking, 1937)

Mantetsu: Minami Manshū tetsudō kabushiki kaisha (South
Manchurian Railway Company)

Chapter One / INTRODUCTION

1. G. Ranis and J. C. H. Fei, "A Theory of Economic
Development," in Eicher and Witt (1964), p. 181.

2. See Liu and Yeh (1965), Table 24, p. 102. In 1952
less than 13 percent of the population was urban, but this
proportion may have been higher at the height of the prewar
economy. The 70% agricultural proportion relies in part on
Buck's estimate of the proportion of the agricultural
labor force engaged in subsidiary work, which may be exaggerated due to sample bias.

3. A. Eckstein, "The Economic Heritage," in Eckstein,
Galenson and Liu (1968), p. 78.

4. Feng Ho-fa (1935), II, pp. 546-547.

5. See for example discussions by Eckstein in Eckstein,
Galenson and Liu (1968) and Liu and Yeh (1965). The latter
also consult other sources, but generally weight the results
of the Buck survey (LUC) at least equally, despite consis-

tent differences in magnitude.

6. Dwight Perkins (1969), Appendix D, pp. 268-269;
Eckstein in Eckstein, Galenson and Liu (1968), p. 78.

7. Ramon Myers (1968), Appendix B., pp. 306-321.

8. Feng Ho-fa (1935), II, pp. 598-600

9. See J. L. Buck, LUC, I, Table 23, p. 197, and
Table 3, p. 291 for Winter wheat-kaoliang area.

Chapter Two / A THEORY OF DISTRIBUTION IN THE AGRARIAN SECTOR

1. A survey of the literature before 1964 on the subject
may be found in Kao, Anschel and Eicher, "Disguised Unemployment in Agriculture: A Survey," in Eicher and Witt
(1968), pp. 129-143.

2. Ibid., p. 130.

3. Ibid., pp. 130-131.

4. Folke Dovring (1967), pp. 163-173.

5. Jacob Viner, "Some Reflections on the Concept of
Disguised Unemployment," Contribucoes a Analise do
Desenvolvimento Economico (Rio de Janeiro, 1957), p. 343;
cited in Eicher and Witt (1964), p. 131.

6. See Kao et al., in Eicher and Witt (1964), pp.
135-141.

7. Morton Paglin (1965), p. 825. See also Heady and
Dillon (1961), pp. 620-624.

8. Heady and Dillon (1961), pp. 627-629.

9. See Kao et al., in Eicher and Witt (1964), p. 132.

10. R. S. Eckaus (1955), republished in Agarwala and Singh (1958), pp. 348-378.

11. Ibid., pp. 364-365.

12. W. Arthur Lewis (1954), pp. 139-191.

13. Stephen Marglin, "Comment" on Jorgenson model, in Adelman and Thorbecke (1966), p. 64.

14. Dale W. Jorgenson, "The Role of Agriculture in Economic Development: Classical versus Neoclassical Models of Growth," and Comments by Bruce Johnston and Vernon Ruttan, in C. R. Wharton, Jr. (1970), pp. 320-360. A condense version of the Jorgenson paper may also be found in Adelman and Thorbecke (1966), pp. 45-60 with a comment by Stephen Marglin.

15. Bent Hansen (1966), pp. 367-405.

16. Harvey Leibenstein (1957), pp. 58-76.

17. See comments of V. M. Dandekar, "Economic Theory and Agrarian Reform," in Eicher and Witt (1964), p. 172.

18. Thomas B. Wiens (1967), pp. 25-27.

19. N. Georgescu-Roegen (1960), pp. 1-40.

20. See the analysis of P. K. Bardhan and T. N. Srinivasan (1971), pp. 48-64. Further discussion of sharecropping will be found below in this chapter.

21. Georgescu-Roegen (1960), p. 24.

22. The 17th century (late Ming dynasty) saw the rise

to dominance of wage labor; contractual tenancy became the rule much earlier. See Mi Chu Wiens (1973), pp. 241-299.

23. Georgescu-Roegen (1960), p. 20 and p. 26.

24. A. V. Tschajanow (Chayanov)(1966). The original was published as *Die Lehre von der bauerlichen Wirtshaft, Versuch einer Theorie der Familien wirtschaft in Landbau* (Berlin, 1923).

25. Chayanov (1966), p. 109.

26. *Ibid.*, p. 113.

27. *Ibid.*, pp. 115-116.

28. Morton Paglin (1965), p. 831.

29. These observations were in part made by Chayanov (1966), pp. 68, 79, 101-102, etc. However, pre-Communist Russian repartitional tenure resulted in a closer relationship between family productive labor potential and farm size than would be observed elsewhere.

30. See Fei Hsiao-t'ung (1945), pp. 202 and 228 for description of such devices for exchange of land for capital.

31. See Charles E. Ferguson (1969), pp. 254-270 for a discussion of the conditions under which neoclassical distribution conclusions would break down.

32. Chayanov (1966), pp. 115-116.

33. For instance, see J. L. Buck, *CFE*, Appendix Tables 1 to 18, pp. 431-448, line 9.

34. See John W. Mellor (1966), pp. 364-371; Theodore

W. Schultz (1964), pp. 110-124; Guy Hunter (1969), pp. 141-148.

35. Mellor (1966), pp. 365-366. For one reason why, consider Buck's comment: "Poor farmers depend on borrowing animals from relatives or neighbors, and since the animals are not enough to get the work done in the proper season, planting is often delayed because the soil has dried out before it could be plowed and harrowed and the moisture thus conserved." CFE (1930), p. 278.

36. Buck (1930), p. 142.

37. See, for example, C. H. Hanumantha Rao (1971), pp. 578-595.

38. Kenneth Arrow casts a skeptical eye on this theory on the grounds that empirical evidence of the existence of positive pure profits in this sense is negligible (K. Arrow, 1971), pp. 6-7; but Sandmo (1971) establishes an interesting result, that under our definition of uncertainty, a competitive equilibrium in an industry may be established such that relatively 'risk-neutral' firms will have higher output levels and higher profits than 'risk-averse' firms, confirming that profits are indeed a 'reward to risk-bearing.'

39. The formal proof is developed in A. Zellner et al. (1966), pp. 784-795.

40. A priori theory and observed human behavior both strongly suggest that generalized (absolute) risk aversion is characteristic of human economic behavior. See K. Arrow

(1971), pp. 90-120; J. Hirshleifer (1970), pp. 224-231.

41. P. K. Bardhan and T. N. Srinivasan (1971) give a
proof of these propositions for a particular case on pp. 62-64.
A. Sandmo (1971) establishes that with risk aversion and
normally-shaped nonstochastic cost curves, uncertainty
output is smaller than certainty output and is characterized
by MC being less than expected price.

42. See, for example, Chihiro Nakajima, "Subsistence and
Commercial Family Farms: Some Theoretical Models of Subjective
Equilibrium," in C. R. Wharton, Jr. (1970), pp. 165-185, for
an interpretation of Chayanov's theory emphasizing the labor-
leisure choice.

43. Hirshleifer (1970), pp. 224-231.

44. Arrow (1971), pp. 94-96.

45. See references in notes 43 and 44 above.

46. In particular, boundedness of the utility function
from above and below implies non-decreasing relative risk-
aversion (Arrow, 1971, pp. 97-98) and is required for a
solution to the St. Petersburg Paradox (but see Hirshleifer's
objections, pp. 227-228). Arrow also argues that this
explains the commonly observed wealth elasticity of demand
for cash balances of greater than one (see pp. 103-104),
but alternative explanations of this phenomenon are conceivable
Constant relative risk aversion is also frequently assumed,
but again for primarily mathematical convenience (see

Bardhan and Srinivasan, 1971, pp. 62-63; Sandmo, 1971, pp. 68-70.

    47. Hirshleifer (1970), p. 230.

    48. Bardhan and Srinivasan (1971), pp. 51-52, footnote 8.

    49. See S. N. S. Cheung, "Private Property Rights and Share-Cropping," _Journal of Political Economy_, November-December 1968, pp. 1113-1114.

Chapter Three / THE LAND MARKET

    1. D. Perkins (1969), pp. 95-96. Perkins in fact subsequently argues (p. 102) that the rate of return was in any case not as important a factor as the use of land as a store of wealth, which contradicts his previous argument.

    2. _Ibid._, pp. 96-97.

    3. Hsüeh Mu-ch'iao (1937), p. 40.

    4. See Yen Chung-p'ing (1955), Table 32, pp. 295-297 for documented examples.

    5. Perkins (1969), pp. 105-106.

    6. Yen Chung-p'ing (1935), Table 48, p. 317.

    7. Fei Hsiao-t'ung (1939), p. 188.

    8. Feng Ho-fa (1935), II, p. 520; Yen Chung-p'ing (1955), Table 47, p. 318.

    9. Yen Chung-p'ing (1955), Table 48, p. 317.

    10. Hsueh Mu-ch'iao (1937), p. 40; Feng Ho-fa (1935), II, p. 507.

11. Mantetsu (Hokushi No. 7), Appendix Table 6 is the
data source. Expected loss was calculated as the proportion
rent was reduced weighted by the number of times this occurred,
divided by total years of the tenancy.

12. See H. T. Fei (1945), pp. 75-80 for a discussion
of some of the differences in relative bargaining power of
landlords between coastal and interior China.

13. Yen Chung-p'ing (1955), Table 44, p. 315. His
figures differ greatly from our Table 3.4 in some cases,
and their reliability may be questionable.

14. Hsüeh Mu-ch'iao (1937), p. 39; Feng Ho-fa (1935),
II, pp. 582-583.

15. Feng Ho-fa (1935), II, pp. 582-583.

16. Ibid., pp. 573-574.

17. N.A.R.B. Crop Reports, 3:4, April 15, 1935, p. 93.

18. Feng Ho-fa (1935), II, pp. 574-575.

19. Ibid., I, p. 474.

20. Ibid., II, p. 520.

21. Ibid., II, p. 589.

22. J. L. Buck, LUC, SV, Table 13, p. 301.

23. Ibid., I, p. 348.

24. Hsueh Mu-ch'iao (1937), p. 40.

25. According to Buck, LUC, SV, Table 7, p. 311, families
in two other hsien near Shanghai (Ch'angshou and Wuhsi)
derived more than 39% of their income from off-farm sources,

an unusually high percentage for China.

26. Yen Chung-p'ing (1955), Table 34, p. 303.

27. Hsueh Mu-ch'iao (1937), p. 38. Ch'en Han-seng
noted that the system was quite prevalent in E. Kwangtung
(cited in Fei, 1939, p. 184). It also occurred less frequently in Anhwei, Kiangsi, Hupei and even in frontier
regions such as Kansu and Ch'inghai. See Yen Chung-p'ing
(1955), Table 57, p. 324.

28. Feng Ho-fa (1935), II, p. 571. See also Evelyn
Rawski (1972), pp. 19-20; Niidi Noboru (1960), pp. 183-
185.

29. Niidi Noboru (1960), p. 168.

30. Fei Hsiao-t'ung (1939), p. 188.

31. Yen Chung-p'ing (1955), p. 323 provides instances of
such abuses.

32. E. Rawski (1972), p. 20 asserts that tenant rights
were even stronger, but Fei's view (1939), pp. 184-185,
that customary rights made it difficult to evict a tenant,
but rental payments had somewhat stronger sanctions behind
them, is probably more accurate.

33. Yen Chung-p'ing (1955), Table 57, p. 324.

34. Hsüeh Mu-ch'iao (1937), p. 38.

35. Niidi Noboru (1960), pp. 177-178.

36. Yen Chung-p'ing, Table 35, p. 304.

37. Feng Ho-fa (1935), II, p. 504.

38. Feng Ho-fa (1935), II, pp. 505-507. Rawski (1972), p. 122, asserts that in Fukien the rent deposit was not refundable.

39. Examples are given in Rawski (1972), pp. 122-123; Yen Chung-p'ing (1955), Table 52, p. 321.

40. E. Rawski (1972), pp. 122-123 and Feng Ho-fa (1935), II, p. 510 and pp. 512-513.

41. Feng Ho-fa (1935), II, p. 512.

42. Yen Chung-p'ing (1955), Table 51 and fn., p. 320; Feng Ho-fa (1935), II, pp. 512-513.

43. Feng Ho-fa (1935), II, p. 515.

44. Hsüeh Mu-ch'iao (1937), p. 44.

45. Information on Tsao-yang hsien may be found in Buck, LUC, SV, various tables.

46. Feng Ho-fa (1935), II, p. 510.

47. J. Tobin (1958), pp. 65-86.

48. H. T. Fei (1939), pp. 189-191.

49. See Perkins (1969), pp. 93-95, where it is asserted that the rate of return was probably no greater than 5%; Fei (1939), pp. 181-183, discussing the "mystique" attached to land ownership; however, his argument seems more applicable to owner-cultivators than to absentee landlords.

50. The South China average tax on medium grade land was exactly $2\frac{1}{2}\%$ of the average value of irrigated fields of medium grade; other calculations give results falling

between 2 and 4 percent. Buck, LUC, I, Fig. 5, p. 326;
T'u-ti wei-yüan hui (1937), p. 55.

51. Buck, LUC, SV, Table 10-1, pp. 168-169.

52. Yen Chung-p'ing (1955), Table 37, p. 307.

53. Ibid., p. 309fn.

54. See H. T. Fei, (1945), pp. 77-80 for a revealing
discussion·of the situation of the institutional tenant.

55. See Yen Chung-p'ing (1955), p. 309fn.

56. L. P. Van Slyke (1968), pp. 27-33.

57. Feng Ho-fa (1935), II, p. 435.

58. See Fei (1939), pp. 182-183.

59. Feng Ho-fa (1935), I, p. 396.

60. H. T. Fei (1945), p. 127.

61. Feng Ho-fa (1935), II, pp. 471-472.

62. Ibid., I, pp. 396-397.

63. The latter group are emphasized by Fei (1945), p. 125.

64. This adds a twist to a point made by Perkins (1969),
p. 96fn.

Chapter Four / THE LOAN MARKET

1. Feng Ho-fa (1935), II, p. 806. From a 22 province,
850 county survey in 1933 (?).

2. As Tawney puts it, "Everything goes down, so to
speak, in a common account, with the result that there is
no discrimination in the mind of either debtor or creditor

between the borrowing and advancing of money for productive purposes .. and household expenditures which ought, in the absence of exceptional misfortune, to be met out of income." Tawney (1932), p. 62.

3. See, for example, H. T. Fei (1945), p. 125.

4. The influence of opium is discussed extensively in Ibid.

5. Buck's survey of sources of credit (LUC, SV, Table 14, p. 404) seems to suffer from this confusion, as it implied that "relatives and friends" furnished almost all loans, to the relative exclusion of rich peasants, landlords, etc. See Buck, LUC, I, pp. 464-465 for his comments on this issue.

6. Ramon Myers (1970), p. 243.

7. Feng Ho-fa (1935), II, p. 812. See also Yen (1955), Table 76, p. 348.

8. Hsüeh Mu-ch'iao (1937), pp. 96-97; Feng Ho-fa (1935), II, p. 844.

9. A sample survey of villages in central Honan, northern Anhwei and eastern Shantung found that in 3 villages, only 2% of loans involved no interest; in another three, 12-14 %. Chen Han-seng (1939), p. 69. According to Fei, "The most that can be obtained in this way [interest-free, unsecured loans] is a few day's work, a few bowls of rice, or a few dollars. If the need is greater, this sort of assistance is normally not available." (Fei, 1945, p. 119).

10. According to national survey, only 19.8% of loans
involved personal trust only (including short term and
grain loans); 33.9% involved a guarantor; 46.3% involved
actual property pledged as security (Yen,1955, Table 75,
p. 347). In Shantung, Kaomi hsien, verbal guarantees were
frequent only among rich peasants (Feng, 1935, II, p. 890.).
Fei suggests that professional moneylenders required land
as security in Wu-hsi (Fei, 1939, p. 278); such guarantees
also seemed to be the general rule in Yünnan (Fei, 1945,
pp. 201-202). On the other hand, Mantetsu surveys of a
Wu-hsi and a Tsingtao village suggest that the use of a
guarantor was more common than a land guarantee (see references,
notes 3-11 and 4-22).

11. Feng Ho-fa (1935), II, p. 890. Both Mantetsu
surveys cited in the previous note show that many nominally
1 year loans were still regarded as current debts, with
interest payments continuing to be made, despite non-repay-
ment of principal when due.

12. Fei (1945), pp. 199-201. Also Chen Han-seng (1939),
p. 69.

13. Fei (1945), p. 67 and p. 123.

14. Hsüeh Mu-ch'iao (1937), p. 96.

15. Fei (1945), pp. 228-229.

16. Feng (1935), II, p. 901 and p. 831; Hsiao Ting-che
and T'ao Meng-ho (1926), p. 475; Feng (1935), I, p. 396
all discuss this practice as it pertained to different localities.

17. Feng (1935), II, p. 832.

18. Ibid., p. 841.

19. Ibid., pp. 844-845.

20. The above discussion is based primarily on Fei (1939), pp. 267-274; Fei (1945), pp. 120-121 and 289-290.

21. Fei (1939), pp. 275-276.

22. Mantetsu (Shanghai No. 50), Appendices.

23. This may only have been a rough guess, however, as no specific survey compilations of family budgets or consumption were included. Moreover, recent inflation had raised the market value of commodities consumed considerably. Ibid., p. 124.

24. In Hopei, the actual rate charged was not always recorded in loan contracts, for fear of legal interference. Feng (1935), II, p. 834.

25. Ibid., p. 835.

26. Hsüeh (1937), pp. 96-97.

27. Feng (1935), II, p. 835.

28. See Yen (1955), Table 78, p. 349.

29. Buck, LUC, I, p. 315.

30. "National surveys" from 1938-1946 do not indicate substantial rises in interest rates until after 1941, but the same "surveys" found that modern banks and cooperatives were supplying a major proportion of new loans during this period (from 25% in 1938 to 54% in 1943), which suggests

a drying-up of traditional sources and/or a totally unrepresentative sample. See Yen (1955), Table 74, p. 346 and
Table 78, p. 349. A 1939 survey of Wuhsi, Kiangsu found
a small rise in the interest rate (from 15.8 to 17.2%) after
1937, but also a drastic fall in the number of loans extended (but the sample was too small to be reliable).
Mantetsu (Shanghai No. 50), p. 113. For a tentative discussion of the impact of inflation on the loan market (after
one year), see Fei (1945), pp. 105-108 and 121-123.

31. The prices were those prevailing in Lu-ts'un village,
Yünnan, in November 1938 and 1939, cited in Fei (1945),
pp. 105-106 and 121-122. The interest rate on such loans
was close to those current in 1938-39 in this village and
in Yi-ts'un.

32. In 1939, the average loan rate in Yi-ts'un was still
5 piculs of rice per $10, despite the fact that the rice price
there was now $2.80 per picul. (Ibid., p. 199)

33. Hsüeh (1937), p. 92. See also Fei (1945), p. 290;
Yen (1955), Table 68, p. 342 and Table 76, p. 348.

34. See Sun Ching-chih et al., eds., Hua-tung ti-ch'ü
ching-chi ti-li (JPRS 11438), pp. 23, 90, and 93-94.

35. Nationally, .3 to .5 (Hsüeh, 1937, p. 99); .5 in
the vicinity of Peking (Feng, 1935, II, p. 840); .6 to .7
in Tsingtao (Mantetsu, Hokushi No. 7, pp. 26-27). Fei
(1945), p. 229 takes 50% as the average discount.

36. Fei (1945), p. 124 gives a 1938 example where the
rate was about .3; Myers (1970), pp. 52-53 cites a Mantetsu
survey of a locality where the usual rate had been about
.6, but a peasant informant suggested that it now (by 1939)
was about .3; although the "conventional rate" in the
surveyed village near Tsingtao was .6-.7, the actual rate
at the time of the survey (1939) average about .5 (Mantetsu,
Hokushi No. 7, pp. 26-27 and computations based on mortgage
data given in Appendix Table 5).

37. See Fei (1945), p. 228.

38. Fei (1939), p. 279; Fei (1945), p. 290.

39. Mantetsu (Shanghai No. 50), pp. 109-112 and Appendix Table 5.

40. Mantetsu (Hokushi No. 7), p. 113 and Appendix Table 16.

Chapter Five / THE LABOR MARKET

1. Buck, LUC, SV, p. 305 and p. 309. Effect of sample
bias here uncertain.

2. Ibid., I, pp. 292-293.

3. Ibid., SV, pp. 303-304.

4. Hsüeh (1937), p. 51.

5. See Thomas C. Smith (1959), pp. 21-29.

6. Hsüeh (1937), p. 49; Feng (1935), II, p. 727.

7. Hsüeh (1937), p. 49; Feng (1935), II, p. 724.

8. Feng (1935), II, p. 725.

9. Hsüeh (1937), p. 50; Feng (1935), II, pp. 713-714. Daily cash wages in Kwangsi ranged roughly between .15 and .40 yüan (Buck, LUC, SV, p. 328).

10. Hsüeh (1937), p. 50; Feng (1935), II, p. 717.

11. Feng (1935), II, pp. 725-726. In some areas labor exchange was also practiced. This was dependent on differences in work scheduling among farms permitting spreading of requirements and cooperation among farms. See Fei (1945), pp. 64-65.

12. Feng (1935), II, p. 716; Fei (1945), p. 68.

13. Fei (1939), pp. 179-180.

14. Feng (1935), I, p. 114.

15. A survey which asked farm laborers what other laborers they knew did after retiring from this work, found most either unemployed and without support or supported by children (Feng, 1935, I, p. 512). In another survey of the ages of farm laborers (full-time), over half of those whose ages were recorded were over 30 (Buck, CFE, Table 15., p. 348).

16. Buck, LUC, SV, p. 328.

17. Ibid., p. 328 and Feng (1935), II, p. 723.

18. Feng (1935), II, p. 711.

19. Ibid., p. 713.

20. Ibid., p. 714.

21. Ibid., pp. 715-716; Hsüeh (1937), p. 53.

22. Fei (1945), pp. 67-68.

23. Hsüeh (1937), p. 51.

24. Feng (1935), II, p. 718.

25. Fei (1945), p. 67; Feng (1935), II, pp. 769-770.

26. Feng (1935), II, p. 728.

27. Fei (1939), pp. 202-203 and p. 232; Fei (1945), pp. 240-243.

28. See, for example, Fei's discussion of the papermaking industry in Yünnan, in Fei (1945), pp. 192-196.

29. Rudolf P. Hommel (1937), contains considerable information on the technologies involved.

30. This point is made strongly by Fei (1945), pp. 272-275.

31. Ibid., p. 274. To the cited cost of $3000 over 9 years was added $100 per year in foregone labor income and interest of about $1400 (roughly computed).

32. High government jobs generally required university degrees; clerkships or primary teaching positions did not pay so well (see Table 5.2). Fei (1945), pp. 278-279.

33. Hsiao Ting-che and T'ao Meng-ho (1926), p. 216, note (2) describe the compensation of Shanghai factor apprentices.

34. For example, skilled workers in the best paying industries in T'ai-yüan were drawn largely from Tientsin; some from Hupei or Shanghai. Local workers had to be content with low paying jobs in low-skilled professions. Ibid., p. 399.

35. For comparative figures on male/female wage rates

in Shanghai, see U.S. Department of Labor, Bureau of Labor
Statistics, <u>Monthly Labor Review</u>, 33:3, September, 1931,
pp. 189-191 and Bureau of Social Affairs, City Government
of Greater Shanghai, <u>Standard of Living of Shanghai Laborers</u>
(1934).

36. D. K. Lieu (1934), vol. III, various tables.

37. See Hsiao Ting-she and T'ao Meng-ho (1926),
pp. 390-400.

38. Valuation of $3.94 per month and $.30 per day based
on Buck, <u>LUC</u>, <u>SV</u>, p. 328.

39. Kendall's <u>tau</u> differs from the more commonly used
Pearsonian coefficient of rank correlation in that a transformation of it is approximately normally distributed for
N > 10 and therefore is susceptiable to significance tests.
See Kendall (1962). In this instance, our estimate of T
is conservative, since we have accounted for rank ties in
the numerator but not the denominator, reducing our estimated T below its true value. We have ignored the Hunan
and Honan ranks in our tests.

40. Land prices from 1934 from T'u-ti wei-yuan hui, eds.
(1937), p. 56. The prices of medium quality irrigated land
were used in computing rank correlations.

41. Data from Feng (1935), II, pp. 765-766.

42. For examples, see Li Wen-chih (1957), III, pp.
269-278; Feng Ho-fa (1935), I, pp. 118-122 (shows that
tenants take losses in accounting sense); Hsiao and T'ao

(1926), pp. 401-523; Ch'en Han-seng (1939), pp. 59-65.
These and other studies used varying accounting methods,
sometimes neglecting to include all opportunity costs (family labor is sometimes excluded); a few show positive accounting profits for particular localities, although the larger
size of farms sampled is usually responsible.

43. See Buck, CFE, Appendix 1, Tables 1-18, line 9.

44. Mantetsu (Hokushi No. 5), Appendices.

45. Ibid. See also Buck, CFE, Appendix 1, Tables 1-14,
line 29.

46. Buck, CFE, Appendix 1, Tables 1-14, line 29.

47. Feng (1935), I, pp. 575-576 gives figures for a
Chekiang hsien, but this need not have been typical.

48. Buck, LUC, I, Table 13, p. 259. These figures not
only are inconsistent with those in Table 12, but also have
no corresponding source table in the SV. They are also
hardly referred to in the text, suggesting that the author
himself did not consider them very meaningful.

49. The villages were in Feng-jun (1937), Huo-lu (1939)
and P'eng-te (1934) counties, Hopei. In Mantetsu, Hokushi
Nos. 5, 25, and 32.

50. Buck, CFE, p. 311.

51. Buck, LUC, I, pp. 250-254.

52. Livestock at least were a smaller proportion of
total investment in S. China than in N. China. See Buck,

CFE, Table 21, p. 63.

53. See Buck, LUC, I, Table 21, p. 194.

54. Mantetsu (Shanghai No. 50), Appendix Tables. Entirely landless peasants have been excluded (because it is impossible to compute a ratio of labor to land endowments for them), along with non-farmers and one temple attendant who evidently took little interest in his farm (most land left fallow).

Chapter Six / THE AGRICULTURAL PRODUCTION FUNCTION

1. R. G. D. Allen (1949), pp. 284-285 and 340-341.

2. Buck, LUC, I, p. 280.

3. With more than one such source of heterogeneity, separate weights would have to be estimated for, e.g. double-cropped and irrigated, double-cropped and non-irrigated, single-cropped and irrigated land, etc. Unfortunately too many degrees of freedom are used up in the process, so it is necessary to assume that the separate qualitative impacts are multiplicative and independent.

4. Permitting both a larger absolute rent level for landlords and a larger net income for tenants, who would have found it hard to survive at prevailing rent proportions on marginal land.

5. See Arrow, Chenery, Minhas and Solow (1961), pp. 225-250 for this finding.

6. See E. Malinvaud (1966), pp. 517-519.

7. See Irving Hoch (1962), pp. 37-38.

8. Our tests were those suggested by Farrar and Glauber (1967), pp. 92-107.

9. On instrumental variable estimation procedures, see Wonnacott and Wonnacott (1970), pp. 152-160 and Johnston (1963), pp. 165-166.

10. Malinvaud (1966), pp. 263-265.

11. C.H. Hanumantha Rao (1965), p. 14.

12. Heady and Dillon (1961), pp. 621-628.

13. See Mantetsu, Hokushi Nos. 5, 25, and 32.

14. D. Perkins also assumes 20% on the assumptions of a capital-output ratio of 2 to 1 (presumably including land, and thus including financial capital) and a rate of return on investment of 10%; or a K/O ratio of 3.0 and 6-7% rate of return. Of course a K/O ratio of 3.4 (as found by Buck, CFE, Table 18, p. 448) and a rate of return of 10% on land investment, as found in our Chapter III, implies a capital share of 34%, counting investment return as well as the return to capital services. See Perkins (1969), pp. 79-81.

15. The factor of 1.4 is derived from Table 3.10, p. 114. 21% would then be the capital share on neoclassical assumptions only.

16. Studies of production functions in Japan and Taiwan

tend to confirm this result. See Heady and Dillon (1961), pp. 624-629.

17. We tested for such nonlinearities by including quadratic terms in the function. Many were significant.

18. Scott R. Dittrich and Ramon H. Myers (1971), pp. 887-896.

19. Buck, LUC, I, pp. 181-185 and 200-201.

20. Ibid., pp. 312 and 315.

21. Ibid., p. 320.

22. Ibid., p. 333.

23. See Nai-ruenn Chen (1967), Table 9.13, p. 437.

Chapter Seven / AN ACTIVITY ANALYSIS APPROACH

1. Mantetsu (Hokushi No. 5); Mantetsu (Hokushi No. 12); Mantetsu (Hokushi No. 36).

2. Zellner, Kmenta and Dreze (1966), pp. 784-795.

3. An exception is a recent study which assumes, as we do, an efficient frontier production function, to be derived empirically by fitting a Cobb-Douglas function as an envelope to all but the 5% most dominant techniques, which are assumed to be the product of errors in the data. While this method appears a bit too ad hoc in its justification, it does avoid the error mentioned in the text. See Timmer (1971), pp. 776-794.

4. See note 1.

5. Dittrich and Myers (1971), pp. 887-896.

6. Price information was derived from Nan-ching ta-hsüeh ching-chi yen-chiu-so (1958), pp. 70-74 (an unfortunate lacunae is the absence of any figures for 1937) and Chung-kuo k'o-hsüeh yüan (1958), pp. 213, 221 and 229. Also of interest for comparing long-term relative prices of grains and cotton (1905-1924) is information given in Feng (1935), I, pp. 86-87 for Nan-t'ung hsien, Kiangsu.

7. The type of efficiency represented by the "expected efficiency frontier" is what Leibenstein calls 'X-efficiency', as distinguished from allocative or price efficiency, which is determined by choice among frontier techniques. Leibenstein argues that 'X-efficiency' is quantitatively more significant than allocative efficiency and is a function of three elements: (1) intraplant motivation, (2) external motivational efficiency, and (3) nonmarket input efficiency. In relation to our critique of the usual methods for assessing allocative efficiency, he points out that "the conventional theoretical assumption, although it is rarely stated, is that inputs have a fixed specification and yield a fixed performance. This ignores other likely possibilities. Inputs may have a fixed specification that yields a variable performance, or they may be of a variable specification and yield a variable performance." Leibenstein (1966), pp. 406-407. 'X-efficiency' might also be termed non-neutral

technical efficiency, as distinguished from the more commonly
assumed neutral variety. In terms of production function
notation, non-neutral technical efficiency (for a function
of two productive factors) could be measured for each factor
of production separately as the terms γ_1 and γ_2 which convert
measured units of factor services, L and K, into units
of homogeneous efficiency and quality, such as to define
a production function, $Q = f[(\gamma_1 L), (\gamma_2 K)]$. The alternative
(for example, see Lau and Yotopoulos, 1971, p. 95) is to
assume differences in efficiency are represented by a term,
θ, in production function, $Q = \theta f(L,K)$, where L and K are
again measured units of factor services. While the latter
approach greatly simplifies econometric problems, it is
otherwise impossible to justify given the lack of homogeneity
of real-world measurements of L and K.

8. Timmer (1971).

9. If the distribution of yields around their mean is
reasonably symmetric, the assumption that the second
moment is large relative to the absolute value of the
third moment will be fulfilled. For this derivation, see
Pratt (1964).

BIBLIOGRAPHY

CHINESE AND JAPANESE SOURCES

Chang Ch'i-yün. Chung-hua min-kuo ti-t'u chi (Atlas of
the Republic of China). Taipei, 1961-1962.

Ch'iao Ch'i-ming. Chung-kuo nung-ts'un she-hui ching-chi
hsüeh (Chinese Village Socioeconomy). Chungking,
Commercial Press, 1945.

Chung-kuo k'o-hsüeh yüan. Shang-hai chieh-fang ch'ien-
hou wu-chia tzu-liao hui-pien, 1921-1957 (Collection
of Shanghai Price Materials Before and After Liberation).
Shanghai, People's Press, 1958.

Feng Ho-fa. Chung-kuo nung-ts'un ching-chi tzu-liao
(Materials on the Chinese Village Economy). 2 vols.
Shanghai, 1935.

Hsüeh Mu-ch'iao. Chung-kuo nung-ts'un ching-chi ch'ang-
shih (Basics of Chinese Village Economy). Shanghai,
Hsin-chih Press, 1937.

Hsiao Ting-che and T'ao Meng-ho eds. Chung-kuo lao-tung
nien-chien (Chinese Labor Yearbook). 1926.

Li Wen-chih and Chang Yu-i eds. Chung-kuo chin-tai nung-
yeh shih tzu-liao (Historical Materials on Agriculture in Modern China). 3 vols. Peking, San-lien,
1957.

Lieu, D. K. Chung-kuo kung-yeh tiao-ch'a pao-kao, 1933
(Manufacturing Census of China, 1933). Shanghai,
Commercial Press, 1934.

Minami Manshū tetsudō kabushiki kaisha. Nōka kezai chōsa
hōkoku (Hokushi kezai shiryo no. 5) (Feng-jun hsien
village survey). Dairen, South Manchurian Railway,
1939.

-----Nōka kezai chōsa hōkoku (Hokushi kezai shiryo no. 12)
(Feng-jun hsien village survey). Dairen, South Manchurian Railway, 1940.

-----Nōka kezai chōsa hōkoku (Hokushi kezai shiryo no. 36)
(Feng-jun hsien village survey). Dairen, 1940.

-----Nōka kezai chōsa hōkoku (Hokushi kezai shiryo no. 25)
(P'eng-te hsien village survey). Peking, South Manchurian Railway, 1942.

-----Nōka kezai chōsa hōkoku (Hokushi kezai shiryo no. 32)
(Huo-lu hsien village survey). Peking, South Manchurian Railway, 1941.

-----Nōson jittai chōsa hokoku (Hokushi chosa shiryo no. 7)
(Tsingtao village survey). Peking, South Manchurian
Railway, 1939.

-----Nōson jittai chōsa hōkoku sho (Shanghai mantetsu chōsa
shiryo no. 50) (Wu-hsi hsien village survey). Shanghai,
South Manchurian Railway, 1941.

Ministry of Agriculture, Foodgrains Production Bureau. 1958 nien nung-tso-wu mi-chih ching-yen (The 1958 Experience with Dense Planting of Agricultural Crops). Peking, 1961.

Nan-ching ta-hsüeh ching-chi yen-chiu so ed. Nan-kai chih-shu tzu-liao hui-pien, 1913-1952 (A Collection of Nankai Index Materials). Peking, T'ung-chi Press, 1958.

Niida Noboru. Chūgoku hōsei shi kenkyū: Tochihō torihikihō (Studies on Chinese Legal History: Land Law, Transactions Law). Tokyo, 1960.

Shensi shih-yeh k'ao-ch'a t'uan. Shensi shih-wu k'ao-ch'a (Investigation of Shensi Industry). Shanghai, 1933.

Sun Ching-chih ed. Hua-tung ti-ch'ü ching-chi ti-li (An Economic Geography of East China). Peking, 1959. tr. JPRS no. 11,438.

Sun Hsing-tung. Chung-yao lü-fei tso-wu tsai-p'ei (The Cultivation of Important Green Manure Crops). Peking, 1962.

Ting Ying. Chung-kuo shui-tao tsai-p'ei hsüeh (A Study of Chinese Paddy Rice Cultivation). Peking, 1961.

T'u-ti wei-yüan-hui. Ch'üan-kuo ching-chi wei-yüan-hui pao-kao hui-p'ien (Collection of National Economic Committee Reports). 1937.

<u>T'ung-chi yüeh-pao</u> (Statistical Monthly).

Yen Chung-p'ing. <u>Chung-kuo chin-tai ching-chi chih t'ung-chi</u>
(Statistics on Modern Chinese Economic History).
Peking, Scientific Press, 1955.

WESTERN SOURCES

Adelman, Irma and Erik Thorbecke eds. <u>The Theory and Design</u>
<u>of Economic Development</u>. Baltimore, Johns Hopkins,
1966.

Agarwala, A. N. and S. P. Singh eds. <u>The Economics of</u>
<u>Underdevelopment</u>. New York, Oxford, 1958.

Allen, R. G. D. <u>Mathematical Analysis for Economists</u>.
London, Macmillan, 1949.

Arrow, Kenneth. <u>Essays in the Theory of Risk Bearing</u>.
Chicago, Markham, 1971.

Arrow, K. J., H. B. Chenery, B. Minhas and R. M. Solow,
"Capital-Labor Substitution and Economic Efficiency,"
<u>Review of Economics and Statistics</u>, 43: 3(August, 1961),
225-250.

Bardhan, P. K. and T. N. Srinivasan. "Cropsharing Tenancy
in Agriculture: A Theoretical and Empirical Analysis,"
<u>American Economic Review</u>, 61: 1(March, 1971), 48-64.

Brown, Harold D. "A Survey of 25 Farms on Mt. Omei,"
<u>Chinese Economic Journal</u>, 1: 12(December, 1927).

Brown, Lester R. Seeds of Change: The Green Revolution.
    New York, Praeger, 1970.

Buck, John Lossing. Land Utilization in China. 3 vols.
    Nanking, University of Nanking, 1937.

-----Chinese Farm Economy. Chicago, University of Chicago,
    1930.

Burki, Shahid. A Study of Chinese Communes. Cambridge,
    Harvard, 1969..

Chayanov, A. V. The Theory of Peasant Economy. ed. D.
    Thorner et al., A.E.A. Translation Series. Homewood,
    Illinois, Irwin, 1966.

Chen, C. S. comp. Rural People's Communes in Lien-chiang.
    tr. Charles R. Ridley. Stanford, Stanford University
    Press, 1969.

Chen Han-seng. Industrial Capital and Chinese Peasants.
    Shanghai, 1939.

Chen, Nai-ruenn. Chinese Economic Statistics. Chicago,
    Aldine, 1967.

Cheung, S. N. "Private Property Rights and Sharecropping,"
    Journal of Political Economy, 76 (December, 1968),
    1107-1122.

City Government of Greater Shanghai, Bureau of Social
    Affairs. Standard of Living of Shanghai Laborers.
    Shanghai, 1934.

Dittrich, Scott R. and Ramon Myers. "Resource Allocation in Traditional Agriculture: Republic of China, 1937-1940," Journal of Political Economy, 79: 4 (July-August, 1971), 887-896.

Dovring, Folke. "Unemployment in Traditional Agriculture," Economic Development and Cultural Change, 15: 2 (January, 1967), 163-173.

Draper, N. and H. Smith. Applied Regression Analysis. New York, 1966.

Eckaus, R. S. "Factor Proportions in Underdeveloped Countries," American Economic Review, 45: 4 (September, 1955), 539-565.

Eckstein, Alexander, Walter Galenson and T. C. Liu. Economic Trends in Communist China. Chicago, Aldine, 1968.

Eicher, Carl and Lawrence Witt eds. Agriculture in Economic Development. New York, McGraw-Hill, 1964.

Farrar, D. E. and R. R. Glauber. "Multicollinearity in Regression Analysis: The Problem Revisited," Review of Economics and Statistics, 49: 1(February, 1967), 92-107.

Fei Hsiao-t'ung. Peasant Life in China. New York, E. P. Dutton, 1939.

-----Earthbound China. Chicago, University of Chicago, 1945.

Fei, J. C. H. and Gustav Ranis. "Capital Accumulation and Economic Development," American Economic Review, 53: 3(June, 1963), 283-313.

Ferguson, Charles E. The Neoclassical Theory of Production and Distribution. London, Cambridge University Press, 1969.

Georgescu-Roegen, N. "Economic Theory and Agrarian Economics," Oxford Economic Papers, 12 (February, 1963), 1-40.

Gordon, Robert J. "The Incidence of the Corporation Income Tax in U.S. Manufacturing, 1925-62," American Economic Review, 57: 4(September, 1967), 731-758.

Government of India, Ministry of Food and Agriculture. Report of the Indian Delegation to China on Agricultural Planning and Techniques. New Delhi, 1959.

Government of West Pakistan, Agricultural Department. Annual Report on Accelerated Rice Research Program. Karachi, 1966.

Hansen, Bent. "Marginal Productivity Wage Theory and Subsistence Wage Theory in Egyptian Agriculture," Journal of Development Studies, 2 (July, 1966), 367-405.

Heady, Earl O. and J. L. Dillon. Agricultural Production Functions. Ames, Iowa, Iowa State University Press, 1961.

Herdt, Robert and John Mellor. "The Contrasting Response
of Rice to Nitrogen: India and the United States,"
Journal of Farm Economics, 46: 1 (February, 1965),
150-160.

Hirshleifer, Jack. Investment, Interest and Capital.
Englewood Cliffs, N.J., Prentice-Hall, 1970.

Hoch, Irving. "Estimation of Production Function Parameters
Combining Time-Series and Cross-Section Data,"
Econometrica, 30: 1(January, 1962), 566-578.

Hoch, Irving. "Consequences of Alternative Specifications
in Estimation of Cobb-Douglas Production Functions,"
Econometrica, 33: 10(October, 1965), 814-828.

Hommel, Rudolf P. China at Work. New York, John Day, 1937.

Hunter, Guy. Modernizing Peasant Societies. New York,
Oxford, 1969.

Johnston, John. Econometric Methods. New York, McGraw-Hill,
1963.

Kenji, Asakawa. "Four Reforms in Agriculture,"
Chūgoku kenkyū geppo (Chinese Studies Monthly),
154 (January, 1961), 1-34, tr. JPRS no. 9209.

Kendall, Maurice G. Rank Correlation Methods. London,
C. Griffin, 1962.

Kuznets, Simon. Economic Growth and Structure: Selected
Essays. New York, Norton, 1965.

-----"Quantitative Aspects of the Economic Growth of
　　Nations: VIII, Distribution of Income by Size,"
　　Economic Development and Cultural Change, 11: 2,
　　Part II (January, 1963).

Lamson, H. D. "The People's Livelihood as Revealed by
　　Family Budget Studies," _Chinese Economic Journal_,
　　8: 5(May, 1931).

Lau, Lawrence J. and P. A. Yotopoulos. "A Test for
　　Relative Efficiency and Application to Indian
　　Agriculture," _American Economic Review_, 61: 1
　　(March, 1971), 94-109.

Leibenstein, Harvey. "Allocative Efficiency vs. 'X-Effi-
　　ciency," _American Economic Review_, 56: 3(June, 1966),
　　392-415.

-----_Economic Backwardness and Economic Growth_. New York,
　　Wiley, 1957.

Lewis, W. Arthur. "Economic Development with Unlimited
　　Supplies of Labor," _The Manchester School of Economic
　　and Social Studies_, 22: 2(May, 1954), 139-192.

Liu Jung-chao. _China's Fertilizer Economy_. Chicago,
　　Aldine, 1970.

Liu, Ta-chung and Yeh Kung-chia. _The Economy of the
　　Chinese Mainland: National Income and Economic
　　Development, 1933-1959_. Princeton, 1965.

Lockwood, W. W. ed. The State and Economic Development
    in Japan. Princeton, 1965.

Malinvaud, E. Statistical Methods of Econometrics.
    Chicago, Rand McNally, 1966.

Matsuo, Takane. Rice Cultivation in Japan. Ministry
    of Agriculture and Forestry, Japanese Government, 1959.

Mellor, John W. The Economics of Agricultural Development.
    Ithaca, Cornell University Press, 1966.

Myers, Ramon. The Chinese Peasant Economy: Development
    in Hopei and Shantung between 1890 and 1940. Cambridge,
    Harvard University Press, 1970.

N. A. R. B. Crop Reports.

National Bureau of Economic Research eds. The Theory and
    Empirical Analysis of Production Functions. New
    York, Columbia University Press, 1967.

Ogura, Takekazu ed. Agricultural Development in Modern
    Japan. Tokyo, Fuji, 1967.

Ohkawa, Kazushi, B. Johnston and H. Kaneda eds.
    Agriculture and Economic Growth: Japan's Experience.
    Princeton, 1970.

Oriental Economist, The. Japan Economic Yearbook, 1961.
    Tokyo, 1961.

Paglin, Morton. "Surplus Agricultural Labor and Develop-
    ment: Facts and Theories," American Economic Review,
    55: 4(September, 1965), 815-834.

Pan Hong-sheng and O. King. "Preliminary Note on an
    Economic Study of Farm Implements," Economic Facts,
    3(November, 1936).

Perkins, Dwight H. Agricultural Development in China,
    1368-1968. Chicago, Aldine, 1969.

Pratt, John W. "Risk Aversion in the Small and in the
    Large," Econometrica, 32 (January-April, 1964),
    122-136.

Ranis, Gustav and John C. H. Fei. "A Theory of Economic
    Development," American Economic Review, 51: 4
    (September, 1961), 553-558.

Rao, Hanumantha. Agricultural Production Function, Costs
    and Returns in India. New York, Asia Publishing
    House, 1965.

-----"Uncertainty, Entrepreneurship and Sharecropping in
    India," Journal of Political Economy, 79: 3(May-June,
    1971), 578-595.

Rawski, Evelyn Sakakida. Agricultural Change and the
    Peasant Economy of South China. Cambridge, Harvard
    University Press, 1972.

Sandmo, A. "On the Theory of the Competitive Firm under
    Price Uncertainty," American Economic Review, 60: 1
    (March, 1971), 65-73.

Schultz, Theodore W. Transforming Traditional Agriculture.
    New Haven, Yale University Press, 1964.

Sen, A. K. "Peasants and Dualism With or Without Surplus Labor," _Journal of Political Economy_, 74 (October, 1966), 425-450.

Smith, Thomas C. _The Agrarian Origins of Modern Japan_. Stanford, Stanford University Press, 1959.

Solow, Robert. "Technical Change and the Aggregate Production Function," _Review of Economics and Statistics_, 39: 3(August, 1957), 312-320.

Tawney, R. H. _Land and Labor in China_. London, Allen and Unwin, 1932.

Timmer, C. P. "Using a Probabilistic Frontier Production Function to Measure Technical Efficiency," _Journal of Political Economy_, 79: 4(August, 1971), 776-794.

Tōbata, Seiichi and K. Ohkawa eds. _Nihon no keizai to nōgyō_ (Japanese Economy and Agriculture). 2 vols. Tokyo, 1964.

Tobin, J. "Liquidity Preference as Behavior Towards Risk," _Review of Economic Studies_, 25: 67(February, 1958), 65-86.

Tsha, T. Y. "A Study of Wage Rates in Shanghai, 1930-1934," _Nankai Social and Economic Quarterly_, October, 1935.

Van Slyke, Lyman P. ed. _The Chinese Communist Movement: A Report of the U.S. War Department, 1945_. Stanford, Stanford University Press, 1968.

Vogel, Ezra. _Canton Under Communism_. Cambridge, Harvard
    University Press, 1969.

Walker, Kenneth R. _Planning in Chinese Agriculture_.
    Chicago, Aldine, 1965.

Walters, A. A. "Production and Cost Functions: An
    Econometric Survey," _Econometrica_, 31: 1(January-
    April, 1963), 1-66.

Wharton, Clifton R. jr. ed. _Subsistence Agriculture and
    Economic Development_. Chicago, Aldine, 1970.

Wiens, Mi Chu. _Socioeconomic Change During the Ming
    Dynasty_. unpublished doctoral dissertation. Harvard,
    1973.

Wiens, Thomas B. "The Backward-Bending Supply Curve of
    Labor in the British Textile Industry," unpublished
    paper, 1967.

Williams, M. S. and J.W. Couston. _Crop Production Levels
    and Fertilizer Use_. Rome, F.A.O., 1962.

Wonnacott, R. J. and T. H. Wonnacott. _Econometrics_.
    New York, Wiley, 1970.

Yin, Lien-ken. "Returns on Landlord's Capital Investment
    in Farms," _Economic Facts_, 2(October, 1936), 123-132.

Zellner, A., J. Kmenta and J. Drêze. "Specification and
    Estimation of Cobb-Douglas Production Function Models,"
    Econometrica, 34: 4(October, 1966), 784-795.

For Product Safety Concerns and Information please contact our EU
representative GPSR@taylorandfrancis.com Taylor & Francis Verlag GmbH,
Kaufingerstraße 24, 80331 München, Germany

Printed and bound by CPI Group (UK) Ltd, Croydon, CR0 4YY

08/05/2025

01864457-0004